1990

A History of Medieval Philosophy

A History of Medieval Philosophy

Frederick Copleston (signature)

F. C. COPLESTON

HARPER TORCHBOOKS

Harper & Row, Publishers

New York, Hagerstown, San Francisco, London

Contents

Foreword

THIS book is a revision and enlargement of my *Medieval Philosophy*,
which was published in 1952 in Methuen's Home Study Books series.
The general plan of the previous work has, of course, been retained.
But in the present volume a great deal more is said about Christian
thought in the ancient world. Again, accounts of Islamic and Jewish
philosophy in the Middle Ages have undergone considerable extension.
And longer treatments have been provided of leading thinkers such as
Aquinas, Scotus and Ockham. Philosophical discussion of issues raised
by medieval thinkers has obviously had to be kept to a minimum. But
some general lines of thought about medieval philosophy have been
expressed in the first and last chapters.

In references *P.G.* and *P.L.* refer respectively to the *Patrologia
Graeca* and the *Patrologia Latina* in the *Patrologiae cursus completus*
edited by J. P. Migne. In footnotes and the Bibliography the series
Beiträge zur Geschichte der Philosophie des Mittelalters has been referred
to simply as *Beiträge*.

A History of Medieval Philosophy

I

Introduction

I

AT one time there was a widespread impression that the student of the development of philosophy could profitably jump straight from Plato and Aristotle to Francis Bacon and Descartes, omitting consideration both of post-Aristotelian Greek thought and of medieval philosophy. The philosophy of the Middle Ages was thought to be dependent on Christian theology in such a way and to such a degree as to exclude any genuine philosophical reflection. There was also a tendency to think of it as pretty well equivalent to a debased Aristotelianism which lacked the original and creative spirit of Aristotle himself and concentrated on trivial and tiresome questions. Again, it was a common enough idea that no logical developments of any value had taken place in the Middle Ages. If, therefore, one were interested in free metaphysical speculation or in the creation of striking world views, one would be well advised to dismiss medieval speculation as hag-ridden by theology and turn to Descartes, Spinoza and Leibniz. If one mistrusted metaphysical speculation and wished to find a tradition of philosophical reflection which was firmly grounded in experience, one had better study the development of British empiricism. If it were logic to which one proposed to devote one's attention, the profitable procedure would be to go straight from the logic of Aristotle (and possibly that of the Stoics) to the logical developments of modern times. In all these areas medieval thought could be profitably passed over as a dark and barren interlude, as far at any rate as philosophy and logic were concerned.

Nowadays we have a better understanding of the continuity between ancient, medieval, Renaissance and modern philosophy. It is unnecessary to dwell here on the connections between ancient and medieval thought, for they will be illustrated in later chapters. It is sufficient to point out that in the Roman empire Christian thought coexisted for some time with non-Christian Greek philosophy, and that a thinker such as St Augustine, who died in 430 and who exercised a great influence in the Middle Ages, belonged to the ancient world. In later chapters we shall see how Greco-Roman philosophy provided material for philosophical reflection in the Middle Ages and for incorporation, in varying degrees, in medieval systems of thought.

If we turn to the other end, so to speak, we can see the difficulty in fixing definite limits to the medieval, Renaissance and modern periods. Let us suppose, for example, that in describing the Renaissance we emphasize both the increased knowledge of classical literature and the increasing literary use of the national vernacular languages, as distinct from Latin. We have to remember that a large number of writings were translated from the Greek (directly or indirectly) into Latin in the last part of the twelfth century and in the early decades of the thirteenth century. We have also to remember that one of the greatest creations of Italian literature, namely Dante's *Divine Comedy*, was composed in the thirteenth century, while in the following century Petrarch and Boccaccio wrote poems in Italian and Chaucer developed the literary use of English. At the same time the use of Latin was continued, as by Descartes and Spinoza, into the early period of what is generally described as modern philosophy. Again, if we emphasize the scientific achievements of the Renaissance, we have at any rate to consider the claim that there was more in common, so far as their spirit was concerned, between certain embryonic scientists of the late Middle Ages and the great scientists of the Renaissance than there was between some of the Renaissance philosophers of Nature and the great figures of the scientific Renaissance.

In regard to the transition between medieval and modern philosophy, it is easy to be misled by the polemical attitudes adopted by early modern philosophers. Francis Bacon and Descartes may have inveighed against scholastic Aristotelianism; but philosophers continued for many years to use categories of thought and philosophical principles which had been used by medieval thinkers. It would be a mistake to attribute what we might describe as the scholastic elements in philosophies such as those of Descartes, Malebranche and Leibniz to the interest in classical literature which was shown during the Renaissance. Descartes's first philosophical studies were in the scholastic tradition, going back to the Middle Ages. And though his mind came to move in other directions, the influence of his early studies was permanent. Malebranche was deeply influenced by Augustine, while Leibniz had a fairly extensive knowledge of philosophical literature belonging to or stemming from the medieval tradition. Moreover, its influence upon him is apparent in his writings. Again, we can trace a connection between medieval philosophy of law and that of John Locke. For the matter of that, Locke's empiricism is not so completely alien to all aspects of medieval thought as has been sometimes supposed.

The philosophers of the French Enlightenment in the eighteenth century tended to think that with themselves reason had at last come into its own, and that 'Middle Ages' and 'Dark Ages' were synonymous terms. The growth of the sense of historical development in the nineteenth century and serious historical study have obviously changed this outlook. Except for people who have no use for historical studies, nobody would seriously suppose that a coherent and adequate account of the development of European culture and society could be given if the medieval period were simply omitted. And it is commonly recognized, even by those who have little sympathy with the religious beliefs of the Middle Ages, that no adequate account of the development of European thought and philosophy could be given unless medieval philosophy were taken into account. But though an emphasis on the continuity of European philosophy can be and has been of use, this emphasis needs to be counterbalanced by a recognition of discontinuity, of differences.

For example, those historians who emphasized the scholastic elements, deriving from the Middle Ages, in the philosophy of Descartes doubtless performed a useful service. They showed the absurdity of supposing that philosophy, having suffered a demise when the emperor Justinian closed the philosophical schools at Athens in 529, was suddenly reborn with Descartes in France and Francis Bacon in England. At the same time, when Descartes uses a term taken from medieval philosophy, it by no means necessarily follows that he is using it in the same sense in which it was used by his medieval predecessors. Indeed Descartes himself drew attention to this point. Again, when Spinoza employs terms such as 'substance' and 'cause', we would be seriously mistaken if we blithely assumed that he means precisely the same as was meant by St Thomas Aquinas in the thirteenth century.

Talk about historical periods has sometimes been attacked. And it is true of course not only that it is very difficult to assign clear and definite boundary lines to periods such as the Middle Ages or the Renaissance but also that, if we try to do so, we tend to obscure important facts. For instance, there are historical facts which make it possible at any rate to extend the Renaissance backwards, so to speak. And there may well be grounds for hesitation in regard to the classification of, say, Nicholas of Cusa (1401–64) as a late medieval or as a Renaissance figure. One can find arguments in favour of either classification. And it is understandable if the validity of such classifications is called in question.

Though, however, division into historical periods may express the tyranny of general ideas over the mind and obscure any clear perception of overlappings and of elements of continuity, it is an exaggeration to claim that a division of this kind is useless or that it has no foundation in historical fact. To be sure, we cannot assign rigidly delimited boundaries. But it seems idle to deny that there are any roughly distinguishable periods with characteristics of their own. Medieval social structures, for example, had characteristics which were clearly different from those of Greek society and which are not found in our modern industrial society. And the set of beliefs which constituted a common mental background in medieval Christendom and which influenced the selection of philosophical problems for consideration were not present during most of the history of the ancient world[1] and can hardly be said to exercise in our contemporary society the synthesizing and coordinating influence which they exercised in the Middle Ages. Again, whereas in medieval Christendom theology was regarded as the highest science available to man, in the modern world theology has obviously lost its dominating position, and today the word 'science' generally suggests the natural sciences which have developed since the Middle Ages and which have had profound and far-reaching effects on human life, society and thought.

In any study of medieval philosophy, therefore, account must be taken of elements both of continuity and discontinuity. If for the sake of convenience we reckon the period of medieval thought from about 800, the year of the coronation of Charlemagne, the historian has to exhibit the connections between early medieval philosophy and what preceded it. At the same time it is his business to illustrate the peculiar characteristics not only of medieval philosophy in general but also of the leading thinkers and currents of thought. Ideally, philosophical

---

[1] Christianity was, of course, born in the ancient world and came to achieve official recognition before the end of the Roman empire. Early Christian thought and Hellenistic philosophy overlapped for a time.

ideas should be related, when it is relevant to do so, to extra-philo-sophical factors, inasmuch as philosophy does not pursue a purely isolated life of its own, without connection with other cultural elements and with social structures. But to realize this ideal in a short work would be impracticable, even if the writer were competent to do so.

2

It might very well be objected that though what has been said is sub-stantially true, it does very little to show that medieval philosophy is worth studying, except perhaps by historians. If medieval philosophy constitutes, as it does, an integral phase in the total development of European thought up to date, anyone who wishes to study this process of development as a whole should obviously acquire some knowledge of the philosophy of the Middle Ages. Further, some specialists in medieval thought are obviously required. But the legitimacy of historical studies in this area certainly does not prove that a student who is interested in philosophical problems as they present themselves today needs to bother his head about the philosophy of the Middle Ages. The tendency to omit medieval thought and to jump straight from Aristotle to Francis Bacon and Descartes may well be objectionable from the historian's point of view. At the same time it may be perfectly justified in regard to the content of medieval thought. After all, the rather obvious point has already been noted, that emphasis on con-tinuity should be balanced by a recognition of discontinuity and of peculiar characteristics. One of the peculiar characteristics of medieval thought was surely the dominant position of Christian theology. To a considerable extent selection of themes for philosophical discussion was governed by theological presuppositions. And even if religious beliefs did not dictate the conclusions at which philosophers had to arrive, they at any rate dictated, in certain areas at least, the conclusions at which philosophers must not arrive. For this reason alone autono-mous philosophical reflection was severely restricted. Further, medieval philosophy belonged to a pre-critical age. Some of its basic assumptions have been called in question and can no longer be taken for granted. In general, medieval philosophy is part and parcel of a world which has passed away. To be sure, there was such a world. And it is open to anyone who wishes to study it and to endeavour to understand it. But it is not our world. Indeed, the modern student of philosophy who does not share the presuppositions of the medieval thinkers has probably more to learn from Plato or Aristotle than from Bonaventure or Aquinas or Duns Scotus.

Let us consider first the relation between philosophy on the one hand and religious and theological convictions on the other in the Middle Ages. Whatever people's conduct may have been, it is obviously true that in medieval Europe there was a much greater homogeneity of religious beliefs than there is in the contemporary western world.[1] And it is only natural that religious belief should influence philosophy. Philosophical thought is influenced not only by its past but also by the historical context and by extra-philosophical factors. In recent centuries the rise and development of the particular sciences have influenced philosophical thought in a variety of ways. In the Middle Ages the principal extra-philosophical factor which influenced philosophy was religious belief. Moreover, the leading medieval thinkers were mostly theologians.[2] Hence it was only natural that religious and theological convictions should exercise a certain degree of influence on the selection and treatment of topics. Just as in recent centuries the sciences have suggested problems and points of view, so did religious belief and theology in the medieval period.[3]

It by no means necessarily follows, however, that the influence of religious and theological beliefs was simply detrimental to philosophy. In the first place antecedent religious belief could and did widen the scope of philosophical problematics. As will be seen later, in the Faculty of Arts at Paris in the middle of the thirteenth century, there was a marked tendency to identify philosophy with the thought of Aristotle. The theologian-philosophers, however, were much less addicted to thinking that the Greek philosopher was the culmination of human wisdom. And Professor Étienne Gilson in particular has argued that the Jewish–Christian tradition acted as a powerful fertilizing and stimulating influence, suggesting fresh problems and points of view.

In the second place it is a mistake to think that during the Middle

[1] Obviously, there was no complete homogeneity of religious belief in medieval Europe. For a considerable time, for example, there was a flourishing Moorish or Islamic civilization in southern Spain. There were the Jews, who produced their own philosophers. And even in Christendom there was a variety of sects. By and large, however, the statement in the text can stand.

[2] To occupy a chair of theology in one of the leading universities, especially at Paris, was, in the Middle Ages, to reach the culminating point of an academic career.

[3] By saying this I do not intend, of course, to exclude the influence of, say, medieval social structures on the political theory of the Middle Ages.

Ages theology dominated philosophy in the sense that the philosopher's job was simply that of finding arguments to prove the truth of propositions asserted by the Church. Obviously, if a man believed, on religious grounds, that a certain proposition was true, he could not at the same time maintain that the falsity of the proposition could be proved by human reason, unless indeed he was prepared to adopt a double-truth theory, namely that a proposition could at the same time be true in theology and false in philosophy.[1] Hence if a philosopher, who was also a Christian believer, thought that he had demonstrated the truth of a proposition which contradicted an article of Christian faith, he would either have to assume that there was a flaw in his reasoning or abandon his faith or conclude that what he had taken to be a truth of faith was not really what he had supposed it to be. But it by no means follows that if a philosopher believed, as a Christian, in the truth of a certain proposition, he would also have to hold that its truth could be proved by philosophical reasoning. For example, William of Ockham believed in human immortality. But he did not believe that the philosopher could prove that man possesses a spiritual and immortal soul. He did not claim that philosophy could prove the opposite. When he criticized the arguments of his predecessors, he was simply extending the area of truths of faith which lie beyond the range of philosophy. To put the matter in another way, he was narrowing the philosophical field.

As for the statement that medieval philosophy was pre-critical, we have to make a distinction. If by critical philosophy we mean the philosophy of Immanuel Kant, it is obviously true that the medieval thinkers belonged to a pre-critical age. But if by describing the philosophy of the Middle Ages as pre-critical we mean that the medieval thinkers were naïve and incapable of questioning presuppositions, the description constitutes a caricature. They certainly did not believe that human knowledge is simply knowledge of ideas, in the sense of subjective modifications, or that human thinking creates reality. They did not look on the range of human knowledge as unlimited; but realism was a common presupposition. To the subjective idealist or to a man who doubts whether there can be such a thing as knowledge of a

[1] A man might perhaps hold (though it was hardly a medieval point of view) that human reason was so corrupted and blind that it could not recognize truth but could only embrace error. But in this case he would have to abandon philosophy, unless he chose to redefine truth as a biologically useful error or something of the sort. But this again was a procedure alien to the medieval mind.

reality external to the mind, this may appear a naïve assumption. But it is not one which is likely to alienate the sympathies of modern British philosophers. In any case the medieval thinker was as capable, or as incapable, as anyone else of criticizing the assumptions or presuppositions of other philosophers. To become explicitly aware of one's own basic presuppositions and to subject them to critical examination is no easy task. Criticizing other thinkers' ideas, arguments and assumptions is, however, a common enough pastime of philosophers. And the medievals were as much given to it as their successors. Obviously, the fact that there was, generally speaking, a common background of religious belief means that we cannot find in the Middle Ages as clearly different and sharply contrasting world-views as we can find in more recent times. But this does not alter the fact that in the fourteenth century some of the premises and arguments advanced by leading metaphysicians of the preceding century were subjected to radical criticism. The notion that the medieval philosophers were uncritical, as distinct from pre-critical in the sense of pre-Kantian, is largely due to an identification of medieval philosophy with the thought of one or two venerable figures whose arguments are considered, whether rightly or wrongly, to rest on unexamined assumptions.

As for the judgement that philosophers of the Middle Ages devoted themselves to discussion of trivial and tiresome questions, we can dispose easily enough of the notion that they were given to heated arguments about the number of angels who could dance on the point of a pin. This notion is a caricature. For angels were conceived as spiritual beings, whereas dancing requires a body. Hence the question how many angels could dance on the point of a pin would be for a medieval theologian or philosopher a good example of a pseudo-question. At the same time the impression that the philosophers of the Middle Ages were preoccupied with tiresome and outmoded questions need not be based on a caricature of medieval philosophy. It can have other grounds.

Suppose that a man is convinced that there is no God to talk about, and even that such talk is nonsensical. He will obviously find medieval discussion of arguments for God's existence and Aquinas's discussion of the meaning of the terms predicated of God tiresome and unprofitable. But a positivist rejection of metaphysics applies to a much wider field than medieval metaphysics. And there is no need to discuss the matter here, though it is worth remarking that the positivist is likely to have more respect for the medieval metaphysicians, who did their best to give precise and clear statement to what they wished to say, than for some much later metaphysicians, whose obscurity and vagueness of expression is notorious.

One reason why a modern reader may form an unfavourable impression of philosophical discussion in the Middle Ages is the feeling that it is predominantly an academic affair, a discussion which is carried on by teachers in universities as a kind of in-game, and that passionate concern with the fundamental problems of human existence is conspicuous by its absence. It may be recognized, of course, that, given a more or less common background of religious belief, this state of affairs is understandable. But the impression of an arid intellectualism and of a remoteness from 'vital issues' may persist.

Contemporary British philosophy too has been accused of concentrating on trivial and tiresome questions and with passing over issues of importance for human life. Indeed, though modern analytic philosophy has marked affinity with certain phases of medieval thought, the former provides firmer ground for the accusations than does the latter. For questions of importance for human life were certainly dealt with by thinkers of the Middle Ages, even if the modern reader feels that such questions were treated in too arid and intellectualist a manner, largely because men looked to the Christian faith, not to philosophy in the narrow sense,[1] as a guide to life. In both cases, however, in that of medieval thought and in that of contemporary British philosophy, it is pertinent to ask whether they deal with themes which can be properly described as philosophical, the sort of themes which tend to recur, in one form or another, in the life of philosophy. In the opinion of the present writer an affirmative answer must be given in both cases. If someone prefers the philosophizing of, say, Miguel de Unamuno or of Leo Shestov, that is his affair. But if someone maintains that either medieval thought or contemporary British philosophy is not 'real' philosophy, he is recommending a certain use of the word 'philosophy', a use which is narrower than its common and legitimate range of meaning.

Philosophical questions are obviously raised in some context or other. In the Middle Ages this was often a theological context. For example, the question whether or not the concept of an infinite series is

---

[1] As will be seen later, a distinction was made within the Middle Ages between philosophy and theology. And philosophy, as so distinguished, is what is referred to above. With a thinker such as Aquinas, however, philosophy, though methodically distinguished from Christian theology, obviously forms part of a total world-outlook or comprehensive interpretation of reality.

self-contradictory was raised within the context of the idea of divine creation. Is creation 'from eternity' possible or impossible? Often the context of a question was a theory of, say, Aristotle. Given, for instance, the Aristotelian doctrine of substantial forms, and given a distinction between the biological ('vegetative'), sensitive and intellectual levels, are we to say that in man there are several substantial forms or one?

In such cases the questions may seem to a student to be historically conditioned to such an extent that some have no relevance today, while others appear relevant only to those who share the religious beliefs of the medievals. Reflection, however, will show that this point of view can be greatly exaggerated. When, for example, Aquinas maintained that the impossibility of an infinite series (in the sense of a series of events without any assignable first member or without a beginning) had never been proved, he was speaking as a philosopher, not as a theologian. For in his capacity as a theologian, so to speak, he believed that the world had a beginning, that there was an ideally assignable first moment of time. He did not, however, regard what he believed to be a truth of faith as entailing the conclusion that things could not have been otherwise. Hence he was free to discuss the possibility of an infinite series as an open question. Again, in the language of substantial forms the medievals discussed a genuine philosophical theme, the nature of man. We are more accustomed nowadays to discussing the meanings of the terms 'mind' and 'body' and the relation between mind and body. But this is one way in which a recurrent problem presents itself, a problem which was expressed in a different way in the Middle Ages.

It must be admitted that phrases such as 'the perennial problems of philosophy' are open to criticism. Take, for example, the problem of human freedom, in a psychological rather than in a political sense. This problem has been raised and discussed in different contexts in different times, now in a theological context, now in the light of the picture of the world as a mechanical system, now in the light of modern depth psychology. If we state the problem very briefly, we are inclined to speak of the same problem which recurs in different contexts. If, however, we state the problem in precisely the way in which it presented itself to, say, Kant, we shall then be inclined to regard it as distinct from the problem as it presents itself in the light of modern psychology. Each way of speaking has its advantages and disadvantages. And if we adopt the second way of speaking, we shall have to apply it to the problems discussed by medieval philosophers. At the same time it is clear that there are certain persistent data which give rise to basically the same problem or to recognizably similar problems. For example, we make use in an ordinary language of universal terms. So, of course, did the medievals. Hence there is no great difficulty in understanding the protracted medieval discussion of the meaning and reference of universal terms and in seeing that the medieval philosophers were discussing a genuine and recurrent philosophical problem.

Obviously, the fact that genuine and indeed important philosophical problems were discussed in the Middle Ages does not prove that they solved these problems. For the matter of that it would not really make any more sense to speak of the medieval solution of a problem than it would to speak of the Greek solution or of the modern solution. Like the terms 'Greek philosophy' and 'modern philosophy', the term 'medieval philosophy' covers the thought of many people. Some of the medieval thinkers, however, were undoubtedly men of outstanding mental ability; and we certainly cannot exclude in advance the possibility of their having said things which were worth saying and of their having shed some light on the problems discussed. As for solutions, we do not become philosophers simply by adopting other people's solutions to problems. If we do in fact endorse the solution given by this or that philosopher, whether ancient, medieval or modern, it must be the result of our own personal reflection. We can, however, approach philosophy by way of a past philosopher's thought, provided that we do not regard it as a divine revelation or a set of unquestionable dogmas. Many people have found a stimulus to philosophical reflection in the Platonic dialogues. Some at any rate have found it in the thought of a medieval philosopher.

3

Some remarks have already been made about use of the term 'medieval philosophy'. But some further comments may be in place in this introductory chapter.

In the first place the word 'philosophy', in the Middle Ages as in the ancient world, covered a good deal more than it does today. It would be inaccurate to say that it covered all human knowledge arrived at independently of divine revelation or of what was considered to be divine revelation. Medicine, for instance, was regarded as a practical art and was not classified as part of philosophy. Astronomy, however, belonged to natural philosophy. After the Middle Ages the development of the particular sciences led in the course of time to a narrowing of the field to which the term 'philosophy' was applied.[1] But to a thirteenth-century thinker such as Aquinas the term covered what it had covered for Aristotle. A clear distinction was made between philosophy and Christian theology or 'sacred doctrine', inasmuch as theology was regarded as employing premises revealed by God. But the embryonic or primitive forms of the natural sciences counted as philosophical disciplines; and in psychology no distinction was made between what would nowadays be regarded as scientific questions and those which would still be looked on as philosophical. In this book emphasis will be laid on themes which can still count, without linguistic impropriety, as philosophical themes. But we shall be dealing with a period in which the modern distinction between philosophy on the one hand and the particular sciences on the other had not yet emerged.

As for the term 'medieval', we can take this as covering, roughly, the period between the coronation of Charlemagne in 800 and the end of the fourteenth century. But these dates obviously cannot be taken as definitive limits; they are chosen for the sake of convenience. More-over, we cannot well give an account of medieval philosophy without saying something both about St Augustine, and about the period between the fall of the Roman empire and the revival of letters at the time of the Carolingian Renaissance.

Mention has already been made of the rather obvious fact that the term 'medieval philosophy' covers the thought of a great number of people. In other words, medieval philosophy was not a monolithic system. Nor can it be identified with the thought of St Thomas Aquinas, which never enjoyed in the Middle Ages that pre-eminent status which was accorded it by the Catholic Church in recent times. To be sure, we can hardly expect to find in medieval philosophy such great differences of outlook as those between, say, Hume and Hegel or J. L. Austin and Karl Jaspers. There is one obvious reason for this. However much the medieval thinkers may have differed among themselves in their estimate of the philosopher's power to prove truths relating to God, the end or goal of human life and so on, there was a common back-ground of religious belief. At the same time medieval philosophy as a

[1] I do not mean to imply that the narrowing took place immediately after the medieval period. For this is not the case. People continued for a long time to speak, for instance, of natural or experimental philosophy, when what was meant was what we would call physical science. Nor do I intend to imply that there is universal agreement today about the boundaries of philosophy. But there is sub-stantial agreement in *not* describing as philosophy a number of disciplines which were once so described.

whole comprised considerable variety, a variety which becomes more evident the closer we look. Between, for example, the philosophical thought of Aquinas in the thirteenth century and that of Nicholas of Autrecourt in the fourteenth century there are differences of fundamental importance.

At an early period, when philosophy amounted to little more than logic or dialectics, it was natural that theologians should tend to look on philosophy as the handmaid or instrument of theology. For unless logic has been developed as a formal science which can be regarded as a science in its own right, it is natural to look on it as providing tools for use elsewhere. And theology was then regarded as the highest science. In the course of time, as will be seen later, the concept of philosophy was greatly widened, and its autonomy came to be recognized. In the fourteenth century the close union between philosophy and theology, which can be found in the thought of, say, Aquinas, tended to fall apart. The metaphysical arguments of the thirteenth-century thinkers, relating, for example, to the existence of God or the immortality of the soul, were subjected to criticism. The range of philosophical demonstration was greatly narrowed. And one can imagine some of the late medieval philosophers, with their concentration on logical studies and their analytic bent of mind, as feeling more or less at home in the philosophical department of a modern British university. They were indeed religious believers; but they tended to relegate such beliefs to the sphere of faith, which lay beyond the scope of philosophical proof.

4

In one sense at any rate the medieval philosophers are extremely clear writers. That is to say, they try to say in a precise manner exactly what they mean. Their writings may indeed appear to lack profundity, at least if profundity and obscurity are regarded as synonymous terms. But they could hardly be accused of undue prolixity, of woolliness of thought, of failure to make distinctions or of substituting striking metaphors and attractive pictures for precise statement. In comparison with some later philosophers their thought is clear and is often expressed in an extremely bald manner, with a great economy of words.

At the same time the modern student of medieval philosophy is likely to encounter considerable difficulty in understanding the language employed. I do not refer to the use of Latin. The difficulty, which is one of unfamiliar terminology and categories, is encountered also in translations. In this book an attempt will be made to simplify terminology as far as possible. But some preliminary remarks may be appropriate.

In the first place some knowledge of Greek philosophy, especially of Aristotelianism, is highly desirable, though it can of course be replaced by *ad hoc* explanations of the meanings of terms. To take an example, the student of medieval philosophy must be able to see when the term 'matter' is being used in the sense of Aristotle's 'first matter'. Otherwise he might misinterpret such a statement as that matter does not exist by itself and imagine that some form of idealism was being expounded.[1]

In the second place, we are obviously not entitled to assume without more ado that a given word is being used by a medieval writer in the sense which would naturally suggest itself to an English reader. For instance, the Latin word *species* may indeed be used in one context to mean species in the sense in which we speak of species and genuses or *genera*. But in another context it may refer to a mental modification or idea. Again, in one context 'good' may be used in the sense in which good actions are opposed to bad actions, in an ethical context that is to say, while in another context it may be used in an ontological sense, being predicated of anything whatsoever when considered in relation to desire, appetite or will. Another example, to which reference has already been made, is the word 'science' (*scientia*). Nowadays it is used primarily in regard to the natural sciences, though we also speak of the social sciences. When, however, a medieval philosopher talks about a 'science', he means a body of propositions which are known to be true inasmuch as they follow from first principles or premises the truth of which is either self-evident or assured by some higher science.[2] Thus, according to Aquinas, metaphysics is a science, as its first principles are self-evidently true,[3] while theology is a science as its first principles or ultimate premises are revealed by God and their truth is assured by the divine knowledge itself.[4]

---

[1] The statement would mean that formless 'matter' never exists by itself without a 'form' or intelligible structure which makes a thing a certain kind of thing.
[2] From the subjective point of view 'science' would mean certain knowledge of the truth of such a body of propositions.
[3] This may suggest that for Aquinas the whole content of metaphysics can be deduced *a priori* from certain self-evidently true propositions. But it will be seen later that he did not in fact conceive metaphysics in this way.
[4] The attempt to fit theology into the Aristotelian idea of science is open to criticism. However, the point made here is simply that for the medievals Christian theology was the supreme science, whereas with us a reference to science is normally taken as a reference to natural science, unless there is a qualifying epithet

In other words, in order to understand the medieval philosophers, we have to make an effort to learn their language, to master their technical vocabulary or the special uses given to words taken from ordinary language. There is, of course, nothing exceptional in this situation. In the case of Kant, for example, we have to learn the meanings of technical terms, such as 'transcendental analytic', which are certainly not household words. With writers such as Locke and Berkeley we are not indeed faced with the necessity of learning the intended meanings of a host of specially invented technical terms. But we have to try to unravel the special uses of ordinary words such as 'idea'. Martin Heidegger has a vocabulary of his own. And even J. L. Austin, who had little use for linguistic pomposity, coined some technical terms to express his ideas.

In the twelfth century the Englishman John of Salisbury inveighed against the barbarous linguistic inventions of the philosophers and logicians. And from the point of view of a lover of pure classical Latin he was doubtless justified in his criticism. But there can be no philosophically relevant objection to the invention of technical terms in philosophy and logic, provided that they have assignable functions and provided that these functions cannot be fulfilled just as well, and without cumbersome circumlocutions, by already existing terms. The fact of the matter is that if the medievals wished to express both certain concepts of Greek thought and their own ideas in a succinct manner, they could hardly help inventing the sort of vocabulary to which literary minded people such as John of Salisbury took exception.

It must be admitted, however, that the difficulty in understanding the medieval philosophers is not simply and solely a matter of learning a technical vocabulary. For example, when Ockham talks about terms of first intention and terms of second intention, he is using a technical vocabulary; but there is no great difficulty in understanding what he is talking about. Terms of first intention stand for things. For instance, in the statement 'man is mortal' the word 'man' is a conventional sign which is said to stand for men, in the sense that mortality is predicated of men. Terms of second intention stand for other signs. For instance, in the statement that species are subdivisions of genuses the word species stands immediately not for things but for class-names, such as man and lion, which do stand for things. When, however, Aquinas

---

such as 'social'. And the natural sciences are not of course regarded as exemplifying the Aristotelian concept of science.

says that God is his own existence and that he is existence or being itself (*ipsum esse*), he is making a metaphysical statement which, by the criteria of ordinary usage, is clearly odd and which cannot be made of anything else but God. In a sense, of course, to understand the statement[1] is to understand the use of a technical vocabulary. But it is not simply a case of logical classification. A metaphysics is involved.

To put the matter briefly, the language of the medieval philosophers is semi-artificial. Basically they use ordinary language. But the ordinary language is enriched with (some would say disfigured by) technical terms, some invented to render concepts of Greek philosophy, others coined or adapted to express the ideas of the writers.

5

References have been made above to the common background of religious belief and to the relation between philosophy and theology in the Middle Ages. The impression may thus be given that western philosophy in the medieval period was confined to Christendom. In point of fact, however, there were eminent Jewish philosophers, such as Maimonides, and famous Islamic philosophers, such as Avicenna and Averroes (to give them the names by which they were known by the Christian thinkers). The tendency in histories of philosophy is to treat the Jewish and Islamic thought of the Middle Ages in function of its connection with and influence on that of Christian writers. This procedure is obviously open to criticism. And a specialist in the history of Jewish and Islamic thought would write from a different perspective. At the same time the procedure referred to is natural enough, if we are considering medieval philosophy as an integral phase in the development of European thought. In any case something has to be said about Jewish and Islamic philosophy in the Middle Ages, even if what is said is inadequate from the point of view of the relevant specialists.

[1] I am assuming that it is intelligible.

2

Christian Thought in the Ancient World [1]

IT is hardly necessary to say that the Apostles and their immediate successors were concerned with preaching the Christian faith, not with elaborating a philosophical system. They regarded themselves as witnesses to the risen Christ and as mediating to men the word of God and the good news of his regenerative action, not as thinkers who were endeavouring to solve the enigma of the universe or to discover the significance of human life by their own mental powers. For them it was a question not of what the human mind can discover about reality by philosophical reflection, but rather of what God has done, of the divine action, and of his self-revelation in and through Christ. We are indeed told that during St Paul's visit to Athens some philosophers of the Epicurean and Stoic schools disputed with him. But it is clear that the Apostle did not present his message as a set of abstract truths arrived at by metaphysical arguments. He was preaching 'Jesus and the resurrection'.[1]

However, it was soon found necessary to defend the new religion against attacks made on it by non-Christian thinkers, to justify its existence in the eyes of the imperial authorities, and to argue that true wisdom was to be found in Christianity rather than in the writings of the pagan philosophers. There thus appeared works such as the *Apology* of Marcianus Aristides (*c.* A.D. 140), addressed to the Emperor Antoninus Pius, the *Plea for the Christians* of Athenagoras (*c.* A.D. 177),

[1] Acts, XVII, 18.

addressed to the emperors Marcus Aurelius and Commodus and the writings of St Justin Martyr (c. A.D. 100–64). The productions of the apologists could not indeed be described as philosophical works. At the same time the apologists naturally made some use of terms and ideas taken from Greek philosophy. Further, when engaged in answering the accusation of atheism they argued both that rejection of polytheism in favour of monotheism was rational and that this truth had been discerned, to some extent at least, by the wise men or philosophers of the pagan world. In regard to the first point it is useless to look to the apologists for developed philosophical arguments. We can indeed find embryonic arguments, as when Theophilus of Antioch asserts in his *Ad Autolycum* (c. A.D. 180), that just as the soul can be known through the movements of the body, so can God and his attributes be known through creatures. Again, Minucius Felix[1] argued that the cosmic order shows the divine unity. But such remarks are little more than statements which repeat the sort of summary inferences already made in the Bible.[2] In regard to the second point, however, namely that the pagan philosophers, or some of them, approximated to the truth,[3] some further indication is required of the attitudes adopted by Christians in the ancient world to Greek philosophy.

2

Some of the early Christian writers adopted a thoroughly hostile attitude to philosophy. This reaction was doubtless encouraged by the criticism directed against Christianity by some philosophers when the religion became more widely known. Basically, however, it was the expression of the sharp contrast which was drawn between the revealed wisdom which comes from God and human speculation, between the Christian life, made possible and sustained by divine grace, and the self-sufficient life of virtue provided by philosophers such as the Cynics and Stoics. At the same time the adoption by a given Christian writer of a hostile, even contemptuous attitude towards philosophy by no means entailed the conclusion that the writer in question was uninfluenced by non-Christian and non-Jewish thought. A notable example is that of Tertullian (c. 160–c. 220). When he chose, he could express

[1] The dates of Minucius Felix are uncertain. Whether he was senior or junior to Tertullian is disputed.
[2] Cf. Wisdom of Solomon, XIII and Romans, I, 20.
[3] The criterion of truth employed in this context is obviously the Christian faith.

great contempt for the philosophers, especially when he was thinking of the Bible as the one true guide to salvation. In his opinion Athens and Jerusalem, as he put it, had nothing in common. At the same time he accepted ideas which derived from Stoicism.

Generally speaking, a different attitude came to prevail among the more intellectual Christians. Even those who took a rather dim view of the philosophers felt compelled to admit that some pagan writers had come closer than others to religious truths recognized by Jews and Christians. Being reluctant, however, to attribute this fact to the power of philosophy itself, they advanced the extremely questionable theory that thinkers such as Plato had borrowed from the Old Testament.[1] Other Christian writers took a different line, maintaining that the divine Word or *Logos*,[2] which enlightens every man who comes into the World,[3] had enabled the philosophers, though some more than others, to attain a partial recognition of religious and moral truth. The view thus came to be proposed that while the Jews had been enlightened by the Law and prophets, the Greeks had been enlightened, even if in a lesser degree, through philosophy. Both the Law and the prophets on the one hand and philosophy on the other looked forward to the Gospel.

This view obviously attributed some positive value to Greek philosophy. Equally obviously, however, it implied that philosophy, when considered as a search for religious and moral truth or as a way of salvation, had ceased to have a function. From the point of view of the Christian writers the search for the maker and father of the universe, as Plato put it, together with the search for knowledge of man's final end and of the way to attain it, had reached their goal in the Christian religion. Logical and philosophical categories could, of course, be used as instruments in theology and in developing a general Christian interpretation of the world. But as far as knowledge of God and of the end or goal of human life were concerned, the search for truth had been supplanted by the possession of it.

A positive evaluation of Greek thought, especially Platonism, as an approximation to the truth appears even with some of the second

[1] For example, Plato's hypothesis, in the *Timaeus*, of the divine craftsman was thought to incorporate ideas borrowed from Genesis.
[2] For the Christian writers the *Logos* was identified with the second person of the Trinity. As for the discussion about the influence of philosophical ideas on, say, the author of the fourth Gospel, we cannot enter here upon this theme.
[3] John, 1, 9.

century apologists, notably in Justin Martyr's *Dialogue with Trypho*.[1]
It is more characteristic, however, of the Christian thinkers of
Alexandria, the city where an impressive and flourishing Christian
intellectual life first arose, centred round the catechetical school. This
school, which is chiefly associated with the names of Clement of
Alexandria (c. 150–c. 213) and Origen (c. 185–c. 254), can be described
as a theological institute, devoted to biblical exegesis and to the understanding and theological statement of the content of Christian belief.
The leading thinkers of the school were considerably influenced in
their speculation by Greek thought.

Clement of Alexandria, a convert to Christianity, developed the
line of thought adumbrated by Justin Martyr. That is to say, he
represented Greek philosophy as a positive preparation for Christianity,
as a schoolmaster with the function of educating the Greek mind to the
point at which it would be open to the truth revealed through Christ.
Like Justin Martyr before him, Clement accepted the idea that Greek
philosophers had borrowed from the Old Testament and had distorted
what they borrowed. This idea was combined, however, with the
conviction that the philosophers, especially Plato, had arrived at some
knowledge of the truth through the illumination of the divine *Logos*.
Further, Clement regarded philosophical speculation not simply as a
preparation for Christian wisdom, but also as an instrument for
penetrating, grasping and stating this wisdom. He contrasted Christian
gnosis or knowledge, possessed by the more intellectual Christian
believers, not only with uninstructed faith but also with the alleged
higher and esoteric knowledge of the heretical Gnostics.[2] For example,
it is only the more intellectual Christians who understand that all the
names predicated of God are in a real sense inapplicable to him, inasmuch as he transcends our conceptual grasp. In this matter Clement

[1] The attitude shown by Justin Martyr is not surprising, as he had made his way
to Christianity via the philosophical schools and had found some light in Platonism in particular.

[2] The Gnostic systems of the first centuries A.D. offered doctrines of reality as bases
for a way of salvation. Gnosticism has often been regarded as an offshoot of
Christianity and as constituting an esoteric or allegedly higher form of the
Christian religion. But though some Gnostic systems incorporated a greater or
less degree of scriptural elements, others seem to have had no positive relation
to Christianity, while those which contained scriptural elements were compila-
tions of Biblical, Greek and oriental elements. Among the second century Gnostics
we can mention Marcion, Basilides and Valentinus. Among the Christians who
wrote specifically against the Gnostics were St Irenaeus in the second century
and Hippolytus in the first half of the third century.

seems to have been influenced by Philo,[1] though he also refers to Plato's remarks in the *Republic* about the transcendent nature of the Good. At the same time Clement's appreciation of Greek philosophy is far from being unqualified. For he attributes positive value to it only in so far as it can be represented as approximating, in some cases, to Christian truth. He is interested in it as a preparation for Christianity, not for its own sake. And in common with other Christian writers of the ancient world he regards the Christian thinker as the true philosopher and Christianity as the true 'philosophy' or wisdom.

The most remarkable figure of the Christian school at Alexandria was Origen. A man who underwent torture for his religion in the reign of the emperor Decius, he was a convinced and fervent Christian. At the same time he was endowed with a powerful mind, given to speculative thought; and certain features of his doctrine led to accusations of unorthodoxy. In general, he can be said to have developed a Christian world-view with the aid of philosophy, especially of Platonism in the form which it had assumed in the Hellenistic world at his time,[2] but also to some extent of Stoicism. His treatise *On First Principles* expressed the outlook of a philosophically minded theologian, while in his later apologetic work *Against Celsus* he felt able to appeal to certain aspects of Greek thought against a philosopher's attack on the Christian religion.

In Origen's vision or interpretation of reality there is an outgoing from and a return to God, conceived as the One, which is identified with the Father. The One transcends essence and being but can be described as good or, rather, as the Good itself, absolute goodness. Creation is the expression or communication or diffusion of goodness, proceeding from God by a necessity of his nature, because, that is to say, he is what he is. The medium of creation is the *Logos*, which contains the Ideas or eternal patterns of creation, the archetypes in the divine mind, which is identified with the second Person of the Trinity, the Word of the prologue to the fourth Gospel. As the Platonic idea of the Soul of the world is seen as an approximation to the Christian doctrine of the Holy Spirit, Origen can be said to have interpreted

[1] The famous Jewish writer, Philo of Alexandria (*c.* 20 B.C.–A.D. 40), exercised a very considerable influence on Christian thinkers. Himself strongly influenced by Greek philosophy, he endeavoured to find in the Scriptures, which he allegorized, the philosophical theories which seemed to him to be true.

[2] Origen is said to have heard lectures by Ammonius Saccas, the teacher of Plotinus.

Christian trinitarian belief in the light of the Neoplatonic hierarchy (or, more accurately, in the light of Middle Platonism), or to have used the latter to elucidate the former.

As for human souls, Origen proposed the theory of pre-existence, according to which human souls existed before their union with terrestrial bodies. In this state of pre-existence they became alienated from God by a free act of sin and descended, so to speak, into this mortal life. This falling away from God is a centrifugal movement, away from the soul's true centre, which is balanced by the centripetal movement of the soul's return to God and its eventual clothing with a spiritual body. In the end all souls, and even, apparently, the fallen angels, will return to God who will then be, in the words of St Paul, 'all in all'.[1]

Some of Origen's theories are doubtless out of accord with the Bible as ordinarily understood. But he distinguished different levels of interpretation, corresponding to different distinguishable levels in man. Literal interpretation of the Scriptures constituted for him the lowest level, which was coordinated with the level of the 'flesh' in man. A higher level was that of ethical or moral significance, coordinated with the level of the soul, while allegorical interpretation of the Scriptures corresponded to the level of spirit in man. Allegorizing of the Scriptures was not, of course, a novelty. The practice had been extensively employed by, for example, Philo. The point is, however, that, given this scheme of levels of interpretation, there was plenty of room for a philosophical or speculative interpretation of the Bible. In terms of a later distinction between theology and philosophy we can say that Origen was developing Christian speculative theology with the aid of ideas derived from or suggested by philosophy. He looked on himself, however, as developing Christian 'philosophy', in the sense of wisdom, for which non-Christian philosophy had been a preparation.

3

The Fathers of the Church of the fourth and fifth centuries were chiefly occupied in working out basic doctrines of the Christian religion and in

[1] I Corinthians, xv, 28. The idea of the soul falling away from its true centre into the sphere of matter is found in Neoplatonism. Philosophical interpretations of the doctrine of the Fall recur in much later periods, for example with the German mystical writer Jakob Böhme (1575–1624) and with the philosopher Schelling (1775–1854).

participating in the theological controversies which led to conciliar definitions. Their employment of philosophical terms and concepts in the development of trinitarian and christological doctrines belong more properly to the history of theology than to that of philosophy.[1] Nowadays the cry is sometimes raised that Christian theology ought to be dehellenized, the emphasis being placed sometimes on a need to return to more biblical ways of thought, sometimes on the need to make Christian beliefs intelligible to modern man and to exhibit their relevance to the world and life as we know it.[2] This is not a matter which can be discussed here.[3] We may note, however, that by using ideas taken from Greek philosophy (especially from the Platonic tradition, though also from Stoicism) in the development of predominantly theological themes the Fathers helped to counterbalance, in the medieval period, the impact of Aristotelianism. In spite of the attacks made on Christianity by Neoplatonists such as Porphyry in the third century, the Fathers naturally tended to turn for philosophical terms, concepts and arguments to the philosophy, namely Neoplatonism, which laid most stress on spiritual reality and on the ascent of the soul to God and which happened to be the last great current of metaphysical speculation in the ancient world.[4] And if in the thought of such a thirteenth-century admirer of Aristotle as St Thomas Aquinas there was a strong dosage of Platonism, this was due in some measure to the writings of the Christian thinkers of the ancient world.

The statement that the Fathers of the Church were so preoccupied with theological themes and controversies that to describe them as philosophers is to misdescribe them is doubtless a valid generalization; but it stands in need of certain qualifications. If the term 'philosophy' is

[1] The Latin Fathers obviously had to find equivalents for terms used by the Greek Fathers. And the associations and images suggested by Latin equivalents might be different from the associations and images suggested by the Greek originals. For the matter of that, the meaning of a philosophical term might undergo alteration in its theological use, whether it was Greek or Latin.

[2] A champion of such dehellenization, though not of a return to biblical thought, is Professor Leslie Dewart, in *The Future of Belief* (London, 1967) and *The Foundations of Belief* (London, 1969).

[3] If anyone imagines that the Bible gives rise to no philosophical problems, he is mistaken. But it does not necessarily follow, of course, that they have to be treated in terms of, say, the philosophy of Aristotle.

[4] Needless to say, not all the Fathers of the Church were speculatively inclined. St Gregory of Nyssa, a Greek Father, certainly was; but St Ambrose, a Latin Father, was not. Cicero was more to Ambrose's taste than Neoplatonist metaphysicians.

understood in the sense which the early Christian writers tended to give it, the statement is untrue. As we have seen, the early Christian writers emphasized those aspects of the philosophy of the ancient world under which it could be seen as a search for happiness and salvation. And they naturally looked on Christianity as the true 'philosophy', the fulfilment of previous desires and groping. If, however, the word 'philosophy' is understood in terms of a later sharp distinction between philosophy on the one hand and theology on the other, it would indeed be extremely misleading to describe the Fathers of the Church as philosophers. For the use in theology of concepts derived from philosophy does not by itself convert theology into philosophy. At the same time, the statement that the Fathers were not philosophers, in the sense in which this term would generally be understood today, leaves out of account the fact that with some of them at any rate we can find lines of thought which clearly count as philosophical even in terms of later ideas of what constitutes philosophy. This is notably true of Augustine.

The point which I am trying to make can be illustrated in this way. St Basil (d. 379) and St Gregory of Nazianzus (d. c. 390), after having been schoolfellows for a time, were later students together at Athens. There they imbibed the literary culture (the 'rhetoric') of the ancient world. This, at any rate in its broader humanistic forms, included some knowledge of the doctrines of the philosophical schools. But philosophy as practised by Cynics, Stoics, Epicureans and Platonists in the Hellenistic world tended to be presented as a way of life, not simply as a set of doctrines about the world. There was thus a difference between the humanistic, anthropocentric education and culture of the rhetoricians and philosophy in the sense of a way of life, especially when this way of life involved, as in Platonism, the location of the true reality in a spiritual sphere and the turning of the human soul to God. Christian thinkers such as Basil and Gregory of Nazianzus could thus find values in literary humanism, in so far as it did not divert man from the Christian life, whereas their attitude to philosophy considered as a way of salvation was complex. They naturally sympathized with the search for virtue, happiness, the divine reality; and they could on occasion find positive value in actual philosophical theories.[1] Believing that Christianity was the true revealed wisdom, they had no sympathy with

[1] For example, in his *Oration* 43 Gregory of Nazianzus approves of the philosophical doctrine that to every virtue there is a corresponding vice (see Migne, *P.G.*, 36, 581B).

the pretensions of philosophical schools to expound the saving truth; and they tended to dismiss a great deal of philosophical discussion as useless or as battles about words.[1] This was, basically, the common attitude among Christian writers of the period, though they differed, as we have seen, in the emphasis placed on the notion of a preparation for the Gospel and in the extent to which different Christian writers employed philosophical ideas in their expositions of Christian doctrine and ethics.

From the point of view of speculative thought, St Gregory of Nyssa (c. 335–c. 395) is, among the Greek Fathers, of particular interest. He was indeed primarily a Christian theologian, who presented a Christian world-view. But as in the case of Origen[2] this Christian world-view is impregnated with ideas derived from or suggested by Greek philosophy, so that it appears as a fusion or synthesis of Platonic, Middle Platonist and Neoplatonic elements with Christian belief.[3] The One is the Trinity;[4] the *Logos* or Word became incarnate in Christ; man's likeness to God, referred to by Plato, is the work of divine grace; and the human soul's return to God is not simply a solitary flight of the individual but is achieved in and through Christ as head of the Church.[5] Gregory was a mystical theologian, who insisted that it is only through mystical experience that man can perceive the divine presence. At the same time he also insisted that branches of study such as natural philosophy are not to be despised or rejected. And he himself speculated about such subjects as the ontological status of the qualities of which bodies are composed.[6]

Of the Greek Fathers of the Church Gregory of Nyssa is the most philosophically inclined. And his thought constituted one of the main

[1] For instance, Gregory of Nazianzus poured scorn on Pythagorean or Orphic talk about beans, on Plato's theory (a myth) on transmigration, on disputes about the void, and so on (see *Oration* 27; Migne, *P.G.*, 36).

[2] Gregory of Nyssa often followed Origen, but not without qualifications. By traditional standards of orthodoxy, Gregory was the more orthodox.

[3] Gregory's mystical interests naturally inclined him to view Neoplatonism with sympathy. But his thought shows evidence of the influence not only of Plato and Platonism but also of Aristotelianism and Stoicism.

[4] In other words, Gregory tries to avoid the Neoplatonic theory of a descending hierarchy. The three divine Persons or hypostases are one God.

[5] Gregory maintained that in view of their common nature all men are really one. This philosophical position naturally favoured Origen's theory of the return of all men to God.

[6] The presupposition of this discussion is presumably derived from the *Timaeus* of Plato.

sources of inspiration of the first outstanding philosopher of the Middle Ages, John Scotus Erigena.

4

The Latin Fathers in general were not much given to philosophical speculation. St Jerome was a great Scripture scholar who in his moments of backsliding (as he evidently considered them) was given to reading the Latin literary classics rather than to philosophizing. St Ambrose's taste, as has already been mentioned, was for ethics rather than for metaphysics. And St Gregory the Great, though an eminent occupant of the Holy See, was no Plato or Aristotle. St Augustine, however, was an outstanding thinker. Though he was first and foremost a theologian, his philosophical reflections, according to Bertrand Russell, who was no great friend of Christianity, showed 'very great ability'.[1] Hence it is appropriate to devote to him a separate chapter.

[1] *History of Western Philosophy* (London, 1946), p. 372.

3

Christian Thought in the
Ancient World [2]

AUGUSTINE was born at Tagaste in what is now Algeria in 354. His mother, Monica, was a Christian, his father, Patricius, a pagan. His education, first at Tagaste, then at Madaura and finally at Carthage, was pretty well entirely literary.[1] A youth of strong bodily passions, when he went to Carthage he soon became estranged from the religion in which he had been brought up by his mother.[2] At the age of eighteen his reading of Cicero's dialogue *Hortensius* impelled him to seek wisdom; but he failed to find it in Christianity. He found the Old Testament repellent in many ways. And the Judaeo-Christian doctrine that God created all things seemed to him quite untenable. For it made God responsible for the existence of evil. And how could this be the case if God was, as Christians maintained, absolutely good? Augustine's search for enlightenment led him to embrace the dualistic doctrine of the Manichees, according to which there were two ultimate principles, one responsible for good and for the human soul, the other for evil and

---

[1] Augustine studied a restricted number of Latin classics. He learned Virgil by heart and greatly appreciated him. Greek, however, was not to his taste; and his knowledge of the language was severely limited. This meant that when he later became interested in philosophy, he had to rely for his knowledge on Greek thought, on Latin summaries of the philosophers' opinions and on Latin translations.

[2] Augustine was not baptized as a child. Deferment of baptism for many years was not uncommon at the time.

matter, including the body.[1] The responsibility for turbulent passions could therefore be attributed to the evil principle, the author of the kingdom of darkness.[2]

In 383 Augustine, who had become a teacher at Carthage, left Africa for Rome; and in 384 he took up the position of municipal professor of rhetoric at Milan. By this time his faith in Manichaeism was shaken; but he was inclinded to Academic scepticism more than to Christianity. However, a reading of some 'Platonic treatises' in the Latin translation of Victorinus[3] led him to think better of Christian doctrine. For Neoplatonism convinced him of two things. First, there could be, and indeed was a spiritual reality, the possibility of which Augustine had come to doubt. Secondly, the presence of evil in the world could be reconciled with the doctrine of divine creation. For evil, according to Plotinus, was not a positive thing but a privation. To say this was not to say that evil was unreal, an illusion. Blindness, a physical evil, is the privation of sight; but it is a real privation. Similarly, moral evil is a privation of right order in the will; but it is real enough. At the same time privations such as blindness or darkness (the privation of light) are not positive things which must have been created by a God who created all things.[4]

We learn from Augustine himself that Neoplatonism facilitated his conversion to Christianity. But it did not resolve his moral conflict. He listened to St Ambrose's sermons at Milan, read the New Testament and acquainted himself with accounts of the conversions of

[1] The religious and ethical system of the Manichees was founded in the third century by Mani, who appears to have been of Persian origin. It included elements taken from various sources, including Zoroastrianism. The Albigensians and Cathari in the Middle Ages can be regarded as spiritual descendants of the Manichees.

[2] The Manichees held that man could awaken to the light and attain purity. And some of them undoubtedly led austere lives. But in the fifth Book of his *Confessions* (10, 18) Augustine refers to the way in which Manichaean doctrine enabled him to claim that it was not he who sinned but something else in him.

[3] Most probably the 'Platonic treatises' referred to by Augustine were the *Enneads* of Plotinus or included part of them.

[4] No great amount of reflection is required in order to see that the theory of evil as privation of good by no means provides the complete solution of the problem of reconciling the existence of evil with existence of an omnipotent, omniscient and all-good creator. But Augustine did not claim that it provided a complete solution. At the same time he saw in it a way of escaping the conclusion that the presence of evil in the world was sufficient evidence of the need for accepting the dualism of the Manichees.

Victorinus to the Christian faith, and of the life of St Anthony of Egypt. Finally in 386 there occurred the famous episode related in the eighth Book of *Confessions*;[1] and in the following year Augustine was baptized by St Ambrose.

Returning to Africa, Augustine was ordained a priest; and in 395 he was consecrated assistant bishop to Valerius, whom he succeeded in the see of Hippo in 396. He died in 430, while the Vandals were besieging his episcopal city.

2

In his life as a bishop Augustine's attention was naturally devoted to the Scriptures rather than to the writings of pagan philosophers, and to the development of theology rather than to the construction of anything which we would be likely to describe as a philosophical system. Moreover, he became actively engaged in theological controversies with Donatists,[2] Pelagians[3] and others, which absorbed a great deal of his time and stimulated a substantial part of his literary output. It is therefore perfectly understandable that some writers on Augustine should emphasize the way in which his philosophical interests diminished. Though, however, this emphasis serves as a corrective to overemphasis on the influence of Neoplatonism on Augustine's thought, any suggestion that he abandoned philosophy stands in need of qualification.

Philosophy, at any rate the sort of philosophy to which he was

[1] 7–12.

[2] When Christianity spread in the Roman world and came to enjoy imperial recognition and official standing, there arose the danger of the Church's compromising with the world about it and of an increasing dilution of the Christian spirit. The Donatists, called after Donatus, a bishop of Carthage, regarded themselves as a chosen people whose mission it was to maintain the purity of the Church and its separation from 'the world'. Augustine emphasized the unity of the human race and the ideal of the Church's becoming coextensive with society. But what most excited his opposition was the Donatists' schismatic tendencies, their tendency to create and maintain a Church distinct from the Church which they regarded as contaminated and impure.

[3] Pelagius, a contemporary of Augustine, came to Rome from Britain. He was a man of high ideals and genuine sensitivity to social evils. In Augustine's opinion, however, Pelagianism laid too much emphasis on human freedom (completely restored by baptism) and self-reliance, disregarding human weakness and corruption and the need for divine grace. We can say perhaps that for Augustine Pelagian ethics bore far too close a resemblance to the ethics of Stoicism.

attracted and which he considered as worth pursuing, meant for Augustine the knowledge of where true and lasting happiness was to be found and of the means to attain it. Man's desire for happiness is the cause or ground for philosophy. Philosophizing is the search for wisdom. True wisdom is to be found only in the knowledge and possession of God. From the time of his conversion Augustine naturally believed that the search for wisdom which could be seen at work in Greek philosophy, or at any rate in certain currents of thought, attained its goal in Christianity. But he obviously did not believe that self-commitment to the Christian religion immediately conferred wisdom and happiness in the full sense of the terms. The Christian could grow in wisdom and in likeness to God through grace. And the goal of lasting happiness could be fully attained only in heaven, in the vision of God. If, therefore, the word 'philosophy' is understood in terms of the pursuit of happiness and of knowledge of God, it is clear that Augustine never abandoned philosophy. Philosophy as a search could be left behind only when the object of the search was fully attained.

If, however, we choose to understand the word 'philosophy' in the restricted sense in which it is distinguished from theology, it is doubtless quite correct to say that Augustine's purely philosophical interests diminished in proportion as he became absorbed in theological speculation and in theological controversies. It is also doubtless true to say that the influence of Neoplatonism diminished. This can be seen, for example, in his handling of St Paul and his doctrine. However, though Augustine as a bishop was absorbed in what we would describe as theological topics, his *Confessions*, which were written not long after his consecration, contain passages which can properly be described as philosophical even according to our use of the term today. And his *City of God*, written late in life, has some philosophical interest, even if, as a whole, it would now be described as a theological work.

In point of fact Augustine did not make that clear distinction between philosophy and theology which was made later on in the Middle Ages. As we have seen, he used the term 'philosophy' in a very broad sense. At the same time he was quite capable of distinguishing between the acceptance of a proposition as true simply on authority, as when a child believes something to be true on the word of its parents, and seeing that a proposition is true as the result of a process of reasoning. In regard to Christian faith, he maintained that faith precedes but that it should be followed, wherever possible, by understanding.[1] The intellectual penetration of the faith and its implications is, of course, in our terms, a theological activity. But in pursuing this activity Augustine made use of philosophical concepts, even if, as we have remarked, the influence of Neoplatonism diminished.

Though, however, Augustine did not make any clear distinction between philosophy and theology, there are in his writings discussions which can be described as philosophical in the sense borne by the term even when the distinction has been made. And it is on such discussions, on some of them that is to say, that we shall concentrate here. To do this is admittedly to mutilate Augustine's thought. For if we understood philosophy in his sense, an account of his thought as a whole would have to be given. Further, the discussions which can be described as philosophical in a modern sense are often embedded in a theological context. However, in a book such as this a policy of selective extraction has to be pursued, with a view to illustrating the quality of Augustine's mind and his lines of thought in the area of what the modern student would regard as philosophical themes.

3

It has been mentioned that when Augustine's faith in Manichaeism was shattered, he felt an inclination to Academic scepticism. But though a flirtation with scepticism was a natural enough phase after the breakdown of a set of beliefs, scepticism was not a philosophy in which Augustine could find satisfaction. For one thing, he was a passionate seeker after a truth by which a man could live. For another thing, he soon came to see that we cannot in fact entertain real or genuine doubt about everything. For example, reflection will convince anyone that he cannot be deceived in thinking that he exists. 'For if you did not exist, you could not be deceived in anything.'[2] Here Augustine anticipates Descartes, so far as the *si fallor, sum* (if I am deceived, I am) is concerned, though he does not try, as Descartes was to try, to make this truth the basis of a philosophical system. With Augustine it is simply an example of the certainties which we undoubtedly possess.

[1] Augustine's mind was too acute to fail to see that acceptance of truths on authority, to be a rational act, must have some basis in reason. The child's acceptance of what it is told by its parents is not irrational, though the reasons which justify belief are implicit rather than explicit, as far, that is to say, as the child is concerned.
[2] *De libero arbitrio* (*On Free Will*), 2, 3, 7.

Augustine is quite well aware that problems arise in regard to sense-knowledge. He assumes indeed that we become directly aware of external objects. Thus a child can be taught by description the meanings of many terms referring to corporeal things; but this process of learning through description is ultimately dependent on knowledge by acquaintance, on learning the meanings of some terms by what we call ostensive definition.[1] And Augustine does not doubt that there are external objects which can be pointed out. The possibility of there not being an external world at all is not one of his problems. But he sees, of course, that there are cases which seem, at first sight, to cast doubt upon the testimony or reliability of the senses. Converging railway lines do not indeed fall within the field of Augustine's experience; but there are other old friends (familiar enough to all who have followed the discussions about the modern sense-datum theory) which do, such as the hackneyed case of the oar which, when partially immersed in water, appears bent. If in such cases I assent to the testimony of the senses, am I not in error?

Augustine gives a negative answer to this question. If the oar, when partially immersed in water, appears bent, and if I say 'the oar looks bent', I am saying what is true. But if I say, 'the oar really is bent', I am going beyond the testimony of sense. In other words, the error lies in my judgement about the testimony of sense, not in the testimony itself. Sight shows me how the oar appears in certain circumstances; but it does not tell me what the oar is 'in itself', apart from its appearance in the given circumstances. Hence sight cannot be said to lie.

It is worth drawing attention to the picture of the situation which Augustine has in mind. External things cause modification in the sense organs; but, in his opinion, the corporeal cannot act upon the incorporeal or spiritual. The soul, noticing or observing the modifications in the sense organs,[2] forms its judgements, whereas the senses make no judgements. As, therefore, logical truth and falsity are predicated of judgements, we cannot properly speak of the senses as erring or as giving false testimony, though they may of course provide occasions for false judgements by the mind.

We may be inclined to think that to locate error in the judgement

---

[1] If a child has seen a cat, it can obviously be given some idea of the meaning of 'tiger' by being told that it signifies a very large cat-like animal with such and such markings. But it probably learns the meaning of 'cat' by hearing the word applied to actual specimens.

[2] See *De quantitate animae* (*On the Greatness of the Soul*), 23, 41 and 25, 48.

rather than in modifications of the sense organs or in sensation does little or nothing to help us to distinguish between appearance and reality. It is arguable, however, that it is not the philosopher's job to tell us how to distinguish between, for example, an oar which appears bent simply because it is partially immersed in water and an oar which is really bent. For we know how to do this already. And if we do not we should not expect the philosopher to tell us. What the philosopher can do, it may be said, is to try to clear up a theoretical puzzle which has little to do with practical life. Many people at any rate have thought that Augustine makes a contribution to showing the fly the way out of the bottle (to use a Wittgensteinian expression), even if the picture of the soul observing modifications in the senses is not particularly helpful.

Augustine thus tries to dispose of scepticism based on the alleged unreliability of sense experience. Like Plato before him, however, his attention is chiefly focused on the propositions which seem to him to possess the characteristics of immutability, necessity and universality. Consider, for example, mathematical propositions. A proposition such as $8+2=10$ is for Augustine immutably true.[1] Further, it is necessarily true. It does not just happen to be true, when it might be false. Nor is it sometimes true and sometimes false. It rules over minds, as it were, rather than the other way round. Finally, the proposition is universally true. It may be true for one man and false for another that a current of air is a pleasant breeze. For to the other man it may be a detestable draught. But the truth of a mathematical proposition is unaffected by personal factors. And the same truth can be seen independently by people living in different parts of the world and in different historical periods.

4

According to Augustine, we see such truths in a manner analogous to that in which we see bodily objects. That is to say, we see a tree because it is there to be seen. Analogously, the eternal truths form an intelligible world of truth. They are in some sense there to be seen to

[1] It may be said that we could change the meanings of the symbols in such a way that it would no longer be true that $8+2=10$. Augustine would doubtless reply that if we changed the meanings of the symbols so as to make it true that $5+2=10$, what would be expressed by the new mathematical statement would be precisely the same as what was previously meant by $8+2=10$. If we chose to call cats 'dogs' and dogs 'cats'; the statement that cats bark would be true, but it would say the same as what was previously meant by 'dogs bark'.

be grasped intuitively. Further, this intelligible world of truth reveals itself to reflection as grounded on the absolute truth itself: God. If we turn to Augustine with the hope of finding a series of developed proofs of the existence of God, we shall be disappointed. He starts from the standpoint of faith. And though in the process of faith seeking under-standing of itself Augustine reflects on the evidence or signs of the divine presence and activity, the 'arguments' which he gives are generally little more than summary statements, reminders to those who already believe. His favourite argument, however, is from the eternal truths, a line of argument which reappears in some modern philo-sophies, notably in that of Leibniz. The general idea is that as the human imagination and its products reflect the changeable human mind, so the eternal truths, which are discovered by the mind and compel its acceptance of them, reflect an eternal ground, an eternal being.

This line of argument is hardly likely to impress minds which have imbibed Hume's doctrine of propositions which state 'relations of ideas' or Wittgenstein's theory of tautologies. What, it may be asked, have analytic propositions to do with the existence of God? We must, however, bear in mind the fact that Augustine was profoundly impressed by truths which seemed to him to be in a sense above the human mind, in the sense, that is to say, that they could be recognized but not altered by man, and which were eternally true, whereas the human mind was changeable. At the same time he did not think of the sphere of eternal truths as existing simply 'out there', independently of any mind.[1] He saw them as pointing to God, as manifesting an eternal basis or ground. The precise way in which eternal truths are related to God is not made clear, any more than it is in the philosophy of Leibniz. It is clear, however, that Augustine thought, as Leibniz did at a much later date, that they required a metaphysical basis, which was itself eternal.

However this may be, Augustine raises the question, how can a mutable and fallible mind grasp immutable truth with infallible certainty? A modern philosopher might reply with the question: why not? Is there really anything odd in a changeable and fallible human being enjoying the ability to recognize the truth of analytic proposi-tions? Augustine, however, thinks of the human mind as rising in a sense above itself, or, rather, above its dependence on the senses and

[1] We may be inclined to say that an 'eternal truth' is a proposition which is true whenever it is enunciated, unlike, for example, 'Socrates is drinking a cup of hemlock'.

entering the sphere of eternal truth. And he asks how this is possible. Plato, it will be remembered, proposed the theory, or myth, of 'reminiscence', according to which the mind recalls what it saw in a previous existence.[1] Though, however, Augustine apparently toyed for a time with the notion of the soul's pre-existence, he rejected it. And for the Platonic theory of reminiscence he substituted his own theory of divine illumination, an illumination which enables us not only to see eternal truths but also to judge of things in relation to eternal standards or ideas.[2]

The themes of light and of illumination are of course widespread. In the Manichean religion, for example, the good principle was described as light. More relevant, however, are the words of Plato in the *Republic*, when he speaks of the Good as 'cause of all things right and beautiful, giving birth to light and the lord of light in the visible world and originating truth and reason in the intelligible world.[3] The Neoplatonists developed this theme of light. Thus Plotinus represents the whole process of creation or emanation as a process of radiation or diffusion of light from its ultimate source. When a man turns from the comparative darkness of matter to the sphere of eternal truth and of spiritual reality, he turns towards the light and is illuminated. Augustine takes up the Platonic idea of illumination and combines it with Christian belief in the light which enlightens 'every man who comes into the world'.[4]

As Augustine had behind him a long and respected tradition, his use of the metaphors of light and illumination doubtless meant more to many of his contemporaries than they mean for people today. We are hardly prepared to take his ideas for granted. On the contrary, we are inclined to ask questions about the precise nature and functions of divine illumination as he conceived them. And it is extremely difficult to answer such questions, as Augustine himself gave no clear account of the matter.

To the present writer at any rate it seems clear that Augustine is not

[1] With what degree of seriousness Plato proposed this theory is a question which we can leave to specialists to discuss. We should not, however, allow admiration for Plato to lead us into attributing to him only those theories which we ourselves regard as sensible or tenable.

[2] As when we judge that things are more or less beautiful or that actions are more or less just. For Augustine, as for Plato, such judgements manifest implicit recognition of an absolute standard of comparison.

[3] *Republic*, 517c.

[4] John, 1, 9.

talking either about a special mystical enlightenment or about an illumination which enables us to see God himself or the contents, so to speak, of the divine mind. It can hardly be denied that some passages give the impression that Augustine did mean something of the sort. But reflection shows that this was not really his meaning. After all, a man can perfectly well see the truth of mathematical propositions without believing in God and without being even a good man. Moreover, as we have seen, Augustine argues from eternal truths to the existence of God. So he can hardly have supposed that to perceive the immutability and necessity of a proposition is to see God.

Again, Augustine followed the Neoplatonists in locating in the divine mind (identified with the Word or *Logos*) eternal ideas as archetypes or exemplars of creation. And he thought, in a thoroughly Platonic manner, that comparative judgements of value refer implicitly to an eternal or absolute standard, an eternal idea of, say, beauty. Even if, however, some passages seem to imply that divine illumination enables us to see these eternal ideas, Augustine can hardly have intended seriously to maintain that the divine mind is an open book to anyone who makes correct comparative judgements of value. For a professed unbeliever can make such judgements. So can people whom it would be absurd to describe as mystics.

At the same time there is a difficulty in following the otherwise attractive policy of interpreting the divine illumination as meaning no more than God's creative and sustaining activity in regard to the human intellect. For Augustine speaks of a light which is *sui generis* or of a special kind.[1] And it is clear that in his opinion the human mind needs a divine illumination to apprehend truths which in some sense transcend it or are superior to it[2] and thus exceed its capacity when it is left to itself. In other words, Augustine speaks as though the theory of divine illumination is not simply a way of referring to the ordinary, natural operations of the mind but rather a hypothesis required to explain how the mind can achieve what it could not otherwise achieve.

An at any rate partial solution to problems of interpretation is provided by Augustine's analogy of the sun's light. We see corporeal objects in the light of the sun, and (prescinding from artificial light) we cannot otherwise see them. But it by no means follows that we see the light which illuminates things, nor that we can look at the sun without being blinded. Analogously, it appears, the divine illumination makes

[1] *De Trinitate (On the Trinity)*, 12, 15, 24.
[2] *De libero arbitrio (On Free Will)*, 2, 13, 35.

visible to the mind the elements of immutability, necessity and un-changeability in eternal truths, though it does not follow that we actually see the divine activity. Again, in some undefined way the eternal ideas exercise a regulative action on the mind, enabling us to judge in accordance with changeless standards, though the eternal ideas are not themselves seen.[1]

The Augustinian theories of the divine ideas and of divine illumination passed into the Middle Ages. Thinkers such as Aquinas tried to state the theory of divine ideas in such a way as to free it from an anthropomorphism which would be incompatible with belief in the divine infinity and simplicity. In the fourteenth century, however, Ockham rejected it. Or, more accurately, he interpreted it in a manner which was equivalent to rejection.[2] As for the theory of divine illumination, it was given a minimizing interpretation by Aquinas. When the theory was discarded, as by Duns Scotus, on the ground that it was neither a necessary nor an effective help in explaining human knowledge, this was because the theory was taken as claiming something more than that God created the human mind and sustains it in its activity. Augustine himself was firmly convinced that to enter the sphere of eternal truth the mind needs a special divine activity. But in his references to the matter he spoke in somewhat different ways and this provided the basis for different interpretations. Nowadays there is obviously a strong tendency to eliminate from analytic propositions the element of mystery which was so strongly felt by Augustine.[3] And philosophical analysis of the value-judgement is a controversial matter.[4]

[1] I have assumed throughout that Augustine does not intend to say that God infuses concepts (ready-made, as it were) into the human mind. Some writers have, however, understood him in this sense.

[2] Given the authority enjoyed by Augustine in the Middle Ages, it required a bold man to say simply 'he was wrong' or 'he was talking nonsense'. Interpretation was a more prudent policy.

[3] Bertrand Russell once thought of pure mathematics in a Platonic manner, as forming a serene intelligible world of changeless truth, a haven for the mind from the changing world. Under Wittgenstein's influence, however, he adopted a theory of 'tautologies' And in any case he soon became caught up in social and terrestrial problems.

[4] Even today there are, of course, philosophers who think in terms of the recognition of absolute values. Probably there always will be, as the reasons for this way of thinking are always with us. So, however, is the difficulty in explaining clearly what one means.

5

Reference has been made to the fact that Augustine's philosophical reflections are often made in connection with theological themes or in the course of scriptural exegesis. A case in point in his theory of the germinal forms or principles which he calls *rationes seminales*.[1] In Ecclesiasticus it is asserted 'that God created all things together',[2] whereas in Genesis we are presented with the picture of successive acts of creation on six consecutive days. Moreover, experience shows that new things are constantly coming into being. Augustine wishes, therefore, to harmonize the assertion that God created all things in the beginning with the evident fact that new things are constantly being produced. And his solution of the problem is the theory that the things which came into being after the original creation of the world by God were present from the start in the form of invisible latent potentialities which are actualized only in the course of time.

The exegetical problem does not seem to present much difficulty, even if we take the biblical account or accounts of creation as being more than myths which express the dependence of finite things on the ultimate ground of being.[3] But what of the theory of *rationes seminales* when considered in itself? It is understandable that at a time when the hypothesis of transformistic evolution[4] was regarded with suspicion in official ecclesiastical circles some writers who wished to allay this suspicion should have appealed for support to the great African theologian. But the Augustinian theory does not seem to have anything to do with transformistic evolution. It may be possible to interpret the theory in such a way as to allow for biological evolution. But it is also possible to interpret it in terms of the fixity of species. In any case modern theories of evolution stand or fall by their merits or demerits as

---

[1] The term *rationes seminales*, sometimes given the literal rendering 'seminal reasons', is a Latin translation of the Greek term *logoi spermatikoi*, which was taken over from the Stoics by the Neoplatonists. By referring to the germinal forms as 'principles', I mean of course that they are *principia* in the sense of beginnings. They are postulated as active, originating factors, not as logical principles.

[2] XVIII, 1.

[3] The Genesis account obviously allows for the continuation of species, while the statement in Ecclesiasticus need not, I suppose, be taken so literally as to be incompatible with Genesis.

[4] The reference is, of course, to the transformation of one species into another or the emergence of a new species from an already existing one.

empirical hypotheses. We certainly cannot decide the matter by appealing to Augustine. And at a time when there is a strong tendency to regard Teilhard de Chardin as a kind of Doctor of the Church, the anachronism of looking to Augustine for support in a campaign either for or against the evolutionary hypothesis seems to be superfluous.

More to the point is Étienne Gilson's contention that Augustine's theory plays down the productive role of secondary causes, of finite causes that is to say.[1] Just as in his account of human knowledge Augustine emphasizes the activity of God (by his theory of divine illumination), and just as in his Christian ethics he emphasizes the role of divine grace and combats Pelagianism, so in his account of the production of things he stresses the divine causality. For if God created all these things in the beginning, in the *rationes seminales*, a finite efficient cause of something new seems to do little, if anything, more than provide the occasion for the actualization of something which already exists in an embryonic state. What seems to be new is not really new.[2]

6

A more elaborate and impressive example of philosophizing in a theological context is provided by Augustine's celebrated discussion of time in the eleventh book of the *Confessions*. Speaking of the Christian doctrine of creation, he refers to those who ask what God was doing before the creation of the world. This question, Augustine comments, assumes that it makes sense to talk about a time 'before' creation. The assumption however is erroneous. For to say that God created the world is to say that he created time. Apart from the world there is no time, and 'if there was no time, there was no "then" '.[3] Hence to ask what God was doing then (i.e. before creation) is to ask a meaningless question.

To say, however, that God created time is not the same as explaining what time is. In a well known passage, which is quoted by Wittgenstein,[4] Augustine remarks that if nobody asks me what time is, I know what it is, whereas once someone raises this question I do not know

[1] See Gilson's *The Christian Philosophy of St Augustine* (London, 1961), pp. 207–8.
[2] Gilson remarks that this view of the matter would hardly fit in with the theory of creative evolution, which envisages the emergence of the genuinely novel and unforeseeable.
[3] *Confessions*, XI, 13.
[4] *Philosophical Investigations*, I, 89.

what answer to give. For all practical purposes, that is to say, we know quite well what is meant by terms such as 'before', 'after', 'past', 'present' and 'future'. We can use temporal expressions correctly. But if we are asked for an analysis of time, we may very well be at a loss for a reply.

Suppose that we divide up time, in the manner suggested by ordinary language, into past, present and future. The past has ceased to be. The future does not yet exist. If, therefore, we say that time *is* or that time exists, we must surely be referring to the present. But what is the present? The present century perhaps? Or the present day? Or the present hour? Any of these can itself be divided into past, present and future. And the same can be said of any assignable stretch of time. Thus the present seems to shrink into an ideal limit, a limit which we can never grasp in such a way as to be able to say of it that it *is*. 'The present cannot possibly have any duration.'[1] For practical purposes we can quite well talk about, for example, measuring time by the movements of the heavenly bodies. But what is measured? What is the basic nature or essence of time?

It is tempting to say with Wittgenstein that to look for the essence of time is a misguided enterprise, and that we should remind ourselves instead of the temporal expressions which we actually use. But this is not Augustine's point of view. He is not prepared to claim that the solution of the problem lies in its dissolution. And he makes the tentative suggestion that time is not something objective, 'out there'. The past exists in the memory, and the future in expectation. We might say, therefore, that there are 'three times, a present of past things, a present of present things, and a present of future things. . . . The present of past things is the memory; the present of present things is direct perception; and the present of future things is expectation.'[2] In other words, time may be explicable in terms of three mental functions, memory, attention and expectation, though Augustine still feels doubtful whether he really knows the nature of time.

Augustine's discussion of time, whether one agrees or not with what he says, shows very clearly his ability as a thinker. It is not surprising that Bertrand Russell, while expressing disagreement, remarks that 'it is a great advance on anything to be found on the subject in Greek philosophy'.[3] When, however, Russell goes on to claim that Augustine

[1] *Confessions*, XI, 15.
[2] Ibid., XI, 20.
[3] *History of Western Philosophy*, p. 374.

gives a better and clearer statement of the subjective theory of time than that given at a much later date by Immanuel Kant, the statement, though possibly true, is somewhat misleading. What Augustine's theory of time looks forward to in modern philosophy seems to be not so much the Kantian theory as the interpretations of time given by such philosophers as Heidegger and Sartre.

7

Mention has been made of Wittgenstein's reference to Augustine's puzzle about the nature of time. Wittgenstein also quotes the passage from the *Confessions* in which Augustine recalls how he learned to speak as a child.[1] Wittgenstein then comments that the picture of language conveyed by this passage is that of individual words naming objects and of sentences as combinations of such words. 'Augustine does not speak of there being any difference between kinds of words.'[2] Every word has a meaning; and what it means is the object for which it stands.

Augustine certainly says what Wittgenstein quotes him as saying. And it must be remembered, of course, that Wittgenstein is concerned with using a particular passage to illustrate a naïve and inadequate theory of language, not with expounding Augustine's ideas as such. However, as modern students of philosophy are likely to be much better acquainted with the writings of Wittgenstein than with those of Augustine, it should be pointed out that the youthful reminiscences contained in the first book of the *Confessions* are far from representing all the views about language proposed by its author.

For example, in the second chapter of the *De Magistro* (*On the Master* or *On the Professor*) Augustine had already remarked that we cannot point to objects signified by prepositions such as *ex* (out of or from). Again, in the early *Principia dialecticae* (*Principles of dialectic*), which was probably written when he was a professor of rhetoric, Augustine distinguished between, for instance, the spoken word, its meaning as grasped by the mind, the use of a word as a sign for itself (as when we think about the word 'man') and its use as signifying or standing for an object or objects. Further, he refers to the force (*vis*) of words, to the effects which words are capable of having on their hearers.

[1] *Confessions*, I, 8.
[2] *Philosophical Investigations*, I, 1.

Augustine's later remarks about language tend to be prompted by some theological discussion, as in the *De Trinitate*. The total impression, however, is of a set of ideas which, though undeveloped and doubtless comparatively primitive by modern standards of semantics, are considerably more sophisticated than Wittgenstein's observations suggest.

8

When we turn to Augustine's view of man, we are confronted with an obviously Platonic theory. For example, in one place man is defined as 'a rational soul using a mortal and earthly body'.[1] The soul's relation to the body is thus conceived according to the model of someone using an instrument or tool. To be sure, Augustine does not need to be told that there is a difference between Tom's relation to the hammer which he is using and the relation between Tom's soul and body. He maintains that man is a unity and not simply two juxtaposed substances. At the same time his ability to explain how man is a unity is limited by the model or analogy according to which he conceives the relation between soul and body. As we have already seen, he will not admit that the body can act on the soul, the material on the spiritual. And he concludes that sensation is an act of the soul which notices, as it were, changes in the body and is then the subject of sensation, the body being an occasion for sensation, an instrument by which the soul is in touch with other material things.

We may be inclined to think that Augustine was a prisoner of Platonic language. But he obviously thought that the way of speaking which he sometimes adopted fitted in with Christian belief and experience. And it can hardly be denied that this way of speaking is frequently encountered in Christian spiritual literature. Moreover, the implied concept of the relation between soul and body makes it much easier to defend belief in the immortality of the soul than does the Aristotelian account of the soul as the 'form' of the body, which was later accepted by Aquinas.[2] Conversely, the Aristotelian theory emphasizes the

[1] *De moribus ecclesiae catholicae* (*On the Way of Life of the Catholic Church*), 1, 27, 52.

[2] In the third book of Aristotle's *De Anima* (*On the Soul*) we find indeed some notoriously obscure statements about the immortal intellect. But elsewhere in this work Aristotle likens the relation of soul to body to, for instance, the relation between the imprint of the seal and the wax on which it is made. And this model is clearly not a promising basis for a doctrine of immortality.

unity of man and perhaps fits in better with belief in the resurrection of the body, on the assumption, that is to say, that there is personal survival of death.

Whatever our attitude to Augustine's way of speaking about the relation of soul to body, we ought to recognize his merits as a psychologist. He was a master of self-analysis, and in the *Confessions* we find plenty of examples of psychological insight. Again, his discussion in the *De Trinitate* of the human soul as the image of God leads him into interesting psychological excursions, on memory for example. In general, he is concerned with the inner life of the soul much more than with Nature; and he shows an acute perception of both the grandeur and the misery or weakness of man, viewed from a religious perspective.

9

Given Augustine's passionate interest in man's search for the happiness which can be found only in God, we might perhaps expect him to follow Plotinus in emphasizing the mystical 'flight of the alone to the Alone'[1] and in depreciating the historical events to which men are inclined to attach importance. Plotinus described the course of what Hegel called world-history as a kind of stage play or puppet show, as something which was of little significance in comparison with the return of the soul to its true centre, the One. And if we focused our attention simply on the Neoplatonic elements in Augustine's thought, we might expect a similar attitude on his part.

As a Christian bishop, however, Augustine could hardly adopt the Plotinian view of history. As a believer in a unique divine Incarnation, for which God's manifestation of his will to the Jewish people was a preparation, in the divine redemptive activity in history and in the Church's mission in the world, he could hardly look on history as unimportant. For God had himself entered, so to speak, into history; and Christ's mission was perpetuated within history. The Greek philosophers tended to think of human history in terms of recurrent cycles. Augustine, however, was convinced that history has a goal, that it is a teleological process which moves towards an end, even if the end or goal is not fully attained within the historical process itself. This conviction enabled him to develop a theologically based interpretation of history in his *De Civitate Dei* (*On the City of God*), which was finished

[1] *Enneads*, 6, 9, 11.

only three years before his death in the period of the crumbling of the Roman empire.

Augustine sees the fundamental dialectic of history in the struggle between two loves. That is to say, ever since the Fall men are divided basically according to the kind of love which effectively inspires the life of each individual. The lives of some are governed by love of the immutable and infinite good, God, while the lives of others are governed by the love of finite, mutable goods to the exclusion of God. Members of the first class compose the City of Jerusalem, while members of the second class compose the City of Babylon.

The matter might be expressed in this way. Behind the foreground movement of the rise and fall of kingdoms and empires there is the process of divine love restoring fallen man and building up the City of Jerusalem. Those who cooperate with God's grace (those who, as Augustine would say, are predestined to eternal life) form the citizens of Jerusalem, while those who refuse grace form the citizens of Babylon.

It is clear that Jerusalem and Babylon cannot be simply identified, without more ado, with Church and State. A man might be a baptized Christian and yet spiritually a citizen of Babylon. Another man might be a high official of the State, even the emperor, and at the same time a citizen of Jerusalem. To be sure, when Augustine looks back at the empires of Egypt, Assyria and Babylon (in a historical sense) and at pagan Rome as a persecuting power, he may speak as though the State were the embodiment of the concept of the City of Babylon. In itself, however, the idea of the two cities of Jerusalem and Babylon must be understood in a spiritual sense. Each City exemplifies indeed Augustine's definition of a society as 'a multitude of rational creatures associated in a common agreement as to the things which it loves'.[1] But the societies in question are not clearly delimited before the public gaze in the way that Church and State are visible organizations. There are assignable empirical criteria for deciding whether a man is or is not a Roman citizen. But it is only God who really knows who are citizens of Jerusalem and who are citizens of Babylon.

As for the State Augustine regards it as conditionally necessary. Its necessity, that is to say, presupposes the Fall. The pagan Roman empire, for instance, was indubitably a state, even if it persecuted the Christian Church. It maintained peace and order within its frontiers; it defended its citizens against external aggression; it punished crimes such as murder, theft and brigandage. It thus fulfilled the functions of a state.

[1] *De civitate Dei*, XIX, 24.

But the exercise of these functions would not have been required if there had been no Fall. Human beings would, of course, have lived a social life. But there would have been no need of the coercive and punitive power which we call the State.

There is thus a considerable difference between Augustine's theory of the State and that adopted by, for example, Aquinas in the Middle Ages. Whereas Augustine emphasized the coercive and punitive functions of the State and looked on man's need for the State as consequent on the Fall, Aquinas regarded the State as a 'natural' institution, demanded, that is to say, by the nature of man as such. He agreed of course with Augustine that if there had been no Fall, there would have been no need for armies, prisons and so on. But he was far from looking on the State as being simply a necessary instrument for checking the evils resulting from man's fallen condition. Aquinas placed emphasis much more on the idea of political society as responding to the social needs of man as such. Hence he could maintain that even if there had been no Fall, the State would nevertheless have come into existence.

The historian of philosophy is likely to draw attention to the influence on Aquinas of the Aristotelian idea of the State, an idea which he had to harmonize with his concept of the function of the Church in human life. But though Aquinas was certainly influenced by Aristotle's political theory, there are other aspects of the situation which have to be borne in mind. Augustine, though he actually lived after the triumph of Christianity in the Roman empire, was very conscious of the fact that for years the empire had indulged in periodic persecution of the Christians and had thus, from the Christian point of view, done what it could to prevent man from attaining his supernatural end, eternal salvation. At the same time the pagan empire was obviously a state. And it clearly performed some useful functions, the sort of functions to which St Paul had explicitly referred.[1] It is therefore understandable that Augustine should tend to restrict the State's functions to those which any state, including pagan Rome, could be expected to fulfil. Aquinas, however, lived in the thirteenth century, when the Christian State had long existed together with the Church. To say this is obviously not to claim that all medieval rulers were eminent for their Christian conduct, nor that relations between Church and State were free from tensions. The point is that the medieval State to which Aquinas was accustomed was an integral part of Christendom, of

[1] Romans, XIII, 1-4. Cf. I Peter, II, 13-14.

Christian society. and that, whatever struggles there may have been between civil and ecclesiastical rulers, the State did not stand to the Church in the relation in which Assyria stood to the Jewish people or pagan Rome to the early Christians. In other words, the historical situation made it much easier for Aquinas to utilize Greek political theory and to regard the State as an institution which was natural to man, irrespective of the Fall.

Given Augustine's view of the State, we might expect him to maintain that it was not the business of the civil authorities to interfere in matters of religious belief and practice, unless perhaps a situation arose in which citizens were performing, in the name of religion, actions which were so clearly criminal or injurious to public peace and order that they could not be permitted. In fact, however, Augustine came to give his approval to restrictive measures by the civil power against the Donatist schismatics in north Africa. He did not indeed regard the State as such as concerned with man's supernatural vocation. But if a state had become officially Christian, Augustine did not think that Christian rulers could remain justifiably indifferent to the eternal welfare of their Christian subjects. And though he was certainly not an enthusiastic and rabid persecutor, he came to accept and endorse the idea of subjecting heretics and schismatics (as distinct from Jews and Gentiles who had never embraced Christianity) to coercion. Hence those who in later centuries encouraged repressive action by the State against heretics were able to appeal to the authority of the man who was regarded throughout the Middle Ages as the greatest of Christian theologians.

If we look at the matter from one particular point of view, we might be inclined to think that Augustine's political theory looks forward to the idea of the religiously neutral secular State. For the basic functions of the State are described in such a way as not to tie up the concept of political society with acceptance of what Augustine would regard as the true religion. As we have seen, however, the Cities of Jerusalem and Babylon cannot be simply identified with Church and State respectively, as distinct visible organizations. Ideally, the City of Jerusalem should include all mankind. This means that the Church, as communicating the divine grace required for man's eternal welfare, has a mission to Christianize the whole of human society. And though a pagan state exemplifies the definition of a political society, Augustine comes to the conclusion that it is both the right and the duty of Christian rulers to assist the Church in its mission by repressing impiety and heresy. He thus lays the foundation for the view that though Church and State are distinct societies, the end for which the Church exists, namely man's eternal salvation, takes precedence of the temporal ends of the State as such, and that it is the duty of the Christian State to assist the Church in the exercise of her divine mission.

These remarks are certainly not intended to imply that in the present writer's opinion religious persecution is justifiable. For the matter of that, it might well be argued that intervention by the State in affairs of religious belief and practice is, in fact, very far from constituting a genuine help to the Church in her mission. The aim of the remarks is simply to show how Augustine could start with the idea of two societies and then arrive, albeit reluctantly, at the conclusion that religious and civil authorities should cooperate in repressing heresy and schism. As his definition of a society does not specify the kind of basic interests agreement about which unites a body of human beings in a community, we can say that by implication it allows for a lay or secular state. At the same time Augustine's thought moves in the direction of the theocratic State, at any rate to the extent of making it possible to appeal to him in later centuries in support of this idea.

As for Augustine's view of history, it is a comprehensive vision in the sense that it extends from the creation of man up to the final completion of the City of Jerusalem. Apart, however, from giving expression to Christian eschatological beliefs of a general nature, Augustine does not, of course, undertake to predict future events. Nor does he aim at recapitulating all human history. He is selective; and he is more concerned with laying bare the basic motives of fallen man and the possibilities of a higher life than with entering into competition with the chronicler of events. As a Roman citizen, he is conscious of Rome's greatness, of Roman virtues and achievements; but in his account of the rise of the city to power and dominion he is far from idealizing the motives of the conquerors. And he refuses to admit that the disasters overtaking the empire in his own day signify the end of all things or the final collapse of Christian civilization. The continuing dialectic of the two loves possesses for him a much profounder significance than the rise and fall of kingdoms and empires.

10

History is thus interpreted by Augustine in the light of Christian belief. It is not, however, simply a question of history. As we have seen, faith is the presupposition of all his thought as a Christian. His programme is that of faith seeking understanding, understanding of itself, its content and its implications. To avoid misunderstanding, however, statements of this sort, namely about the priority of faith in Augustine's thought, stand in need of some amplification and explanation.

In the first place it would be absurd to claim that all the positions adopted by Augustine are logically dependent on Christian beliefs in such a way that a man who rejected Christianity would be committed, from the logical point of view, to regarding his judgements and theories as false or valueless. For example, Augustine's conviction that the rise of states to power through conquest is simply successful brigandage obviously fits in well with his view of the ways of fallen man. And we can say, if we like, that he is seeing the history of empires in the light of his belief about the Fall. So he is. At the same time Augustine's judgement is clearly a piece of realism which could perfectly well be endorsed by the non-believer, if he thought it a valid generalization from the available data. If we say, therefore, that Augustine sees history in the light of belief in the Fall of man, it by no means necessarily follows that this perspective distorts his vision. In this particular case at any rate it might be claimed that his antecedent belief enables him to take, or facilitates his taking, a detached and realistic point of view, instead of, for example, idealizing the rise to power of the empire of which he was a citizen. Needless to say, the judgements which Augustine makes about human actions in history are made in the light of his own religious and ethical convictions. And his general assessment of the basic significance of the historical process is made within the framework of a Christian world-vision. He certainly sees history from a Christian perspective. And the non-Christian would doubtless reject this particular perspective, while a good many people would reject any teleological presuppositions, whether theological or metaphysical, whether Augustinian, Hegelian or Marxist.[1] But there is no good reason why a Christian thinker should not offer a possible interpretation of history as seen in the light of Christian beliefs.

[1] Some Marxists try indeed to avoid committing themselves to the view that history is moving towards a goal, a view which seems to imply teleological presuppositions which fit in far better with idealism than with materialism. But it can hardly be denied that Marxism in general has given ground for the impression that it is a secularized version of an originally religious eschatological interpretation of history.

Again, when Augustine is reflecting on man, what he has in mind is clearly man as seen by the Christian, man fallen and redeemed, drawn by the impulses of fallen human nature on the one hand and by divine grace on the other, called to the lasting happiness for which he has a basic desire but capable of sin and alienation from God. For man as seen in this way is, for Augustine, concrete historical man, man as he actually exists. Within, however, this general view of the human being there is obviously room for discussion of themes which we would label as psychological, epistemological or phenomenological, and for the proposal of theories which are not logically dependent on theological assumptions or on a theological context.

For various reasons the eventual drawing of an explicit distinction between theology and philosophy was doubtless inevitable. And we may therefore tend to look on the absence of any such distinction in Augustine's thought as the expression of a comparatively primitive and outdated attitude. This is understandable. We must remember, however, that, given Augustine's own idea of genuine philosophy, introduction of the distinction would be a questionable procedure. If philosophy is equated with, for instance, conceptual analysis or the mapping out of ordinary language, it must obviously be distinguished from Christian theology and Christian ethics. But if philosophy is regarded as exhibiting a way of salvation and as legitimately dealing with such themes as the meaning of human existence,[1] the Christian thinker can hardly pursue themes of this kind while prescinding altogether from his Christian beliefs. It is thus not simply a question of introducing a clarificatory distinction. Ideas of the nature and scope of philosophy are also involved. And it is at any rate arguable that there is room even today for the Christian thinker who offers an interpretation of the world and of human life which is frankly inspired by Christian beliefs but which at the same time does not claim that the positions adopted are logically deduced from such beliefs where this is not in fact the case.

[1] Not simply in the sense of analysing the concept of meaning in this context, but rather as assigning a meaning.

4

Christian Thought in the Ancient World [3]

I

St Augustine was the most outstanding Christian thinker of the ancient world; and he exercised a far-reaching influence on medieval thought. There are, however, one or two other writers of whom mention should be made. One of them is the gentleman who passed himself off as Dionysius the Areopagite, St Paul's Athenian convert, and whose writings consequently came to enjoy a high degree of authority in the medieval period. He was probably a Christian monk who composed his treatises at the end of the fifth century. For it seems clear that they reflect the teaching of Proclus, the fifth-century systematizer of Neoplatonism. There have been conjectures about the identity of the author; but it seems unlikely that we shall ever know it with certainty. Meanwhile the author of the treatises in question has been saddled with the cumbersome name of the Pseudo-Dionysius.

The Pseudo-Dionysius tried to synthesize Christianity and Neoplatonism or, more accurately perhaps, to express Christian doctrines in the framework of Neoplatonic philosophy. For example, he endeavoured to harmonize the Christian doctrine of the Trinity with the Neoplatonic theory of the One and the Christian concept of divine creation with the Neoplatonic idea of emanation. Whether we regard the results as a Neoplatonizing of Christianity or a Christianizing of Neoplatonism is to a large extent a question of where we choose to place the emphasis. To be sure, those modern theologians who believe that theology should steer clear of philosophy would doubtless look on the treatises of the Pseudo-Dionysius as a disaster. For our present purposes, however, the important point is that the treatises were one of the channels through which a strong dosage of Platonism entered medieval thought. As will be seen later, in the course of time Aristotle came to occupy an extremely prominent position in medieval philosophy. At the same time it is a mistake to think that the Platonic tradition had no influence on the thought of the Middle Ages but had to await the Italian Renaissance.

One of the ways in which the Pseudo-Dionysius influenced medieval thought was through his theories about our knowledge of God and our language about him. Following Proclus, he distinguished two approaches to God by philosophical reasoning, the negative and affirmative approaches. The way of negation, of which the Pseudo-Dionysius writes in his *Mystical Theology*, consists in denying of God the names or terms which we apply to creatures. For example, while the creature is said to be mutable, God is said to be immutable, non-mutable that is to say, or unchangeable. Again, whereas the creature is finite, God is described as non-finite or infinite. The negative approach thus expresses a recognition of the inadequacy of human concepts when applied to God and emphasizes the divine transcendence.

The affirmative approach, exemplified in the treatise on *The Divine Names*, consists in predicating of God those attributes of creatures which are judged to be compatible with infinite spiritual being. For example, God is described as good and as wise. This way of speaking expresses a recognition of the reflection of the divine being in creation.

Clearly, a conflict can arise, or at least can appear to arise, between the two ways of speaking. For instance, the negative approach appears to demand that we should deny wisdom of God, inasmuch as it is found in human beings, whereas the affirmative way permits its predication of God. The Pseudo-Dionysius tries to surmount this opposition by speaking of God as super-wise rather than as wise, as super-being rather than as being, and so on.

Evidently, the problem is one of reconciling the predominantly positive way of speaking about God which is found in the Bible with a philosophy of religion which emphasizes the divine transcendence and severely restricts the range of terms which can be properly predicated of God.[1] The problem was taken up again in the Middle Ages; and

[1] Plotinus affirmed the unity of the Godhead, as the term 'the One' indicates; and he predicated goodness of the One. But intellectual activity was attributed to the second hypostasis (Nous or Mind), not to the One.

Aquinas, for instance, allowed for the negative and affirmative approaches of the Pseudo-Dionysius. But with Aquinas, a professional theologian, the influence of Neoplatonism is somewhat diminished; and we find a more sophisticated account of analogical predication.

Another theme discussed by the Pseudo-Dionysius was the nature of evil. It has already been mentioned that Augustine took over from Neoplatonism the theory of evil as a privation. As developed by the Pseudo-Dionysius it passed into medieval thought and was used, for example, by Aquinas in his attempt to reconcile the presence of evil in a divinely created world with belief in an all-good, omnipotent and omniscient creator. Later on we find the same idea being employed by philosophers such as Leibniz and Berkeley.

The Pseudo-Dionysius was also a channel through which the Neoplatonic metaphysics of light passed to the Middle Ages. God, identified with the Neoplatonic One, is light itself (the spiritual or intelligible, not material light) and the source of all light.[1] The hierarchic structure of being, the various levels or general types of beings, that is to say, conceived as forming a descending series of levels of perfection, represent so many degrees of created or participated light, flowing, to use a Neoplatonic metaphor, from the ultimate source of light. Further, the return of human beings to God is represented as a process of ascending degrees of illumination. Here the Pseudo-Dionysius introduces specifically Christian themes. For example, the Church and its sacraments are means whereby divine illumination is imparted to men in their ascent to God.

Use of this light-language, as we might describe it, was common enough in the Middle Ages. With those thinkers who were profoundly influenced by Aristotelianism talk about divine illumination tended to become little more than a convention, a sign of respect for Augustine. With certain philosophers, however, among whom we can count even the empirically minded Franciscan Roger Bacon, the influence of the Neoplatonic light-metaphysics is evident. It is indeed difficult to know what to make of the ontological side of the doctrine, the representation, that is to say, of degrees of perfection as degrees of light. And it is hardly surprising that after the Middle Ages the light-language became more or less a preserve of spiritual and mystical writers. There are

[1] The ideas of light and radiation go back to Plato himself. In the *Republic* (517–18) the absolute Good is said to be the source of light in the intelligible world or sphere of being and to be the parent or producer of the source of light (the sun) in the visible world.

doubtless psychological reasons for the prevalence of the light-theme; but this is a matter for psychologists.

As for the doctrine of a hierarchy of levels of being, this had become a characteristic of the Platonic tradition as expressed in Middle Platonism and Neoplatonism. The philosophers of this tradition thought it necessary to postulate a graduated series of intermediary beings between the One and the material world. This idea of intermediary beings, which can be found also in the writings of Philo, was pushed to extraordinary lengths by some of the Neoplatonists, notably Iamblichus in the first decades of the fourth century. The idea enabled pagan Neoplatonists, such as Proclus, to find room for the Greek deities, not of course in the anthropomorphic forms attributed to them in popular mythology and in poetry but as identified with metaphysical realities in the hierarchy of being. With the Pseudo-Dionysius the idea takes two forms. In the *Celestial Hierarchy* he treats of the orders or graded classes of angels, while in the *Ecclesiastical Hierarchy* he deals with the reflection on earth of the heavenly hierarchy. This hierarchic conception of the universe passed to the Middle Ages, though there is an important difference between the idea as found in Neoplatonism and the idea as found in medieval Christian thought. One of the reasons why the Neoplatonists postulated a series of intermediary beings in the process of emanation was their conviction that the transcendent One could not be directly responsible, so to speak, for the creation of the material world, for the creation, that is to say, of what, in comparison with pure light, is relatively speaking darkness. For the Christian philosopher of the Middle Ages, however, creation was an expression of divine freedom and will.

In passing we can note that according to some Marxists the medieval concept of a hierarchic universe was a reflection of the feudal structure of society. An obvious objection to this interpretation is that the theory of a hierarchic universe was already present in the philosophy of the ancient world. The retort of the Marxists in question is that the idea, though present in ancient philosophy, was tailored to medieval conditions. Though, however, there may be some truth in this contention, the fact remains that the idea was also tailored or adapted to Christian beliefs which were certainly not simply the reflection of the structure of medieval society.

The treatises of the Pseudo-Dionysius were not the only channel by which Neoplatonic themes were transmitted to the medieval world. Apart from Fathers of the Church such as Augustine, there were works such as the *Liber de Causis* (*Book on Causes*), to which reference will be made later. But this work, though derived from Proclus's *Elements of Theology*,[1] became available in Latin translation only in the twelfth century, whereas the writings of the Pseudo-Dionysius were translated from Greek into Latin by John Scotus Erigena in the ninth century.

2

To turn from Neoplatonism to Aristotle. In the early Middle Ages the Christian West did not possess the Aristotelian *corpus* as a whole. A knowledge, however, of a considerable part of the logic of Aristotle was transmitted from the ancient world by means of the writings of Boethius, who lived from about 480 until 524. He held high office under Theodoric the Ostrogoth king; but he was eventually accused of treason, perhaps on the charge of having carried on a correspondence with Byzantium, and after a period of imprisonment suffered execution. During his imprisonment he wrote his famous work *De consolatione philosophiae* (*On the Consolations of Philosophy*).

Boethius intended to translate into Latin and to furnish commentaries on all the works of Aristotle.[2] In effect he translated the *Categories*, the *Prior* and *Posterior Analytics*, the *Hermeneutics* (*De Interpretatione*), the *Sophistical Arguments* and the *Topics*. He also translated the *Isagoge* (*Introduction*) of Porphyry the Neoplatonist. He wrote two commentaries on the last named work, and he also commented on the logical writings of Aristotle mentioned above, as well as on Cicero's *Topics*. In addition he wrote a number of logical and theological treatises of his own,[3] as well as some introductory textbooks on mathematics and music.

It can hardly be claimed that Boethius was a philosopher of much originality. But this does not alter the fact that in addition to being a channel whereby some knowledge of the logic of the ancient world was transmitted to the Middle Ages he made a powerful contribution to the creation of a Latin vocabulary of logical terms. Regarding logic as concerned with discourse, he transmitted to the medievals the distinction, attributed by Porphyry to the Peripatetics, between written, spoken

[1] For a time the *Liber de Causis* was wrongly attributed to Aristotle.
[2] Boethius planned to do the same for Plato, hoping to be able to exhibit a harmony between Plato and Aristotle.
[3] Boethius was a Christian, even if in his *De consolatione* Stoic and Neoplatonic themes are more evident than specifically Christian doctrines.

and mental discourse, though the precise nature of mental discourse and of its relation to the other kinds of discourse was left obscure. Further, Boethius supplied the medievals with the distinction between words of first intention or imposition (such as 'man' in 'Socrates is a man') and words of second intention or imposition (such as 'man' in 'man is a noun'). Again, it was in connection with a text of Boethius that the problem of universal terms was raised,[1] a problem which was discussed, with varying degrees of sophistication, throughout the Middle Ages. Boethius also provided the medievals with some classical definitions, such as that of a person, defined as 'an individual substance of a rational nature'.

This particular definition occurs in Boethius's theological treatise *Against Eutyches*. Here and in other theological treatises, such as that *On the Trinity*, Boethius refers to a number of Aristotelian metaphysical concepts. But these references were not taken much notice of by the early medievals, for whom Aristotle was above all a dialectician or logician.

3

In the fourth century Chalcidius, who seems to have been a Christian, translated into Latin and commented on part of the *Timaeus* of Plato,[2] a work which was used in the twelfth century by members of the School of Chartres. Another fourth-century writer, Marius Victorinus, who became a Christian in late life, translated into Latin the *Isagoge* of Porphyry, part of the *Enneads* of Plotinus,[3] and one or two of Aristotle's logical works, besides composing some treatises of his own, for example on definitions.

Early in the fifth century Martianus Capella, a learned pagan, wrote his work *De Nuptiis Mercurii et Philologiae* (*On the Nuptials of Mercury and Philology*), a kind of encyclopedia of the liberal arts. And in the following century the Christian writer Cassiodorus, a pupil of Boethius, wrote on the same subject, dividing the seven liberal arts into two groups, called respectively the *Trivium* (grammar, rhetoric and dialectic,

---

[1] It may be objected that there are several distinguishable problems. But the problem was discussed in the Middle Ages as primarily one of reference (what do universal terms stand for?), and as relating primarily to generic and specific terms.

[2] This work by Chalcidius is published in the *Corpus Platonicum Medii Aevi* (Leiden, 1962).

[3] As we have seen, this was read by Augustine before his conversion.

the three linguistic sciences) and the *Quadrivium* (arithmetic, geometry, music and astronomy). The liberal arts, together with a multitude of other subjects, were also treated in the *Etymologies* of bishop Isidore of Seville, who died in the first half of the seventh century. This encyclopedia or compilation was much used in the early Middle Ages. For the most part these works were collections of ideas and did not aim at or show originality of thought. But they were found in monastic libraries, served as textbooks and transmitted at any rate some acquaintance with the learning of the past to the early medievals. The two groups of liberal arts formed the basis of medieval education.

5

Early Middle Ages

I

IN 455 the Vandals took and pillaged Rome, which had already been entered by the Visigoths under Alaric in 408. In 476 the nominal Roman emperor, who resided at Ravenna, was deposed by Odoacer, who had risen to a position of eminence among the German mercenaries in Italy. Odoacer, with the title patrician, was effective ruler of Italy until in 493 Theodoric, king of the Ostrogoths, made himself master of the land. The Ostrogoth kingdom in Italy lasted until Belisarius, general of the Byzantine emperor Justinian, took Rome in 536 and Ravenna in 540. In the second half of the sixth century the Lombards invaded and occupied northern Italy, while the representatives of the Byzantine emperor resided at Ravenna. Rome passed under the temporal sovereignty of the pope.

It is hardly to be expected, of course, that philosophy would flourish during the turbulent years of the fall of the Roman empire and the successive invasions. It would be indeed an exaggeration to describe the period following the collapse of the empire as a period of unmitigated barbarism. As we have seen, Boethius lived in the Ostrogoth kingdom; and mention has been made of Isidore of Seville who died about the year 636 in the Visigothic kingdom in Spain. At the same time the educational system of the Roman empire broke down; and what learning existed was to be found chiefly in the monasteries. St Benedict lived from 480 until 543; and the monasteries which owed their inspiration to his Rule became the channel whereby remnants of the old culture were preserved and transmitted to the 'barbarian' peoples.[1]

In England the situation began to improve from about 669, when a Greek monk, Theodore of Tarsus, arrived as archbishop of Canterbury and, together with his associates, developed the monastic school in that city. The Venerable Bede (674–735), Scriptural exegete and historian (or at any rate chronicler), was a monk at Jarrow. And it was a pupil of Bede, Egbert, who was mainly responsible for the growth of York as an educational centre.

A rebirth of letters in Europe came in the time of Charlemagne. In 406 Clovis, king of the Franks, was converted to Christianity; and under his rule and that of his successors all the Frankish lands were united under the Merovingian dynasty. After the death of Dagobert I in 638 the Merovingian kings became only nominal rulers, the real power being exercised by the Mayors of the Palace.[2] In 751, however, the Merovingian dynasty came to an end with the acclamation of Pippin the Short as king of the Franks. Pippin left his kingdom to his two sons, Charles and Carloman. The latter died in 771, and Charles, who was to be known as Charles the Great or Charlemagne, became the sole monarch. After an invasion of Lombardy, several conquests of the Saxons, the annexation of Bavaria, the subjection of Bohemia and the conquest of parts of Spain Charlemagne was the greatest Christian ruler in western Europe. On Christmas Day in the year 800 he was anointed emperor by the pope at Rome, an act which marked a decisive breach between Rome and Byzantium and also emphasized the Christian responsibilities of the monarch and the theocratic character of the State.

In addition to being a conqueror Charlemagne was a reformer, interested in educational work and aiming at the cultural reconstruction of society. For this purpose he gathered about him a band of scholars. In view of the fact that in the sixth and seventh centuries the old Roman culture of Gaul had sunk to an extremely low level, the emperor had to rely mainly on scholars from outside the Frankish kingdom. At his invitation some came from Italy and Spain; but his chief instrument, Alcuin, came from York. In 782 Alcuin took over the organization of

[1] There was also the cultural influence of the old Celtic monasticism, which spread from Ireland to Scotland and northern England.
[2] Thus Charles Martel, who in 732 defeated the Saracens at Poitiers and halted the Moslem invasion of the West, was not the king of the Franks in name, even if he was their ruler in fact.

the Palatine school, the academy attached to the imperial court, where he instructed his pupils in the Scriptures, ancient literature, logic, grammar and astronomy. Alcuin also busied himself with composing textbooks and with the accurate copying of manuscripts, particularly of the Scriptures. Among his pupils was Rhabanus Maurus, known as the 'preceptor of Germany', who became abbot of Fulda and subsequently archbishop of Mainz.

It cannot be said that much original work was done by Alcuin and his associates. Their task was rather that of disseminating existing learning. This was done both in monastic schools, such as those attached to the monasteries of St Gall and Fulda, and in the episcopal or capitular schools. These institutions existed primarily, though not exclusively, for those who were to become monks or priests. The Palatine school, however, was doubtless intended by the emperor to be an instrument in the creation of what we might describe as a civil service, required for the administration of the Carolingian empire.[1]

The language employed in education was Latin. Even if the use of Latin had not followed naturally from the predominantly ecclesiastical character of education, it would have been necessary from the administrative point of view, given the medley of peoples comprising the empire. The content of education consisted of the seven liberal arts, mentioned in the last chapter, and of theological studies, taking the form of a study of the Scriptures. Besides promoting education in this sense Charlemagne's cultural reform resulted in the multiplication of manuscripts and the enrichment of libraries.

In the Carolingian era philosophy, generally speaking, amounted to little more than dialectic or logic, which was included, as we have noted, in the *Trivium*. With the great exception mentioned in the next section speculative philosophy existed only in rudimentary forms. For example, in the *Sayings of Candidus about the Image of God*, attributed to a monk of Fulda in the early part of the ninth century, there is an argument for the existence of God, based on the idea that the hierarchy of being demands the existence of an infinite divine intelligence. Again, we can find some indications of the beginning of the controversy about universal terms, a subject which will be treated later. In a period of salvage and transmission one would hardly expect to find much original philosophizing.

[1] Some people have liked to regard the Palatine school as the remote ancestor of the University of Paris, in spite of the fact that Charlemagne's court was at Aachen.

2

The great exception, to which reference has been made above, is the thought of John Scotus Erigena,[1] the first eminent philosopher of the Middle Ages. Born in Ireland, John Scotus studied in an Irish monastery, where he doubtless acquired his knowledge of Greek.[2] By 850 he had become attached to the court of Charles the Bald, where he taught in the Palatine school. Charles was king of the western part of the empire, Neustria, from 843 until 875, when he was crowned emperor. He died in 877, and it seems probable that John Scotus died about the same time, though the date and place of his death are unknown.[3]

In a work *On Predestination* (*De praedestinatione*) John Scotus intervened in a current theological controversy on the side of human freedom. As a reward for his pains he incurred the suspicion of heresy and prudently turned his attention to other subjects. In 858 he began his translation into Latin of the writings of the Pseudo-Dionysius, on which he also commented.[4] In addition he translated some writings of Gregory of Nyssa and Maximus the Confessor, and he appears to have written commentaries on St John's Gospel and on certain works by Boethius. His chief title to fame, however, is his work *On the Division of Nature* (*De divisione naturae*), which was probably composed between 862 and 866. Consisting of five books, the work is written in dialogue form, the participants being a master or professor and a pupil. It reveals a considerable dependence on the writings of the Pseudo-Dionysius and of Fathers of the Church such as Gregory of Nyssa. Nevertheless the work is a remarkable achievement, setting out an overall system or world-vision and manifesting a powerful and outstanding mind, limited indeed by the intellectual life of the time and by

[1] The combination of the epithets Scotus and Erigena (born in Ireland) may seem to amount to a contradiction in terms. But in the ninth century Ireland was commonly described as Greater Scotland and the Irish as 'Scots'.

[2] It would be extremely rash to assume that all Irish monks knew Greek. At the same time, in the ninth century a knowledge of Greek was more or less peculiar to the Irish monasteries. When it is found elsewhere, as at St Gall, it can generally be traced to the influence of Irish monks.

[3] The story that John Scotus became abbot of Athelney and was murdered by the monks seems to be either pure legend or due to a confusion between the philosopher and some other John.

[4] The writings of the Pseudo-Dionysius had been presented by the emperor Michael Balbus to Louis the Fair in 827. The commentaries by John Scotus did not include the *Mystical Theology*.

the paucity of the available philosophical material for reflection but rising far above the rather mediocre abilities of contemporary thinkers.

The word 'Nature' in the title of John Scotus's work signifies the whole of reality, including both God and creatures. The author tries to show how God in himself, described as 'Nature which creates and is not created', generates the divine Word or *Logos* and, in the Word, the eternal divine ideas. These ideas are created in the sense that they are logically, though not temporally, posterior to the eternally generated Word; and they are creative at any rate in the sense that they are the exemplars or archetypes of finite things; together, therefore, they form 'Nature which is created and creates'. Finite things, created according to their eternal patterns, constitute 'Nature which is created and does not create'. They are the divine self-manifestation, the theophany or appearing of God. Finally John Scotus speaks of 'Nature which neither creates nor is created'. This is the conclusion of the cosmic process, the result of the return of all things to their source, when God will be all in all.

There does not seem to be any cogent reason for doubting that John Scotus intended to expound a Christian vision of the world, an overall interpretation of the universe in the light of the Christian faith. His initial attitude, that is to say, seems to be that of faith seeking understanding. But the instrument of understanding is speculative philosophy, ultimately derived from Neoplatonism. And the modern reader can hardly avoid receiving the impression that in the hands of John Scotus Christianity tends to undergo transformation into a metaphysical system. It is indeed most unlikely that the philosopher himself thought in terms of transformation. He doubtless thought rather in terms of penetration, of penetration, that is to say, by the intellect of the Christian view of reality. In the process of understanding, however, he leaves us with a number of ambiguities, or of tensions between what Christianity was popularly supposed to teach and John Scotus's philosophical interpretation of this teaching. We can refer to two or three examples.

The Bible speaks of divine wisdom and of God as wise. The way of negation, however, which for John Scotus is of fundamental importance, demands that wisdom should be denied of God, inasmuch as it is an attribute of some creatures. The philosopher attempts dialectical harmonization of the relevant biblical statements with the way of negation by interpreting the assertion that God is wise as meaning that super-wisdom is to be predicated of God. The biblical assertion that God is wise is not contradicted; but the use of the word 'super' indicates that the divine wisdom transcends human understanding. And inasmuch as creaturely wisdom, the wisdom of which we have experience, is negated of God, the way of negation remains supreme. Evidently, John Scotus is drawing on the ideas of the Pseudo-Dionysius. What he says is not an unheard of novelty. The point is, however, that he starts, as it were, with a biblical idea of God and then proceeds in a direction which leads logically, so it can be argued, to agnosticism. First it is asserted that God is X. Then it is denied that God is X. Then God is asserted to be super-X. The question naturally arises, do we have any notion what we are predicating of God when we say that he is super-X?

A second example. In the first book of the work *On the Division of Nature* John Scotus makes it clear that he accepts belief in free divine creation of the world 'out of nothing'. He then goes on to argue that the statement that God made the world implies change in God and the untenable notion that God existed 'before' the world. Of course, Augustine would have allowed that creation should not be interpreted as implying the temporal priority of God (that God exists in time) or that God underwent a change through the act of creation. John Scotus suggests, however, that belief in creation should be understood as meaning that God is the essence of all things, and even, rather surprisingly, that he is made in the things of which he is said to be the maker. The Neoplatonic idea of emanation, of things flowing out from the One, is doubtless at work here; but some of John Scotus's statements, taken by themselves, give the impression that for him the world is the divine objectification or, to use an Hegelian phrase, God-in-his-otherness. At the same time John Scotus maintains that God in himself remains transcendent, unchangeable and impassable. And though it is indeed clear that he is trying to interpret the Judaeo-Christian belief in divine creation with the aid of philosophical instruments, it is none too clear what the reader should make of the results of this process.

A final example. John Scotus accepts Christian belief in man's return to God through Christ as incarnate Son of God; and he states explicitly that individual persons will be transformed rather than annihilated or absorbed. Further, he accepts belief in reward and punishment in the next life. At the same time he maintains that creatures will return into their eternal foundations in God (the archetypal ideas) and will cease to be called creatures. Moreover, the idea of eternal punishment of the finally impenitent is explained as meaning that God will eternally prevent the perverse will from fixing itself on the images, conserved in memory, of the things which the sinner desired on earth.

Here John Scotus's problem is to a considerable extent internal to the Christian religion, a problem treated by Origen and St Gregory of Nyssa. How, for instance, can we reconcile the doctrine of hell with St Paul's statement that God will be all in all, and indeed with belief in the universal salvific will of God? At the same time the philosopher evidently tries to understand Christian eschatology in the light and with the aid of Neoplatonist belief in the cosmic emanation and return to God. His problematics are determined by his study of the Scriptures and of treatises by the Pseudo-Dionysius, Gregory of Nyssa and others.

It may seem to be a gross anachronism if we mention the name of Hegel in connection with a ninth-century thinker. And so it is in certain important respects. In spite, however, of the great and obvious differences in mental background, historical context, approach and philosophical convictions, we can find in both men the impulse to explore the philosophical or speculative significance of Christian beliefs. As for the dispute among historians whether John Scotus should be labelled as a theist, a panentheist or a pantheist, it is hardly profitable to pursue this theme unless one is prepared to offer clear definitions of the senses which one proposes to give to these terms. We can indeed say that John Scotus assumes Christian theism, tries to understand it and, in the process of understanding, offers what may fairly be described as a panentheistic system. But unless theism is taken as equivalent to deism, it must presumably be in some sense panentheism.

The remarkable achievement of John Scotus seems to have aroused very little interest at the time. This was doubtless due in some measure to the conditions prevailing after the break-up of the Carolingian empire. The *De divisione Naturae* was indeed used by a few writers in the early Middle Ages; but it did not acquire notoriety until it was appealed to by Amalric of Bene (Amaury de Bène), who died soon after the beginning of the thirteenth century and who was apparently accused of pantheism.[1] The result of Amalric's patronage was that the *magnum opus* of John Scotus, considered to be the root of the trouble, was condemned in 1225 by Pope Honorius III.

[1] We know very little of Amalric's ideas. It seems, however, that his writings were interpreted, whether justifiably or not, as identifying God with creatures.

3

The empire of Charlemagne turned out to be a political failure. After the emperor's death his dominions were divided. Further, a wave of invasions occurred. The year 845 witnessed the burning of Hamburg and the sack of Paris by the Northmen or Vikings, while in 847 Bordeaux suffered a like fate. The Frankish empire was ultimately split into five kingdoms, frequently engaged in war with one another. Meanwhile the Saracens were invading Italy and nearly captured Rome. Europe, apart from the flourishing Moslem culture in Spain, was involved in a second Dark Ages. The Church fell victim to exploitation by the new feudal nobility. Abbacies and bishoprics were used as rewards for laymen or unworthy prelates; and in the tenth century the papacy itself was under the control of local nobles and factions. In such circumstances the educational movement inaugurated by Charlemagne could not be expected to bear much fruit.

This is not to say, of course, that learning simply disappeared in Europe. In 910 the abbey of Cluny was founded; and the monasteries of the Cluniac reform, which was introduced into England by St Dunstan, contributed to keeping letters alive. For example, the monk Abbon, who died in 1004, directed a monastic school on the Loire, where, in addition to study of the Scriptures and the Fathers, attention was given to grammar, logic[1] and mathematics. A more prominent figure, however, is Gerbert of Aurillac. Born about 938, Gerbert became a monk of the Cluniac reform and studied in Spain, where he seems to have acquired some knowledge of Arabic science. Later he became director of the school at Rheims. After having occupied successively the posts of abbot of Bobbio, archbishop of Rheims and archbishop of Ravenna, he was elected pope in 999, taking the name of Sylvester II. In his period of teaching at Rheims he lectured on logic; but he is more remarkable for his study both of the classical Latin literature then available and of mathematics. He died in 1003.

One of Gerbert's pupils at Rheims was a certain Fulbert, who is regarded as founder of the school at Chartres and who became bishop of that city. There had been a cathedral school at Chartres for a considerable time; but in 990 Fulbert laid the foundations of a centre of humanism and of philosophical and theological studies which was to

[1] Logic included Aristotle's *Categories* and *De Interpretatione* (the so-called 'old logic') and the treatises of Boethius on the *Prior* and *Posterior Analytics*.

become famous in the twelfth century, until the regional schools were eclipsed by the prestige of the University of Paris.

4

We have seen that dialectic or logic formed one of the subjects of the *Trivium*. As a liberal art it had therefore long been studied in the schools. In the eleventh century, however, we find logic coming to life as it were, and being used as an instrument for asserting the supremacy of reason even in the domain of faith. In other words, there arose a class of dialecticians who were not content simply with studying Porphyry's introduction, a couple of Aristotle's logical works and commentaries and treatises by Boethius. It seems indeed that there was a certain amount of verbal acrobatics on the part of dialecticians who wished to dazzle and impress. But there were those who applied logic within the field of what was then regarded as the chief and most sublime science, namely theology.

To express the matter in this way is, it is true, misleading. For theology had never been regarded as immune from every logical criterion. Nor had the theologians disdained the use of logical deduction. The point is that whereas the theologian regarded certain premises or doctrines (from which conclusions could be deduced) as revealed by God and to be accepted on authority, some of the eleventh-century dialecticians paid little attention to the idea of authority and tried to turn revealed 'mysteries' into conclusions of reason. In some cases at any rate they altered the doctrines in the process. It was this rationalistic attitude which excited the hostility of a number of theologians and led to some lively controversy. The dispute was about the scope and limitations of the human reason. As, however, philosophy at the time did not amount to much more than logic,[1] we can also say that the controversy was about the relation between philosophy and theology.

One of the chief sinners, from the point of view of the theologians, was the monk Berengarius of Tours (*c.* 1000–88), a former pupil of Fulbert of Chartres. Berengarius was understood as denying, for logical reasons, that in the eucharist bread and wine are 'substantially converted' (transubstantiated, that is to say) into the body and blood of Christ. Lanfranc, who died in 1089 as archbishop of Canterbury,

---

[1] This statement prescinds from the question whether logic should be considered a part of philosophy, a propaedeutic to philosophy or a separate and purely formal science. At the time it was considered part of philosophy.

accused Berengarius of disregarding authority and faith and of trying to understand 'those things which cannot be understood'.[1] It is not indeed very easy to make out precisely what Berengarius held: but in his work *On the Sacred Supper against Lanfranc* he certainly exalted dialectic or logic as 'the art of arts' and maintained that 'to turn to dialectic is to turn to reason',[2] which is something which any enlightened person should be prepared to do. As for the application of dialectic to the eucharist, he apparently held that it was nonsense to talk about accidents existing without their substance. In the formula of consecration 'this is my Body' (*hoc est corpus meum*) the pronoun 'this' must refer to the bread, which therefore remains. The subject of the proposition is bread, and though through consecration the bread becomes a sacramental sign of Christ's body, it cannot be identified with the actual body born of the Virgin Mary. The real conversion or change is effected in the souls of the communicants.

Berengarius seems to have based his doctrine on a work by Ratramnus of Corbie (d. 868), which he attributed to John Scotus Erigena. As proposed by Berengarius, the doctrine was condemned by a Council held in Rome in 1050. It does not appear, however, that this condemnation made much impression on Berengarius. For in 1079 he was required to subscribe to a statement in which he asserted his belief in the substantial conversion of bread and wine into the body and blood of Christ. Apart from having to retract his former teaching in this way he was not otherwise molested.

A case such as that of Berengarius helps to explain the hostility shown by certain theologians to dialectic or, as we can say when speaking of the period in question, philosophy. At the same time it would be a mistake to suppose that all the eleventh-century dialecticians set about rationalizing Christian dogmas. A more general reason for disparagement of philosophy was the conviction that it had little value in comparison with study of the Scriptures and the Fathers, and that it made no contribution to the task of saving one's soul. Thus St Peter Damian (1007–72) made it clear that in his opinion the liberal arts were of little value. And though he did not say with Manegold of Lautenbach (d. 1103) that the use of logic was superfluous, he maintained that the role of dialectic was purely subordinate, being that of a 'hand-

---

[1] *On the Body and Blood of the Lord* (*De corpore et sanguine Domini*), Migne, *P.L.*, 150, col. 427.

[2] *De sacra coena adversus Lanfrancum*, ed. A. F. and F. Th. Vischer (Berlin, 1834), p. 101. This is an edition of a manuscript discovered in 1770.

maid' to theology.[1] To be sure, this view was not exceptional. It was shared, for example, by Gerard of Czanad, a native of Venice who died in 1046 as bishop of Czanad in Hungary. Nor indeed was the view, taken in itself, particularly odd. For, as has already been noted, unless logic is developed as a science in its own right, it is natural to think of it as an instrument for use in developing some other science. St Peter Damian, however, went further than saying that the role of dialectic in theology is subordinate or ancillary. He maintained that it could not be taken for granted that the principles of reason were of universal application in the realm of theology. Some other writers, such as Manegold of Lautenbach, apparently held that the pretensions of human reasoning were overthrown by such truths as the virgin birth and resurrection of Christ. But this was a question of exceptional events rather than of a contradiction of logical principles. Peter Damian went further, by maintaining, for example, that God in his omnipotence could undo the past. Thus though it happens to be true today that Julius Caesar crossed the Rubicon, God could in principle make the statement false tomorrow, by cancelling out the past.[2] If this idea was at variance with the demands of reason, so much the worse for reason.

The number of theologians who depicted philosophy as a useless superfluity was, of course, restricted. Lanfranc, who, as we have seen, attacked Berengarius, remarked that the trouble lay not with dialectic itself but with its abuse. And he recognized the fact that the theologians themselves made use of dialectic in the development of theology, a fact which was exemplified in the writings of his pupil St Anselm, of whom something will be said in the next chapter. In general, it is a mistake to be so hypnotized by the rationalizing activities of certain dialecticians on the one hand and by the exaggerated pronouncements of certain theologians on the other that one conceives the situation in the eleventh century as being simply a matter of a fight between reason, as represented by the dialecticians, and obscurantism, as represented by the theologians.[3] If, however, we take a broader view and consider

[1] On the Divine Omnipotence (De divina omnipotentia), Migne, P.L., 145, col. 63.
[2] Obviously, this thesis is different from the claim that God could have prevented Julius Caesar from crossing the Rubicon at all. The thesis presupposes historical events and then asserts that God could in principle bring it about that they should no longer be historical events.
[3] It is doubtless tempting to look on Berengarius as a spiritual ancestor of the Protestant reformers. But he was not concerned with ecclesiastical reform, nor with appealing to the authority of the Scriptures against that of the Church. He was concerned with applying the demands of reason, as he saw them, for the

theologians such as St Anselm, we can see that in the development of intellectual life in the early Middle Ages, both theologians and dialecticians had their parts to play. The views of Berengarius, for instance, can of course be regarded from the point of view of theological orthodoxy. But we can also see in them an expression of the reawakening of intellectual life.

5

The statement, made above, that in the eleventh century philosophy was more or less equivalent to logic stands in need of some qualification. It overlooks, for example, the metaphysical elements in the thought of a theologian such as Anselm. And if we turn to the controversy about universals, we can see that the ontological aspect of the problem figured prominently in medieval discussion of the topic.

Consider the sentence 'John is white'. The word 'John' is used as what the dictionary would call a proper name. It designates or refers to an individual. It is true that one might lay down conditions which any word had to satisfy before we were prepared to recognize it as a proper name, and which a word such as 'John' would not satisfy. If, for example, we demanded that a proper name should designate, in principle, one and only one individual thing, 'John' could not be classified as a proper name. For many people are called John. And even if in fact only one person were named John, other people could be so named. In other words, we could, if we wished, legislate proper names out of existence. As things are, however, 'John' is obviously a proper name. It is a word used to name people, not to describe them.[1] 'White', however, in the sentence 'John is white', is not a name but a universal term which has a descriptive meaning. To say that John is white is to say that he has a certain quality. But the same can be predicated of other individuals, say Tom, Dick and Harry. And as the meaning of 'white' is, or can be, the same in each case, we may be led to ask whether John, Tom, Dick and Harry all participate in a certain reality called whiteness. If so, what is the ontological status of this reality? It may be the case that such a question is the product of logical confusion. But as it stands, it is an ontological question.

understanding of what his opponents believed to be a 'mystery' transcending human understanding.
[1] It seems clear to me that proper names such as 'John' do not have descriptive meaning, though this view has been challenged.

One of the sources of the discussion of universals in the early Middle Ages was a text in Boethius's second commentary on the *Isagoge* of Porphyry.[1] Boethius quotes Porphyry as asking whether species and genuses (such as dog and animal) actually subsist or whether they have reality only in concepts, and, if they are subsistent realities, whether they subsist apart from material things or only in them. As Boethius notes, Porphyry does not answer his questions in this particular text. Boethius himself, however, discusses the problem and solves it on Aristotelian lines, not, he remarks, because he approves of the solution but because Porphyry's *Isagoge* is an introduction to the *Categories* of Aristotle. The early medievals, while noticing the questions, did not properly appreciate Boethius's discussion of the matter. We may add that trouble was caused by Boethius's remark in his commentary on Aristotle's *Categories* that the work was about words, not things.[2] For this statement suggested the idea of a simple dichotomy. Are universals words or are they things?

Already in the ninth century we find evidence of an ultra-realism which was the expression of the unwarranted assumption that there must be some real entity corresponding to every noun. For example, Fredegisius of Tours (d. 834), a pupil of Alcuin, wrote a *Letter on Nothing and Darkness*, in which he maintained, among other things, that there must be something corresponding to the word 'nothing'.[3] It does not follow, however, that Fredegisius thought of absolute nothingness as a special kind of something. What he was concerned with maintaining was that as God created the world 'out of nothing', and as every noun must refer to a corresponding reality, God must have created the world out of a pre-existing undifferentiated material or stuff. To philosophize in this way is to philosophize as a grammarian. The same can be said of Remigius of Auxerre (d. 908) who apparently held that as 'man' is predicated of all individual men, they must all have one substance.

When considering ultra-realism in the Middle Ages, we have to allow for the influence of theological factors. For example, when Odo of Tournai (d. 1113) maintained that there was only one substance in all men and that the coming into being of a new individual meant that this one substance existed under a new modification, he was not simply

---

[1] See, for example, Migne, *P.L.*, 64, col. 82, or *Selections from Medieval Philosophers*, edited by R. McKeon (London, 1930), I, p. 91.

[2] See Migne, *P.L.*, 64, col. 162.

[3] Ibid., 105, cols. 751–6.

in the grip of a naïve 'one noun—one thing' theory. Nor, for the matter of that, was he concerned with expounding Spinozism before Spinoza, even if his thesis logically demanded some such development. Odo was unable to see how the doctrine of original sin, as transmitted from Adam to his descendants, could be preserved, unless it was held that one substance, contaminated in Adam, was handed on, as it were in human generation. Hence to convince Odo of the absurdity of his position logical analysis would have to be supplemented by a theological account of original sin which did not involve ultra-realism of the type which he apparently defended.[1]

If ultra-realism goes back to the ninth century, so does opposition to it. Thus Eric of Auxerre seems to have maintained that if we wish to explain what is meant by 'whiteness', 'man' or 'animal', we have to point to individual specimens of white things, men or animals. There are no extramentally existing universal realities corresponding to the names of qualities, species and genuses. Only individuals exist. What the mind does is to 'gather together', for example, individual men and form the specific idea of man, for purposes of economy.

To jump to a much later date, an anti-realist position was trenchantly stated by Roscelin, a canon of Compiègne, who taught at various centres and died about 1120. It is indeed very difficult to ascertain precisely what he held, because his writings, apart from a letter to Abelard, have perished or at any rate have been lost. We have to rely on the testimony of other writers, such as Anselm, Abelard and John of Salisbury. It is Anselm who credits Roscelin with the statement, always associated with his name, that universals are mere words.[2] As Anselm's knowledge of Roscelin's teaching was obviously superior to ours, we can hardly call his report in question. At the same time it is not at all clear what precisely Roscelin meant by saying that universals are simply words. He may have intended his assertion to be taken literally; but we are not compelled to interpret him as denying universal concepts and as identifying universals with words considered simply as spoken or written entities. According to Abelard, Roscelin maintained that when we speak of a substance as consisting of parts, 'part' is a mere

---

[1] The theological theory which supplanted 'traducianism' was that original sin consists in the privation of sanctifying grace. That is to say, in human generation God creates a new individual soul which, because of Adam's sin, is deprived of sanctifying grace as an initial state. How theologians understand original sin today is not clear to me.

[2] *Flatus vocis* is the phrase. Migne, *P.L.*, 158, col. 265A.

word.[1] This could mean that in the case of a given thing, such as an undivided apple, it is we who conceive and designate the parts. As the apple is *ex hypothesi* undivided, the parts are not really there, as they would be if we had divided the apple. The statement that 'part' is a mere word need not necessarily be taken as meaning that Roscelin is identifying the conceived or designated parts of the undivided apple with the *word* 'part'. And it may well be the case that his statement about universals should be taken simply as an emphatic way of saying that there are no universal entities out there, apart from the mind.

However this may be, Roscelin aroused some hostility by his application of his theory to the doctrine of the Trinity. He maintained, for example, that if the divine nature or essence or substance is really one and the same in the three divine Persons, we ought to say that all three Persons became incarnate in Christ. But this is not what theology teaches. Must we not admit, therefore, that the divine nature is not one and the same in all three Persons, and that the Persons are distinct individual beings? Having drawn attention to this puzzle, Roscelin was accused of tritheism, an accusation which he rejected. In any case the attack on him does not seem to have interrupted his career.

In the early Middle Ages ultra-realism was known as the 'ancient' doctrine, while the opposing doctrine, based on the slogan that only individuals exist, was described as 'modern'. The dispute between the two parties came to a head with the famous controversy between William of Champeaux and Abelard, in which William, an upholder of the 'ancient' doctrine, was made to look pretty foolish. But further mention of this controversy had better be left until we treat of Abelard.

[1] Ibid., 178, col. 358B.

6

Anselm and Abelard

I

THE most outstanding theologian of the eleventh century was St Anselm (1033–1109). Born at Aosta in Piedmont, Anselm studied in France, joined the Benedictine order and became prior (1063) and later abbot (1078) of Bec. In 1093 he was nominated to succeed Lanfranc in the see of Canterbury.

In the introduction to his lectures on the philosophy of religion Hegel refers approvingly to Anselm as one of those 'great men'[1] who, so far from thinking that the effort to understand was injurious to faith, were convinced that the attempt to understand was essential for the development of faith itself. Hegel's statement is justified, inasmuch as Anselm insisted, with Augustine, that 'I believe in order that I may understand' (*Credo ut intelligam*). In his view the Christian should try to understand the content of his faith and the connections between the articles of belief. He even set out to prove, for example, the doctrine of the Trinity by 'necessary reasons'.[2] True, it would show a misunderstanding of Anselm's outlook or attitude if we were to conclude that he was prepared to reject Christian beliefs in the event of his finding himself unable to provide philosophical proofs. For Christian faith was his point of departure; and if he found that the search for understanding came up against limits, faith would still remain. However, Anselm was not prepared to set limits in advance. He was no anti-intellectualist; and he contributed powerfully to the development of theology in the Middle Ages.

[1] *Philosophy of Religion* (translated by E. B. Speirs and J. Burdon Sanderson), I, p. 21.   [2] Migne, *P.L.*, 158, col. 272 (*De fide Trinitatis*, 14).

It is in this context that we must see Anselm's arguments for the existence of God. In terms of the distinction which was made at a later date between natural or philosophical theology on the one hand and dogmatic theology on the other, these arguments would be classified as belonging to the part of metaphysics called natural theology. But Anselm did not make this distinction. His attitude was frankly that of the Christian who already believes in God but who then reflects on the rational evidence for this belief. His arguments, in other words, were one expression of his general programme of faith seeking understanding (*fides quaereus intellectum*). Needless to say, Anselm recognized dialectic as a distinct liberal art which, considered in itself, belonged to the *Trivium*. And he was convinced that dialectic or logic could and should be employed in theology. But what would later be described as Anselm's natural or philosophical theology was for him part of his programme as a Christian theologian, part of the programme, that is to say, of faith seeking understanding of itself.

The fact, however, that Anselm reasons within, so to speak, the area of faith does not entail the conclusion that what appear to be arguments are really something else. Pious meditations they may be, but not in a sense which excludes serious reflection and reasoning. Anselm was obviously not surrounded by atheists, whom he was trying to convince that there is a God after all. But it by no means follows that he was not trying to exhibit the rational grounds of belief in God as part of the programme of faith seeking understanding. To tear the arguments out of their context and treat them out of any relation to initial faith is one thing. To claim that they are not arguments at all is another thing.

In the *Monologium* Anselm develops a series of proofs of God's existence from degrees of perfection.[1] It is obviously assumed as a fact that there are degrees of perfection in the universe, degrees of goodness for example. It is further assumed as a premise that when a number of beings possess a perfection which does not of itself involve finiteness and limitation,[2] they derive this perfection from a being which is that perfection itself in an absolute and unlimited form. Thus degrees of goodness reveal the existence of absolute goodness, degrees of wisdom the existence of absolute or infinite wisdom, and so on.

---

[1] In the third chapter Anselm gives an argument which starts as an argument from efficient causality but then falls into the general pattern of the arguments contained in the first two chapters.

[2] Quantitative size, for example, implies limitation, in the sense that whatever quantity we conceive, we can always think of a greater.

This line of argument can be described as Platonic in character, though there is a brief expression of it in Aristotle's dialogue *On Philosophy*.[1] Obviously, even if we are prepared to admit the presence in the world of objective degrees of perfection, the validity of the premise on which any inference from the existence of a limited to an unlimited perfection is based is precisely what has to be proved. Moreover, in the argument given in the third chapter of the *Monologium* Anselm seems to assume that existence is a perfection.[2] However, by trying to show that the empirical world, with its varying degrees of perfection, manifests God's existence, Anselm contributed to the development of medieval metaphysics. The line of argument represented by the first three chapters of the *Monologium* reappears in Aquinas's fourth way of proving God's existence.

Anselm is much better known for the famous argument in the *Proslogium*, the so-called ontological argument, which, despite all refutations, has tended to recur in some form or other up to the present day. Wishing to find a brief argument which by itself would be sufficient to prove not only the existence of God but also all that Christians believe about the divine nature or substance,[3] he found what he was looking for in a line of argument which claimed to show the existential implication of the idea of absolute perfection. That is to say, if 'the fool' of the Psalms,[4] who says in his heart that there is no God, really understands what Christians mean by God, he is logically bound to recognize the existence of God. If, in other words, by admitting that he knows what is meant by God he admits that it is possible for there to be a God, he is logically committed to asserting that God actually exists. Though, therefore, he can say with his lips that there is no God, he cannot say this in his heart, really meaning it, provided, that is to say, that he once admits the real possibility of there being a God. That this is in fact the case is what the argument purports to prove.

[1] Aristotle argues that where there is a better, there is a best, and that, as some things are better than others, there must be a best, which is the divine. See *Aristotelis Fragmenta* (Berlin, 1870), Fragment 15.

[2] It is obvious that existence cannot be a perfection in the same sense as, for example, wisdom. For nobody can be wise unless he exists. We cannot say with propriety that Tom is white, kind, existing and intelligent. For unless he exists, he can be neither white, kind nor intelligent. Whether there is another sense in which existence can be described as a perfection has been a matter for dispute.

[3] Anselm is thinking of attributes such as omniscience and omnipotence, not of the Trinity.

[4] Psalms, XIII, 1 and LII, 1.

In the second chapter of the *Proslogium* the argument runs on these lines. If the doubter is told that God is defined as that than which no greater can be thought, he understands what is said. In this case he admits that God has subjective existence, in the sense that he exists intramentally, in the concept of him which is shared even by the doubter. But God has been defined as absolute perfection, as that than which no greater can be thought. And that which exists objectively, extramentally, as well as subjectively, is obviously 'greater' (more perfect) than that which exists only in idea. If, therefore, God is that which no greater can be thought, he must exist objectively.

In the third chapter of the *Proslogium* Anselm adds what he seems to think of as a complement to the argument already given, though some commentators see in it a separate or logically independent argument.[1] We can think of some things as not existing. For example, the tree out there in the field did not always exist. Nor will it always exist. In other words, its existence is contingent, not necessary. But to exist necessarily, to exist in such a way that non-existence is excluded, is 'greater' (more perfect) than to exist contingently. Hence that than which no greater can be thought must be conceived as existing necessarily. In other words, God cannot be merely a possible being. If he exists or can exist at all, he exists necessarily.

From the concept of that than which no greater can be thought Anselm goes on to deduce divine attributes, such as omnipotence (Chapter 7) and infinity (Chapter 13). For such perfections are implicitly contained in the idea of absolute perfection, of that than which no greater can be thought.

A Benedictine monk named Gaunilo wrote a criticism of Anselm's argument. His general thesis can be summed up in the statement that no concept implies its own reference.[2] Taking the example of a fabled lost island which was said to be more beautiful or excellent than any known island, he argued that though we might conceive or imagine such an island, it would by no means follow that there actually was such an island. Anselm very naturally denied that there was any parity between the case of the concept of the island and that of the concept of God. For

---

[1] On this subject see, for example, *St Anselm's Proslogion*, translated with an introduction and philosophical commentary by M. J. Charlesworth (Oxford, 1965), pp. 73 f.

[2] That is to say, no concept logically implies its own instantiation, that there is an existent being to which it is applicable.

it is only the latter concept which is that of something than which no greater can be thought.[1] In Gaunilo's opinion, however, Anselm had not shown that God exists in the mind in a different way from that in which we have ideas the instantiation of which can certainly be doubted or denied. It is all very well to talk about God existing in the mind. But though 'the fool' may have some notion what is meant when he hears the words 'that than which no greater can be thought', he does not possess the clear and distinct understanding of the divine nature or essence which would be required to see that God must exist. The fool can therefore doubt or deny God's existence.

Anselm's argument has had a chequered history. Used, in some form or other, by certain medieval thinkers, it was rejected by Aquinas.[2] After the Middle Ages Descartes and Leibniz defended their own versions of the argument.[3] But Kant rejected it; and most modern philosophers have assumed that his criticism was decisive. The argument, however, has recently been given a new lease of life. Thus Professor N. Malcolm[4] and Professor C. Hartshorne[5] have tried to show that God's existence is either logically necessary or logically impossible, and that, as it has not been shown to be logically impossible, it is logically necessary.

Discussion of Anselm's argument (or arguments) in the *Proslogium* has been conducted on the assumption that what appears to be an

[1] Even the most beautiful island possible (if it makes sense to speak in this way) would lack certain perfections, such as wisdom. But that than which no greater can be thought lacks no perfection. Hence if necessary existence is a perfection, the idea of existing reply is that though the idea of necessary existence may belong to the idea of God, this is not enough to show that the idea is instantiated. The fool might think that there was no necessarily existing reality.

[2] Aquinas argued, among other things, that though the proposition 'God exists' is the one necessarily true (or analytically true) existential proposition, it is not so 'for us'. In other words, we lack the positive insight into the divine nature which would be required for arguing from God's possibility to his actuality. When God's existence has been proved in another way (*a posteriori*), we can then see that the proposition 'God exists' must be necessarily true. But we cannot see it simply by analysis of the proposition.

[3] Leibniz tried to prove that the possibility of God is shown by an inability to discern any contradiction in the idea of a perfect being, and that, as the idea of perfection includes the idea of existing necessarily, God must exist.

[4] See 'Anselm's Ontological Arguments' in the *Philosophical Review*, vol. 69 (1960), reprinted in *Knowledge and Certainty* (Englewood Cliffs, N.J., 1963).

[5] See, for example, *The Logic of Perfection* (La Salle, Illinois, 1962), Chapter 2, and *Anselm's Discovery: A Re-examination of the Ontological Proof for God's Existence* (La Salle, Illinois, 1965).

argument is intended to be such. The question asked has been, is the argument valid or invalid? This interpretation has, however, been challenged.[1] It has been claimed, for example, that Anselm is concerned not with developing an argument to convince agnostics or atheists but with clarifying for Christians their idea of God. To believe in God is to believe in one who is absolutely perfect and who differs radically from all finite things inasmuch as he does not just happen to exist but exists necessarily. Anselm's reflections are set in a religious context, and they can serve to elevate and deepen the Christian's understanding of the divine uniqueness, of the fact that God is conceived not as the relatively supreme being but as the unique transcendent object of adoration and worship. To treat his reflections as a proof of God's existence, addressed to the unbeliever, is a mistake.

It is true that Anselm's reflections are set in a religious context. The argument is indeed developed in the form of an address to God himself. Further, Anselm writes as a Christian believer, from the point of view of faith seeking understanding; and there is no good reason for denying that he tries to bring home to the Christian the nature of the God in whom he believes. At the same time it seems clear enough that Gaunilo was perfectly justified in interpreting the argument as an argument. It may be said that Anselm is claiming that 'God exists' is an analytically true proposition. If so, it can hardly be denied that he tries to prove that it is an analytically true proposition. We can grant that the more we abstract the argument from its context and consider it purely of itself, the more do we move away from the atmosphere, so to speak, of faith seeking understanding of itself. Though, however, Anselm states in his preface to the *Proslogium* that he writes from the standpoint of one who is trying to raise his mind to God and to understand what he believes, he also states explicitly that he was looking for one single argument which would prove that God exists and that he is what Christians believe him to be. It is therefore difficult to see any impropriety in considering the argument as an argument.

To embark on such a discussion here is not possible. It would carry us too far afield.[2] We can, however, make the following two remarks. First, if we come to the conclusion that Aquinas and Kant were right

[1] See *Anselm: Fides Quaerens Intellectum* by Karl Barth (London, 1960).
[2] For example, we would have to discuss the question whether there is any sense in which existence can be described as a perfection. There is also the question whether it makes any sense to talk about necessary existence. A discussion of analytic propositions would also be required.

in rejecting Anselm's *Proslogium* argument,[1] we still have to explain why the argument tends to recur in different forms. Is it simply a case of persistent grounds for logical confusion? Or is it a case of belief in an ultimate divine reality imposing itself, as it were, on certain minds? If so, why? Secondly we can note that Anselm's reasoning and his controversy with Gaunilo show a level of sophistication which we would not expect, if we thought of the eleventh century as a time of practically unrelieved intellectual backwardness and darkness.[2]

Anselm's sophistication can be seen in his analysis of the phrase 'out of nothing' in the statement that God created the world out of nothing. He explains that 'out of nothing' does not mean out of nothing as a pre-existing material, a peculiar kind of something, but that it is equivalent to 'not out of anything'. Anselm may well have had in mind the sort of view expounded by Fredegisius of Tours, who has been referred to above (p. 69), a view which he intended to correct. The point is, however, that in this instance Anselm showed an appreciation of the fact that there can be a difference between the grammatical and logical forms of a proposition. It is quite wrong to think that the medievals were all blind to this difference, and that the light first dawned with Bertrand Russell.[3]

It is worth adding that in his treatise *De Grammatico* (*On the Grammarian*), which takes the form of a dialogue between a professor and a student, Anselm shows a tendency to appeal to rational or ordinary language.[4] He is treating of the subject of paronyms, a topic which he tells us was much discussed by eleventh-century dialecticians.[5] And

[1] It is true that in his criticism of the argument Kant appealed to an example which was even less apt than Gaunilo's example of the beautiful island. But he also put his finger on some important relevant points.

[2] In an essay on Anselm (*Medieval Humanism and Other Studies* (Oxford, 1970), pp. 9–18) R. W. Southern draws attention not only to the brevity and conciseness of Anselm's arguments and his refusal to clutter them up with appeals to authorities but also to the way in which Anselm asks questions which are still relevant and tries to answer them in a fresh and original manner.

[3] Russell doubtless stated the difference in the form of a generalized logical theory, whereas Anselm was concerned with the meaning of a particular theological statement. But what Anselm says clearly implies a perception of the difference between logical and grammatical forms.

[4] There is an edition with Latin and English texts by D. P. Henry. *The De Grammatico of Saint Anselm: The Theory of Paronyms* (Notre Dame, Indiana, 1964).

[5] The discussion arose from Aristotle's *Categories* (10a, 27f.), when Aristotle remarks that many things are called or described paronymously, as a pale man from paleness, the grammatical from grammar, and so on.

he selects for special consideration the case in which a word can function either as a concrete noun or as an adjective. The example which he chooses is *grammaticus*, which can function as a noun, as in *grammaticus loquitur* (the grammarian is speaking), or as an adjective. In English, however, we cannot use 'grammatical' as a noun, so we might take the word 'drunk'. In sentences such as 'drunks are a nuisance' or 'there was a drunk in the corner' the word 'drunk' functions as a noun, whereas in 'Peter was drunk' it functions as an adjective. Anselm's question is whether such a word signifies a substance or a quality. Most people would probably reply that it signifies sometimes the one and sometimes the other. According to Anselm this answer will not do. We can indeed use 'drunk' as an adjective; but if we use it by itself to signify a quality, by saying, for example, that 'drunk is deplorable', not only grammarians but even peasants will laugh. We have to say, for instance, 'drunkenness is deplorable' or 'to become drunk is deplorable'. Anselm's conclusion is that a word such as 'drunk' signifies drunkenness, the state of being drunk, directly and a person indirectly, or that it signifies drunkenness and 'appellates' a person.[1] Indeed, ordinary usage shows us that 'drunk' appellates a person. For the sentence 'drunkenness is drunk' is excluded. Anselm argues similarly that in a sentence such as 'Tom is white', 'white' signifies the possession of the quality of whiteness and 'appellates' Tom.

These samples of Anselm's dialectic are not presented as evidence of a highly developed logic. But it is of interest to observe how he distinguishes between meaning (*significatio*) and reference (*appellatio*), and how he tries to support the theory of which he approves by showing that a rival theory leads to or authorizes the production of sentences which are absurd or nonsensical by the standards of ordinary usage.[2] As logic developed, it was to become more formalized. But in the early Middle Ages it was pursued in association with the semantics of natural or ordinary language.

[1] As an animal can be made drunk, it is true that Mr D. P. Henry's example of 'illiterate' is preferable. For we do not speak of anything but a human being or person as being literate or illiterate.

[2] 'Drunk is deplorable' is an example. Similarly, Anselm argues that if 'white' is taken as signifying or meaning a thing or substance, absurd sentences will be authorized.

2

To turn from Anselm to Abelard may seem equivalent to turning from a theologian to a dialectician, and from a saint and highly orthodox and edifying writer to an heretically inclined philosopher. But though Abelard was indeed the most outstanding dialectician of his time, he was also a theologian.[1] And though he was no saint but a man of combative disposition who made enemies, notably St Bernard, and seems to have been difficult to live with in community, he was no archheretic, as some of his opponents made him out to be. In any case he was an original thinker of great ability, who made a powerful contribution to raising the standard of intellectual life.

Born at Le Palais near Nantes in 1079, Abelard studied first under Roscelin and then under William of Champeaux (d. 1120), both of whom became victims of his dialectical skill. He then started lecturing, first at Melun, then at Corbeil, and afterwards at Paris. Turning to theology, Abelard studied this subject with Anselm of Laon. It appears, however, that his combative disposition led to trouble; and in 1113 he started teaching theology in the cathedral school at Paris. His career was interrupted however by his famous association with Héloise and its sequel; and he retired to the abbey of St Denis. Having stirred up trouble there, he withdrew to the neighbourhood of Nogent-sur-Seine, where he founded the school of Le Paraclet for the students who came to him in his place of retreat. He then became abbot of St Gildas in Brittany, after turning over the property of Le Paraclet to Héloise. His relations with the monks of St Gildas however were far from peaceful;[2] and after some years in which his movements are uncertain he returned to Paris and lectured at Ste Geneviève, with John of Salisbury among his pupils. Abelard also devoted himself to literary activity, the result of which was that he was accused of heresy by St Bernard and condemned by a synod at Sens in 1141. An appeal to Pope Innocent II led to a further condemnation and a prohibition to lecture. Meanwhile Abelard had made some sort of retraction. And he died in peaceful retirement at the Cluniac monastery of St Marcel-sur-Saône in 1142.

It has been mentioned above that Abelard studied for a time under

[1] See, for example, *The Logic of Divine Love: A Critical Analysis of the Soteriology of Peter Abailard*, by R. E. Weingart (Oxford, 1970).
[2] Abelard appears to have tried to introduce reforms which were not to the taste of the monks. And according to his own account of the matter they attempted his assassination.

William of Champeaux. Though William had studied under Roscelin, the expounder of the *flatus vocis* theory, he himself expounded an ultra-realist theory of universals. William maintained, for example, that there is in all men one common essence, present indivisibly in each of them, and that it is to this common essence that the word 'man' refers in a statement such as 'man is mortal'. Abelard objected, however, that this theory led to absurd consequences. If, for instance, John and Tom had numerically the same essence, they would be the same man. Hence if John were in Paris and Tom in London, the same man would be in two places at once. Further, as we can speak of the divine essence or substance, William's theory leads logically to the conclusion that all essences or substances are identical with God's essence or substance.[1]

Under pressure of criticism by Abelard, William of Champeaux abandoned his theory and maintained instead that in the members of a species the same nature or essence is present 'indifferently' (*indifferenter*). Abelard appears to have regarded this as a mere verbal change, as though William were claiming that while two human beings are not the same, neither are they different. But from the extant fragments of William's logical writings[2] it seems fairly clear that what he meant was that in two men their human nature is not identical but similar. It is present 'indifferently' in each of them in the sense that they cannot be distinguished from one another simply by mentioning the defining characteristics of human nature. It is hardly possible, however, to determine William's position or series of positions with certainty.[3] What is clear is that as a result of Abelard's sustained attack he abandoned ultra-realism. In 1108 he left his chair in the cathedral school of Paris and went to teach at the abbey of St Victor near Paris. He was a theologian of stature and subsequently became bishop of Châlons-sur-Marne.

As for Abelard's own opinion about universals, in his introductory work on logic (known as *Ingredientibus*) he inquires whether universality is to be ascribed to words alone or to things as well; and he

---

[1] That is to say, if we hold that the word 'man' refers to a human nature which is numerically the same in all human beings, we are logically committed to holding that if one word, such as 'essence' or 'substance', is predicated of both God and creatures, it refers to what is numerically the same reality in both God and creatures.

[2] Most of our knowledge of the controversy between Abelard and William comes from Abelard's *History of Calamities* (*Historia Calamitatum*; Migne, *P.L.*, 178).

[3] It has been held, for instance, that William first proposed his identity theory, then the theory of indifference and finally a clearer anti-realist theory.

replies that it is to be ascribed to words alone.[1] He does not, however, intend to claim that it is the word itself, the spoken sound or series of sounds, the *flatus vocis*, which is the universal. For he distinguishes between *vox* (the word considered as a physical entity) and *nomen*, later called *sermo* (the word considered as having a logical content or meaning). When a universal term, such as 'man', is predicated of the members of a class, it is predicated according to this logical content. It is the *sermo*, not the *vox*, which is predicated. And it is to *sermones* alone that universality can properly be ascribed.

The point is, of course, that there are no universal entities or things. For example, there are only individual men. At the same time these individuals are similar or resemble one another in various assignable ways. And the mind can attend to these similarities, while disregarding or leaving out of account or abstracting from all differentiating factors.[2] Abelard speaks in different ways about the results of this process of abstraction. Sometimes he speaks of the universal concept or 'understanding' as though it were a confused image, which can stand for a plurality of things precisely because it is confused or blurred. At other times he is clearly not thinking of an image. He says, for instance, that the concept of man consists of the ideas of being animal, rational and mortal. We have therefore to think twice before suggesting that Abelard anticipates Berkeley in identifying universals with confused images. In any case Abelard lays emphasis not so much on the precise nature of the mental modifications involved in predicating universal terms as on the fact that universality belongs not to things but to certain words or terms when considered in respect of their logical function.

A universal term such as 'man' is not of course a proper name like 'Socrates'. But inasmuch as it is predicable of all men, Abelard can speak of it as naming them. In other words, universality is ascribed to common nouns in virtue of their function of naming or referring to a plurality of individuals indeterminately. It then occurs to Abelard, however, that we make true statements about, say, roses or 'the rose' when, as in winter, there are no roses to name or refer to. He therefore makes a distinction between the denominative and significative functions of a term. If we assert, for instance, that there is no rose, the

---

[1] *Ingredientibus*, edited by B. Geyer in *Beiträge*, XXXI, 16.
[2] Abelard notes that when differentiating factors are omitted, things are represented otherwise than they actually exist. But he insists that inasmuch as the universal idea does not comprise any characteristics which are not present in the relevant particulars, it cannot be said to distort reality.

term 'rose' is obviously not used to name existing entities or things. But equally obviously, it has a meaning, a significative function.

In the field of logic Abelard wrote commentaries on Porphyry's *Isagoge*, Aristotle's *Categories* and *De Interpretatione*, and on Boethius's *De differentiis topics*. He also wrote a treatise on dialectic (*Dialectica*) in which he dealt with propositions and their constituent parts, with syllogisms, with definition and with the idea of logical consequences. He worked with the so-called 'old logic', the heritage, for the most part, of Boethius; but in his handling of the matter he tended to turn away from the notion of logic as treating of entities, including mental entities, to the idea of it as treating of terms and propositions.[1]

Among the writings of Abelard is a work entitled *Sic et Non* (*Yes and No*), in which a number of contrasting Scriptural and theological statements are collected. The historical importance of the work lies in the fact that it contributed to the development of the scholastic method of mentioning different opinions and the reasons given for them and attempting solutions of the problems raised. It is true that in the *Sic et Non* contrasting or incompatible statements are generally given without any attempt at harmonization. But the work was doubtless intended to provide students with material for reflection and the exercise of dialectical ingenuity. We are not entitled to conclude that in Abelard's opinion no solutions consonant with the Christian faith were possible. Apart from the fact that even in the *Sic et Non* Abelard states some opinions of his own, positive theological positions are developed in writings such as the *Theologia Christiana* (*Christian Theology*), the commentary on Romans and the treatise on the *Trinity*. Abelard may have been a rationalist in the sense that he tried to understand and give reasons for the content of Christian belief. And some of his opinions aroused hostile criticisms and accusations of heresy. But there is no good reason for depicting him as a rationalist in the modern popular sense of the term, or for thinking that in the *Sic et Non* he was primarily concerned with bringing Christian belief into disrepute.[2]

In his work *Scito teipsum* (*Know Thyself*) Abelard dealt with ethical

[1] For example, if we say that the proposition 'man is an animal' is true in virtue of its terms (an analytically true proposition), its truth is dependent on the inclusion of 'animal' in the definition of man as a rational animal.

[2] Abelard's statement to Héloise is well enough known, namely that he would not be a philosopher if it meant denying Paul, nor an Aristotle if it involved separation from Christ (*Letter* 17).

topics, though not all the subjects treated would be recognized nowadays as pertaining to moral philosophy. A notable feature of the work is the emphasis placed on intention. Considered purely in themselves, acts are morally indifferent. It is the intention which places them in the moral order, making them right or wrong. There are indeed inclinations which can be described as good or bad; but a bad inclination is not of itself a sin.[1] For a man may fight against it; and to do so is meritorious. Sin arises when a man consents to evil or, more precisely, when he does not abstain from doing what he ought not to do.[2] If it is asked what consenting to evil means, the answer is that it means acting with disregard to the divine will. Sin consists essentially in a perverted will, in an interior act involving contempt or disregard for the divine will, while right action consists essentially in an interior act involving respect for the divine will. The exterior action does not add anything. If an executioner legitimately hangs a man out of respect for justice and law, his exterior action is the same as it would have been if he had hanged the man from motives of private revenge or enmity. It is the intention which makes the difference. The moral status of human acts cannot depend on consequences. For the consequences of our actions are by no means always subject to one's own control. Intention is thus all-important.

As Abelard equates sin with contempt for the divine will, whether known through the natural law (mediated by reason) or in the form of commandments revealed by God, he insists there can be no culpability or sin where there is ignorance of the divine will. Nobody, he says, can be judged guilty of contempt of God if he contradicts the truth in ignorance or if he does not act against his conscience.[3]

Abelard reflects as a Christian about man's moral life, introducing discussion of topics which a present-day moral philosopher would be inclined to leave to the theologian. But it would be an anachronism to expect anything else, quite apart from the fact that there is no good reason why a Christian should not reflect, as a Christian, about man's moral life. In any case the salient features of his ethics are probably his emphasis on intention and on personal conscience as the subjective ethical norm. To be sure, he may well have exaggerated the role of

[1] See *Scito teipsum*, 3; Migne, *P.L.*, 176, col. 639A.
[2] Abelard expresses the matter in this negative way in order to show that sin is not a positive entity but a privation of right order in the human will.
[3] *Scito teipsum*, 12; Migne, *P.L.*, 176, col. 667. Abelard's doctrine that ignorance excuses from culpability was censured at the Synod of Sens.

intention at the expense of other factors which should be borne in mind. But nobody claims that Abelard's ethics are final and definitive. What can properly be claimed is that he drew attention to and discussed moral problems of interest and importance, and that he contributed to raising the level of ethical discussion.

7

Twelfth Century Schools

I

REFERENCE has already been made, in connection with the Carolingian Renaissance, to the monastic and cathedral schools. The schools attached to monasteries were, naturally enough, domestic or internal in the first instance. That is to say, they catered primarily for young monks and candidates for the monastic life, though some monasteries maintained external schools as well. And in the eleventh century certain monastic schools, such as that of Bec, attracted pupils from different parts. The cathedral schools were also clerical in character, in the sense that they existed for the education of clerks in holy orders. In the twelfth century some of these schools were notable centres of learning, such as those of Chartres and Paris.

Studies in law and medicine were at first centred in Italy. Some Italian cities, such as Pavia, possessed urban schools of law, though in the twelfth century the rest were eclipsed by the rise of Bologna. In the first half of the century Irnerius lectured and commented at Bologna on the Justinian code. And it was at Bologna that the Camaldolese monk Gratian produced his code of canon law which facilitated the education of trained canon lawyers in the service of the Church. As for medical studies, the first important centre was at Salerno. In the eleventh century the monk Constantine of Monte Cassino translated some treatises by Hippocrates and Galen from Arabic into Latin; and it was at Salerno that some sort of professional training for physicians, based on Greco-Arabic medicine, was first developed. Later on other medical schools, such as that of Montpellier in France, became prominent. But at the end of the eleventh century Salerno was the chief centre for the study of medicine.

At Oxford there was a flourishing school in the first half of the twelfth century, at which Robert Pullen, later Cardinal, lectured on theology before going to Paris. The lawyer Vacarius of Lombardy, who had gone to York in the middle of the century, afterwards lectured at Oxford. As for Paris, the Parisian schools came more and more to the fore in the course of the twelfth century, and were already attracting teachers and pupils from other centres.

Bologna, Paris and Oxford were all to become celebrated universities. In this chapter we are concerned primarily with schools which reached their zenith in the twelfth century and declined. In France regional or local schools, such as those of Chartres and Laon,[1] were to be completely eclipsed by the University of Paris.

2

It is generally stated in histories of philosophy that Chartres was a centre of humanistic studies in the twelfth century. So it was in a sense, in the sense, that is to say, that the liberal arts were cultivated there. Thus Bernard of Chartres, who was master of the school from 1119 until 1124, was extolled by John of Salisbury as a successful teacher of Latin grammar.[2] Again, Thierry (Theodoric) of Chartres[3] composed a collection of texts on the seven arts, known as the *Heptateuchon*, and was praised by John of Salisbury as a most diligent student of the arts. The same English worthy, John of Salisbury, described William of Conches as the most gifted grammarian after Bernard.

It must be remembered, however, that the seven liberal arts, forming the *Quadrivium* and the *Trivium*, were the basis of education in the early Middle Ages. Their study was not peculiar to Chartres, though it may have occupied a more prominent position in the school there than it did in some other schools which were noted for, say, theological studies. What is more, John of Salisbury's praise of Thierry and William of

---

[1] The school of Laon enjoyed its *floreat* while Anselm of Laon (*c.* 1050–1117) and his brother Ralph were teaching theology there. As we have seen, Abelard studied theology with Anselm of Laon for a time.

[2] John of Salisbury did not study at Chartres, certainly not in Bernard's time. So he must have obtained his information from pupils of Bernard.

[3] Thierry also commented on Cicero's *De Inventione*, on Genesis and on Boethius's treatise on the Trinity.

Conches does not prove that either man actually taught in the school of Chartres. Thierry certainly taught at Paris; and in 1141 he became chancellor at Chartres. He may have taught in the school, whether before going to Paris or as chancellor or during both periods; but there does not appear to be any firm evidence that this was the case. As for William of Conches, who died about 1154, he seems to have been a pupil of Bernard of Chartres; but in all probability it was at Paris that he had John of Salisbury as a hearer for three years.[1] And though he may have taught at Chartres, we have no proof that he did so. In other words, John of Salisbury's eulogies of teachers who were in some way associated with Chartres does not necessarily provide us with evidence that they actually taught in the school of that city.

In the field of philosophical speculation twelfth-century Chartres has been traditionally associated with Platonism. The main ground of this view is the use which was made of Plato's *Timaeus*. Thus Bernard of Chartres, described by John of Salisbury as 'the most perfect among the Platonists of our time',[2] showed the influence of the Platonic dialogue on his thought by maintaining that matter existed in a formless or chaotic state before order was brought out of disorder, and that Nature is an organism which is informed by a world-soul. Again, William of Conches, who had at any rate studied at Chartres, derived his cosmological ideas largely from the *Timaeus*, with additions from other sources such as Macrobius. William is also notable for having identified the world-soul of the *Timaeus* with the Holy Spirit. He was doubtless thinking of God's creative activity and of the Spirit brooding over the waters.[3] His theory, however, caused some eyebrow-raising and excited opposition; and in a second version of his commentary on the *Timaeus* he withdrew it, remarking that he was a Christian and not a member of the Academy.

The idea of harmonizing Aristotle with Plato goes back to antiquity. And though the thinkers associated with Chartres were not well acquainted with Aristotle,[4] we can find among them a desire to bring together the Platonic theory of eternal ideas or forms and the Aristotelian theory of the immanent forms or intelligible structures in virtue

---

[1] Opposition to William's teaching at Paris led to his retirement to his native Normandy, where he was tutor to the future King Henry II of England.

[2] *Metalogicon*, 4, 35.

[3] Genesis, 1, 2.

[4] For the matter of that, they were not well acquainted with Plato. But they had Boethius's translation of the *Timaeus* or of parts of it.

of which each material thing is the kind of thing that it is. For example, Bernard of Chartres made a distinction between the eternal ideas or exemplar archetypes of Plato and Augustine on the one hand and the 'native forms' (*formae nativae*) on the other, which are copies of images of the archetypes and which make things members of this or that species. The effort to combine the Platonic–Augustinian theory of divine ideas with Aristotelian hylomorphism[1] was not indeed peculiar to Chartres. It is true, however, that the writers in question took notice of the Aristotelian theory as mentioned by Boethius.

The interest taken in the *Timaeus* by William of Conches was devoted in large measure to Plato's scientific theories, if one can dignify them by this title. In William's *Philosophy of the World* (*Philosophia mundi*), which was a systematic treatise on God, the world and man, in which much of the then available learning was collected, the derivation of his ontological theories from the *Timaeus* was clear. William's later *Dragmaticon Philosophiae*, which was based on the *Philosophy of the World*, showed his increasing interest in physical and astronomical theories and also his utilization of the medical treatises translated into Latin by the monk Constantine.

As for William of Conches's identification of the world-soul of the *Timaeus* with the third Person of the Trinity, we have already had occasion to note excursions into theology by dialecticians and philosophers. Roscelin provides us with an example. William provides us with another. We may add that Thierry of Chartres[2] maintained that God is the 'form of being' (*forma essendi*) of all things. And he was followed by a one-time pupil, Clarembald of Arras. It is understandable that some historians have detected in this way of speaking a marked tendency to pantheism. For it certainly suggests that all things are part, as it were, of God. Both Thierry and Clarembald, however, seem to have explained that in their view the actual forms of things were copies or images of the eternal archetypes in God. The statement that God is

[1] A material thing, for Aristotle, was composite, the two basic constitutive principles being 'matter' (*hyle*) and 'form' (*morphē*). Matter in this sense was purely indeterminate and formless and could not exist by itself, but only in combination with a form or dynamic principle which made a thing a member of a certain class or species. Thus it was the form, not matter *as such*, which made a man a man and distinguished him from other kinds of living things. 'Form' did not, of course, mean external shape. In the case of a dog, for instance, it was the vital principle or 'soul', responsible for biological and sensitive functions.

[2] Besides writing his *Heptateuchon* on the liberal arts, Thierry commented on Cicero's *De Inventione*, on Genesis and on Boethius's treatise on the Trinity.

the 'form of being' of things appears to amount to no more than to saying that God is the cause of things, creating and maintaining their being.

3

Mention can be made here of two writers, Gilbert of Poitiers and John of Salisbury, who had some association with Chartres, though to describe them as members of the school would be misleading.

Gilbert of Poitiers (c. 1076–1154), sometimes known as Gilbertus Porreta or Gilbert de la Porrée, seems to have been a pupil of Bernard of Chartres and then to have studied theology with Anselm of Laon. In 1126 he succeeded Bernard as chancellor at Chartres; and it is possible that he taught in the school. The fact, however, of which we have firm knowledge is that he was teaching at Paris in 1141, when John of Salisbury attended his lectures. In 1142 Gilbert became bishop of Poitiers. He wrote a number of Scriptural commentaries, on the Psalms and on Romans for example, and some commentaries on Boethius. The *Book of the Six Principles* (*Liber sex principiorum*), which treats of the last six Aristotelian categories and which has been traditionally ascribed to Gilbert, is however of doubtful authenticity.

Developing a statement by Boethius, Gilbert made a distinction in all created things between the concrete being (*id quod est*, that which is) and that by which (*id quo*) the thing is what it is. For example, humanity or human nature cannot be simply identified with a given human being; but it is through participation in human nature that a man is a man. Gilbert did indeed maintain that the mind forms a specific concept by 'collecting' the similar 'native forms' of the members of the species, while it constructs the generic concept of comparing things which differ in species but have some essential determinations in common. In other words, he had some idea of the mental activity of abstraction. But he combined this idea with insistence on the participation by members of a species in a common form, which makes them what they are.

Gilbert then proceeded to apply this distinction in the area of Trinitarian theology. Each of the three divine Persons, he argued, is constituted as God by a common form of divinity, the divine essence. To his critics he appeared to be denying the divine 'simplicity', the apparent implication of his theory being that just as individual human beings are constituted as human beings in virtue of their participation in a human nature which cannot be identified with any one individual, so the three Persons are made divine by participating in a common form of divinity which is distinguishable from them and so not itself God. St Bernard, that great detector of heresies, succeeded in getting Gilbert brought to trial in 1148. But there was no official condemnation,[1] though Gilbert had already been vehemently attacked at Paris in the preceding year by such worthies as Peter Lombard and Robert of Melun.

Robert of Melun was an Englishman who died as bishop of Hereford in 1167 after having spent most of his career in French schools such as Melun and Paris.[2] In the twelfth century there were no centres of learning in England which could really compare with those in France; and theologians such as Robert Pullen and Robert of Melun studied and taught on the other side of the channel. A distinguished figure among such Englishmen is John of Salisbury (c. 1115–1180), who crossed to France in 1136 and studied logic at St Geneviève until 1138. From 1138 until 1141 he studied under William of Conches, Thierry of Chartres, Adam du Petit-Pont (Parvipontanus) and others. For a time it was claimed that he spent these years at Chartres. But it is much more probable that they were spent at Paris where he went to study theology with Gilbert of Poitiers.[3]

Though he was evidently a diligent student, John of Salisbury was never a professional theologian or philosopher. After having been attached to the Roman Curia he became secretary to Archbishop Theobald of Canterbury; and after Theobald's death he was closely associated with Thomas Becket, whom he supported in the famous controversy with the King of England.[4] He was thus a man of affairs. At the same time he was a close observer of the thought and personalities of his time. And he had a particular distaste for barbarities in style and diction, being an admirer of the eloquence of Cicero. Those who

[1] Gilbert denied any intention of impairing the divine simplicity by dividing the divine essence or nature from the three Persons.
[2] Whatever Robert of Melun may have thought of Gilbert, he found St Bernard's attacks on Abelard exaggerated and, in fact, the result of misunderstanding.
[3] It is to John that we owe an account of the dispute between St Bernard and Gilbert.
[4] After Becket's murder John worked for the archbishop's canonization. But he evidently had some reservations about Becket's mode of procedure. Apropos of the murder he remarked that the archbishop seemed to be the only member of the party who was keen on dying for the sake of dying.

studied for purely utilitarian purposes were dubbed by him 'Cornifi-cians', though we do not know who Cornificius was. In 1176 John became bishop of Chartres. So though he probably never studied at Chartres and certainly never taught there as a professor, he was at any rate bishop of the city during the last years of his life.

In his *Metalogicon* John of Salisbury makes it clear that in his opinion discussion of philosophical topics will get us nowhere or at any rate will be a haphazard affair, arriving at the truth by good luck rather than by sound reasoning, unless it is based on logical principles and method as expounded by Aristotle. At the same time he deplores the use of dialectic as a sort of game, as an instrument, that is, of verbal acrobatics or in the discussion of unimportant questions, and, still worse, as an instrument for gain.

These ideas may not reveal a startling profundity; but they show John's sound common sense, a quality which is evident in what he says on the subject of universals. Anyone, he trenchantly remarks, who looks for species and genuses outside the mind is wasting his time.[1] Universals are mental constructions or products of the human reason, not extra-mental realities. It does not follow, however, that they are *flatus vocis* or mere arbitary constructions. Human beings, for example, are objectively similar in ways which distinguished them, or constitute an objective basis or ground for distinguishing them from other kinds of things. The mind compares things, notes basic similarities and dis-similarities, and by a process of abstraction forms specific and generic concepts. These concepts are indeed mental constructions, and it is useless to look, for example, for a common human nature existing extramentally alongside individual human beings. But the concept of man is not void of objective reference. For it represents, in an abstract way, the real similarity of human beings, the similarity between what Aristotle called the substantial forms of human beings. To John of Salisbury the truth of this line of thought was pretty obvious. That is to say, it seemed to him that both ultra-realism (which postulated extramentally existing universal realities) and the type of nominalism which identified universal concepts simply with words were both clearly false.

John of Salisbury's rambling *Polycraticus*, which, according to its subtitle,[2] deals with the vanities of courtiers and the traditions of philosophers, is remarkable as being one of the first medieval writings

[1] *Metalogicon*, 2, 20.
[2] *De nugis curialium et vestigiis philosophorum.*

in which political theory is treated at all extensively. His general idea of the state is thoroughly theocratic or hierocratic. It is true that as an observer of Roman law and a believer in its civilizing mission in Europe John is prepared to accept the maxim of Ulpian, the Roman jurist, that what pleases the prince has the force of law. That is to say, the prince is the legislator, and his will is the fount of law. At the same time John makes it clear that he has no intention of encouraging arbitrary legislation by the monarch.[1] The prince is under a moral obligation to respect the natural moral law and Christian faith and ethics. John makes use of the analogy, common enough at the time, of the relation between soul and body. In the Christian community the soul is represented by the Christian faith and by Christian ethical concepts. Hence in a manner analogous to that in which the soul expresses itself in and through the body, Christian faith and Christian ideas of justice and law should express themselves in the positive law of the state. This means in effect that the Church is superior to the State, and that the prince is, or should be, subordinate to the authority of the Church. When legislating he should listen to the opinion and advice of the clergy, as being the persons best qualified to judge whether a proposed law is or is not in accordance with Christian faith and ethics.

John draws the conclusion that the more the prince legislates in a sense contrary to Christian faith and morals, the more does he take on the character of a tyrant. In the case of a persistent tyranny the citizens are entitled, or even in extreme cases obliged, to make away with the tyrant,[2] at any rate if their prayers for his conversion have proved ineffectual, and provided of course that there is no less drastic means of deposing him. It would be an anachronism, however, if we took the doctrine of justifiable tyrannicide as implying a concern for political democracy in our sense. John doubtless shared the common conviction that the monarch should respect the customs and traditional laws of the country. And he insisted on the monarch's duty to care for the welfare of his subjects, especially for those who were most in need. But all this was common medieval doctrine and was regarded as quite compatible with a theocratic conception of the Christian State. The limitations on royal power were represented by John as due to the claims of the moral

---

[1] In point of fact Ulpian's maxim was intended to explain the legality of the Roman emperor's enactments, not to encourage a political absolutism which would involve a disregard of natural justice and moral principles.

[2] *Polycraticus*, 8, 10. In John's opinion poisoning the tyrant should be barred, a somewhat curious proviso perhaps.

law and the Christian faith rather than to the political rights of citizens to participate in government.[1]

4

We have seen how already in the twelfth century the Parisian schools were becoming a centre of attraction. One of these schools was associated with the Augustinian abbey of St Victor outside the walls of Paris. It was here that William of Champeaux retired after having been worsted in debate by Abelard. And the school subsequently attained a high reputation under Hugh of St Victor, who was perhaps a German, and the Scotsman Richard of St Victor. Professor David Knowles is most probably right when he suggests that one main reason for the comparative neglect of the Victorines (in comparison, that is to say, with the attention paid to other schools and individual teachers of the time) has been their reputation as mystical writers.[2] For this reputation tends to give the impression that a study of the Victorines belongs more to the history of spirituality than to that of medieval philosophy. In point of fact, however, the Victorines by no means confined themselves to the theme of mystical contemplation and the ascent of the soul to God in prayer. They certainly shared St Augustine's conviction that the goal of the search for truth is lasting happiness, which is ultimately found in God himself. And it is true that Richard of St Victor in particular developed a theory of mysticism, and that he allegorized the Scriptures in a manner which is alien to the minds of most modern exegetes. At the same time both Hugh and Richard of St Victor contributed to the development of theological and philosophical thought in the Middle Ages.

Hugh of St Victor (d. 1141) is said to have been born of noble parentage in Saxony and to have made his early studies near Halberstadt, though it is not certain that he was actually born in Germany. In any case he continued his studies at Paris, in the abbey of St Victor, where he was subsequently engaged in teaching and writing. From the philosophical point of view his main work is the *Didascalion* in seven

---

[1] In the eleventh century Manegold of Lautenbach, one of the gentlemen who considered dialectic a superfluity for the theologian, maintained that the monarch owes his power to election and has a trust to fulfil. He thus implied a compact theory of government. But he was doubtless thinking primarily of the relation between princes and nobles on the one hand and the monarch on the other.
[2] See *The Evolution of Medieval Thought* (London, 1962), pp. 141 f.

books. His work *On the Sacraments of the Christian Faith* (*De sacramentis christianae fidei*) is of importance for the development of theological teaching. Among other writings Hugh composed a commentary on the *Celestial Hierarchy* of the Pseudo-Dionysius, as translated into Latin by John Scotus Erigena.

One of Hugh's sayings is 'learn everything: you will see afterwards that nothing is superfluous'.[1] The word 'everything' refers of course to the various branches of study of the time. In his *Didascalion* Hugh gives a classification of the arts and sciences, derived principally from Aristotle through Boethius, but also from some other writers. Logic, which is said to treat of concepts rather than of things and which is divided into grammar and the art of reasoning, is represented as a preparation for science proper.[2] Science itself is divided into theoretical science, comprising theology, mathematics[3] and physics,[4] and practical science, comprising ethics, economics and politics. In addition there are the various 'illiberal' or 'adulterine sciences',[5] including such varied pursuits as carpentry, commerce, agriculture, medicine and theatricals.

Hugh of St Victor thus gives a systematic programme of education. Though, however, he says that all knowledge is useful, he certainly does not look on the liberal arts and physical science or natural philosophy as subjects to be studied simply and solely for their own sake. In his *Didascalion* he treats first of the liberal arts, then of theology and finally of religious contemplation. And it is clear that he regards the liberal arts and a study of this world as a preparation for the higher science of theology. This point of view was of course natural enough for a theologian who believed that the world was the creation and manifestation of God. That is to say, it was natural enough for him to think of the mind as passing from a knowledge of divine effects to a knowledge of their author. It was also natural for him to see theology, considered as conceptual knowledge about God, as subordinate to the knowledge of God by acquaintance which can be obtained in mystical prayer, and to see mysticism as a preparation for the beatific vision of God in heaven.

Obviously, the comparative paucity of empirical knowledge at the

---

[1] Migne, *P.L.*, 176, 800C.

[2] Needless to say, 'science' must be understood in the wide sense of reasoned knowledge, not in the restricted modern sense of the term.

[3] Mathematics includes arithmetic, music and astronomy.

[4] Physics deals with the nature and qualities of things and is thought of as delving deeper than astronomy, which is concerned with the movement of things.

[5] *Scientiae adulterinae.*

time made the task of arranging all the branches of study in such a way that each had its place in an overall scheme appear much easier to the medievals than it would seem to anyone today. We have also to bear in mind the hierarchic conception of the universe and the prevailing teleological view of it, which formed a background for the attempts at systematizing knowledge which we find in writers such as Hugh of St Victor. It is true that the idea of overcoming the fragmentation of knowledge is not necessarily dependent on religious beliefs.[1] But religious beliefs obviously influenced the structure or general plan of medieval systematization.

Both Hugh and Richard of St Victor contributed to the development of philosophical theology by offering proofs of the existence of God. But Hugh's arguments were more sketchy than those of Richard and more obviously dependent on presuppositions or assumptions which were taken for granted. However, his line of thought, based on internal experience, on an experience, that is to say, of ourselves, has some interest. 'Nobody', Hugh argues, 'is truly wise who does not see that he exists; and if a man begins truly to consider what he is, he sees that he is none of all those things which are either seen in him or can be seen.'[2] Again, the rational soul is 'distinguishable by reason from the substance of the flesh and is seen to be different therefrom'.[3] In other words, reflection shows, Hugh claims, that the human soul transcends the corporeal and cannot be identified with any of its passing modifications. The soul, however, did not always exist. Nor could it have brought itself into being. Hence its existence must be ascribed to the activity of God. This line of thought may not appear convincing to most people today; but the fact that Hugh bases his argument on experience of the self is of some interest, as we probably think of medieval proofs of the existence of God in terms of the Five Ways of Aquinas, which take the external world as their point of departure.[4]

[1] We can think, for example, of August Comte and, at a later date, of the logical positivist attempt to construct a common language for the empirical sciences. But this attempt followed the development of the particular sciences and increased specialization, whereas medieval encyclopaedic schemes preceded the emergence of modern science.　　　　　　　　　　　　　　[2] Migne, *P.L.*, 176, col. 825A.
[3] Ibid. In his idea of the relation between soul and body, described as one of 'apposition' (176, col. 409), Hugh follows Augustine's line of thought rather than Aristotle's.
[4] Hugh gives other kinds of argument as well, as that the totality of things which come into being and pass away must have had a beginning, and so a cause external to itself.

Richard of St Victor, said to have been a Scotsman by birth, went to Paris in his early years and entered the abbey of St Victor, where he eventually became prior. He died in 1173. Author of a treatise on the Trinity (*De Trinitate*) in six books, he also wrote two works on religious contemplation, the *Beniamin minor* and the *Beniamin maior*.

Like Anselm, Richard presupposes faith and tries to understand its content. He has often read, he tells us, that there is but one God, that God is eternal, omnipotent and so on, that he is one in substance and three in Persons. 'But I do not remember that I have read how all these things are proved.'[1] Well, if we are concerned with the existence of God, what point of departure should we select? Richard's answer is that we must start with reflection on those things the existence of which is given in experience and of which we can have no real doubt. These are things which come into being and pass away. We know by experience that there are such things. Indeed, this is the only way in which we can know of their existence.[2] And we cannot seriously doubt whether there are any such things.

Now everything which exists has its being either through itself or through something other than itself. Further, whatever exists either does so from eternity or begins to exist in time. We cannot, however, combine the concepts of a thing existing through itself and of its having a temporal beginning. For the concept of beginning to exist in time excludes the concept of something existing from itself (*a se*), of necessary existence that is to say. If something exists necessarily, it must exist always and cannot have a temporal beginning. There are therefore three possible modes of existence. Something may exist through itself and from eternity, necessarily, that is to say, or in virtue of its essence or nature. Something may exist neither through itself nor from eternity. And, finally, something may exist from eternity but not through itself or necessarily.[3]

The things which come into being and pass away, the existence of which we know by experience, must belong to the second class. For

---

[1] Migne, *P.L.*, 196, col. 893BC. In terms of the later concept of 'natural theology' the Trinity would be excluded from the class of truths which could be proved by philosophical reflection.

[2] That is to say, the existence of what comes into being and passes away is not necessary and cannot be proved by *a priori* demonstration.

[3] This allows for the possible existence of a being which is created from eternity, a being, that is to say, which is ontologically dependent but which does not come into existence in such a way that there is an ideally assignable first moment of its existence.

if they came into being, they do not exist from eternity. And if they do not exist from eternity, they cannot exist necessarily or through themselves. To explain or account for their existence we must therefore assert the existence of a being which exists through itself and from eternity. If there were no such being, nothing at all would exist here and now, whereas our point of departure is precisely recognition of the fact that there are existing things.

If it were objected that the being which exists of itself might very well be the world, Richard would presumably have to reply that what we call the world consists of things which come into being and pass away, and that the world is not something over and above or in addition to them. At any rate it seems that he would have to argue in this way in order to justify the mind's transcending the world in search of a being which exists of itself or necessarily.

Richard also offers an argument on Anselmian lines from degrees of perfection to an eternal and necessarily existing cause of all finite perfection. Of greater interest, however, is his argument to God as the ground of all possibility.[1] In brief, a thing which lacked the possibility of existing would be, to speak paradoxically, nothing at all. The concept of such a thing would be self-contradictory. A theory, however, which has the possibility of existing but does not exist necessarily or through itself must receive this possibility or capacity for existing from something other than itself. Ultimately we must assert the existence of God as the ground and origin of all possibility or of all 'possibles'.

Needless to say, Richard draws on previous writers. At the same time the systematic way in which he develops his arguments for the existence of God and the care which he shows in making clear the line of argument employed and the premises which he himself is conscious of employing represent a considerable development in philosophical theology.

When setting out to treat of the Trinity, Richard follows Anselm by saying that he intends, so far as God permits, to give not only probable but also necessary reasons for what Christians believe.[2] God, he points out, is necessarily all that he is. He does not just happen to be three Persons in one Nature, when he might be two or four Persons. God must be three Persons in one Nature and cannot be anything else. There must therefore be necessary reasons for what is necessarily the case. And though we cannot fully understand the mysteries of the faith, we are

[1] Migne, *P.L.*, 196, col. 896.
[2] Ibid., col. 892C.

not barred from trying to understand as much as we can. Richard attempts therefore to show why God must be three Persons in one Nature; and his line of thought is to construct a kind of dialectic of love, based on the belief that God is not simply loving but love itself. In other words, it is only in the light of the idea of the internal love-life of Father, Son and Holy Spirit that we can do justice to the statement that God *is* love.

The thought of Richard of St Victor is a signal example of the use of dialectic in theology, a use to which, as we have seen, some worthies of the early Middle Ages took exception. But his thought is free from the sort of application of dialectic which aroused the hostility of St Peter Damian, St Bernard and others. In spirit Richard is closer to Augustine and Anselm than to Roscelin. In his account of the spiritual life of the Christian and of mystical experience he places the emphasis, and St Bernard did, on the affective life of man. And this treatment of the soul's ascent to God and of religious contemplation exercised an influence on later writers such at Bonaventure.

Among the other Victorines we can single out for mention the re- doubtable conservative Walter of St Victor (d. *c.* 1180), who composed a work against the four sources of confusion in France (*Contra quattuor labyrinthos Franciae*). The offending thinkers were Abelard, Peter Lombard, Peter of Poitiers and Gilbert of Poitiers. In Walter's opinion these gentlemen were puffed up with the spirit of Aristotle. They treated with a shocking levity of the ineffable mysteries of the faith, vomited out heresies and were guilty of a multitude of errors. In fine, Walter highly disapproved of contemporary developments in the theological field and of the use made of dialectic in the effort to penetrate revealed truths. He did not of course reject theology as such. But he evidently thought that the writers of whom he disapproved represented the triumph of philosophy over faith or, to put the matter in another way, the triumph of Aristotle over the Fathers of the Church.[1]

5

We have had occasion to mention Abelard's *Yes and No* (*Sic et Non*), his collection of contrasting Scriptural passages and theological opinions. In his *Introduction to Theology* (or *Theologia Scholarium*)

[1] Godfrey of St Victor (d. 1194) tried to combine the spiritual tradition of the school with dialectic. But Walter adopted a more uncompromising and rigid position.

Abelard divided theology into the subjects of faith, charity and sacrament. There were, of course, other grouped collections of opinions, such as the *Summary of Opinions* (*Summa Sententiarum*), an early twelfth-century work, the author of which is unknown.[1] But the work which became the most widely used textbook in medieval universities and which set the general pattern for the division and treatment of theology was the *Four Books of Opinions* (*Libri quattuor sententiarum*) composed by Peter Lombard, one of the writers singled out for attack by Walter of St Victor. The work is commonly known as the *Sentences* of Peter Lombard.

Peter Lombard (*c.* 1095–1160) was born, as the name implies, in Lombardy. He probably studied at Bologna before going first to Rheims and then to Paris, where he taught in the cathedral school. In 1159, a year before his death, he became bishop of that city. In the early part of his teaching career he composed commentaries on the Psalms and on St Paul's epistles. But his name is chiefly associated with the *Sentences*, in which he gathered together a large number of quotations and opinions from the Fathers, especially St Augustine, but also made copious use of quotations and ideas taken from later theologians and writers, such as Anselm of Laon, Abelard, Hugh of St Victor and Gratian. The material was arranged in four books, dealing respectively with God, creatures, the incarnation and redemption and the sacraments and four last things. Peter cited different authorities, drawing attention to real or apparent contrasts and divergences, analysed the meaning of the passages referred to, tried to reconcile *prima facie* incompatible statements and drew theological conclusions.

Historians are accustomed to draw attention to the fact that the work was largely a compilation of opinions, and that Peter was not an original thinker. At the same time he was certainly a man of talent. In any case his work enjoyed a great success and was made the subject of commentaries by such famous thinkers as St Bonaventure, St Albert the Great, St Thomas Aquinas, Duns Scotus and Ockham. Lecturing on the *Sentences* of Peter Lombard was a recognized stage in the academic career in the medieval university. It is true that the use made of the work raised some criticism even within the Middle Ages. Thus in the thirteenth century Roger Bacon complained that it had come to usurp

---

[1] In Migne's *Patrologia Latina* (176) the *Summa Sententiarum* is included among the writings of Hugh of St Victor. It has been ascribed by different scholars to a number of authors. But we do not know with certainty who wrote it. Indeed, in its full form it appears to be a compilation rather than the work of one man.

the place which should properly belong to the Bible. It is possible to argue, as some modern theologians have argued, that the work contributed to the development of a situation in theological studies in which the Scriptures were used more or less as a quarry for texts selected with a view to supporting conciliar or other ecclesiatical pronouncements and the conclusions of theologians. It has also been argued that by becoming a successful and widely used textbook the *Sentences* contributed to the neglect of important theological themes which the author had himself neglected or had treated only very summarily. Though, however, such objections are perfectly understandable when one looks back at the past in the light of modern theology, the fact remains that the work fulfilled a need. The growth and expansion of the medieval schools naturally called for a systematic arrangement of theological material. And the use of Latin as a common language for theological instruction and writing obviously facilitated the movement of both masters and pupils from one centre of learning to another and thus made desirable the widespread use of a given textbook or manual as a basis for lecturing.

The *Sentences* of Peter Lombard is primarily of course a theological work. But within the theological framework and context themes are treated which we would describe as philosophical or which would fall, for the author, into the class of truths which can be known independently of faith.[1] In Peter's opinion this class of truths includes the existence of God, the divine creation of the world and the immortality of the human soul. How much treatment was given to philosophical themes by those who lectured and commented on the *Sentences* obviously depended to a great extent on the interests and abilities of the individual lecturers. In some of the major commentaries on the work we can find a great deal of philosophy.

6

The Aristotelian ideal of science was that of a body of propositions systematically derived in a logical order of dependence on ultimate premises or principles. In a 'subordinate' science these principles would be ultimate in a relative sense. That is to say, they would be proved in a wider science, though not in the science in which they functioned as premises. Ultimate principles in an absolute sense would be self-

[1] Cf. *Sentences*, III, 24, 3.

evidently true propositions or propositions which could not be denied without contradiction.

As theology was regarded in the Middle Ages as a science, or rather as the queen of the sciences, it was fitted into the general Aristotelian concept of a science. The premises, however, were regarded as truths revealed by God. And though it was believed that God could reveal truths which the human mind was in principle able to discover for itself, it was also believed that God had revealed truths which transcended the capacity of the human mind. At the same time there was, as we have seen, a continued effort to understand the content of the Christian faith. Indeed, this was what theology was about, a theology which naturally involved some philosophical reflection. Further, the pressure of the Aristotelian concept of a science would, by itself, tend to promote a 'rationalistic' view of theology. Needless to say, when theologians were lecturing to or writing for students who could be presumed to share their masters' religious beliefs, the ideas of revelation and of truths transcending the capacity of the human mind but revealed by God could be assumed, in the first instance at any rate. But what if a writer were addressing non-Christians? He could not assume, for example, that the New Testament was revealed by God. He had to appeal not to authority but to reason. And this practical need, combined with the pressure of the Aristotelian concept of science, might push him in the direction of turning the Christian faith into a kind of metaphysical system. We can find at any rate one or two examples of this kind of thing.

A notable example is the work entitled *De arte fidei catholicae* (*On the Art of the Catholic Faith*). The author, aware of the uselessness of appealing to authority against the views of those who do not recognize the authority in question, tries to develop theology in a quasi-geometrical manner. The theologian, he points out, has no power of coercing non-Christians such as the Moslems. He has to appeal to reason. This means that theology must be made to conform, as much as possible, to the Aristotelian ideal of science. And this means, for the author, achieving as close an approximation as is feasible to the model of mathematical reasoning as exemplified in geometry. The writer starts with definitions of terms, with axioms which are taken to be self-evidently true propositions and with certain postulates; and he then attempts to deduce in a logical order truths relating to God, creation, redemption, the sacraments and the resurrection. He does indeed admit that arguments used to prove the mysteries of the Christian faith are probable arguments rather than rigorous demonstrations. In other words, he allows that the geometrical ideal cannot be fully realized in theology. But he is convinced that exemplification of the model should be aimed at.

In Migne's *Patrologia Latina* this work is included among the writings of Alan of Lille (d. 1203), who taught at Paris and ended his days as a monk at Citeaux. Martin Grabmann attributed the work to Nicholas of Amiens. But Professor Balić has argued for its re-attribution to Alan of Lille. If Alan is indeed the author, the work fits in with his polemical treatise against heretics, Jews and Moslems, and with his *Rules of Sacred Theology (Regulae de sacra theologia)*. It can hardly be claimed that his remarks about heretics and non-Christians express what we might describe nowadays as an ecumenical spirit. But this is irrelevant. The point is that Alan sees that it is idle to rely on appeals to authority with those who refuse to recognize it. And in his *Rules of Sacred Theology* he attempts to exhibit theology as a deductive science, based on self-evident principles.

It would be a mistake to interpret this attempt as an expression of rationalism, in the sense of expressing a deliberate intention of converting Christian theology into a metaphysical system, worked out with the aid of a method analogous to that employed in Spinoza's *Ethics*. The motive is apologetic. To convince heretics and non-Christians the author of the work *On the Art of the Catholic Faith* tries to carry to an extreme point the application of dialectic to theology of which we have noticed a number of examples. Moreover, even St Anselm had looked for 'necessary reasons' when treating of a doctrine such as the Trinity. At a time when no clear division had been made between metaphysics and theology, it was natural that the programme of faith understanding itself should sometimes tend to take a form which, to our eyes, seems to foreshadow Hegel's attempt to reveal the philosophical content of Christian doctrines.

8

The Philosophy of Islam

I

THERE is a natural tendency to think of medieval philosophy as coterminous with the philosophical thought of medieval western Christendom. To put the matter in another way, the term 'medieval philosophy' brings to mind, in the first instance at least, names such as Anselm, Abelard, Aquinas, Duns Scotus and William of Ockham. We cannot, however, make a close study of the thought of Aquinas or of the philosophical situation in the university of Paris in the thirteenth century without becoming aware of the existence of Islamic philosophers such as Avicenna and Averroes and of Jewish thinkers such as Maimonides.

This particular approach has its disadvantages. In particular it encourages a study of Islamic and Jewish philosophy in the Middle Ages simply in function of its influence on Christian thinkers and of their reactions to it. While, however, it must be granted that both Islamic thought and Jewish thought in the Middle Ages are proper subjects of study for their own sakes, it would be a mistake to suppose that Christian prejudice is the reason for their being generally treated as peripheral themes in histories of philosophy written by Europeans and Americans. Apart from the fact that any extended or deep study of philosophy in the Moslem world of the Middle Ages requires a knowledge of Arabic, we have to remember that, as far as Europe is concerned, Islamic philosophy ceased with the Middle Ages or, rather, well before the end of the Middle Ages, whereas in western Christendom philosophy gradually separated itself from the dominance of theology and led a flourishing life of its own, with roots in the medieval thought of Christian centres but without any contact worth speaking of with Islamic thought. As for Jewish philosophy, we naturally think of Jewish thinkers such as Spinoza and Bergson as belonging to the main stream of European thought. In other words, they happened to be Jews but can hardly be described as specifically Jewish philosophers. It is only natural, therefore, if European and American historians tend to look on Islamic and Jewish philosophy in the Middle Ages as being, so to speak, closed chapters.

This is not to say that either Islamic or Jewish philosophy in the Middle Ages lacks interest. In both cases we find philosophy coming up against religious orthodoxy; and in both cases we can observe efforts at synthesis and also mutual enmities. The interaction between the philosophy of the ancient world on the one hand and the Koran and the Old Testament and Law on the other is certainly not without interest. It is also interesting to see what Moslem and Jewish thinkers made of Neoplatonism and Aristotelianism.

Jewish philosophy in the Middle Ages was dependent, to a considerable extent, on the philosophy of Islam. This statement is not intended to imply that Jewish thinkers were devoid of originality, nor that they had no problems of their own to cope with. The fact remains however that Jewish philosophy grew and developed, for the most part, in the Islamic world. When Aristotelianism came to the fore in Jewish medieval philosophy, it was Aristotelianism as interpreted and developed by Islamic thinkers which constituted a datum for acceptance, rejection or rethinking and modification. Jewish philosophers in Moslem Spain often wrote in Arabic. And, with certain notable exceptions, they tended to take over from Islamic thinkers the treatment of philosophical issues which were not clearly connected with religious problems involved in the rational justification of Judaism.

It is only appropriate therefore to outline the development of Islamic philosophy in the Middle Ages before considering Jewish thought. This policy entails, of course, retracing our steps chronologically when we turn to Jewish philosophy. And this may seem objectionable. But whatever cross-influences there may have been, each set of thinkers operated within a different religious tradition; and it might be confusing if one attempted to treat them together, at any rate in an introductory book of this kind.

2

The religious point of departure in Islam is obviously the Koran, believed to have been revealed to the prophet Mohammed. In the eighth century reflection on the Koran, stimulated by ideas from outside Islam, led to the development of speculative theology, known as the *kalām*. One group of theologians, the Mu'tazilites, raised and discussed a number of problems relating, for example, to human freedom and to man's ability to discern moral principles or precepts independently of revelation. The Mu'tazilites discussed and solved these problems in a theological setting. The problem of freedom, for instance, was raised and discussed in the light of the Moslem concept of God. Historians are therefore inclined to describe the Mu'tazilites as theologians rather than as philosophers. At the same time these theologians were regarded by their opponents as rationalists and as surrendering orthodoxy in favour of a humanistic approach. For the time being orthodoxy triumphed. The rise of Islamic philosophy in a more restricted sense presupposed the translation into Arabic of a considerable amount of Greek philosophical literatures which had survived the Moslem conquests.

The first stage of translation had taken place in Christian schools of the Orient. Works by Aristotle and Porphyry and other Greek philosophers, mathematicians and writers on medicine were translated from Greek into Syriac at the Nestorian school of Edessa in Mesopotamia,[1] the schools of Nisibis and Gandisapora in Persia, and the Monophysite schools in Syria. The second stage was the translation into Arabic of the Syriac version of Greek writings, though some translations were made directly from the Greek. In 750 the dynasty of the Abbasides came to power, and a welcome was extended by the Arab rulers to Syrian scholars. In the reign of the Caliph Al-Mamun al-Rashid a regular school of translators was set up at Baghdad.

Among the works translated into Arabic were the so-called *Theology of Aristotle* (a compilation from the *Enneads* of Plotinus) and the *Book on Causes* (based on Proclus's *Elements of Theology*). The erroneous attribution of these two works to Aristotle meant of course that Aristotelianism, for which the leading Islamic philosophers had a profound respect, was seen and presented in a partly false light. It is true that in their amalgamation of Aristotelianism and Neoplatonism the Islamic thinkers were also influenced by the Neoplatonic or Neo-

[1] This school was closed by the emperor Zeno in 489.

platonizing ancient commentators on Aristotle. But Avicenna, probably the most outstanding Islamic philosopher of the Middle Ages, was strongly influenced by the misnamed *Theology of Aristotle*, whereas Averroes tried to get back to the thought of Aristotle himself.

As has already been mentioned, it was not only Greek philosophical writings which were translated into Arabic. The Moslems had little use for classical literature; but they came to possess a considerable number of Greek scientific and medical writings. And scientific and medical studies flourished in the Islamic world at a time when such studies in the Christian West were in a much more rudimentary state.

3

Al-kindi, who held a position at the court of Baghdad and died shortly after 870, is commonly reckoned as the first Arab philosopher of importance. He seems to have taken the position of the Mu'tazilites as a point of departure and then to have developed ideas on the basis of a Neoplatonized Aristotelianism. Al-kindi maintained the harmony of revelation and reason, and that the human reason can work out a valid philosophical theology. For example, reason can prove the truth of the theological belief in divine creation out of nothing.[1] Some of Al-kindi's ideas may be difficult to reconcile with the Koran;[2] but he certainly did not set philosophy over against theology, nor did he maintain its superiority. On the contrary, he maintained that knowledge acquired through the sacred writings and through inspired prophecy is superior to that acquired simply through philosophical reasoning. Some later Islamic philosophers clearly believed that philosophy was superior to theology. But this cannot be said of Al-kindi.

Al-kindi composed a treatise on the intellect, in which he introduced into Islamic thought the Aristotelian distinction between the active and passive intellects and more or less followed the interpretation proposed by Alexander of Aphrodisias. That is to say, he regarded the active intellect as a single intelligence which comes 'from outside' to perform its function in individual human minds.[3]

[1] This does not prevent Al-kindi from making use of the Neoplatonic concept of emanation.
[2] His belief in astrology as a genuine science may not be in conflict with Moslem theology, but it seems to involve ideas which are alien to the Koran.
[3] This view, taken by itself, does not entail denial of personal immortality. This denial is entailed only when the passive intellect too is regarded as a separate and unitary intelligence.

In the twelfth century this treatise was translated into Latin as the *De intellectu* and thus became available to the Christian west. Twenty-four of Al-kindi's writings were discovered only recently and were printed for the first time in two volumes published at Cairo in 1950–3.[1]

4

In the following century philosophy in the Islamic world was greatly developed by Al-Fārābī (*c.* 875–*c.* 950), whose main teacher was a Christian Aristotelian at Baghdad. In addition to introductions to philosophical subjects and monographs on psychological and political themes, he wrote commentaries on Aristotle, an activity which was to be brilliantly pursued at a later date by Averroes.[2] In his commentaries on the *Organon* Al-Fārābī devoted attention to non-categorical syllogisms and to the problem of propositions relating to the future, to which he ascribed truth-value.

Unlike Al-kindi, Al-Fārābī maintains, and makes it clear that he maintains, the superiority of philosophy in the field of human knowledge. It is in fact the highest exercise of the human mind. In his work on the ideal state[3] he argues that philosophers become aware of the truth through strict logical demonstration and their own insight. Non-philosophers can know the truth about reality by means of symbols. Knowledge acquired in this way is inferior to philosophical knowledge; and whereas the latter is the same for all who possess it, symbolic knowledge can take different forms in different societies. It is true that symbolic expressions can differ in their adequacy, in their degrees of approximation, that is to say, to philosophical knowledge. But there is no one perfect symbolic expression of truth, which is suited to all nations or societies.

This line of thought was hardly such as to commend philosophy in the eyes of orthodox theologians. Al-Fārābī was, of course, continuing the Aristotelian idea of philosophy as the highest activity of the human mind. But Aristotle was not faced with any set of religious doctrines which were ascribed to divine revelation. Al-Fārābī was. And his theory of symbolic knowledge clearly implied that whereas there was

---

[1] Edited by Abū Rīda.
[2] Al-Fārābī's commentary on the *De Interpretatione* was published by W. Kutsch and H. Marrou at Beyrouth in 1960, and his Short Commentary on the *Prior Analytics* by N. Rescher at Pittsburgh in 1963.
[3] The title was *On the Principles of the Views of the Citizens of the Excellent State.*

in principle one true philosophy, there could not be a religion of which it could properly be assumed that it was suited to all peoples. Al-Fārābī did indeed find room for prophetic revelation. But he looked on this as being impressed upon the prophet's imagination (rather than on his passive intellect) by the separate active intellect, and so as clothing or expressing itself in symbolic form. Though, therefore, he was able to accept the Koran as revealed, he could hardly, in view of his premises, regard the religion of Islam as suited to all nations. And in any case Moslem theology was subordinate to philosophy.[1]

In Al-Fārābī's cosmological scheme the active intellect is the tenth and lowest in the hierarchy of pure intelligences. At the summit of the hierarchy of being is the One of Neoplatonism, identified with the Aristotelian First Cause and self-thinking intellect or mind[2] and also with Allah. From the One, God, there emanates or proceeds eternally the first subordinate intelligence, which gives rise to the second intelligence and, on the physical side, to the highest celestial sphere. The lowest intelligence, the active intellect, has no sphere corresponding to it but acts as an intermediary between the realm of intelligences and individual human minds. For Al-Fārābī creation, the process of emanation that is to say, is eternal. As for man, it is only those minds which, under the illumination of the active intellect, apprehend philosophical truth or the truth in approximately adequate symbols who attain immortality.

Al-Fārābī composed commentaries on Plato's *Republic* and *Laws*, besides writing his own treatise on the ideal State.[3] Like Plato, he attributed to philosophy an important role in political life. Ideally, the ruler should be philosopher and prophet in one. Philosophy would provide the theoretical knowledge required for the proper organization of society according to the model of the hierarchy of being. But this knowledge would have to be communicated to the mass of citizens in symbolic form. Hence the need for prophetic gifts in the ideal ruler. The role of the prophet of Islam cannot, however, be repeated. And the combination of philosopher and prophet is in any case unlikely to be

[1] The Persian physician and philosopher Al-Razi, who died somewhere around the year 925, went a great deal further, maintaining that philosophy and allegedly revealed religion were incompatible, and that there was no need for prophets.

[2] Strictly speaking, of course, the self-thinking thought of Aristotle should not be identified with the Neoplatonic One, which transcended thought.

[3] This treatise has been translated into German by F. Dieterici as *Der Musterstaat von al-Fārābī* (Leiden, 1900) and into French by R. P. Jaussen, Y. Karam and J. Chlala as *Idées des habitants de la cité vertueuse* (Cairo, 1949).

realized in any ruler or Caliph. So in practice philosopher and politician will have to work together.

The Plotinian idea of mystical union with the One was looked at askance by Al-Fārābī. In his view no such union was possible for man, not in this life at any rate. Philosophy was the highest activity open to man. It is not surprising, therefore, that while Al-Fārābī criticized the type of state which caters only for the citizens' material welfare, he also criticized the type of state in which the citizens despise this world and place all their hopes in happiness to be attained in another life.

Some of Al-Fārābī's writings were translated into Latin in the twelfth and thirteenth centuries.

5

Some Arabic writers looked on Al-Fārābī as the most notable Islamic philosopher of the Middle Ages. Generally, however, this position is attributed to Abu Ibn-Sīnā (980–1037), who was known to the Christian medievals as Avicenna. A Persian by birth,[1] Avicenna was a precocious youth who soon ran ahead of his instructors and, to a great extent, taught himself theology, physics, mathematics, medicine, logic and philosophy.[2] He started practising medicine as a youth, and he was also interested in astronomy. His life was not altogether a tranquil one. He was in the service of various princes, sometimes in the position of vizir, sometimes in that of physician; and after the fall of one of his patrons he suffered a period of imprisonment. But he had the gift of studying and writing, even in unfavourable conditions. He died at Hamadan at the age of fifty-seven.

A very considerable quantity of Avicenna's literary production has survived. His works, written mainly in Arabic,[3] cover a wide variety of topics. From the philosophical point of view the most elaborate treatise is the *Al-Shifā*, which became known to the Christians as the *Sufficientiae*.[4] The *Al-Najat* is mainly a summary of this voluminous treatise, though the matter is arranged somewhat differently.

---

[1] Avicenna was born near Bokhara, then the seat of a Persian dynasty.

[2] According to Avicenna's own account he read Aristotle's *Metaphysics* forty times without really understanding it until he chanced upon a commentary written by Al-Fārābī.

[3] Some works were written in Persian. In 1951 the University of Tehran published a number of volumes containing these works.

[4] A critical edition of successive portions of the *Al-Shifā* (in Arabic) has been

Avicenna's general division of philosophy into its branches is on Aristotelian lines. Logic is regarded as a propaedeutic to philosophy, and philosophy proper is divided into theoretical or speculative philosophy (including physics, mathematics and theology) and practical philosophy (including ethics, economics and politics). Theology is subdivided into first theology, comprising both what was later to be known as ontology and natural theology, and second theology, which includes topics relating specifically to Islamic thought.

If somebody tells us that there are no dinosaurs or that dinosaurs do not exist, the statement is not unintelligible. We can know what is meant by the word 'dinosaur'. We can have an idea or concept of the nature of a dinosaur. And if we have such an idea, and if someone then tells us that the concept is not instantiated or that there are no actual exemplifications of the concept in the world, we know perfectly well what is meant. Again, we know what is meant if someone tells that the geometer's definition of the 'essence' of a straight line is such and such, but that there are no actually existing straight lines which instantiate the definition or essential concept. In other words, if we assume that there are or can be essential definitions, we can make a distinction between essence and existence. To explain what 'man' means is not the same as to assert that there are men.

It would be misleading if one were to say, without qualification, that Avicenna gave to the logical distinction between essence and existence an ontological application. For this statement might be taken to imply that he was the first to do so, whereas Al-Fārābī had already made such a distinction, interpreting existence as an 'accident' which accrues to an essence. Even though, however, Avicenna was not the first philosopher to distinguish between a thing's essence and its existence, he certainly made the distinction. For example, let us suppose that there is an actually existing man, Tom Smith. He exists, but he came into existence and he will pass away. Before he came into existence his 'essence' was merely possible. It could be conjoined with existence, but it was not. Indeed, even while Tom Smith exists, his essence, taken in itself, remains simply possible, in the sense that it can either exist or not exist. If this were not the case, Tom Smith could not cease to exist; he could not die.

One mode of being, therefore, is possible being. And a thing which may or may not exist requires a cause in order for it to exist. This cause may, of course, be another possible being. And so on indefinitely. But here again we must make a distinction. A being can be hypothetically necessary, in the sense that it must exist if some other being exists. Or a being can be absolutely necessary, in the sense that it must exist in virtue of its essence. That is to say, an absolutely necessary being is one which exists *per se* (of itself or because it is what it is), whereas a hypothetically necessary being exists *per aliud* (through something else). 'That which exists necessarily through itself is such that, if it is said not to exist, there follows a repugnance (logical contradiction).'[1] In other words, its essence is to exist. In it essence and existence are identical.

The general idea is thus that the existence of possible beings (in the sense of things capable of coming into being and passing away) implies the existence of an absolutely necessary being. And as there obviously are possible beings in this sense, Avicenna argues that there is an absolutely necessary being, God. He employs also the Aristotelian argument to the existence of a first unmoved mover. But he adapts it in such a way as to represent the becoming of things as due to the will of the first unmoved, an idea foreign to the mind of Aristotle himself but one which brought the Aristotelian concept of God more into line with Moslem belief. Avicenna's main argument for God's existence, however, is from possible to absolutely necessary being.

The absolutely necessary being is for Avicenna not only the ultimate cause of all other beings but also a personal being who knows all that proceeds from him.[2] To this extent, therefore, Avicenna effects a harmonization between philosophy and the religious beliefs of Islam. At the same time he finds himself quite unable to accept the idea that the temporal series of events had a beginning or that creation took place in such a way that it would make sense to speak of God existing when there were no creatures. God is unchangeable and transcends time. The philosopher cannot conceive him as becoming one day a creator, after a period in which he created nothing. If God is the absolutely necessary being and also, as Avicenna believes, absolute good-

---

[1] *Avicennae Metaphysices Compendium*, translated into Latin and annotated by N. Carame (Rome, 1926), p. 68. This work contains the third part of the *Al-Najat* of Avicenna.

[2] God does not know things in such a way that he is dependent on them. According to Avicenna, he knows all things by knowing his own essence. Indeed, it is the divine self-knowledge which generates the world.

ness, this goodness must diffuse or communicate itself eternally. This means in effect that creation is necessary, not of course because God is coerced into creating, but because he is what he is. 'Whatever proceeds from the necessary being must necessarily exist.'[1] The relation of creator to creature is thus assimilated to the relation of logical implication.

It follows from this, in the first place, that the whole hierarchical series of separate or subsistent intelligences proceeds from God necessarily and eternally. The intelligences, which are intermediary beings between God and the material world, are of course other than God himself. In each of them there is a distinction between essence and existence, a distinction which does not apply to the unique absolutely necessary being. But the intelligences are all hypothetically necessary beings. If God exists, the first subordinate intelligence must proceed from him, and so on down the series.

These intelligences differ from one another in virtue of their different degrees of proximity to the absolutely necessary being. The tenth intelligence is the giver of forms. That is to say, it is through its activity that forms are received in matter as pure potentiality. And as matter in the principle of individuation, there can be a plurality of things possessing similar forms and so belonging to the same species.[2] These things come into being and pass away.

The things which come into being and pass away are obviously different, in this respect, from the created but eternally existing separate intelligences. We may therefore be inclined to conclude that for Avicenna there is one absolutely necessary being (God), a small number of hypothetically necessary beings (the separate intelligences) and a vast number of contingent beings which came into existence and pass away and are neither absolutely nor hypothetically necessary. This would, however, be a mistake. A thing which comes into being and passes away depends for its existence on an external cause, which in turn depends on another cause, and so on indefinitely. But the series cannot be other than it is. If it could, God could not know things by knowing his own essence as the source of all that exists.

In effect, therefore, we can say that even trees, animals and men are hypothetically necessary, provided that we allow for the difference between such beings, which come into existence and pass away, and the

---

[1] *Avicennae Metaphysices Compendium*, p. 138.
[2] Within the material thing Avicenna postulated a plurality of forms, the basic one being the 'form of corporeity'.

immaterial intelligences which, though proceeding from God, do so eternally. In other words, Avicenna's universe is one of necessary connections. It is deterministic through and through. There is no room for human freedom, except, of course, in the sense that a man's actions proceed from himself.[1]

The tenth intelligence, the giver of forms, also has the function of illuminating the human mind. That is to say, it exercises the function of Aristotle's active intellect. In his account of the way in which we come to know Avicenna follows Aristotle; but whereas the Greek philosopher's remarks on the ontological status of the active intellect are notoriously obscure and open to various interpretations, Avicenna makes it perfectly clear that in his opinion the active intellect is not simply a function or power of the human mind but a separate intelligence. In particular, its activity is required for the apprehension of the universal concept or essence.[2] Otherwise the potential intellect would actualize itself by its own power. And this, for Avicenna, is not possible.

This doctrine, however, does not entail denial of personal immortality. For Avicenna the pronoun 'I' refers to the soul rather than the body. Personal identity can thus be preserved without the body. And the rational soul is immortal. Further, there are sanctions in the next life. It is true that Avicenna regards the pictures of the after-life found in the Koran as mythical, and that he interprets reward as the knowledge or vision of purely intelligible realities and punishment as the deprivation of such knowledge.[3] But though he demythologizes, as we may put it, popular conceptions of the next life, he accepts the Moslem doctrine of immortality, as far as the soul is concerned.

[1] That is to say, there is no room for the claim that, everything else being the same, a man could have acted differently from the way in which he did act. If by freedom we simply mean acting consciously and deliberately, freedom in this sense is not incompatible with Avicenna's premises.

[2] Avicenna distinguished between the universal as an exemplar pattern (the universal *ante rem*, as the Christian medievals put it), the universal in the sense of the essence of an actual thing (the universal *in re*), and the universal concept (the universal *post rem*). The reference here is to the universal concept.

[3] 'The proper perfection of the rational soul is that it should become an intellectual world, namely inasmuch as there is comprised in it the image of the universe, and of the intelligible order of the universe, and of the goodness diffused in all things' (*Avicennae Metaphysices Compendium*), pp. 230–1). It is possible, however, for people in this life to avert their minds from such sublime matters and concentrate all their attention on, say, the pleasure of sense. A soul, of this kind, when deprived of the body by death, is in torment.

Avicenna finds room for specifically Islamic themes. He emphasizes, for example, the role of the prophet. Ordinarily, intuitive vision is the culmination of a reasoning process. The prophet, however, receives illumination in such a way as to exclude the preliminary ratiocinative process. This illumination affects the prophet's imaginative power (by way of what Avicenna calls the 'internal sense') and expresses itself in ways which are understandable by men in general and is capable of moving them. The prophet thus becomes a law-giver. Further, in the work entitled *Ishārāt* Avicenna develops a doctrine of stages of the soul's ascent to mystical union with God.

Mention has already been made of Avicenna's interest in scientific and medical studies. He also pursued independent studies in logic. That is to say, though he learned from Aristotle and other logicians, such as the Stoics, he also developed ideas of his own. For example, he improved on the Aristotelian and Stoic interpretation of the modality of necessity. Whereas 'all As are necessarily Bs' had been interpreted as 'at any time t all As at t are Bs', Avicenna distinguished, for instance, between 'at every time during its existence every A is a B', 'at most times during their existence every A is a B' and 'at some time during their existence every A is a B'. After all, the statement that all men necessarily die could hardly be interpreted as equivalent to 'at any time t all men at t necessarily die'. Avicenna also made a study of conditional propositions.

6

It would be a mistake to regard Avicenna's attempts at reconciling his philosophy with the Moslem religion as being simply the expression of prudence or a way of satisfying the demands of expediency. He was clearly a genuinely religious man. At the same time he denied free creation by God, asserted the eternity of the world and rejected resurrection of the body. And we have seen how Al-Fārābī had subordinated theology to philosophy and exalted the latter as the highest activity of the human mind. It is not surprising, therefore, if the philosophers were attacked in the name of religious orthodoxy and as attributing a greater value to Aristotle than to divine revelation.

The most notable attack was made by Al-Ghazālī (c. 1058–1111), known to the medieval Christians as Algazel. A Persian by birth, Algazel taught for a time at Baghdad. In a treatise entitled *Intentions of the Philosophers* he summarized the views of Al Fārābī and Avicenna, principally of the latter. This work was translated into Latin in the twelfth century and was taken to represent the author's own opinions. Thus we find William of Auvergne, who flourished in the first half of the thirteenth century, criticizing Algazel along with Al-Fārābī and Avicenna. In point of fact Algazel had attacked these two thinkers in his *Incoherence of the Philosophers*.[1] In the first-named work he had simply expounded what he was afterwards to subject to trenchant criticism.

When he was thirty-six Algazel left his post at Baghdad and passed a number of years in spiritual exercises and pilgrimages to Moslem shrines. In his *Revival of the Religious Sciences* he attempts to fuse the Moslem doctrines of predestination and universal divine causality with mysticism. This work had a considerable influence on the Sunnite Moslem tradition.

In his *Incoherence of the Philosophers*, Algazel tried to show, by refuting the arguments of the philosophers, that human reason is unable to prove such theses as the eternity of the world. A particular target of attack was the Avicennian picture of the universe as pervaded by necessary causal relations. He objected to it, however, not in order to leave more room for human freedom but in order to maintain the doctrine of God's universal causality. This concern with the divine causality led to an occasionalistic interpretation of empirical causality. What the philosopher takes to be a relation between cause and effect, a *propter hoc* relation, is in fact simply a *post hoc* relation, a case of one event being followed by another. The philosopher mistakes regular sequence for a necessary causal relation and attributes to a secondary cause (a created cause, that is to say) what should be attributed to God alone. On the occasion of event *a* God causes event *b*. This doctrine may seem to imply a form of pantheism; but this was certainly not Algazel's intention.

Algazel seems to have thought of himself as attacking philosophy as such, represented by Aristotle as interpreted by the Islamic philosophers. But it is obvious that his criticism does not simply take the form of confronting philosophy with Moslem orthodoxy and condemning the former as heresy when it is incompatible with the latter. It involves philosophical analysis and reflection. This was seen by Averroes, who was to reply to the *Incoherence of the Philosophers* by writing a work entitled *The Incoherence of the Incoherence*.[2] Further, Algazel

---

[1] When this work was translated into Latin in the thirteenth century, it was given the title of *Destructio Philosophorum* (*The Destruction of the Philosophers*).

[2] The title given to the Latin translation was *Destructio destructionis philosophorum* (*The Destruction of the Destruction of the Philosophers*).

made use of metaphysical ideas in his mystically oriented speculation.

7

The Islamic philosophers whom we have been considering belonged to the eastern group. There was, however, a flourishing Islamic culture in southern Spain. In 756 Islamic Spain was separated from the caliphate of Baghdad; and in the ninth century the independent dynasty became the caliphate of Córdoba. A culture developed, of which several famous architectural monuments still survive, such as the Alhambra of Granada, the Giralda of Seville and the mosque of Córdoba, which was later to be converted into a Christian church. Among the philosophers of Moslem Spain we can mention the names of Ibn Bājja, known to the Christians as Avempace, who was born at Saragossa and died in Morocco in 1138, and Ibn Tufayl, known to the Christians as Abubacer, who was born in the province of Granada and died in Morocco in 1185. Ibn Bājja is best known for his *Rule of the Solitary*, in which he traces the stages of the ascent of the human spirit from concentration on embodied forms to union with the active intellect.[1] Ibn Tufayl composed a philosophical story or allegory designed to convey the idea that religious doctrine is the symbolic expression of a truth which is known by the philosopher in a higher and purer form but which cannot be grasped in its esoteric form by the ordinary man.[2]

The most famous of the Islamic philosophers of Spain is undoubtedly Ibn-Rushd, known to the Christians as Averroes. Born at Córdoba about the year 1126, Averroes seems to have come under the patronage of the sultan or caliph of Marrakesh, who commissioned him to write the series of commentaries on Aristotle which was to earn him the title of Commentator in Christian circles. In 1169 he was appointed to a judicial post at Seville; and from 1171 he was similarly employed at Córdoba. From 1182 until 1195 he appears to have acted as physician to the caliph of Marrakesh. Falling into disfavour and accused of unorthodoxy, he then seems to have retired to Spain. Recalled to Morocco, he died at Marrakesh about the year 1198.

[1] Ibn Bājja also wrote some commentaries on Aristotle and interested himself in medicine, mathematics and astronomy.
[2] This work was not known to the Christian philosophers of the Middle Ages. Ibn Tufayl became known to them through the fact that Averroes, writing on Aristotle's *De Anima*, criticized one of his psychological doctrines.

The writings of Averroes fall under different headings. In addition to the impressive body of commentaries on the works of Aristotle he wrote philosophical and theological treatises and also concerned himself with matters relating to astronomy and medicine. The commentaries on Aristotle were of three kinds. Some were paraphrases or compendia, more or less confined to giving Aristotle's conclusions. Then there were the so-called middle commentaries in which Averroes explained the content of Aristotle's doctrine and added his own ideas. Finally there were the greater commentaries in which Aristotle's text was followed by Averroes's detailed commentary. The three classes were not exclusive, in the sense that a given work by Aristotle was accorded only one type of treatment. In the case of some works we possess commentaries of all three kinds, while in other cases we possess commentaries of two kinds or of one only.[1]

Averroes looked on Aristotle's genius as the culmination of human intellectual activity, a fact which helps to explain why he devoted so much time and energy to the study and explanation of the Greek philosopher's writings. In his commentaries Averroes aimed at expounding the real thought of Aristotle. He was, of course, himself influenced in his interpretation by commentators such as Alexander of Aphrodisias; but his aim was to exhibit and clarify the genuine thought of Aristotle, which, he believed (rightly, of course) to have been distorted to some extent by previous Islamic philosophers. As for religion, we cannot know with certainty Averroes's real opinions about Moslem theology. But there is no very good reason for refusing to accept his profession of adherence to the religion in which he had been brought up. He seems to have thought that a clarification of the genuine thought of Aristotle would help to free philosophy from the bad reputation which it had come to have in the minds of conservative theologians. It cannot be said, however, that his efforts in this direction were conspicuously successful. In point of fact they were a conspicuous failure.

In his endeavour to reconcile philosophy with the religion of Islam Averroes distinguished different ways of understanding the Koran, corresponding to different types of mind or to the different capacities of human minds. The mass of mankind is hardly able to conceive a reality transcending the level of the sensible or perceptible. Such people can be moved only by rhetorical or persuasive arguments and can

[1] Averroes wrote a commentary on Plato's *Republic*. He did not possess Aristotle's *Politics* and apparently thought that Plato would do very well instead.

apprehend the truth only when presented in imaginative or pictorial form. The Koran caters for such minds, through its pictures of the after-life for example. Secondly, there are minds which can grasp dialectical arguments leading to probable conclusions. Their requirements too are met by the Koran, when taken together with theology. Thirdly, there are those minds which seek for strict logical demonstrations and are capable of apprehending the truth in its rational essence. The Koran caters for them in so far as it provides material for philosophical penetration.

Averroes maintains therefore that the Koran can be understood at different levels; and he sees in this a sign of its being the embodiment of revelation. Provided that philosophy is not communicated to people incapable of appreciating it, it constitutes no danger to religious belief. It is pretty obvious, however, that Averroes's way of reconciling philosophy with the Koran was hardly such as to dissipate the suspicions of the conservative theologians of Islam.

In his metaphysics Averroes follows Aristotle as faithfully as he can. The subject-matter of metaphysics is being, which is the object of the intellect and intelligible. Being exists primarily in the form of substances,[1] which are distinct entities. There are no universal things or substances. A material substance has indeed a form which makes it a member of a certain species, and which is individuated (constituted as the specific form of this particular substance) by the matter of the substance in question. And the mind can form a universal concept by attending to the form and prescinding from differentiating factors. But this is no good reason for postulating, for instance, subsistent universal ideas in the manner of Plato. Forms exist only in substances, though they can be conceived separately by the mind. These immanent forms are the intelligible element in material substances; and this intelligibility shows that things are the product of the intelligence.

Every material substance is composed, from the metaphysical point of view, of act and potentiality. It is something of a definite kind; but it can change, whether substantially or accidentally. And as change, becoming, 'movement', requires a cause, we can argue with Aristotle to the existence of a first or supreme unmoved mover and first cause. Averroes does not accept the view, proposed by Al-Fārābī and Avicenna, that existence is an 'accident' of created substances. But he is

[1] That is to say, substance is primary, accident secondary, in the sense that the existence of quantity, quality, relation and so on logically presupposes the existence of substance.

prepared to accept Avicenna's argument from possible to necessary being, provided that certain important changes are made, the absence of which renders the argument, in his opinion, invalid.

Averroes is, however, far from being simply an Aristotelian. He is not content with a supreme unmoved mover who moves the world by drawing it. For him, as a Moslem, God is creator, 'drawing forth the universe from non-existence to existence and conserving it'.[1] Following Aristotle, Averroes postulates the existence of intelligences of the spheres, leaving it to the astronomers, if they can, to determine the number of spheres and so of intelligences. But he is not prepared to accept the emanation theory of Avicenna, according to which God can produce directly only one intelligence. Avicenna's fundamental mistake was to assume that 'from the one only one can proceed'.[2] By assuming this, he made the emergence of plurality inexplicable. For all we know, God may have created directly all the separate intelligences. We cannot legitimately assert that God could not create a plurality, not at any rate in the sense intended by Avicenna. We can, however, say that the oneness of the creator is reflected in the unity of the universe, in the inter-relations between things. Further, God acts in all things, conserving them as long as they exist and acting through them. Averroes does not indeed accept the occasionalism of Algazel. Causal relations between things are an empirical reality. But Averroes combines the recognition of empirical causal relations with the doctrine of the universal causality of God. Indeed, we can say with the mystics (Sufis) that 'there is no reality besides Him'[3] and that all things are in God, though this is not a doctrine to be preached to all and sundry.

According to Averroes, God creates all things by knowing them.[4] This is of course nonsense, if we interpret the divine knowledge on the model of human knowledge. For human knowledge of things pre-supposes their existence. God, however, in knowing himself, knows all that can exist, and his knowledge is productive, not representative. In other words, the self-thinking thought of Aristotle becomes for Averroes creative thought, or thought and will in identity.

We can say, therefore, that Averroes's account of the relation between

[1] *Averroes' Tahafut Al-Tahafut* (*The Incoherence of the Incoherence*), translated with introduction and notes by S. Van den Bergh (London, 1954), Vol. I, p. 90.
[2] Ibid., p. 148.
[3] Ibid., p. 281.
[4] According to Averroes, God knows all particulars, all individuals, but through knowing himself, his own essence.

the world and God is less Neoplatonic and more in accordance with Moslem belief than that given by Avicenna. It does not follow, however, that Averroes is prepared to admit that the world had a temporal beginning. Nor could he admit it, not at any rate unless he was prepared to commit a flagrant act of inconsistency. For if the world is created by eternal and unchanging thought, it must be eternally created. Averroes writes about this theme at considerable length. It is nonsense, he claims, to speak of there having been nothing (apart from God) 'before' the world began. For the word 'before' can have no application in this context.[1] If popular theology represents creation as an event in time, this is doubtless because it is the best way of conveying the truth of the world's dependence on God to those who can think only in imaginative or pictorial ways.

Of Averroes's philosophical doctrines the one which caused the most excitement in the academic world of western Christendom was his interpretative development of Aristotle's account of the intellect in the third Book of the *De Anima*. Avicenna's theory of the active intellect as a separate and unitary intelligence did not arouse passionate opposition, even from those who rejected it. For, as we have noted, room was left for personal immortality. Averroes, however, was understood as maintaining the unicity of the intellect in a sense which would exclude personal immortality and the idea of reward and punishment in the next life. As for Averroes's assertion that he, as a Moslem, believed in personal immortality, it has sometimes been taken as evidence that he held a double-truth theory, namely that a given proposition could be true in philosophy and demonstrable by reason, while a contrary proposition could be simultaneously true in theology and known to be true by revelation.

When commenting on the *De Anima* Averroes remarks that 'this word *intellect* is used in this book in four ways'.[2] First[3] there is the

---

[1] See *Beiträge*, III, 4, pp. 66–70, where a version of an essay by Averroes on the question of the eternity or temporal creation of the world is printed as an appendix to *Die Lehre der Anfangslosigkeit der Welt bei den mittelalterlichen arabischen Philosophen* by M. Worms. The opening discussions in the *Tahafut Al-Tahafut* are devoted to this subject.

[2] *Averrois Cordubensis Commentarium Magnum in Aristotelis De Anima Libros*, edited by F. Stuart Crawford (*Corpus Commentariorum Averrois in Aristotelem*, Vol. VI (Medieval Academy of America, Cambridge, Mass., 1953), p. 452. This volume will be referred to as *CM*.

[3] For convenience of exposition I have rearranged the order in which Averroes mentions the different senses of the word 'intellect'.

imaginative power or faculty, called by Aristotle the passive intellect. When Aristotle says that the passive intellect is corruptible or mortal, 'he understands by this the imaginative power'.[1] Secondly there is the active intellect which 'abstracts' intelligible forms from the images or phantasms in the imaginative power or illuminates the intelligible elements. The active intellect is pure activity and a separate, unitary intelligence. Thirdly there is a potential principle, the material intellect,[2] which receives intelligible forms from the active intellect. Averroes compares it to a transparent surface which can be affected by light and receive all colours, though in itself it has no colour. As, therefore, the material intellect is in itself without form or determination, there is no way of distinguishing between one material intellect, considered purely in itself, and another. Besides, 'the human species is eternal',[3] not of course in the sense that its individual members are eternal but in the sense that, according to Averroes, the species is without beginning or end. As, therefore, the active intellect is one and eternal, and as it requires a potential element to activate, the material intellect too must be one and eternal.

In his work *On the Unity of the Intellect against the Averroists* Aquinas objects that if both the active and potential intellectual principles were numerically one in all men, we could not properly say that John thinks or that William thinks. We should have to say that 'it' (the intellect of the species or race) thinks in both men. Further, the theory of the unicity of the intellect cannot account for the obvious empirical fact that John and William can think differently and have different ideas and convictions.

This undoubtedly relevant line of objection is anticipated by Averroes. 'If what was understood by me and by you were one in every way, it would be the case that when I understood something, you too would understand the same thing; and there would be many other impossible consequences.'[4] Objections of this kind are met by Averroes through the introduction of a fourth sense of the term 'intellect'. An individual man has his own life of sense-experience and has his own images in the imaginative power or faculty. When, therefore, the active intellect illuminates the intelligible forms potentially contained in the

[1] *CM*, p. 409.
[2] The word 'material' must not be understood as meaning corporeal. The material intellect is pure potentiality, like Aristotle's 'first matter'.
[3] *CM*, p. 499.
[4] Ibid., p. 411.

imaginative power, the material intellect is actualized in respect of these particular forms. This actualization of the material or potential intellect in respect of a particular man gives rise to the 'acquired intellect'. This is the intellect of an individual human being. Hence John or William can have their own ideas, based on their respective sense-experience. Indeed, each has, so to speak, his own stock of ideas, on which he can draw. And the acquired intellect, when considered in this way, can be described as the habitual intellect or the intellect 'in habit'.

As the acquired intellect arises through the interaction of the active and potential intellects in a particular man, it obviously cannot be eternal. But does it survive death? As Averroes, like Aristotle, regards generation and corruption as complementary, the answer would, at first sight at any rate, appear to be 'no'. It is true that in so far as the human mind apprehends eternal truths, it rises above particularity (as understood in terms of a particular individual's sense-experience and imagination) and takes on a universal character. But it would appear that if the human mind can achieve inimortality in this way, it does so not as a particular mind but as a moment in the life of the eternal intellect, the intellect of the human race. And this is not what is ordinarily meant by personal immortality. Besides, Averroes endorses the Aristotelian doctrine that matter is the principle of individuation within a species; and he draws the conclusion that the existence of a multiplicity of disembodied souls is impossible.[1] On this account alone, therefore, it would appear that personal inimortality is excluded.

Yet Averroes clearly states his belief in human immortality as a tenet of Moslem belief. And the question arises, how can we reconcile this belief with the conclusions which seem to follow from his philosophy? We cannot claim that in his commentaries on Aristotle and other philosophical writings he is simply reporting and explaining the Greek philosopher's ideas without committing himself to their truth. For Averroes regards Aristotle as expounding demonstrated or demonstrable truths. Nor can we suppose that Averroes seriously held the double-truth theory, especially when he explicitly says that truth cannot contradict truth, and that philosophy and revelation must be in accord.[2] It may of course seem reasonable to suppose that Averroes regarded the Moslem doctrine of personal immortality as a popular or

---

[1] *Tahafut Al-Tahafut*, p. 14.
[2] *Averroes on the Harmony of Religion and Philosophy*, a translation, with introduction and notes, of the *Kitāb faṣl al-maquāl* by G. F. Hourani, p. 50 (London, 1961).

imaginative expression, suitable for the mass of mankind, of a philosophical theory of impersonal inimortality. But the trouble with this
interpretation is that he asserts an obligation to accept the Moslem
doctrine of personal immortality.

It seems that a solution of the problem can only be found in the
following line of thought. Individual human souls cannot persist after
bodily death as distinct disembodied entities. For without bodies they
cannot be distinct. If, however, the body is raised, the soul can persist
as an individual entity, informing the risen body. And the resurrection
is precisely what revelation teaches. The philosopher, however, cannot
accept literally the doctrine of the resurrection as popularly understood,
as meaning, that is to say, that numerically the same body is raised to
life. 'That which has perished does not return individually, and a thing
can only return as an image of that which has perished.'[1] What happens
is that the soul informs a new body, an astral or pneumatic body.[2]

To claim that this theory makes everything crystal clear would be to
claim too much. It does, however, enable us to see how Averroes could
feel himself justified in saying on the one hand that the individual human
soul cannot survive as such in a disembodied state and on the other hand
that he, as a Moslem, accepts the doctrine of personal immortality. The
reconciliation of the two positions is found in the belief in bodily resurrection, even if resurrection is interpreted as meaning the emergence
of a new and 'spiritual' or very rarefied body.

It has sometimes been said that the death of Averroes at the end of
the twelfth century coincided with the disappearance of philosophy in
the Islamic world for a long time, and that religious orthodoxy reigned
supreme. This is true up to a point. Móslem theology (the *kalām*),
somewhat enlarged in its scope to include a theological treatment of
philosophical problems, certainly won a victory over Greco-Islamic
rationalism. Forms of Sufi philosophy, however, centring round the
theme of the soul's mystical ascent to God, continued to exist. At the
same time Averroes was the last of the line of medieval Islamic thinkers
to exercise a real influence on the Christian philosophers of the Middle
Ages. Indeed, his influence on European thought lasted beyond the
close of the medieval period.

[1] *Tahafut Al-Tahafut*, p. 362.
[2] The theory of astral bodies was present in Neoplatonism.

9
Jewish Philosophy

IN the ancient world Judaism produced a notable thinker in Philo of Alexandria (*c.* 20 B.C.–*c.* A.D. 40), who tried to show that Greek philosophy and the Jewish religious tradition were substantially compatible. In the process he had to have recourse to a certain amount of allegorizing in his interpretation of the Scriptures; but he was evidently a sincere Jewish believer, who was convinced that religious faith had nothing to fear from genuine philosophy. For him genuine philosophy was to be found in the Platonic tradition.[1] Thus he accepted the theory of the divine *Logos* as an intermediary being between God and the world and as the 'place' of the eternal archetypes or exemplar ideas. But the theory of the *Logos*, which combined Platonic and Stoic ideas, fitted in, or could be made to fit in, with the rather obscure doctrine of the divine Wisdom as found in the Old Testament and with Jewish angelology, at least if suitably interpreted. It was not, however, simply a question of interpreting the Scriptures to accommodate Platonic and Stoic theories. To allow for the revelation of the Law through Moses, Philo had to find room in his theory of cognition for prophetic knowledge. And the Greek idea of historical cycles had to be changed so as to permit the representation of historical change as guided by the *Logos*, the divine Wisdom, towards the attainment of a goal, a goal which was for Philo the building up of a worldwide and rationally organized and governed society.

[1] Platonism for Philo was Platonism considered as moving in the direction of Middle Platonism and Neoplatonism.

It seems that the thought of Philo was more influential in Christian than in Jewish circles. In any case Jewish philosophy did not show much further sign of flourishing until it reawakened in the Islamic world. In the Islamic world during the early Middle Ages the Jews could become not only wealthy but also influential men. In the capacity of physicians, for example, they could meet Moslems pretty well on terms of equality. There was no bar to the development of thought and learning in the Jewish community. Further, the development of philosophy among the adherents of Islam can reasonably be seen as constituting an incentive to its development among the Jews. In both bases there was belief in a transcendent God and in divine revelation. If therefore philosophy was capable of coexistence with the Koran, why should it not also be capable of harmonization with the Old Testament and the Law? As the Jews were not outcasts from Islamic society but, to a large extent, members of it, it was only natural that intellectual trends in Islam should make their influence felt in Jewish circles.

In the first half of the tenth century we find a Jewish thinker, Saadia ben Joseph (882–942), who developed philosophical ideas within a theological setting or framework, possibly under the influence of the Mu'tazilites in Islam. Born in Egypt, Saadia left the country as a young man; and in 928 he became head of the rabbinical academy at Sura in Babylonia. He translated the Old Testament into Arabic and commented on a number of Talmudic treatises, besides writing original works on legal topics. From the philosophical point of view his main work is *The Book of Beliefs and Opinions*, which can be described as an essay in philosophical apologetics on behalf of the Jewish religion.

At the beginning of the work Saadia discusses human knowledge and its sources. These are the senses, reason (considered as discerning self-evidently true propositions), inference and reliable testimony. Saadia then goes on to argue that knowledge derived from the first three sources, namely sense-experience, reason and inference, is in harmony with testimony, when this is understood as revealed truth. For example, the Bible speaks of God as creator. And this testimony agrees with the result of human reasoning. For it is evident to the human mind, if it reasons correctly, that the world cannot have existed from eternity and so must have been created. If the world had existed from eternity, an infinite tract of time would have elapsed before the present moment. But this is not possible. In other words, Saadia conceives demonstration of the creator's existence as presupposing demonstration of the impossibility of the world having existed from eternity.[1]

In the field of ethics Saadia was at one with the Mu'tazilites in holding that the human reason is capable, without revelation, of discerning basic ethical truths or principles. At the same time he had no wish to provide grounds for concluding that the Law was superfluous. So he argued that reason itself can show the need for a revealed Law to define concepts such as murder and to determine appropriate penalties for wrong-doing. Again, while reason can see man's general obligation to worship God and to show gratitude to him, the Law reveals the particular ways in which such obligations are to be fulfilled.

Saadia was an upholder of rabbinical Judaism and engaged in polemics with the Jewish sect of Karaites,[2] who accepted the Old Testament but rejected the Mishnah and Talmud. As one would expect, the elements of Greek thought which he adopted were well tailored to Jewish religious belief. When, however, we turn to Isaac ben Solomon Israeli (c. 855–c. 955, if his biographers are to be trusted) we find both a more extensive use of Greek philosophy and a lack of harmonization between various component elements in his total world-view.

Israeli was born in Egypt. After studying medicine he became physician to a Moslem ruler in north Africa. Among other writings, he was the author of *The Book of Definitions*, *The Book on the Elements* and *The Book of Substances*. In his philosophical thought he introduced Neoplatonism into Jewish speculation; but he tended to leave Neoplatonist and Jewish beliefs in a state of juxtaposition. For example, Israeli asserted, as a Jew, that God created all things out of nothing, and that his will sustains them in existence. At the same time he expounded a Neoplatonist theory of emanation, according to which the levels of being emanate from God through a hierarchy of stages, from the intellect or divine mind down to the visible world. And if we ask how the belief that the personal God created all things and conserves them through his will can be reconciled with the Neoplatonist belief in the emergence of multiplicity from the One through a graded series of intermediary beings, no clear answer is forthcoming. Perhaps no clear answer could be given in any case.

[1] In the thirteenth century Aquinas made demonstration of God's existence independent of the question whether the world had or had not a beginning in time.
[2] This sect was founded by Anan ben David in the eighth century. It produced philosophers such as the eleventh-century thinkers Joseph ben Abraham al-Basir and Joshua ben Judah.

Historians have also drawn attention to the ambiguities in Israeli's account of prophecy. In the *Book of the Elements* he gives what amounts to a psychological and naturalistic account, based on the idea of the intellect communicating its spiritual lights or ideas to the soul, these ideas becoming semi-materialized in the process and then being able to impress themselves on the imagination and memory. But Israeli also gives another account of prophecy in terms of the distinction between two classes of men. The prophet conveys revealed truth or the divine will; and prophecy is intended to affect both the enlightened and those who cannot appreciate truth unless it is expressed in images drawn from the world of sense. This is the reason why prophetic truth is expressed sometimes in conceptual form and sometimes in the form of images derived from sense-experience. This second explanation assumes that prophecy is the result of divine activity, of a divine communication to the prophet; and it is difficult to see how it fits in well with an explanation based on a psychological theory of what happens in dreaming. Perhaps the two can be reconciled, as Israeli thought that they could. But, if so, he failed to make their harmony clear.

There are other ambiguities in Israeli's thought, such as the difficulty in harmonizing his acceptance of belief in divine reward and punishment after death with a Neoplatonist account of the soul's return to its ultimate source. But sufficient has been said to indicate why he was not highly esteemed as a thinker by his coreligionists. Maimonides went so far as to refuse to see in Israeli a philosopher at all. Among Christian scholars in the Middle Ages, however, Israeli enjoyed posthumous fame as a physician and medical authority. And in philosophy he certainly possesses some historical importance as the first Jewish thinker to import Neoplatonic theories.[1]

2

The leading Jewish Neoplatonist, however, was an eleventh-century thinker, Solomon ibn Gabirol, who lived in Spain. Born about the year 1025, he seems to have died in 1058 or thereabouts, though Abraham ibn Daud, a Jewish philosopher of the following century, gave 1070 as the date of death. Gabirol was a celebrated Hebrew poet, and he enjoyed the patronage of Moslem rulers in Spain. His main philosophical work, *The Fountain of Life*, was written in Arabic. So was his ethical treatise *The Improvement of the Qualities of the Soul*. It was not

[1] Philo, of course, lived long before Neoplatonism.

until the nineteenth century that the author of *The Fountain of Life* was identified, by Solomon Munk, with the Hebrew poet.

When *The Fountain of Life* came to be translated into Latin, with the title *Fons Vitae*, Christian scholars of the Middle Ages thought that Gabirol, whom they called Avicebron or Avicebrol, was a Moslem. This was natural enough in view of the facts that the original version of the work was in Arabic and that they were unaware that the author was a Hebrew poet. But there was another reason why it was natural that Christians did not suspect that the writer was a Jew. Though in his ethical treatise Gabirol did make some references to the Bible, *The Fountain of Life* was free of any references to the Bible or the Talmud. Close attention to the work may reveal some signs of concern with allowing for Jewish religious belief; but there is no overt attempt to argue that the philosophy expounded is biblical in spirit or in harmony with the Scriptures and Jewish tradition. The author simply expounds and defends a metaphysical system. He uses the form of a dialogue between master and pupil, the latter being very much the pupil.

Gabirol presupposes the general Neoplatonic ideas of a hierarchy of levels of being proceeding from the One and of the emergence of plurality from the supreme unity or One. But the whole structure is rethought in terms of the Aristotelian concepts of matter and form, which are extended to apply to all creation. Concrete existing things or substances are obviously of different kinds. Each is the kind of thing which it is in virtue of its form. If, however, we think away all such determinations, all forms, we arrive at the concept of matter, considered as pure potentiality for receiving forms. 'If you try to imagine matter without form, you will not be able to do so, inasmuch as matter in itself has no form.'[1] But though we cannot imagine pure matter, we can conceive it as a basic component element in all created beings. This is what Gabirol calls 'universal matter', matter considered as common to all things. It is correlative to universal form, which is said to sustain the forms of all things. This universal form, in which all forms are contained, is the same as the form of the intelligence, the cosmic intelligence, that is to say, or the Neoplatonic *Nous*. The intelligence knows all forms, but they do not, of course, exist within it as the actual forms of distinct substances. The multiplicity of things comes into being through the derivation of particular forms from the form of the intel-

[1] *Fons Vitae*, V, 4 (Latin translation edited by C. Baeumker in *Beiträge*, I, 2–4, p. 263).

ligence and their union with matter, which is the principle of individuation.

It would be a mistake to conclude that according to Gabirol all things are corporeal, inasmuch as matter is one of their basic constituent elements. Matter in itself, universal matter, is, to speak in an apparently paradoxical way, immaterial. It does not exist by itself: it has actual existence only through the advent of form. And it becomes corporeal matter only through union with the form of corporeality. As present in the cosmic intelligence, for example, or in the rational soul, it is not corporeal or quantitative matter.

To the present writer it seems that what Gabirol does is to distinguish the elements of potentiality and determination or form in the things which fall within the range of an experience and then to hypostatize these elements under the labels of universal matter and universal form. If we abstract from all definite forms, we are left with the simple concept of the pure capacity of receiving form. And if we consider forms in themselves and then abstract or prescind from all kinds of forms, we are obviously left with the concept of form in itself. Universal matter and universal form are then seen as pervading and being concretized in every level of being. If we mean by 'matter' corporeal matter, it is only certain kinds of things which are composite. Gabirol can thus speak of incorporeal substances, such as the intelligence, as 'simple'. But if we understand by 'matter' universal matter, which, considered in itself, is not corporeal, everything apart from the First Essence (the One of Neoplatonism) is composite. Gabirol can thus say that 'the essence of universal being'[1] is composed of universal matter and universal form. The co-presence of these two factors unifies the whole of creation. The First Essence is 'above all things and is infinite'.[2] And, being infinite, it transcends our comprehension and can be human only through those things which proceed from it. Matter and form, being co-principles of being and 'terminating' one another, should not be described as infinite.

As matter, considered by itself, cannot be said to exist, the question of its being brought into existence by creation hardly arises. It comes into existence as the matter of a created thing only through the advent of form. But what is the process by which the substances inferior to the First Essence come into existence? Some of Gabirol's ingenious accounts of the matter seem to imply a theory of spontaneous and

[1] *Fons Vitae.* (*Beiträge*, p. 7).
[2] Ibid., I, 5 (*Beiträge*, p. 6).

necessary emanation. But he also introduces the concept of will. Things come into existence only through the union of matter and form; and it is the divine will which effects this union. This will 'penetrates everything, and nothing exists without it, for the being and constituting of all things comes from it'.[1] Again, 'to describe the will is impossible; but it is also described when we say that it is the divine power, making matter and form and uniting them, and which is diffused from the highest (level of created being) to the lowest, as the soul is diffused throughout the body, and that it is the will which moves all things and disposes all things.'[2]

As Gabirol finds a duality in all creation, the co-presence of matter and form, we may be inclined to think that the notion of a lower level of being reflecting a higher level pushes him into finding a ground for duality within the First Essence itself, and that a distinction between the divine essence and will provides this ground. While, however, this line of thought may have exercised an influence on Gabirol's mind, it is also reasonable to suppose that he is concerned with finding room for the religious ideas of divine creation and causal activity. As has already been indicated, Gabirol makes no overt attempt to harmonize his philosophy with Jewish beliefs, by referring, for example, to biblical doctrine. But it does not necessarily follow from this that Jewish religious belief has no influence on his thought. And when he says, for instance, that the will is other than matter and form, inasmuch as it is the maker of them,[3] it is pretty obvious that he is including in his philosophy a doctrine of divine creative activity which goes further towards satisfying the demands of Jewish religious belief than would a theory of spontaneous and necessary emanation.

Gabirol's extension of the distinction between matter and form influenced some thirteenth-century Christian philosophers, principally Franciscans such as St Bonaventure and Matthew of Aquasparta. They saw in the theory of matter and form a way of differentiating between God and creatures. God, that is to say, is pure act, whereas in all creatures there is 'matter', considered as potentiality. Those who accepted this theory, according to which even the angels were composed of matter and form, had also of course to accept the idea of a form

[1] Ibid., V. 39 (*Beiträge*, p. 327).
[2] Ibid., V, 38 (*Beiträge*, p. 326).
[3] Ibid., V, 37 (*Beiträge*, p. 325). Sometimes Gabirol says that it is only form which is due to the divine will, matter being a reflection of the divine essence (cf. *Fons Vitae*, V, 42; *Beiträge*, p. 335).

of corporeality, in order to distinguish between spiritual matter, as found in the angels, and corporeal matter.

3

These were some other Jewish Neoplatonists, such as Bahya ben Joseph ibn Paquda in the eleventh century and Joseph ibn Saddiq in the first half of the twelfth century. The former, however, while influenced by Neoplatonism, was principally concerned with promoting a genuine religious spirit and attitude. In his *Guide to the Duties of the Heart*[1] he distinguished between external observances (the duties of the limbs) and interior morality and religion (the duties of the heart). Paquda insisted, however, that man cannot achieve and maintain the proper relationship to God without theoretical knowledge. True, he admitted both revelation and Jewish tradition. But it is his treatment of the contribution of reason which wins for him the title of philosopher. In his proofs of the existence and unity of the creator he combined, or set side by side, cosmological arguments and characteristically Neoplatonic lines of thought. Though, however, he attached great importance to philosophical knowledge of God and deplored its absence in so many believers, he envisaged such knowledge as leading to attitudes of worship and of trust in and love of God rather than to any mystical absorption in the One. In other words, however much he may have used Neoplatonic ideas, the end which he sought was a deepening and interiorization of Jewish ethics and piety.

A very different attitude to metaphysical philosophy is shown in *The Book of Argument and Proof in Defence of the Despised Faith* by Yehuda Halevi (*c.* 1080–*c.* 1141), a native of Toledo and a Hebrew poet. Referring to an account of the conversion to Judaism of a Khazar king and his people in the first half of the eighth century, Halevi imagines the discussions preceding the king's conversion and introduces a philosopher, a Christian, a Moslem and a Jewish rabbi.[2] The philosopher is a follower of Islamic Aristotelianism rather than of Neoplatonism. The relevant point, however, is that the claims of metaphysics to

[1] Written in Arabic about the year 1040, the work was translated into Hebrew some twenty years later.
[2] Needless to say, the advocates of philosophy, Christianity and Islam fail to make their respective cases. In Halevi's story the king did not originally intend to summon any advocate of Judaism, as he regarded its adherents as a miserable and despised lot of people. Hence the reference to 'the despised faith'.

provide a basis for religion are, in Halevi's work, successfully rebutted by the rabbi. Halevi is prepared to admit that a philosophical explanation of the world in terms of the idea of a divine creator is superior to other explanations. But in his view the claims of metaphysicians to provide genuine knowledge are groundless. This can be seen easily enough by considering the fact that whereas in mathematics we do not find mutually opposed schools, agreeing about practically nothing at all, this is just the kind of thing which we find in philosophy. As for religious truth, this comes through God's revelation of himself, as recorded in the Old Testament. And as for the moral life, while reason certainly suggests certain prudential or utilitarian lines of conduct, man is unable by his own efforts to live a life pleasing to God. Philosophers may have preached ways of salvation, attainable by human effort; but in point of fact it is God alone who can show us the way to union with himself. In fine, a religion based on metaphysical philosophy is a sham religion.

Halevi's attack on the philosophers in the name of religion is not, of course, an isolated phenomenon. In Islam Al-Ghazālī had already attacked them in his *Incoherence of the Philosophers*. And there were attacks to come in the future. Whereas, however, Al-Ghazālī was a Moslem, Halevi was a fervent adherent of the Jewish faith. For him the Jewish Scriptures were the purveyors of religious truth and the Jewish people the elect of God, the chosen people. He denied that certain knowledge is attainable in metaphysics; but he did so not to promote scepticism but in what he supposed to be the interests of genuine religion.

4

Historians of Jewish philosophy in the Middle Ages are accustomed to say that Neoplatonism was eclipsed by Aristotelianism, and this was one main reason why the thought of Gabirol, for example, did not exercise much influence in Jewish circles. This statement is doubtless true in a sense. It must be added, however, that the Aristotelianism in question was the philosophy of Aristotle as developed by Islamic thinkers in the light of Neoplatonizing commentators and of writings erroneously attributed to Aristotle. For example, Aristotle's first unmoved mover took on some of the characteristics of the Neoplatonic One, becoming the ultimate source and origin of the world. At the same time some Neoplatonic theories were reinterpreted in the light of, or made to fit in with, the doctrine of Aristotle. It was not a question of Islamic Aristotelians consciously distorting or changing the philosophy of Aristotle. It was rather that they tended to interpret his thought in the light of Neoplatonic ideas which they believed to be Aristotelian in origin or a fair development of his ideas. This impregnation of Aristotelianism by Neoplatonic theories made it in some ways easier and in some ways more difficult for Islamic and Jewish thinkers to harmonize Aristotelianism with the Koran and the Old Testament. In so far as Aristotle's philosophy became more religious, the harmonization was made easier. In so far as a Neoplatonic theory such as that of necessary emanation tended to appear, there arose the problem of reconciling this idea with belief in free creation or of interpreting emanation in such a way as to be compatible with belief in free creation by a personal God.

Aristotelianism made its first appearance in Jewish circles in the Islamic east. In Spain its influence is usually said to have shown itself first in *The Exalted Faith* (or *The Book of Sublime Religion*) by Abraham ibn Daud, who lived at Toledo and died in the second half of the twelfth century. This work was originally written in Arabic, apparently in 1161, and, according to the author, was intended to solve the problem of free will. But the actual subject-matter, which reveals the influence of the Islamic philosopher Avicenna, is much more general.

For ibn Daud, as for Avicenna, God is not only the supreme unmoved mover and ultimate final cause of movement or becoming[1] but also the first or supreme cause and absolutely necessary being, the source and origin of all finite things. Like Avicenna again, he postulates intermediary beings between God and the world, the separate intelligences of Aristotle, the active intellect being the lowest member of the hierarchy.[2] As for creation, ibn Daud evidently wishes to maintain the Jewish doctrine of free creation by God. At the same time he makes use of the Neoplatonic idea of emanation. This idea, taken by itself, implies that the beings subordinate to God proceed from him necessarily. To meet this difficulty ibn Daud suggests that the doctrine of emanation, when taken as implying necessity, is the result of a neglect of the limits

[1] Aristotle used the word *kinesis* in a broad sense, to include not only locomotion but any transition from one state to another.
[2] Aristotle postulated an active principle in intellection, which he called the *nous poietikos* or active intellect. Its precise relation to the individual human mind was left obscure. Philosophers such as Avicenna, however, took Aristotle to mean that the active intellect is a separate unitary intelligence which fulfils a certain function in the life of individual human minds.

of human thought. We can know by philosophical reasoning that the world proceeds from God, but not how it proceeds from him. Ibn Daud thus allows room for the thesis that though the separate intelligences were created from eternity, the material world had a temporal beginning.

The Aristotelian idea of the soul as the form of the body is accepted by ibn Daud. At the same time he follows Avicenna in defending the theory of personal immortality. In his opinion our ability to form universal concepts shows clearly the spiritual nature of the human soul. The universal concept can apply to an infinite number of particulars[1] and, unlike the body, it is indivisible. As a thing's nature is shown by its operations, our activity of conceiving universals reveals a difference between soul (more accurately perhaps, the mind or the soul as thinking) and the body. The soul therefore has a certain independence of the body and can survive death. In reply to the objection that if the soul is really the form of the body, it is so united to the body that it is inseparable from it and must perish when the body perishes, ibn Daud follows Avicenna in maintaining that though this is true of the sensory or sensitive soul, we are not entitled to say the same of the rational soul or mind. To do so would be to go beyond what observation warrants.

In regard to the question whether human beings enjoy freedom or whether all their actions are determined, ibn Daud comes down strongly on the side of freedom. What then of divine omniscience? If God knows all events, must not man's future actions be known by him in advance? And, if so, how can they be free? Some earlier Jewish thinkers had maintained that though man's future acts are indeed known by God, divine foreknowledge is none the less compatible with human freedom. Ibn Daud, however, takes the somewhat drastic step of subtracting future contingent events from the scope of divine knowledge. By endowing man with freedom God limited, to this extent, his knowledge of future events, just as he limited his own omnipotence when he left man freedom of choice.

Ibn Daud is of some interest as exemplifying the influence of Avicenna's brand of Aristotelianism. But, as we have seen, he adjusts Avicenna's doctrine to the demands of Jewish religious belief, as in regard to human freedom. In the sphere of ethics he utilizes Aristotle's concept of practical philosophy, and also the Aristotelian theory of virtue as a mean between two extremes. He goes on, however, to

[1] That is to say, it is predicable of an indefinite number of possible exemplifications or instantiations.

identify philosophical ethics with the Torah and then to give it a religious orientation. Thus the Aristotelian idea of theoretical activity as constituting the highest achievement of man is interpreted in terms of the knowledge and love of God.

5

The most famous Jewish philosopher of the Middle Ages is undoubtedly Moses ben Maimon (1135–1204), generally known as Moses Maimonides. Born at Córdoba, Maimonides left his native town when it was overrun by the Almohades, a fanatical Moslem sect, and in 1159 crossed with his family to north Africa, where he settled first at Fez. As this city, however, was subject to Amohad rule, Maimonides went to live near Cairo, becoming in the course of time head of the Jewish community in Egypt. Besides being a physician and a writer of medical treatises, Maimonides was the leading authority of the time on Jewish law and undertook to systematize and codify it.

The philosophical reputation of Maimonides rests chiefly on his *Guide of the Perplexed*. It is generally asserted that the perplexed in question were those who had some knowledge of philosophy but who did not see how it could be reconciled with Jewish religious beliefs and ethical convictions. The assertion is indeed true, but it can none the less be misleading. For it might be taken to mean that Maimonides writes from the point of view of a pure philosopher, who then sets about reconciling philosophy with the Jewish faith for the benefit of people who are devout Jews and suspicious of philosophical speculation. In point of fact, however, Maimonides explicitly states that 'the first purpose of this Treatise is to explain the meanings of certain terms occurring in books of prophecy',[1] and that the work's second purpose is 'the explanation of very obscure parables occurring in the books of the prophets'.[2] In other words, Maimonides is writing as a Jewish believer, intent on explaining the inner meaning of prophetic parables. At the same time he makes it clear that he is addressing what he says to readers who have become philosophers and possess knowledge of the sciences but who are perplexed about the meaning of the Scriptures and the Law and put off or repelled by the externals and *prima facie* sense of what they have read. If we presuppose a religious Jew who has

[1] *The Guide of the Perplexed*, translated with an introduction and notes by Shlomo Pines (University of Chicago Press, 1963), p. 5.
[2] Ibid., p. 6.

studied the sciences and philosophy and who finds himself 'distressed by the externals of the Law'[1] and by equivocal or ambiguous language, several choices are open to him. He can follow what he believes to be the demands of intellectual integrity and renounce the Law. Or he can hold fast to what he believes to be the meaning of the Scriptures and the Law and resist the clamouring demands of his intellect. He is in a perplexed state of mind. And Maimonides wishes to show him that he is not forced to choose one of these two paths. For the man can come to understand the inner meaning of the Scriptures and the Law and to see that it agrees with the teaching of genuine philosophy, and if it goes beyond philosophy, this is due to the limitations of the human reason which leave room for prophetic revelation.

It can hardly be denied that the *Guide of the Perplexed* is itself a rather perplexing work. For one thing, Maimonides's own attitude is none too clear. His admiration for Al-Fārābī, the Islamic thinker, suggests that Maimonides thought of philosophy as exhibiting the truth of religion, as revealing, that is to say, the rational truth expressed in religious doctrines in a mythical or pictorial manner. It can also be maintained, however, that he clearly thought of prophetic illumination as superior to philosophical reasoning. For another thing, Maimonides has a good deal to say about the pedagogical role of contradiction and inconsistency. He mentions, of course, types of case in which apparent or *prima facie* contradictions can be resolved. But he also remarks that 'in speaking about very obscure matters it is necessary to conceal some parts and to disclose others'[2] and claims that in such cases it is sometimes necessary to use one premise in one place and a contradictory premise in another place, care being taken that 'the vulgar must in no way be aware of the contradiction'.[3] The reader is warned that this sort of procedure is to be found in the *Guide of the Perplexed*. This suggests that Maimonides intends to make things difficult for readers of meagre intellectual capacity, whereas the philosophically gifted will be able to overcome the stumbling blocks put in the way of the less talented, who are presumably judged unfit for understanding the inner meaning of doctrines and beliefs. Indeed, Maimonides says explicitly that both the greater part of natural science and also divine science 'should be withheld from the multitude'.[4]

[1] Ibid., p. 5.
[2] Ibid., p. 18.
[3] Ibid.
[4] Ibid., p. 42.

Maimonides starts by discussing the saying, attributed to God, 'let us make man in our own image and likeness'[1] and explains that it is not to be understood in any sense from which it would follow that God is corporeal. Through an examination of this and other ways of speaking he shows the reader how he should or should not think of God. We can say, therefore, that before undertaking to demonstrate God's existence Maimonides clarifies the concept of that the existence of which he proposes to prove. To put the matter in another way, he first explains what the word 'God' means, or at any rate what he thinks it ought to mean or what he intends to understand by the term. In the first part of the *Guide of the Perplexed* he goes into the matter at considerable length. He explains, for example, that there is no multiplicity at all in God, and that when we predicate of God a variety of attributes, we are referring, or should be referring, to the multiplicity of God's effects, unless we are simply denying of God the privation of a certain perfection.

The last clause is important. When we make positive statements about God, for example that he is wise, we are using terms equivocally. And we do not know what they mean when applied to God, except that they deny something of him. To say, for instance, that God is powerful is to say that he is not powerless. The divine power in itself is the divine essence; and this transcends human understanding. The same can be said in regard to the statement that God exists. To say that God does not exist, in the sense that the world is self-sufficient and that there is no divine reality, would be to say what is false. We have therefore to assent that God exists. The statement is true; but God's existence is 'not according to the notion of that existence which is in us'.[2]

For Maimonides, therefore, the confession that we know of God what he is not rather than what he is expresses the proper human attitude in face of the divine mystery and transcendence. A critic might indeed object that this emphasis on the way of negation provides a pretty weak basis for proving God's existence. Does Maimonides propose to demonstrate the existence of an I-do-not-know-what? The philosopher would presumably reply that he is proposing to show that finite things, which fall within the field of our experience, must depend for their existence on a reality other than ourselves, a reality which transcends human experience and comprehension, and that a claim to

[1] Genesis, 1, 26.
[2] *Guide of the Perplexed*, p. 144.

enjoy positive insight into the nature of the divine reality is not required for this purpose.

As Maimonides is well aware, proofs of the existence of God involve presuppositions. At the beginning of the second part of the *Guide of the Perplexed* he lists twenty-five premises, the truth of which, he assures the reader, has been demonstrated by Aristotle and his followers. For the sake of argument he adds a further premise, the eternity of the world. This matter has already been discussed at considerable length in the first part. Maimonides has made it clear that though he believes that time had a beginning, he also believes that philosophy has never succeeded in proving that the world did not exist from eternity. Proofs of God's existence therefore should be independent of the question whether the world did or did not exist from eternity. This means in effect that the eternity of the world should be taken as a premise for the sake of argument. If we can demonstrate God's existence even on this premise or presupposition, the demonstration will hold, *a fortiori*, if the world did not exist from eternity. If, however, we assume that the world had a temporal beginning and argue that it must therefore have been created by God, the natural conclusion to draw will be that if the premise were proved false, there would be no God, or at any rate that his existence could not be proved.

In proving God's existence Maimonides makes use of Aristotle's argument to the existence of a first or supreme unmoved and non-corporeal mover, presenting the argument in several ways. He also makes use of Avicenna's argument to the effect that the existence of 'possible' things (things, that is to say, which come into being and pass away) implies the existence of a being which cannot not exist, a necessarily existent being. If there were no such being, nothing would exist. For that which is merely possible cannot bring itself into existence. Further, in the absolutely necessary being, God, existence and essence must be identical. For the necessary being exists because of what it is. Its essence is to exist. In other beings, however, existence is an 'accident' or accidental determination.[1]

The world of Avicennian Aristotelianism was pervaded by necessity. The first subordinate intelligence proceeded necessarily from God, the second from the first, and so on down to the terrestrial world. God was not, of course, coerced by anything external to himself; but all things other than himself came into being through a process of emanation

[1] In making existence an accident in creatures Maimonides is following Al-Fārābī.

which implied necessity. This view of the world was not, however, acceptable to Maimonides, who regarded the Jewish faith as including belief in the free creation of the world by God. The first cause of all things is 'God's will and free choice'.[1] As for an individual thing, 'if he wills, he causes the thing to pass away; and if he wills, he causes it to last'.[2] This is not perhaps altogether consistent with Maimonides's doctrine on providence, according to which God watches over human beings, whereas events affecting other things are due to 'pure chance'.[3] However, it is clear that Maimonides ascribes the creation of the world to the free choice of God, as indeed he must if he wishes to hold, as he does, that the world was not in fact created from eternity. That is to say, if he wishes to leave room for the religious belief that the world had a temporal beginning, he can hardly depict creation as following from the eternal thought of God. In this case the world would exist from eternity. So Maimonides claims that in his wisdom God freely willed to create the world in such a way that there would be an ideally assignable first moment of time.

The critic might well object that according to Maimonides divine thought and will are identical with the unchanging and unchangeable divine essence. He might also object that as, according to Maimonides, such terms as 'thinking', 'knowing' and 'willing' are predicated equivocally of God, to say that creation was due to God's free will and choice does not tell us anything. Presumably the philosopher would reply that the statement that God created the world freely is equivalent to saying that God did not create necessarily. We know what God did not do rather than what he did. We cannot understand how God created the world. It takes on for us the character of a miraculous event.[4]

Like Aristotle, Maimonides sees ethics in a social context. The two aims of moral precepts are to secure for man 'the welfare of the soul and the welfare of the body'.[5] These aims, however, can be achieved only 'through a political association, it being already known that man

---

[1] Guide of the Perplexed, p. 409.
[2] Ibid., p. 332.
[3] Ibid., p. 471.
[4] Once we accept the idea of God's free creation of the world, we can envisage the possibility of his miraculous intervention in Nature. It does not follow that Maimonides understands in a literal sense all the miraculous events narrated in the Old Testament. But he allows in principle for miracles.
[5] Guide of the Perplexed, p. 510.

is political by nature'.[1] Maimonides is not, however, simply an Aristotelian. He is a Jew and a great authority on the Law. And he sees the two aims mentioned as achieved through observance of 'the true Law',[2] the Mosaic Law that is to say, which brings to man welfare of soul and body 'through the abolition of reciprocal wrongdoing and through the acquisition of a noble and excellent character'.[3] In other words, the perfecting of man in society, which is the end of moral conduct, is brought about through observance of the Law of Moses as understood and developed in Jewish tradition. This Law presupposes or implies certain correct beliefs, in the existence and unicity of God, for example, and in man's duty to obey God.

Now the idea of law, taken by itself, may suggest the idea of arbitrary commands or precepts. But Maimonides wishes, of course, to bring together and fuse the Mosaic Law and philosophical ethics. He looks therefore for the causes or reasons of the commandments of the Law. And he maintains that they are all justified by their utility, by their being the means, that is to say, of achieving welfare of soul and body. Maimonides finds, however, that he has to make a distinction. The utility of certain commandments is clear enough. For instance, human society could not prosper if indiscriminate homicide were permitted. Again, if we presuppose belief in God and man's relationship to God, it is clearly desirable that man should reverence and worship God. But when we consider the detailed prescriptions of the Mosaic Law in regard to sacrifice, their utility is by no means manifest. Why is this particular action commanded rather than that?

In discussing this sort of question Maimonides dismisses the claim that all particular prescriptions of the Law have their assignable particular causes or reasons, which are hidden from us, either because of the limitations of the human intellect or because God did not choose to reveal them. If it is asked, for example, why a lamb should be sacrificed rather than a ram, it is useless to look for some particular reason for choosing the former. It is sufficient to say that sacrifice to God is of manifest utility, and that if sacrifice were to be offered, something had to be offered. In other words, the prescription that a particu-

[1] Ibid., p. 511. The word 'political' must be understood of course in an Aristotelian sense. To say that man is political by nature is to say that he is social by nature, that he can perfect himself only in and through membership of a human society. It is not to say that he must be a politician in our modern sense of the term.
[2] Ibid.
[3] Ibid.

lar kind of animal should be sacrificed is a positive enactment which defines the general law of worshipping God but cannot be deduced from it. It is in accordance with the general commandment but does not follow logically from it.

Although Maimonides considers moral precepts in the context of the Mosaic Law and bases the distinctions which he makes between different classes of laws on reflection about the Law of Moses and the Jewish ethical tradition, he shows clearly enough the influence of Aristotelianism in his doctrine of man's ultimate perfection. This consists not in moral action nor in the possession of moral qualities but in knowledge, especially knowledge about God. 'This is what gives the individual true perfection, a perfection belonging to him alone; and it gives him permanent perdurance; through it man is man.'[1] Maimonides adds, however, that the man who has achieved this perfection will assimilate his actions, as far as he can, to the divine actions. Thus a higher or more perfect morality is envisaged than a purely utilitarian morality.

The *Guide of the Perplexed* was written in Arabic; but it was translated into Hebrew in Maimonides's lifetime.[2] Some Jewish writers attacked it violently on the ground that it represented the abandonment of pure religion in favour of Greco-Islamic philosophy. To put the matter another way, when philosophy came under fire, Maimonides's work tended to be singled out for attack. This did not, however, prevent commentaries being written on the work by those who favoured Maimonides's point of view. And the *Guide* became pretty well a philosophical textbook for Jewish students. The work was translated into Latin in the thirteenth century and exercised a considerable influence on Christian thinkers, Aquinas for example. At a much later date Spinoza studied the *Guide*, and in the *Tractatus theologico-politicus* he criticized Maimonides, though often without mentioning him by name.

6

Maimonides was a contemporary of Averroes; and in a letter to Samuel ibn Tibbon (who translated the *Guide* into Hebrew) he commended Averroes's commentaries. But there does not seem to be any evidence that at the time of writing the *Guide* he had been influenced by

[1] *Guide of the Perplexed*, p. 635.
[2] Several translations into Hebrew were made in the Middle Ages. When the Christians reconquered southern Spain from the Moslems, Jewish scholars took to writing in Hebrew instead of in Arabic.

the Islamic philosopher. Nor does he mention the Averroistic theory of the intellect. Ibn Tibbon, however, translated into Hebrew some of Averroes's smaller treatises, while his son-in-law, Jacob Anatoli, translated some of the Islamic philosopher's commentaries on Aristotle's logic.

Needless to say, Jewish thinkers differed in their attitude to Averroes. In the thirteenth century a Jew of Italy, Hillel ben Samuel, attacked the Averroistic psychology, making use for this purpose of Aquinas's work *On the Unity of the Intellect against the Averroists*.[1] In the same century, however, Isaac Albalag was a fervent admirer of Averroes and made it pretty clear that in his opinion philosophy took precedence of the Scriptures and the Torah. Sometimes indeed he tried to interpret Jewish beliefs in such a way as to show their accordance with philosophical doctrines, such as the eternity of the world. In other words, he sometimes represented religious beliefs as esoteric or imaginative expressions of esoteric philosophical theories. His real opinion, however, seems to have been that the Jewish sacred writings were concerned not with truth but with laying down laws conducive to social utility. He may have said or implied on occasion that a man could maintain the truth of a given proposition from the point of view of a religious believer and the truth of an incompatible proposition from the point of view of a philosopher. But he can hardly have seriously believed that a given proposition could be true and false at the same time. It is much more probable that those are right who interpret him as anticipating the position of Spinoza, namely that whereas philosophy is concerned with truth, the Scriptures are concerned with practical conduct, with inculcating obedience to useful laws or precepts, and that what seem to be metaphysical doctrines in the Old Testament or the Law should be given a pragmatic meaning and not taken as giving us revealed information about reality.

Commentaries on Averroes's commentaries and Aristotle's *Organon and Metaphysics* were written by Levi Ben Gerson (1288–1344), known as Gersonides. A native of the south of France, Gersonides was a mathematician and astronomer,[2] who also commented on the Penta-

---

[1] Hillel evidently knew Latin, as he translated some works from Latin into Hebrew. We can add that in the course of time some texts by Christian writers were translated into Hebrew, and that several Jewish philosophers were influenced to some extent by Christian thought, even if they did not always make explicit acknowledgement of this influence.

[2] Gersonides is credited with the invention of two astronomical instruments.

teuch and some other biblical writings. His chief philosophical work was *The Wars of the Lord*, comprising six parts, in which he expounded his ideas, to a great extent, by interpreting Aristotle in the light of the commentators.

For example, when treating of the Aristotelian psychology Gersonides examines at length the interpretations given by Alexander of Aphrodisias, Themistius, Averroes and others. He accepts Alexander's view that the potential intellect (the intellect considered simply as capable of actualization) is dependent on the soul as the form of the body. It cannot be, as Averroes supposed, a separate immaterial substance, one in all men. For if it were, it would be impossible to explain the evident fact that one man knows something which another man does not know. The potential intellect must be individualized. In this case, however, it is dependent on the body and perishes with it. At the same time Gersonides maintains that the actualization of the potential intellect by the active intellect (a separate immaterial substance or intelligence) gives rise to the acquired intellect, which survives the death of the human organism. This may sound as though Gersonides is asserting personal immortality. So he is in a sense. But not in the ordinary sense. For the acquired intellect consists simply of its ideational content. It consists, that is to say, of concepts or, more precisely, of the concept which subsumes in itself the concepts which a man has had in his lifetime.[1]

In his interpretation of the idea of God Gersonides returns, under the influence of Averroes, to Aristotle's own idea of God as self-thinking thought, rejecting the Neoplatonic doctrine of the One which is beyond thought. Further, Gersonides rejects the negative theology of Maimonides, according to which terms predicated of God are predicated purely equivocally. If Maimonides were right, it would follow that we could know nothing about God. In Gersonides's opinion the terms predicated of God and creatures apply primarily to God and derivatively to creatures. Wisdom, for example, is predicated in a primary sense of God, as the source of all wisdom, and derivatively of certain creatures, in so far as they reflect the divine wisdom. But the meaning of the term is the same in both cases. It is therefore easier to understand Gersonides's limitation of the divine knowledge. God does

---

[1] In other words, Gersonides looks on a man's concepts as so interrelated that what comes later subsumes in itself what came earlier. Hence if we say that for him the acquired intellect is the sum of a man's concepts, this does not imply that what survives death is a string of concepts.

not know the individual as such but only as a member of the universal order of things. In other words, the divine knowledge, like human knowledge, is limited to universals. Man's future contingent acts thus elude divine knowledge and are free.

As for creation, Gersonides rejects the theory of emanation and ascribes creation to the divine will. At the same time the idea of creation 'out of nothing' seems to him quite unacceptable. Things came into being through the creative activity of God; but becoming presupposes the potentiality of becoming. In other words, creation presupposes formless and indeterminate matter.[1] It does not follow, however, that pre-existing matter was in time. Temporality began only with creation with, that is to say, the conferring of form on the pure potentiality for receiving form.

7

In some important respects Gersonides doubtless approached the historic Aristotle more closely than did those Jewish philosophers whose Aristotelianism was strongly imbued with Neoplatonic theories. Neoplatonism, however, was more profoundly religious than original Aristotelianism. In any case the world-vision of Aristotle was hardly that of the Bible. And it is understandable if efforts at harmonizing philosophy, whether Neoplatonic or Aristotelian, with the Bible and Jewish tradition seemed to some Jews to express a surrender to rationalism. To some minds the philosophers appeared to be primarily philosophers and only secondarily Jewish believers. That is to say, the philosophers seemed to take their view of reality from Greco-Islamic thought and then to set about reconciling their world-vision with Jewish belief, with varying degrees of success.

At the same time the reflective mind could obviously not be content with taking literally the more anthropomorphic statements about God in the Bible, not at any rate if they were understood as factually informative statements. Moreover, quite apart from philosophy, one would expect a religiously-motivated tendency to find a spiritual significance in the external observances and actions prescribed by the Law. In other words, the growth of some kind of esoteric Judaism was natural enough. And we find this in the Cabbalistic writings. The Cabbala (tradition) seems to have been a mixture of elements derived

[1] Obviously, Gersonides finds no great difficulty in interpreting Genesis in this sense.

from Judaism, Persian thought, Hellenistic philosophy and Gnosticism. But even if philosophical ideas were employed, it was presented as a set of doctrines (especially in regard to creation, revelation and salvation or Messianism) which were superior to rationalistic philosophy and which appealed to the more mystically and theosophically inclined.

In the thirteenth century the Cabbalistic movement developed in southern France and in Spain.[1] A theory of emanation, tending towards pantheism, was developed; and systems of symbolism, in terms of letters and numbers, were worked out for use in biblical exegesis. A summary of Cabbalistic doctrines, *The Book of Splendour*, in the form of a commentary on the Pentateuch, was composed about the year 1290 by Moses ben Shentob de Leon, a Spanish Jew.[2]

There were, however, some writers who aimed, in opposition to the philosophers, at returning to the biblical concept of God while arguing on philosophical grounds against their opponents, without having recourse to the esoteric doctrines of the Cabbala. Prominent among them was Hasdai Crescas (c. 1340–1410), a Spanish rabbi who was born at Barcelona. When his son perished in a persecution in 1391, he moved to Saragossa. A scholar in the Jewish Law, Crescas believed that Judaism should be purified from contamination by Aristotelianism, and that Maimonides had not gone far enough in this direction. At the same time he tried to support basic Jewish beliefs by philosophical arguments. Hence his criticism of philosophy as such hardly squares with his actual procedure.

Crescas wrote in Spanish a *Refutation of the Principal Dogmas of the Christian Religion*, which has survived in a Hebrew translation. But we are concerned here only with his effort to defend Judaism from the corrosive effects of philosophical ideas alien to Jewish belief and tradition. In this field his principal work is entitled *The Light of the Lord*, intended originally as an introduction to an exposition of the Talmud which was not in fact written.

In this work Crescas subjects the Aristotelian physics to a critique which is certainly not without interest. For example, in his opinion Aristotle fails to distinguish between space and place. The place of an object in a box, for instance, is the inner limit of the container. In the case of a boat being carried down a river, its place is determined in relation to the whole river, when this is considered as at rest. In other

---

[1] There was a somewhat earlier development among Jews in Germany.
[2] In the sixteenth century another exposition, *The Garden of Pomegranates*, was produced by Moses ben Jacob Cordovero.

words, place is the limit within which a body is contained, when this limit is considered as immobile. Crescas objects that if space is confused with place and defined in the same way, the outermost sphere would not be in space at all, as it would have no containing limit. Further, there would be no empty space, no vacuum. But the outermost sphere must be in space; and space beyond this sphere is empty. Hence there can be a vacuum.

Crescas evidently looks on space as logically prior to bodies, as an infinite 'receptacle', as Plato put it in the *Timaeus*. And if space is infinite, so is time. Against Aristotle, Crescas argues that time should not be defined in relation to the motion of bodies, as it is independent of such motion. Against Gersonides he argues that it is by no means impossible to conceive time as without a beginning. There is no good in claiming that if time were infinite, the present day would never have been reached. For to say that time is infinite is simply to say that any selected period of time is preceded by another period, and so on indefinitely. And between any selected period and the present day the distance is finite.

All this sounds like the usual game of philosophers criticizing one another on philosophical grounds. So it is, if we consider Crescas's critique of Aristotelian physics by itself. His aim, however, is to show the invalidity of Aristotle's argument to prove the existence of a first unmoved mover. And he tries to do so by arguing that, if time is infinite, there can be a causal series without a beginning.[1] The reason why Crescas is opposed to Aristotle's argument is evidently that, in his opinion, the argument concludes only in the assertion of a cause of 'movement', of becoming that is to say, and that this concept of God does not square with the biblical concept. He accepts, therefore, the argument from 'possible' being to the existence of the absolutely necessary being,[2] as this argument represents God as the ultimate reality from which all else derives its existence.

As for the question whether the world was or was not created from eternity, Crescas regards it as of secondary importance. Provided that God is recognized as creator, as the ultimate productive source of all other beings, it does not matter much if we assume that the divine goodness expressed or manifested itself from eternity in the created world. Maimonides may have thought that if creation was the expression

[1] Presumably Crescas understands Aristotle as meaning that the first unmoved mover is first in a temporal sense.

[2] This argument, employed by Maimonides, was taken over from Avicenna.

of the divine will, the world must have had a temporal beginning. But the conclusion does not follow from the premise. The divine will could perfectly well have willed creation from eternity. However, as the Torah teaches that the world had in fact a temporal beginning, this doctrine must be accepted.

The essence of God, Crescas insists, is not thought, as Aristotle maintained, but goodness. God is absolute goodness, and, as such, he knows and loves individuals. Further, the end of man, the goal of human life, is not, as Aristotle imagined, philosophical knowledge of God but love. This love is shown in obedience to the Law. And obedience to the commandments of God is not confined, as philosophy is, to a select few. Again, though Crescas accepts the Aristotelian concept of the soul as the form of the body, he tries to combine this acceptance with the view that the soul of man is spiritual and immortal, and that it is not simply the intellect which survives death. Love of God, the end or goal of human life, is not confined to this life.

By insisting that the divine essence is goodness and not thought, and that attainment of man's highest perfection is not confined to an intellectual élite, Crescas is obviously rejecting Aristotelianism in favour of religious belief. When, however, he discusses the subject of human freedom he makes a concession to Avicennian Aristotelianism.[1] If we consider the human will in itself, we must describe it as free, in the sense that its choices proceed from the man himself. That is to say, when I am not coerced into doing something, the decision to do it is mine. If, however, we go further back and inquire into the causes of a man's choice, we must admit that the choice could not be other than it is. Crescas rejects Gersonides's theory that the divine omniscience is limited. God knows in advance, so to speak, how a man will act in any given set of circumstances. And this is the way in which the man will act. If it is objected that in this case punishment in the next life for wrongdoing in this life is unjust, the reply can be made that if a man puts his hand into the fire, it will burn.

As Crescas is primarily interested in developing a religious system of thought in harmony with the Scriptures, we would hardly expect him to devote attention to logic for its own sake. Logical questions arise, however, in the course of his reflections. For example, against Averroes he argues that existence and essence cannot be identical in creatures. If they were, any proposition asserting the existence of a finite thing or

[1] Aristotle himself does not appear to have seen human freedom as a problem. He simply assumed that man enjoys freedom.

substance would be a tautology. And this is clearly not the case. Against Al-Fārābī, Avicenna and Maimonides, however, Crescas argues that existence cannot be regarded as an accident of creatures. If this were the case, a given thing, such as a man, would come into being through one of its accidents. This is an absurd supposition, inasmuch as substance is logically prior to its accidents or modifications. Existence, Crascas maintains, is the precondition of essence. What precisely is meant by this, is not made clear. But perhaps we can interpret Crescas as meaning that nothing can have attributes unless it exists. He would then be claiming that existence is not a predicate.

Spinoza refers to Crescas in a letter; and it is probable that he derived some stimulus from his thought, as also from that of Maimonides. At the same time the influence of Jewish medieval philosophy on the mind of Spinoza can be exaggerated.[1] As we have seen, Crescas intended to support orthodox Jewish belief against Greco-Islamic philosophy; and he was certainly no pantheist. Spinoza, however, was far from being an orthodox Jew. Nor did he address himself to his fellow-Jews in the way that Crescas did. It has indeed been argued that the Jewish concept of God, when thought through philosophically, tends to become the Spinozistic concept. And Crescas might agree, if, that is to say, the word 'philosophically' were understood in the sense in which he was suspicious of philosophy. If, however, the word were understood as being equivalent simply to 'rationally', he would not agree. For in his criticism of views which met with his disapproval he employed rational argument rather than simple appeals to revelation.

Jewish philosophy, in the sense of an attempt to state and defend Jewish religion and ethics in philosophical terms, did not end with Crescas. But though Spinoza was certainly influenced by Jewish medieval thinkers, his system belongs to the main stream of European philosophy rather than to specifically Jewish thought. And it is obvious that when we speak of a given modern philosopher as a Jewish thinker, we often mean little more than that he happened to be a Jew.

[1] As for the Cabbalists, Spinoza had little use for them and spoke of their 'insanity'.

10

Thirteenth Century:
Universities and Translations

I

WE have seen that in the twelfth century there were schools, as at Paris, to which students came not only from the neighbourhood or from the country in which the school was situated but also from abroad. Further, the teachers were often of different nationalities. A centre of learning of this kind was known in the Middle Ages as a *studium generale*. Some of these more or less internationally organized schools declined and died out. Others became universities. The term 'university' (*universitas*) meant in the first instance the body of professors and students teaching and studying in a certain centre. Its original use did not therefore correspond with our modern use. There could be the 'university' of teachers or the 'university' of students or, of course, of both combined in a single society. In the course of time, however, some centres of learning in which there were faculties of theology or law or medicine became universities in the sense that they possessed charters and statutes and established forms of government and that the professors had the right to teach anywhere.[1]

In the case of the older medieval universities the granting of a charter by papal or imperial or royal authority does not necessarily mean of course that there was not already in existence what might

---

[1] The *ius ubique docendi* might be restricted in fact. For example, professors of law at Bologna had to take an oath not to leave the University to take up more congenial or better paid posts. But this local restriction did not affect the basic right.

fairly be described as a university. And in such cases it is obviously difficult to fix a precise date for the founding of the university in question. The University of Paris grew out of the cathedral school of Notre Dame; and though the date of foundation is often given as 1215, the year in which the statutes were sanctioned by Robert de Courçon, the papal legate, it is clear that statutes existed before this date. Oxford seems to have been given a chancellor in 1214, Cambridge somewhat later.[1] Montpelier, already a flourishing medical school, became a university early in the thirteenth century, while the University of Toulouse was founded by papal authority in 1229. In Spain the University of Salamanca was founded by royal authority in 1220.

In universities such as Paris and Oxford a system of colleges arose, with the doctors or teachers in control. South of the Alps, notably in the law university of Bologna, we can find a different situation. At Bologna there was a student rector and student control. This seems to have been due partly to the fact that the appointment and payment of teachers fell into the hands of the municipality, while the great mass of the student body came from outside the city and was concerned with asserting its rights over against the municipality.

In the thirteenth century Paris was undoubtedly the foremost university in the field of theology and speculative philosophy. An important event in the life of the university, and indeed in the life of other universities too, was the introduction of houses of study maintained by the new religious orders. The Order of Preachers, commonly known as the Dominicans (after their founder St Dominic), might be expected to be friendly to the study of theology. But St Francis of Assisi, with his devotion to the literal following of Christ and the Apostles in the way of poverty, did not envisage his disciples as possessing houses of study and libraries and as teaching in universities. However, transformation of the original band of disciples or companions of the Saint into an organized institution, with priest members, obviously made necessary provision for study. Moreover, the Holy See was quick to realize the potentialities of the new and fervent mendicant orders; and Gregory IX in particular, who as a cardinal had contributed to the development of study among the Franciscans, did all he could to introduce the Dominicans and Franciscans into the life of the University of Paris and to maintain them there. In 1217 the Dominicans estab-

[1] The University of Cambridge is said to have originated in an exodus of students from Oxford in 1209. But this does not exclude the previous existence of a school or schools in the town.

lished themselves at Paris, and in 1229 they obtained a chair of theology. In the same year the Franciscans, who had established themselves at Paris a little later than the Dominicans, also obtained a chair, their first professor being an Englishman, Alexander of Hales. Both orders soon erected *studia generalia* in other universities too, such as Oxford. And other religious orders presently followed their example.

Entry of the religious orders into the University of Paris did not take place without a good deal of opposition from the secular clergy.[1] From the point of view of the orders this opposition doubtless seemed to be the expression of prejudice and the desire to protect vested interests. But from the point of view of their opponents the friars appeared to be claiming unjustifiable exemptions and privileges. Opposition to the religious orders lasted for a considerable time, sometimes amounting to attack on the religious life itself.[2] But the Dominicans and Franciscans enjoyed the support of the Holy See, and the opposition they met with, though vigorous, was overcome. The great majority of the well-known philosophers of the thirteenth century were members of religious orders.

The course of studies lasted a long time. But in those days students entered the university at a very much earlier age than they do today. Thus at Paris, in the thirteenth century, students had first to study in the Faculty of Arts for six years. During this period the student could become a 'bachelor' (*baccalaureus*) and help with the teaching in a subordinate capacity. But he could not take the mastership until he was twenty. The content of the course consisted of the 'liberal arts'; but the study of literature had practically disappeared in favour of emphasis on grammar. Logic was, of course, primarily the logic of Aristotle, though Porphyry's *Introduction* (*Isagoge*) was also studied.

The course of theology lasted at first for eight years; but it underwent a process of lengthening. After completing his course in the Faculty of Arts and teaching for some years the student gave four years to the study of the Bible and two to that of the *Sentences* of Peter Lombard. He could then become a bachelor and lecture for two years

[1] The term 'secular Clergy' refers to those members of the clergy who do not belong to a religious order. Soon after the middle of the century the college of the Sorbonne was founded (named after Robert de Sorbon) for the theological education of secular clergy.
[2] In this context 'religious life' does not mean religion. It means the state of belonging to a religious order.

on the Bible and one on the *Sentences*. The mastership or doctorate could be taken after another four or five years.

Some students might, of course, go through the long period of studies with a view to ecclesiastical preferment. But the course of studies itself was obviously geared to teaching, to the production of doctors or professors. And as the arts course was preparatory for higher studies and theology was regarded as the queen of the sciences, the mastership or doctorate in theology, conferring the right to teach, was naturally looked on as the crown of the academic career.[1] We can thus easily understand how it was that most of the leading thinkers of the Middle Ages were theologians.

The basis of teaching was the lecture (*lectio*), originally taking the form of the reading of a text, with glosses, explanations and notes by the lecturer, but gradually becoming freer and more elaborate. I addition disputations formed a prominent feature of university life. In the case of the formal 'disputed questions' (*quaestiones disputatae*) a problem was raised, different or contradictory opinions were stated and argued, and a reply (*responsio*) was given by a student, followed by the decision (*determinatio*) of the professor. At certain times in the year there were freer discussions, open to teachers, students and visitors, when any problems could be raised. These were known as *quaestiones quodlibetales*.

2

Reference has already been made, in connection with Islamic philosophy, to the translation of Greek works into Syriac and then Arabic and, in some cases, directly from the Greek into Arabic. In the second half of the twelfth century and during the thirteenth century many works were translated into Latin. It has sometimes been said that the Latin translations used by the Christian theologians and philosophers of the Middle Ages were translations of Arabic translations of Syriac translations of Greek writings. This is inaccurate. For example, in the twelfth century James of Venice translated logical works by Aristotle directly from the Greek. James operated at Byzantium. In Sicily Henricus Aristippus, archdeacon of Catania, translated the *Meno* and *Phaedo* of Plato, while others translated Euclid and some writings by Ptolemy. In Spain a flourishing school of translators was established at

[1] Reference here is of course to universities such as Paris and Oxford. In a medical or law university arrangements were obviously somewhat different.

Toledo by Archbishop Raymond (1126–51). Among the translators were Gerard of Cremona, Dominic Gundisalvi (Gundissalinus) and, later, Michael Scot. Philosophical works by Islamic and Jewish thinkers, such as Avicenna and Avicebron, were translated into Latin; and also Arabic scientific writings. As for works by Greek authors, it is true that some Latin translations were made from the Arabic. For instance, a large part at any rate of Aristotle's *Metaphysics* was translated in Spain from Arabic into Latin. But this version has been preceded by a partial translation from the Greek (the so-called *Old Metaphysics, Metaphysica vetus*); and it was itself supplanted, after the middle of the thirteenth century, by William of Moerbeke's new translation from the Greek.[1] Again, the translation of the *De Anima* from the Arabic by Michael Scot was preceded by a translation from the Greek and followed by another translation from the Greek by William of Moerbeke, who also translated the *Politics*. As for the *Nicomachean Ethics*, a translation from the Greek of the second and third books was available in the twelfth century, while a translation of the first book was made early in the thirteenth century. These were known respectively as the *Old* and *New Ethics*. About 1240 Robert Grosseteste undertook the labour of translating the whole work from the Greek.

The work of translation lasted over a very considerable span of time. And Christian scholars at the beginning of the thirteenth century were not as well off, for available material, as later generations. For example, the writings of Averroes did not begin to penetrate into the University of Paris until about 1230. Again, it was William of Moerbeke's translation of the *Elements of Theology* by Proclus which enabled Aquinas to see that the *Liber de causis*, previously attributed to Aristotle, was really based on the work of Proclus. At the same time scholars at the beginning of the thirteenth century possessed a considerable part of the *corpus* of Aristotle's works, the *Timaeus, Meno* and *Phaedo* of Plato,[2] some writings by Al-Kindi, Al-Fārābī and Avicenna, two works of Isaac Israeli and Avicebron's *Fountain of Life*.

3

The greatest impact on the thought of the thirteenth century was made by the extended knowledge of Aristotelianism. By means of the trans-

---

[1] It was on this translation that Aquinas based his commentary.
[2] The medievals had no extensive knowledge of Plato. And their direct knowledge of Neoplatonic texts was also extremely limited.

lations Aristotle was converted from being more or less a logician into the expounder of a comprehensive system. As this system obviously owed nothing to Christianity, it came, we may say, to represent philosophy, while its author was known as 'the Philosopher'. Aristotle was naturally read in the light of comment and elaboration by Islamic and Jewish thinkers. And, as we have seen, certain writings were attributed to him which were really of Neoplatonic origin. So up to a point he was seen through coloured spectacles. But this does not alter the fact that his philosophy as a whole was greatly superior to the philosophizing which preceded it in the Christian medieval world. No very great effort of the imagination is required, therefore, in order to appreciate the interest and enthusiasm aroused by the extended knowledge of Aristotelianism which had been made possible by the translations.

This enthusiasm was however by no means universally shared. In 1210 a provincial synod at Paris forbad the use of Aristotle's writings on 'natural philosophy' in the Faculty of Arts, whether in public or in private, under pain of excommunication.[1] In 1215 the newly sanctioned statutes of the University of Paris prohibited professors in the Faculty of Arts from lecturing on Aristotle's works on metaphysics and natural philosophy or on summaries of them.[2] In 1231 Pope Gregory IX issued a bull (*Parens scientiarum*) in which he declared that the works prohibited in 1210 should not be used at Paris until they had been expurgated from all suspicion of error.[3] In 1245 Innocent IV extended the prohibitions of 1210 and 1215 to the University of Toulouse, which had previously prided itself on its freedom. These prohibitions were not extended to Oxford; but it is clear that they were observed for a time at Paris. From about 1255, however, all the known works of Aristotle were being lectured on at Paris, a fact which makes it all the more surprising that in 1263 Urban IV confirmed the bull of Gregory IX, including Gregory's endorsement of the prohibitions of 1210. Various

[1] The prohibition did not affect private reading in our sense. The phrase 'in private' referred rather to instruction given to students in private, apart from the ordinary lectures that is to say. 'Natural philosophy' doubtless included metaphysics, but neither the *Organon* nor the *Ethics*. In addition to Aristotle, Amaury of Bene, David of Dinant and a certain Maurice of Spain were named. David of Dinant is said to have interpreted Aristotle in a materialistic sense.

[2] The 'summaries' in question probably included those of Avicenna; but the date was too early for the commentaries of Averroes to be included.

[3] The Pope appointed a commission of three theologians to expurgate the offending works. But nothing seems to have been done, possibly because of the death of William of Auxerre, who headed the commission.

explanations have been offered, including the conjecture that the pope had his predecessor's bull reissued without adverting to the fact that it repeated the 1210 prohibition.[1] This sounds odd. But the renewed prohibition is itself odd, as Urban IV must have been well aware that William of Moerbeke was translating Aristotle at his own court. Anyway by 1263 Aristotle was being freely lectured on at Paris.

The interesting question is why the prohibitions were ever made in the first place. The explanation which consists in saying that Aristotle entered Christendom in bad company will not do. Avicenna was not exactly bad company, no worse than Aristotle himself. And Averroes's commentaries had not been translated by 1210. The fact seems to be that, in general, the philosophy of Aristotle seemed to be a comprehensive and naturalistic system, and that, in particular, Aristotle had some theories which were, or could be taken to be, incompatible with Christian theology. In other words, Aristotelianism appeared to some minds as a potential threat to the Christian faith. Professors of theology could be trusted to correct what was erroneous or misleading. But teachers in the Faculty of Arts should not be permitted to indoctrinate or give cause for stumbling to their young charges. This seems to be the most promising line of explanation.

4

The policy of dividing the different currents of thought in the thirteenth century according to the various attitudes adopted towards Aristotelianism is, from some points of view at any rate, both convenient and attractive. For it enables the writer to give a more or less clear picture of the situation and of the conflict which arose. The policy may involve an oversimplification of what is complex and a rather one-sided presentation of thirteenth-century thought. As, however, the new learning in general and Aristotelianism in particular undoubtedly caused a ferment and excitement in academic circles and provoked different reactions, it seems that the various attitudes adopted towards the philosophy of Aristotle can justifiably be used as guiding-lines provided at least that we remember that other approaches are possible.

[1] It has also been conjectured that Urban IV's action was aimed more against Averroes's interpretations of Aristotle than against Aristotle himself. This is possible. But if this were indeed the case, one might expect a reference to the doctrines to which exception was taken, unless perhaps the pope was primarily concerned with saying 'hands off Aristotle' to the Arts Faculty at Paris.

Though, however, all historians agree that the extended knowledge of Aristotle provoked different reactions, there is still plenty of room for dispute. For example, if a given thinker adopts a hostile attitude towards Aristotle, he is presumably rejecting Aristotelianism in favour of something else. What is this something else? If it is simply a case of a theologian feeling that the philosophy of Aristotle constitutes a menace to Christian faith, the situation is clear enough. The theologian doubtless makes some use of Aristotle, of his logic for example; but he looks on certain doctrines, such as the eternity of the world, as incompatible with Christian theology; and he feels perhaps that the metaphysical and ethical world-vision of the Greek philosopher is a naturalistic system. If he makes a recognizable use of certain Aristotelian categories and concepts, we can, if we like, describe him as an incomplete Aristotelian, from the philosophical point of view that is to say. But in so far as he opposes Aristotle, he does so as a Christian believer rather than as a philosopher.

If, however, we wish to claim that some critics of Aristotle in the thirteenth century were speaking as philosophers, what was the philosophy which they were defending? At the end of the nineteenth century Père Mandonnet proposed the view that in the early part of the thirteenth century Aristotelianism encountered the opposition of a long-entrenched Augustinianism going back eventually to Plato and St Augustine and characterized by such theories as divine illumination and *rationes seminales* and by the absence of any clear distinction between philosophy and theology. This view had the obvious merit of recognizing the fact that philosophical thought existed in medieval Christendom before the wave of translations to which reference has been made above. It soon came under fire, however, on the ground, for example, that it was a greatly oversimplified interpretation of the actual state of affairs. And historians such as Étienne Gilson, who have supported the idea of an opposition between Augustinianism and Aristotelianism in the early part of the thirteenth century, have felt themselves compelled to distinguish between different types of Augustinianism.[1]

[1] Gilson distinguished between an Augustinianism influenced more by Aristotle and one influenced more by Avicenna. Maurice De Wulf objected that in this case one should also allow for an Augustinianism influenced more by Ibn Gabirol. He also criticized the basis of Gilson's interpretation, on the ground that it involved an anachronistic emphasis on theories of knowledge. Van Steenberghen sees in the distinction between different types of Augustinianism an implicit recognition of the fact that it was a case of eclecticism rather than of an Augustinian philosophical system.

Professor F. Van Steenberghen of Louvain has, however, maintained that it is a serious mistake if one depicts the situation in the first half of the thirteenth century as a conflict between two philosophical systems, one Augustinianism, the other Aristotelianism. St Augustine was certainly regarded as the great master in theology; but he was no regarded in this way by all parties. As for philosophy, there was no such thing as an Augustinian system. 'On the *philosophical plane*, Augustinianism is non-existent during the first half of the thirteenth century.'[1] There were, of course, thinkers who maintained theories derived from Augustine. But these theories were mixed, in a variety of combinations, with ideas derived from other sources, such as the Pseudo-Dionysius, the Jewish writer Avicebron (Ibn Gabirol) and Aristotle. After all, Aristotelian categories and concepts, such as act and potentiality, matter and form, substance and accident, were widely employed before the thirteenth century. In other words, the conservative thinkers who were suspicious of or hostile to the spread of the Aristotelian system in the first half of the thirteenth century were eclectics. And their philosophical theories derived what units they possessed from their integration into a theological framework of thought, not from any systemization on the purely philosophical level. In the last part of the thirteenth century we find a self-conscious Augustinianism which must be seen in the light of the condemnations of 1270 and 1277. But in the early decades of the century there was no philosophical *system*, Augustinian or otherwise, confronting the growing influence of the system of Aristotle. There was an eclecticism which, in its various forms, constituted part of a theological outlook.

There is undoubtedly a good deal to be said in favour of Van Steenberghen's thesis. It was to a great extent the increased knowledge of the Aristotelian philosophy which, as has already been remarked, obviously owed nothing to the Judaeo-Christian tradition, that necessitated the drawing of a clear distinction between philosophy and theology. Needless to say, there was philosophical reflection and speculation in medieval Christendom long before the thirteenth century. But philosophizing was, as Van Steenberghen maintains, eclectic, and it was pursued within the framework of a Christian theological outlook. Hence we can admit without difficulty that in the twelfth century and in the first half of the thirteenth century there was no one definite system of philosophy which could be labelled 'Augustin-

[1] *La philosophie au XIIIe siècle* by Fernand Van Steenberghen (Louvain and Paris, 1966), p. 187.

ianism' and which, when Aristotelianism became better known, was set over against it and defended by the conservatives as the one true philosophical system. This could hardly have been the case, in spite of the use made of Augustinian ideas. For, as we have seen, some basic Aristotelian categories and concepts had already become common coin, while other ideas of the conservatives derived from Neoplatonism or Ibn Gabirol or other sources rather than from Augustine.

At the same time a good deal depends on the meaning which we give to the word 'philosophy'. Van Steenberghen himself admits that 'the *philosophy* of the men of the twelfth century, understood as a *general vision of the universe*, that is to say philosophy in the broad sense, is essentially Christian and Augustinian.'[1] To be sure, he goes on to say that 'from the point of view of *philosophy as a scientific discipline*, that is to say of philosophy in the strict sense, it would be very inexact to speak of a philosophical Augustinianism in the twelfth century'.[2] Perhaps so; but Augustine himself understood the word in a broad sense.

In any case it seems to the present writer that we can reasonably speak of an Augustinian approach to philosophical reflection, an approach which was different from that of Aristotle. It by no means follows, of course, that this Augustinian approach is characteristic of all those who would be classed as Augustinians according to Père Mandonnet's use of the term. But it is arguable that it is characteristic of St Bonaventure at any rate, of whom something will be said presently. As for philosophy as a 'scientific discipline', discussion of the subject would take us too far afield. It can be granted, of course, that Aristotle looked on philosophy, or on parts of it, as a 'science'. But it is obviously by no means everyone who would be prepared to regard the spread of Aristotelianism as equivalent to the spread of scientific philosophy.

[1] Ibid., p. 70.
[2] Ibid.

I I

St Bonaventure

I

THE Dominicans arrived at Paris in 1217; and in 1229 Roland of Cremona became the first Dominican professor in the University. The Franciscans arrived in 1219; and in about the year 1235 Alexander of Hales, who was already teaching at Paris, entered the Franciscan order. Robert of Cremona was soon joined by a fellow Dominican, John of St Giles; and in 1238 the Franciscan John of La Rochelle joined Alexander of Hales.[1]

The two mendicant orders obtained chairs at Paris during the period when William of Auvergne was bishop of the city (1228–49). William had taught at Paris before being nominated bishop; and he was a good example of an open-minded eclectic. He made use of the new learning and employed ideas derived from Aristotle, Avicenna and Ibn Gabirol, combining them with Augustinian theories and subordinating them to the development of a Christian theological world-view. For example, he adopted the Aristotelian idea of the soul as 'the perfection of a physical organic body having life in potentiality';[2] but though he was prepared to speak of the soul, in Aristotelian fashion, as the form of the body, he also used Platonic-Augustinian expressions in regard to the relationship between soul and body. Further, he rejected Avicenna's theory of the separate active intellect, which he ascribed, as Avicenna had, to Aristotle himself, and had recourse instead to the Augustinian theory of divine illumination. Again, while William accepted Avicenna's

---

[1] Both Alexander of Hales and John of La Rochelle died in 1245.
[2] See William's *De Anima* I, 1. According to this definition the body has actual life through the soul as principle of life.

doctrine of a distinction between essence and existence and used it to distinguish between God and creatures, he rejected the Neoplatonic-Avicennian theory of emanation and argued against the doctrine of the eternity of the world.[1]

Alexander of Hales, who had St Bonaventure as his pupil for a time, is said to have been the first professor of theology at Paris to use the *Sentences* of Peter Lombard as a textbook. As for his *Summa Theologica* (*Summary of Theology*), Roger Bacon, a fellow Englishman and a fellow Franciscan, remarked caustically that it weighed as much as a horse and was of doubtful authenticity into the bargain.[2] Even though the first part of Bacon's statement was an obvious exaggeration, the second part was correct. For the work is a compilation containing elements taken from Alexander himself but comprising also additions made by John de la Rochelle and others. It illustrates, however, the ideas of the Franciscan teachers at Paris at the time; and it shows that though there was an intelligent interest in Aristotle, Avicenna and Ibn Gabirol, this was accompanied by a pretty reserved attitude towards Aristotle and his followers, an insistence that more faith should be put in Augustine and Anselm than in Aristotle, and an expression of the view that no satisfaction was possible without the light of revelation. Alexander cannot be described as an Augustinian if the use of this term is taken to imply that he owes nothing to thinkers other than Augustine. For example, he follows Ibn Gabirol in interpreting 'matter' as equivalent to potentiality and in attributing hylomorphic composition to every creature.[3] But, generally speaking, he certainly continues the Platonic-Augustinian tradition.

2

Giovanni Fidanza, to be known as St Bonaventure, was born at Bagronea in Tuscany. The date of his birth has usually been given as 1221; but good reasons have been advanced for fixing it in 1217. He seems to have studied arts at Paris and then to have joined the Francis-

---

[1] Some of William's arguments to show that the world must have had a beginning reappear with Bonaventure.

[2] There is a critical edition in three volumes (Quaracchi, 1929–30).

[3] William of Auvergne rejected Ibn Gabirol's theory and, following Aristotle, confined hylomorphic composition to material things. The distinction between essence and existence was sufficient to mark off angels from God.

cans in 1243.[1] He studied theology under Alexandes of Hales and John of La Rochelle until their deaths in 1245 and then under Eudes Rigaud and William of Meliton. In 1248 he obtained the bachelorship in Scripture and in 1250 that in the *Sentences* of Peter Lombard. His commentary on the *Sentences* must have been composed between 1250 and 1252. In 1253 he obtained the licence to teach from the chancellor of the University and was in charge of the Franciscan school until 1257. Owing to a quarrel between the secular and regular clergy he was not admitted as a 'master' or professor of the Faculty of Theology until 1257, along with the Dominican Thomas Aquinas. Earlier in this year, however, he had been elected minister general of the Franciscan order, which put an end to his academic career as a professor.

In addition to his chief work, the commentary on the *Sentences* of Peter Lombard, Bonaventure wrote some biblical commentaries, a theological compendium (*the Breviloquium*), a small work *On the Re-direction of the Arts to Theology* (*De reductione artium ad theologiam*), some *Quaestiones disputatae*[2] and his well known *Journey of the Mind to God* (*Itinerarium mentis in Deum*). As Franciscan minister general Bonaventure gave several sets of conferences (*Collationes*) at Paris, including those on the six days of creation (*In Hexaemeron*). By the time in which the conferences were given a rationalistic spirit, inspired by devotion to Aristotle,[3] had developed in the Faculty of Arts; and the conferences exhibit Bonaventure's reaction to it.

In 1273 Bonaventure was nominated a cardinal and bishop of Albano by Pope Gregory X. In this capacity he was involved in the work of the Second Council of Lyons; but he died in this city in 1274, before the end of the council.[4]

Étienne Gilson has said that in reading Bonaventure 'one frequently imagines . . . a Saint Francis of Assisi gone philosopher and lecturing at The University of Paris'.[5] The trouble with this statement is that it is extremely difficult to imagine St Francis turned philosopher and lecturing in any university. He was devoted to the ideal of following

[1] It is related that as a small child Bonaventure was cured of an illness by St Francis of Assisi.

[2] These include *On the Knowledge of Christ* (*De scientia Christi*) and *On the Mystery of the Trinity* (*De mysterio Trinitatis*).

[3] Some of Averroes's theories had made headway in the Faculty of Arts and gave rise to vehement discussion. But Averroes was regarded as the 'Commentator', that is, as expounding Aristotle.

[4] 1274 was also the date of death of St Thomas Aquinas.

[5] *Christian Philosophy in the Middle Ages* (London, 1955), p. 340.

Christ and his apostles in a literal way, especially in regard to poverty; and he did not envisage his friars as occupying chairs in universities and possessing colleges and libraries. Another objection to Gilson's statement is that to describe Bonaventure as a philosopher is somewhat misleading. He philosophized, it is true. But he was primarily a theologian. The same holds good indeed of Aquinas. But the modern reader is more likely to find evidence of what he would probably regard as a philosophical outlook in the writings of St Thomas than in those of St Bonaventure.

At the same time Gilson's statement cannot be simply dismissed. If there was to be an organized and self-perpetuating Franciscan order, consisting partly of priests, there had to be houses of study, even if the ownership was vested in the Holy See. Further, granted the metamorphosis of a band of companions and disciples into an organized institution, it was natural that St Francis's preoccupation with the human soul's relation to God should find an intellectualized expression. It is arguable that Bonaventure's theological-philosophical synthesis constitutes such an expression. The powerful influence of Augustine on Bonaventure's thought should certainly not be underestimated. At the same time it is reasonable to claim that there is a closer connection between Bonaventure's thought and the spirit of St Francis than there is between the thought of Duns Scotus, a later Franciscan thinker, and St Francis's spirit. To say this is not to belittle Duns Scotus. As a philosopher he was much superior to Bonaventure. Indeed it is arguable that he was the most outstanding Christian metaphysician of the Middle Ages. But it is not perhaps without reason that Bonaventure came to be given the honorific title of Seraphic Doctor, while Duns Scotus was known as the Subtle Doctor.

These remarks should not be taken to imply either that Bonaventure fails to distinguish between philosophy and theology or that he denies the possibility of philosophical knowledge. As one would expect of a thirteenth-century thinker, well aware of the existence of non-Christian philosophers, he makes an explicit distinction between philosophy and theology. He says, for example, that theology begins with God, the supreme cause, with whom philosophy ends.[1] That is to say, the theologian presupposes belief in God and takes his data or premises from divine revelation, whereas the philosopher, in his desire to know reality, starts with reflection on finite things and argues to the existence

[1] *Breviloquium*, I, I. Cf. Commentary on the *Sentences*, Book III, Distinction 35, Article 1, Question 2, Conclusion 3.

of God as their creator. When trying to show the relevance of all knowledge to theology, as he does in his *Reduction of the Arts to Theology*, he clearly assumes that philosophical knowledge is possible.

In his own philosophizing Bonaventure makes use, of course, of basic Aristotelian concepts, such as those of act and potentiality, form and matter, substance and accident. He is certainly not an anti-Aristotelian in the sense of simply rejecting the whole philosophy of Aristotle. But the Aristotelian elements in his thought are often combined with ideas derived from other sources, while ideas derived from other sources are sometimes affected by Aristotelian theories. For example, though Bonaventure accepts the Aristotelian theory of the hylomorphic composition of material things, he follows Alexander of Hales (and so Ibn Gabirol) in extending this composition to all creatures, including angels, and is thus committed to interpreting 'matter' as pure potentiality without any intrinsic relation to quantity or to materiality in our sense. Again, while Bonaventure accepts the Aristotelian theory of the soul as the form of the body, he also maintains that the human soul is a spiritual substance, composed of spiritual form and spiritual matter and individuated by the union of its own two component factors. This view seems to make the soul a substance in its own right and is difficult, to put it mildly, to reconcile with the Aristotelian definition of the soul. Again, a theory of perception which is largely Aristotelian is combined with the Augustinian doctrine of divine illumination. As an example of the way in which ideas derived from sources other than Aristotle are sometimes affected by Aristotelian elements, we can mention Bonaventure's theory of *rationes seminales*. This theory is taken from Augustine, a fact of which Bonaventure is well aware. Indeed he explicitly says that in his opinion the theory should be held both because reason suggests it and because the authority of Augustine confirms it.[1] At the same time he has no intention of implying either that forms, latent in matter, all actualize themselves or that God is the sole cause of their actualization. Hence he proposes the view which, he says, seems to have been that of Aristotle that almost all natural forms, at any rate corporal forms, are actualized through the action of a particular finite efficient cause.[2] In other words, matter contains from the beginning forms virtually present, which are

[1] *Sentences*, Bk, II, Dist. 7, Qu. 2, Art. 2.
[2] According to Bonaventure, light (*lux*), the basic substantial form in terrestrial and celestial bodies, was created directly by God. So were purely spiritual beings (angels). The human rational soul is also directly created by God.

made actual by created agents. As the forms are already virtually present, the finite agents do not create out of nothing. At the same time their actions are not mere occasions for the causal activity of God.

If we simply list Bonaventure's opinions in this way, the impression is inevitably given that he is an eclectic who takes ideas from a variety of sources and tries to combine them, the framework of combination or synthesis being a Christian theological outlook. Indeed, the way lies open for devotees of Aristotle to depict Bonaventure as an incomplete Aristotelian, as a thinker that is to say, who makes more use of Aristotle than his predecessors but who does not possess the knowledge of Aristotelianism shown by St Albert the Great and St Thomas Aquinas and who fails to develop an integrated Aristotelian system. The description of Bonaventure as an incomplete Aristotelian is, however, questionable. If it is taken to mean that Bonaventure wished to be a thorough Aristotelian but failed to achieve his aim, this does not seem to be true. If the description 'incomplete Aristotelian' is intended to imply that Aristotelianism and philosophy were synonymous at the time, so that Bonaventure was less of a philosopher than Aquinas inasmuch as he made less use of Aristotle, the identification of philosophy with Aristotelianism is certainly not beyond criticism, even if it is intended to apply simply to the first half of the thirteenth century. As for eclecticism, Bonaventure was obviously an eclectic in the sense that he derived ideas from diverse sources. And Christian belief certainly serves as the central point of reference in combining these different ideas in a comprehensive world-vision. At the same time, unless one persists in equating philosophy with Aristotelianism, it is arguable that we can find Bonaventure's thought a philosophical approach which is common to Augustine and himself and which at any rate contributes to the unification of different elements. In other words, it is arguable that the unifying factors in Bonaventure's eclecticism are not purely external to philosophy, even if Christian belief plays the chief role.

Like Augustine before him, Bonaventure is preoccupied with the soul's relation to God. The title of his *Journey of the Mind to God* expresses the centre and spirit of his thought. It may be said, of course, that in this concern with the soul's relation to God he is thinking precisely as a Christian, and that the work in question is a work of mystical theology. This is doubtless true. But it seems reasonable to suggest that this Christian concern with 'interiority' affects his philosophical reflection and helps to differentiate it from that of Aristotle. Take, for example, Bonaventure's views on evidence for the existence of God. He does not deny that reflection on the external world of things can form the basis for proofs of God's existence. On the contrary he gives a series of Aristotelian or Aristotelian-style arguments.[1] At the same time he asserts that the existence of God is a truth implanted in the human mind. He does not mean by this that human beings have an innate idea of God or an inborn explicit knowledge of him. He means that man has an implicit awareness of God which can be made explicit by reflection. For instance, every human being has a natural desire for happiness, which can in fact be attained only through the possession of the supreme and ultimate good, which is God. The virtual or implicit knowledge of God can indeed be actualized by reflection in his effects. But Bonaventure likes to dwell on the soul's orientation to God and on its making the implicit awareness of God explicit through consciousness of itself and of its basic desires.

It may be objected that Bonaventure's theory of the desire for happiness as involving an implicit awareness of God is a line of thought taken over from the Augustinian tradition, that it is found alongside Aristotelian arguments, and that it is connected more with spirituality than with 'scientific' philosophy. After all, does not Bonaventure assert in his Commentary on the Sentences that God can be known through creatures as cause through effect, and that this way of knowing is natural to man, inasmuch as the objects of sense-perception are the means by which we arrive at knowledge of realities which transcend sense-perception?[2] When he is writing on spiritual and mystical matters, he naturally favours an interior approach, so to speak, to knowledge of God; but when he is speaking as a philosopher, he adopts an Aristotelian line of argument.

This view seems, once more, to presuppose an identification of philosophy with Aristotelianism. In any case it is open to criticism. For Bonaventure assumes, in a Platonic–Augustinian fashion, that recognition of the imperfections and limitations of creatures implies an implicit awareness of a standard in comparison with which creatures are judged to be imperfect. This view is connected with the Augustinian theory of illumination. And it is also relevant to Bonaventure's acceptance of Anselm's argument from the idea of perfection. For the idea of perfection, virtually present at least in the soul, is for him a sign of the divine presence, an effect of the divine illumination. There is therefore a real sense in which, for Bonaventure, arguments from external

[1] In the commentary on the Sentences and in On the Mystery of the Trinity.
[2] Commentary on the Sentences, Bk. I, Dist. 3, Art. 2.

objects of sense-perception to the existence of God presuppose in the soul a virtual or implicit awareness of God. In other words, the Augustinian line of thought is for him fundamental. God is indeed reflected in Nature, which is the shadow or 'vestige' of God; but he is manifested more clearly in the human soul, which is God's image.

It has already been remarked that Bonaventure is not an anti-Aristotelian in the sense that he dismisses Aristotle as a negligible thinker or regards most of the Greek philosopher's theories as false. Bonaventure himself not only uses basic Aristotelian categories and concepts but also looks on Aristotle as in certain respects superior to Plato. For Plato, he claims, opened the door to scepticism by denying that we can have real knowledge of the things of this world,[1] whereas Aristotle by his doctrine of immanent substantial forms provided a theoretical basis for natural philosophy. At the same time Bonaventure subjects Aristotle to pretty trenchant criticism. Plato proposed the theory of exemplar or archetypal ideas. But Aristotle rejected the theory. 'At the beginning of the *Metaphysics* and at the end and in many other places he execrates the ideas of Plato.'[2] For Bonaventure, however, exemplarism is at the heart of metaphysics. It is closely bound up with belief in divine creation. And if a philosopher rejects it, it is not to be wondered at if he conceives God as knowing only himself and as exercising no providence. Aristotle was indeed a great natural philosopher. He had 'the word of science' (*sermo scientiae*). But by rejecting exemplarism he showed his limitations as a metaphysician.

Bonaventure interprets Aristotle as having no idea of divine creation and as looking on the world as having existed from eternity.[3] The idea that motion and time had no beginning is, however, for Bonaventure, an absurd idea. And he gives a series of arguments to prove that this is the case. For example, if the world had existed from eternity, then at any date which one likes to choose an infinite number of solar revolutions would already have occurred. But it is impossible to add to the infinite. The daily occurrence of a solar revolution shows therefore that the

[1] Bonaventure's point is that we do not enjoy a direct vision of the eternal ideas. Hence if we cannot have knowledge of sensible reality, we cannot have knowledge of spiritual reality either. Plato deprived what he regarded as genuine knowledge of its necessary experiential basis.

[2] *In Hexaemeron*, 6, 2.

[3] Bonaventure speaks rather cautiously in attributing this doctrine to Aristotle, remarking that Aristotle never asserts that time had a beginning and that commentators generally interpret him as teaching the eternity of the world. In point of fact there is no reason for supposing that Aristotle believed in divine creation.

world cannot have existed from eternity.[1] Therefore it must have been created.[2] But Aristotle failed to see this very obvious truth.

As Bonaventure's thought centred round the soul's journey to God, he naturally looked on philosophical knowledge as demanding revelation and theology for its completion, and on theological knowledge (knowledge about God) as pointing to the knowledge of God by acquaintance, crowned by the vision of God in heaven. He therefore emphasized the shortcomings of any self-sufficient philosophical system, closed in on itself. Obviously, if we once assume the existence of revealed truths, any philosophical world-vision which ignores such truths must be judged a defective account of reality. To take an example given by Bonaventure, any theory of exemplarism which knows nothing of the Christian doctrine of Christ as the divine *Logos* or Word will fall short of the complete truth. Bonaventure, however, goes further than saying simply that a self-sufficient and self-enclosed philosophical system is bound to be defective. He maintains that the self-sufficient philosopher inevitably falls into error. The human reason, weakened by the Fall, can indeed attain philosophical knowledge. But the more that it tries to know realities which transcend the field of sense-perception, the more will it stumble. For Bonaventure, Aristotle is a signal example of this. He was a great natural philosopher; but when it was a question of God and of the world's relation to God, he fell into error on issues of central importance.

In the remarkable study of Bonaventure's philosophy which he published in 1924[3] Étienne Gilson appealed to this line of thought in support of his contention that Bonaventure was concerned with expounding a distinctively Christian philosophy, which was characterized by a marked hostility to Aristotle and which was different from, though complementary to, the Christian Aristotelianism of St Thomas Aquinas. Gilson's interpretation has, however, been challenged, notably by Van Steenberghen. The latter has pointed out, for instance, that if Bonaventure emphasized the shortcomings of a purely self-

[1] Commentary on the *Sentences*, Bk. I, Dist. I, Qu. 1, Art. 2.
[2] For Bonaventure the idea of the world being created by God from eternity was self-contradictory. In his view the idea of creation entailed the idea that time had a beginning. Conversely, denial that motion and time had a beginning entailed denial of creation. Aquinas took a different view, maintaining that the statement that the world was created 'out of nothing' entailed denial of the statement that the world was created 'out of something' but involved no intrinsic reference to time, to its having had or not having had a beginning.
[3] English translation, *The Philosophy of St Bonaventure* (London, 1938).

sufficient philosophical system, so did Aquinas. Again, Aquinas, no less than Bonaventure, looked on philosophical knowledge as demanding theological knowledge as its completion and on knowledge about God as subordinated, from a theological point of view, to the immediate vision of God. Further, Bonaventure's attacks on Aristotle are found mainly in writings which he composed when a form of heterodox or integral Aristotelianism[1] had become prominent in the Faculty of Arts at Paris, a phenomenon which was resisted by Aquinas as well as by Bonaventure. Van Steenberghen also maintained that the philosophy of St Bonaventure was not a special creation by the saint but rather an eclectic and Neoplatonizing Aristotelianism, subordinated to an Augustinian theology.

A certain amount of what Van Steenberghen has said seems to the present writer to be quite true. It is true, for example, that Aquinas maintained that if men in general were to come to a knowledge of God and if philosophers were to be preserved from mixing error with truth in their views of God, the light of revelation was morally necessary.[2] It is also true that criticism of Aristotle is much more marked in those writings of Bonaventure which fall within the period in which the goings-on in the Faculty of Arts at Paris excited opposition from the theologians. Bonaventure's critical remarks are not, however, confined to these writings. And in any case they cannot be discounted simply because they were written later than the Commentary on the *Sentences* and reflected Bonaventure's reactions to a particular situation. The fact of the matter is that in the field of what we might describe as transcendent metaphysics Bonaventure awarded the palm to Plato and Plotinus rather than to Aristotle, though he believed, of course, that the truths to which Plato and Plotinus approximated had been better grasped by Augustine, who enjoyed the light of Christian faith. Finally, to describe Bonaventure's philosophy as an eclectic and Neoplatonizing *Aristotelianism* seems inappropriate. If we consider Bonaventure's separate opinions, he was of course an eclectic. And the Aristotelian elements in his thought formed part of his eclecticism. But

---

[1] That is to say, the thought of Aristotle, or what was considered to be such, was expounded 'integrally', without any attempt to revise or change it in accordance with the demands of Christian theology. Aristotle was regarded, as Averroes regarded him, as the culmination of the development of human reason.
[2] That is to say, revelation was required if men were to be able to achieve the end for which they were created. For this demanded knowledge of God, a demand which the philosophical speculation of a few intellectuals could not fulfil.

his approach to philosophical reflection, with its marked 'interiority', is much more Augustinian than Aristotelian. And it cannot be counted as simply a matter of Christian theology or Christian spirituality. These factors were doubtless influential. But the point is that they influenced Bonaventure's thought within the philosophical area. To regard him as an incomplete Aristotelian is to fail to do him justice. His approach is not to everyone's taste. To some minds it may seem subjectivist and lacking in the spirit of 'scientific' philosophy. But it is an approach which has tended to recur, in various forms, in the history of philosophy. And it is certainly not a characteristically Aristotelian approach.

3

To turn to a very different type of man, the celebrated English Franciscan Roger Bacon (c. 1215-92). After studying arts at Oxford, Bacon went to Paris in 1236 or 1237. While at Paris, he lectured on the *Physics* and *Metaphysics* of Aristotle, a fact which presumably shows that the prohibitions were not taken very seriously by this time. He also compared a number of commentaries, some of which are lost, on Aristotle's treatises and on one or two works, such as the *Liber de causis*, which were wrongly attributed to Aristotle. Bacon was a great admirer of the Greek philosopher, though he was by no means such a pure Aristotelian as he liked to think himself.[1] He was not, however, an admirer of the Paris theologians, about whom he made caustic remarks. He found fault with them for their excursions into philosophy, for their ignorance of languages and of the sciences, and for the deference which they paid to people such as Alexander of Hales and Albert the Great. Bacon failed, however, to appreciate the work being done by the theological professors in the systematic development of their subject.

About the year 1247 Bacon returned to Oxford, entering the Franciscan order a few years later. At Oxford he gave himself to linguistic and scientific studies and composed his chief work, the *Opus maius* (*Greater Work*), supplemented by the *Opus minus* (*Lesser Work*) and the *Opus Tertium* (*Third Work*). He also wrote on mathematics and scientific subjects, besides composing Greek and Hebrew grammars and a philosophical compendium. For reasons which are not altogether

[1] Van Steenberghen characteristically describes Bacon's philosophy as a 'Neoplatonizing Aristotelianism' (*La philosophie au XIIIe siècle*, p. 150), a description which is doubtless apt within limits but will hardly do as a description of Bacon's thought in general.

clear[1] he was sentenced to imprisonment by Jerome of Ascoli, the Franciscan minister general, in 1277 or 1278. He was subjected to some sort of confinement, though we do not know for how long. He died in 1292, apparently at Oxford, while writing a theological compendium.

Bacon was a strange mixture. In spite of his attacks on the theologians, he was, in some ways, an extremely credulous man. He believed, for example, that God had revealed the secrets of Nature to the Jews, that their secret teaching had been transmitted, by way of the Chaldeans and Egyptians, to Aristotle, and that it could be recovered, given the requisite moral and mental qualities. Again, he inclined to the apocalyptic view expounded by Joachim of Fiore in the twelfth century and tried to prove that the coming of Antichrist was imminent. He was also interested in astrology and alchemy.[2] At the same time he was one of the precursors of empirical science and he did important work in optics, especially in concave lenses, besides foreseeing the possibility of the telescope and other inventions.

It would obviously be a mistake to think that Roger Bacon was the first person in the Middle Ages to take an interest in empirical science. A general background was formed by translation of Arabic scientific writings, the Arabs having themselves been stimulated by Greek works. Moreover, Bacon was strongly influenced by two men, Robert Grosseteste (c. 1168–1253) in England and Peter of Maricourt[3] whom he knew at Paris. Grosseteste, who was for a time chancellor of Oxford and, from 1235 until his death, bishop of Lincoln, was a friend of the Franciscans and was admired by Bacon for his insistence on the use of mathematics in physics, his emphasis on empirical observation and testing[4] and also for his speculations about the nature of light.[5] Peter of

---

[1] 'Suspected novelties' was the reason given. But Bacon had doubtless made a good many enemies by his habit of indulging in vehement invective.

[2] Bacon tried to dissociate astrology from determinism. Men's natural dispositions, he argues, can be affected by the heavenly bodies, as they are by climatic conditions; but it does not follow that all their actions are determined.

[3] Dates of birth and death are unknown. However, Peter took part in a siege in 1269.

[4] Grosseteste shows an awareness of the role of hypotheses in science and of the need for experimental testing of these hypotheses, when possible. As for mathematics he maintained that all local motion can be described in mathematical terms.

[5] Grosseteste maintained the metaphysics of light, according to which light is the basic corporeal form. He also believed that it is light which causes local motion and that its behaviour can be described geometrically. His idea that light is transmitted in pulses was accepted by Bacon and can be regarded as some sort of anticipation of the wave theory.

Maricourt, author of a *Letter on the Magnet*, was praised by Bacon in the *Opus Tertium* as being devoted to the experimental method in science. We are told, among other things, that Peter had been working at the production of a mirror which would produce combustion at a distance.[1]

In the sixth part of the *Opus maius* Bacon asserts that though reasoning may lead the mind to a correct conclusion, it is only experimental confirmation which removes all doubt. He is not thinking however only of sense-experience. There are two kinds of experience. In one kind man uses his senses, assisted by instruments and by the trustworthy evidence of witnesses. The other kind of experience is of spiritual realities and culminates in the higher mystical states. This type of experience is made possible by divine illumination.[2] In other words, experimental knowledge means, for Bacon, knowledge gained by experience, as opposed to knowledge gained simply by inference or reasoning.

The last part of the *Opus maius* deals with moral philosophy, which is said to stand on a higher level than mathematics or empirical science. Indeed, according to Bacon, all science should be ordered or directed towards moral philosophy. But this term is understood in a pretty broad sense. Bacon makes use of the writings of Greek, Roman and Islamic philosophers; but he goes on to treat not only of the reasons for accepting the Christian religion but also of man's incorporation into Christ. He was not an agnostic scientist but a medieval Franciscan who was interested in empirical science. And he could, of course, justifiably claim that in sharing this interest he was walking in the footsteps of Aristotle.

4

Any list of the more interesting Franciscan thinkers of the Middle Ages would certainly include the name of Raymond (or Ramón) Lull (*c.* 1232/5–1315). Born in Majorca, Lull underwent a religious conversion in about 1263 and resolved to devote himself to spreading Christianity in the Islamic world. By way of preparation he gave some nine years to the study of Arabic and philosophy.[3] Becoming a member of the third

[1] *Opus tertium*, Chapter 13.
[2] God, as illuminating the human mind, is identified by Bacon with Aristotle's active intellect.
[3] At that time there were a considerable number of Moslems on Lull's native island.

order of St Francis, he taught for a succession of short periods at Paris; and he made several expeditions to Moslem Africa. Tradition has it that he eventually died a martyr's death in north Africa; but doubt has been cast on this story.

Lull was an extremely profilic writer, the majority of his works being written in Catalan, though some were originally composed in Arabic. Most of the surviving writings have been preserved only in Latin translations. Besides being a poet, Lull wrote on logic, philosophy and theology. He dreamed not only of the reunification of Christendom itself but also of the unification of humanity through the Christian religion. And in *Blanquerna* he outlined a programme for a society of nations presided over by the pope. His sojourns at Paris prompted him to write against the errors of the Islamic philosopher Averroes and of the so-called 'Averrorists', such as Siger of Brabant, in the Faculty of Arts.

In theology, Lull wished to show the Moslems and Jews that Christian beliefs were not contrary to reason; and he spoke, in Anselmian fashion, of proving the articles of faith by necessary reasons. In philosophy he maintained the theory, originally derived from Ibn Gabirol, of universal hylomorphic composition in all creatures and defended such theses as the impossibility of creation from eternity and the primacy of the will over the intellect.[1] But it is not for the inclusion of traditional theories of this kind that Lull's thought is of interest. It is his logical studies and programmes which constitute the interesting element.

When in the twelfth century the Christian scholars' knowledge of Aristotle's *Categories* and *De Interpretatione* (the 'old logic') was supplemented by a knowledge of other books of the *Organon* (the 'new logic') particular attention was paid to the treatment of fallacies in the *De sophisticis elenchis*. The Aristotelian logic was, of course, cultivated in the universities. But in the course of the thirteenth century there arose in the Faculty of Arts what was described as 'modern logic' to distinguish it from the 'ancient logic', comprising both the 'old' and 'new' logics in the above mentioned senses. We shall have to return later on to the *logica moderna*. The point to be made here is that Lull's logical speculations, closely connected with metaphysical convictions

---

[1] Generally speaking, the Franciscans stressed the primacy of love over knowledge, and so of the will over the intellect. Aquinas took a different view. But it was, of course, a question of the comparative 'nobility' of the two faculties, not of attaching an exclusive value to one or the other.

and expressed in such works as *The Great Art* (*Ars magna*), *The Ultimate General Art* (*Ars generalis ultima*) and *The Tree of Knowledge* (*Arbor Scientiae*), stand rather apart from the general development of logic in the thirteenth century.

In Lull's opinion philosophy and the sciences presuppose and logically depend on certain basic categories or concepts. These are the absolute predicates (such as goodness), signifying the attributes which together constitute the nature of God and which are found in limited forms in creatures. And there are the relative predicates, signifying the different types of relations which obtain between creatures (such as difference and equality). These are also, for instance, certain basic questions. The first step in Lull's logic is thus to ascertain the basic concepts, which form a kind of alphabet of thought. The 'combinatory art' (*ars combinatoria*) can then be employed to construct the fundamental principles of all the sciences and so to manifest their unity. To facilitate such combination Lull suggests the use of symbolism.[1] And he goes on to describe mechanical devices, with concentric and rotating circles or discs, which would enable people to see the various possible combinations of the basic concepts.

It has been conjectured that in developing this line of thought Lull was influenced by Jewish Cabbalist writings. In any case his aim seems to have been, in great part, apologetic. That is to say he believed that his combinatory art would be of service in dialogue with Moslems and other non-Christians. It would show, for example, how all the sciences are unified in and depend on the predicates which signify the divine attributes. In other words, his aim seems to have been primarily expository and didactic, even if he does imply on occasion that the combinatory art could be used to discover new truths. When considering Lull himself we have to bear in mind his preoccupation with the conversion of the Moslem world.

If, however, we prescind from the connections between Lull's thought and his historical situation, we can hardly help being struck by the resemblance between his logical speculations and Leibniz's theories of an alphabet of human thought, of mathematical symbolism as providing a suitable language (a *charactistica universalis*), and of a combinatory art. And in point of fact Leibniz derived some stimulus from Lull. Further, though Leibniz was not preoccupied, in the way that Lull was, with the conversion of Moslems, he envisaged, at any rate for

---

[1] Lull used letters to stand for concepts.

a time, the possibility of his logical schemes being of service in the reunification of the Christian confessions. In general, we can find both with Lull in the thirteenth century and with Leibniz in the seventeenth century the ideal of universal harmony.

12

Albert the Great and Thomas Aquinas

I

THE first Dominican professors of theology at Paris were conservative in their views and reserved in their attitudes to Aristotle, though they certainly studied his writings and referred to him. A much more appreciative attitude was shown by St Albert the Great, known for his encyclopedic interests and learning as the 'universal doctor' (*Doctor universalis*).

Albert was born at Lauingen in Swabia. The date of his birth is customarily given as 1206 or 1207, though some have argued in favour of an earlier date. He studied for a short while at Bologna and Padua and then entered the Dominican order in 1223. After completing his noviceship and some further studies at Cologne, he seems to have taught in Germany and to have arrived at Paris in 1240 to study theology.[1] In 1242 he took his baccalaureate; and from 1245 to 1248 at any rate he was teaching theology. In 1248 his superiors sent him to Cologne to organize the Dominican house of studies where he had Thomas Aquinas among his pupils. From 1254 until 1257 he was superior of the German Dominican province, and from 1260–2 bishop of Ratisbon. He then seems to have lived mainly at Cologne, with visits to Rome and elsewhere, until his death in 1280.

In his early days at Paris Albert wrote successively a *Summa de creaturis* and a commentary on the *Sentences* of Peter Lombard, besides

[1] According to Roger Bacon, who thought that undue deference was accorded to Albert as a living authority, Albert never did a proper course of arts.

composing biblical commentaries. His paraphrases of a very large number of Aristotle's works seem to have been published subsequently to his sojourn at Paris.[1] So were his commentaries on Boethius, on the writings of the Pseudo-Dionysius and on the *Liber de Causis*. The date of his little work *On the Unity of the Intellect against Averroes* is disputed; but it cannot have been written before 1256. Albert's handbook of theology, the *Summa Theologiae*[2] belongs to the last decade of his life.

In the course of commenting on the writings of the Pseudo-Dionysius Albert gave the frequently quoted description of ignorant people who wished to attack philosophy in every way they could, 'like brute animals blaspheming what they do not know'.[3] When he turned his attention to philosophical studies, he tried to show that philosophy and the sciences are not in themselves hostile to or dangerous to the Christian faith; and in his paraphrases on Aristotle he undertook to explain the philosophy and science of Aristotle, often adding his personal opinions and additional information. It is often said that in his own philosophical thought Albert was by no means a thorough Aristotelian but mixed Aristotelian theories with ideas derived from Platonism, Neoplatonism and Islamic philosophy. That he maintained theories which were in fact of Neoplatonic origin is quite true. Thus he used the language at any rate of emanation, though he explained the theory in a manner consonant with the Christian theology of creation. Again, though he accepted Aristotle's theory of the soul as the form of the body, he tried to reconcile it with a Platonic–Augustinian view of the soul as a spiritual substance by distinguishing between the essence of the soul and its operational function as a life-giving form. It must be remembered, however, that Albert regarded Aristotle as the author of the *Liber de causis* and that he saw the Greek philosopher partly through the eyes of commentators such as Avicenna. In any case there can be no doubt about the fact that Albert tried to exhibit the value of philosophy and the sciences, of profane learning that is to say, to contemporaries who were often suspicious of such learning or even hostile to it. A real philosopher, in his opinion, should learn from both Plato and Aristotle. But Albert clearly looked on the

[1] The only disputed point is whether the paraphrases were begun at Paris.
[2] Some material may have been inserted in this work by another author.
[3] *On the Letters of the Blessed Dionysius the Areopagite*, Letter 7, No. 2. In the passage there is a reference to the Dominicans. But it is not clear whether Albert is referring to Dominicans as attacking philosophy or as not resisting the attackers.

latter as the chief master of profane or secular science. And though he certainly did not regard Aristotle as infallible and remarked that in matters of faith and morals one should listen to Augustine rather than to the philosopher when they contradict one another,[1] he believed that by and large a synthesis of the new learning, derived from Greek and Islamic sources, with Christianity was both possible and intellectually necessary.

Apart from the impetus which he gave to the development of Christian Aristotelianism, Albert is best known for his scientific work. The label 'scientist' is not perhaps very apt. For it suggests more than was in fact the case. For an adumbration of scientific method, for instance, in the thirteenth century we have to turn rather to Robert Grosseteste. Albert, however, had something of Aristotle's intense interest in empirical studies, and he insisted strongly on the need for observation. In his paraphrases of Aristotle's scientific writings he refers to personal experience and to the need for empirical verification and remarks that traditional ideas cannot be accepted if they conflict with experience. Moreover, he proposed some sensible hypotheses which were empirically testable, at any rate in principle, and he seems to have made some experiments in regard to animals. In any case, even if he did not add a great deal to existing scientific knowledge, his attitude of open-minded curiosity and his appeals to observation and experiment show him as being closer in spirit to Aristotle himself than were many later Aristotelians.

2

We have seen that for a few years Albert the Great had Thomas Aquinas as one of his pupils. Thomas was born at the end of 1224 or the beginning of 1225 at Roccasecca near Naples, his father being the Count of Aquino. After early education at the abbey of Monte Cassino he studied arts at the University of Naples from 1239 until 1243.[2] He entered the Dominican order in 1244, a step which so displeased his family that they kidnapped him and confined him for some months. Thomas may have gone to Paris in 1245 and have been a pupil for a time of Albert the Great. But in any case he was Albert's pupil in the Dominican house of studies at Cologne from 1248 until he went to Paris in 1252. After studying the Bible and then, from 1253 until 1256,

---

[1] Commentary on the *Sentences*, Bk. II, Dist. 13, C, Art. 2.
[2] One of his teachers was Peter of Ireland.

the *Sentences* of Peter Lombard, he obtained the licence to teach in 1256, though he was not officially admitted as a professor until 1257, along with St Bonaventure. During this first period of teaching at Paris Thomas wrote his commentary on the *Sentences*, two commentaries on Boethius, the *De ente et essentia* (*On Being and Essence*), the *De principiis naturae* (*On the Principles of Nature*) and a number of *Questions*, including the *De Veritate* (*On Truth*). He may also have begun work on the *Summa contra Gentiles* (*Summary* or *Manual against the Gentiles*).

In 1260 (probably) Thomas left Paris and passed some years in Italy, where he taught at various places, Orvieto, Rome and Viterbo. He wrote the *Summa contra Gentiles* (or finished it, if it was begun at Paris) and some Biblical commentaries, and began his famous *Summa Theologiae* (*Summary of Theology*). He also wrote the *De potentia* (*On Power*)[1] and started his series of commentaries on Aristotle's writings, being fortunate enough to find at Urban IV's court at Viterbo William of Moerbeke, author of fresh translations of Aristotle from the Greek text.

Returning to Paris at the beginning of 1269 Thomas took up again his professorial work in the university. He continued both his commentaries on Aristotle and his *Summa Theologiae*, wrote some more Biblical commentaries and was responsible for a number of important *Questions*, such as the *De Malo* (*On Evil*). Taking part in the controversy between the theologians and teachers in the Faculty of Arts, he wrote his *On the Unity of the Intellect against the Paris Averroists*.

In 1272 Thomas went to Naples to found a Dominican house of studies in the University. While there, he composed further commentaries on Aristotle and worked on the third part of the *Summa Theologiae*. Early in 1274 he set out for Lyons, to take part in the work of the council; but he had not got far on his journey before he fell gravely ill at the abbey of Fossanuova between Naples and Rome.

The titles of works mentioned above by no means constitute a complete list of Thomas's writings. It will be seen, however, that they include works on Scripture, theology and philosophy. Thomas was a professor of theology; but he was acutely aware of problems raised by the widening of the intellectual field through the translations of Greek, Jewish and Islamic writings. To say that he consequently attempted a synthesis of non-Christian thought and Christian belief is true in a

---

[1] The *Questions on Power* relate to the power of God rather than to power in general. It is a metaphysical and theological work, not a political treatise.

sense; but it can be misleading. If, for example, Thomas relied so heavily on Aristotle and made such use of him, the reason was that he believed that the philosophy of Aristotle was, in the main, true and that, because it was true, it provided a powerful instrument in the construction of a general Christian world-view. Whatever we may think of Aristotle's arguments in this or that field, we cannot understand Aquinas's attitude unless we appreciate the fact that he was not simply pursuing a policy of expediency. That is to say, he was not primarily concerned with so interpreting and adapting a philosophical system as to be able to reconcile it with Christian belief and so draw its sting. To be sure, in order to construct a coherent synthesis he had to do some rethinking. For example, one could hardly content oneself with simply juxtaposing the account of man's highest excellence and activity which is found in Aristotle's *Ethics* with a Christian idea of man and his activity. Thomas was, however, convinced that the teleological ethics of Aristotle was, in general, sound, and that the Greek philosopher's way of thinking provided a philosophical backbone or, if preferred, a philosophical substructure for a Christian ethics. He did indeed tend to interpret Aristotle in what, from a theologian's point of view, might be described as a benevolent manner. But if he thought that Aristotle was wrong on some topic he said so. The point is that for Aquinas Aristotle was 'the Philosopher', in the sense that Aristotelianism represented philosophical truth; and, believing that Christianity had nothing to lose but a lot to gain from truth deriving from any quarter, and especially from philosophy, he naturally tried not only to exhibit the coherence of philosophy with Christian belief but also to use the philosophy which he believed to be true in the systematic development of theology itself.

What has just been said stands in need of qualification. Aquinas is conceived, and rightly so, as the Christian theologian who made a much more thorough and a much wider use of Aristotle than his predecessors had done. It by no means follows, however, that his philosophical thought derived nothing from any other source. In point of fact there are a good many elements in his thought which originally came from other sources than Aristotle. A simple example is talk about the divine ideas, which obviously derives from Augustine, or, to go further back, from Neoplatonism. Again, Aquinas was certainly influenced not only by the writings of the Pseudo-Dionysius but also by Islamic philosophy and by the Jewish thinker Maimonides. He regarded Aristotle as 'the Philosopher' *par excellence*, but we can say that it was philosophy in general, as known to him of course, which he tried to rethink in a coherent system, not indeed as a purely self-sufficient philosophical system but rather as one linked in assignable ways with Christian belief.

The fact that Aquinas derived ideas and stimulus from a variety of sources tends to suggest both that he was an eclectic and that he was lacking in originality. For when we consider this or that particular doctrine or theory, it is very often possible to make claims such as 'this comes straight from Aristotle', 'this has already been said by Avicenna' or 'that is obviously a development of an argument used by Maimonides'. In other words, the more we know about Aristotle and about Islamic and Jewish philosophy, as also of course about previous Christian thought, the more we may be inclined to wonder what, if anything, is peculiar to Aquinas himself. In fact we may be led to wonder whether all the fuss made by Thomists about their hero's theory of the distinction between essence and existence does not represent a rather desperate way of finding something in his multitudinous pages which can be cited as an original idea.

This attitude, though doubtless annoying to devout Thomists, is perfectly understandable. But it is rather unfair to Aquinas. To his contemporaries he appeared as an innovator, partly because he treated problems in a fresh way and introduced new lines of argument, partly because on some matters he rejected traditional positions. He was not, however, a striver after originality, in the sense of one who is at all costs intent on saying something new. His originality lies rather in his patient sifting of diverse opinions to get at what seemed to him to be the truth and in his systematic welding together of positions through the use of wide-reaching philosophical principles and categories. He was an eclectic in the sense that he was open to stimulus and ideas from a variety of sources; but he was not an eclectic in the sense of one who adopts a number of different ideas from different philosophies and juxtaposes them. He had to rethink his material coherently and systematically; and in this rethinking he shows his power as a thinker.

Thomas Aquinas was a professor of theology; and he did not set out to construct a philosophical system. But he certainly distinguished between theology and philosophy. The distinction, as he sees it, is not simply one of subject-matter. To be sure, there are revealed truths (such as the Trinity) which cannot be proved by philosophy, though philosophical concepts can be used by the theologian in his attempt to state them. And there are philosophical truths which have not been revealed by God. But in regard to subject-matter, there is a certain, though limited, overlapping. For example, metaphysics proves the existence of God; and God obviously forms a theme for the theologian. But in 'sacred doctrine' the theologian starts with God, presupposing his existence as a matter of faith and dealing with God's self-revelation and redemptive activity, whereas the philosopher starts with the objects of sense-perception, the things of this world, and comes to knowledge of God only in so far as inference will take him. If we start with Christian faith and explore its content and implications, we are thinking as theologians. If we do not presuppose faith as a premise but rely simply on human reasoning, employing principles based on an ordinary experience, we are thinking as philosophers.

Inasmuch as Thomas himself was a Christian believer all his life and obviously did not suspend his faith when he pursued philosophical reflection, it may seem unrealistic on his part to make such a distinction. Was he not, we may ask, always the theologian? Thomas might, of course, reply that the possession of faith does not entail inability to reason objectively. Further, that he took his position seriously can be seen by considering what he has to say on the eternity of the world. He thought that Christian theology involved the belief that in point of fact the world had a beginning. But he also maintained that no philosopher had ever succeeded in proving that it could not have been created from eternity. And he criticized the arguments offered by Bonaventure and others to demonstrate that the world must have had a beginning. In other words, Aquinas argued that, as far as he could see, the question whether the world did or did not have a beginning could not be answered by the philosopher. For if we cannot show that something is impossible, we must assume its possibility. Of course, this thesis may seem a case of letting Aristotle down lightly, instead of claiming that his theory of the eternity of motion was an absurd notion, as some theologians claimed. However, as Aquinas believed that 'sacred doctrine' was able to answer the question of *fact*, he clearly did not regard the distinction between philosophy and theology as unreal.

It does not follow that Thomas leaves philosophy and theology unrelated. The easiest way, however, of seeing the relation, as Thomas conceives it, is by looking at the different sciences in the light of his convictions about man's supernatural end and vocation. He sees man as called to the attainment, by divine grace and by leading a life pleasing to God, to the direct or immediate vision of God in heaven. Attainment of this goal demands some knowledge of God and of his will for man. Some knowledge of God is attainable in philosophy, through human thought. Indeed, 'almost the whole of philosophy is directed towards the knowledge of God'.[1] That is to say, philosophical theology is the culminating point of philosophical reflection and presupposes other parts. Philosophy, however, is in any case a matter for a few people, whereas all men are called to the knowledge of God. Moreover, philosophical knowledge of God, though genuine, is extremely limited; and it does not extend to God's self-revelation in Christ. Revelation therefore is morally necessary, if men in general are to attain the goal for which they were created. And theology is the science which deals with God's self-revelation in and through Christ. As for human conduct, reason can indeed apprehend basic ethical principles. Philosophical ethics, however, if taken completely by itself, knows nothing of man's supernatural end and of the life in Christ by which it is to be attained. Though therefore it is valid in itself, in that it demonstrates the rational bases of the moral life, it is limited in a variety of ways and needs to be subsumed in Christian ethics. Finally, knowledge *about* God, whether philosophical or theological, is subordinate and teleologically orientated to the experimental knowledge of God, knowledge by acquaintance, which is attainable, imperfectly in mystical states, perfectly in the vision of God in heaven.

This general scheme is not, of course, peculiar to Aquinas. It is common to theologians and can be found, for example, in Bonaventure. With Aquinas, however, we find a much greater appreciation than can be found among many theologians both of the value of philosophical and scientific studies and of the fact that they have their own proper methods or procedures, in which appeals to authority have no decisive weight. Theology, 'sacred doctrine', presupposes and appeals to the Scriptures and to conciliar definitions; but in philosophy an appeal to authority constitutes the very weakest of arguments.[2]

The medievals wrote a good deal about knowledge from the psychological point of view; but they were not tormented by such questions as whether or not we can know anything at all. For Aquinas it was obvious that we know some truths and that we know that we know them. In the context of a discussion of the soul's knowledge of itself he remarks that 'nobody perceives that he understands except through the fact that he understands something, for to understand something is

prior to understanding that one understands'.[1] Similarly it is by knowing something that we know that we know. And it is by knowing that
we know something that we are able to assert the mind's capacity to
know. It would be, for Aquinas, a mistake to suppose that we could
profitably *begin* by asking whether we are capable of knowing anything
at all. To be sure, we may think that we know something when we do
not. Erroneous judgement is clearly possible. But there are ways of
correcting error. And the whole process of recognizing and correcting
erroneous judgements implies that we can and do apprehend true
propositions and know that we do so.

The mind's capacity for knowledge does not, of course, entail the
conclusion that it starts its life with a stock of innate ideas or of inborn
knowledge. For Aquinas the mind is initially a capacity for knowing;
and, as far as the natural order of things is concerned at any rate, it
cannot come to know anything except through or in dependence on
experience, the primary form of experience being sense-experience or
sense-perception. This does not mean that the mind is a passive
recipient of sense-impressions. For example, once the mind has had
experience of concrete causal relations in the world about it and has
formed the abstract ideas of cause, of thing and of beginning to be, it
sees a connection between a thing's coming to be and its being caused.
It can thus come to enunciate universally and necessarily true propositions, such as that everything which comes into being does so through
the agency of a cause external to itself. And it is then able to transcend
the visible world, in the sense that is to say, that it can relate the objects
of sense-experience to that which transcends sense-experience. Even
so, however, our rational knowledge 'can extend only so far as it can be
brought by (reflection on) the things of sense'.[2] And 'when we understand something about incorporeal things, we have to have recourse to
the images of bodies'.[3] Although, Thomas insists, the primary objects
of human knowledge are material things, the mind is not limited to
them in its potential field of knowledge. At the same time by its own
resources it can know the existence of purely spiritual beings only in
so far as material things reveal themselves to the active and reflective
mind as dependent on that which transcends them. Further, in thinking
or conceiving spiritual beings the mind, according to Aquinas, cannot
help employing images which depend on our life of sense-perception.

[1] *De veritate*, 10, 8.
[2] *Summa Theologiae*, Pt 1, Qu. 12, Art. 12.
[3] Ibid., Pt 1, Qu. 84, Art. 7, Reply 3.

The reason for this is the status of the rational soul of man as 'form' of the body. The human soul is by its nature the life-giving principle in the organism; and its thought and knowledge are coloured, as it were, by this fact.

In view of the emphasis on the dependence of human knowledge on sense-perception it is natural that Thomas should regard the study of physics or natural philosophy as preceding the study of metaphysics. For metaphysics culminates in the inferential knowledge of what is further removed from sense-perception. The natural order, that is to say, is to study bodies in motion before one goes on to inquire into the ultimate cause of bodies in motion or of the world of becoming. Logic, however, is presupposed by philosophy, and natural philosophy presupposes a study of mathematics. To what extent Thomas expects the philosopher to be acquainted with the science of the time is difficult to say. He did not expect the philosopher to be learned in medicine. But medicine was not considered as part of philosophy, whereas the general principles of astronomy fell under the heading of physics or natural philosophy. It is relevant, however, to mention the fact that while Thomas thought that there were propositions which must be true of corporeal things and would count as philosophical principles, he allowed for empirical hypotheses which 'save the appearances' but which are not necessarily true on this account, as the phenomena might be equally well explained on some other hypothesis. He applies this idea to, for example, the Ptolemaic theory of epicycles and Aristotle's theory of homocentric spheres.[1] In other words, though it would be an anachronism to look to Aquinas for any clear distinction between philosophy and the sciences as we conceive them today, he supplies some material for the making of a distinction.

In Thomas's vision of the world all finite things, whether corporeal or spiritual, exemplify the basic distinction between essence and existence. In an early work he remarks that 'I can understand what a man or a phoenix is and yet not know whether they exist in nature'.[2] If the distinction is expressed in this way, it may seem clear enough. A child might learn the meanings of the terms 'whale' and 'dinosaur' without knowing that there are whales but that, so far as we are aware, there are no dinosaurs.[3] In other words, from the concept of a possible

[1] Cf. *Summa Theologiae*, Pt 1, Qu. 32, Art. 1, Reply 2 and *De caelo et mundo*, Bk II, Chapter 12, Lecture 17.
[2] *De ente et essentia*, 5.
[3] I am assuming, of course, that the meaning of 'dinosaur' is not so defined as to

kind of finite thing we cannot infer that the concept is exemplified or instantiated. Though, however, this line of thought may serve as a way of approaching Aquinas's thesis, the distinction associated with his name is one between two inseparable but distinguishable metaphysical constituents or components of a finite substance. In Tom Smith, an actual human being, we can distinguish between what he is, his human nature and his existence. Al-Fārābī, for instance, had spoken of existence as an 'accident'. But Aquinas is careful to avoid the absurdity of claiming that existence is an accident occurring in an already 'existing' essence.[1] When a thing comes into being, it comes into being in regard to both essence and existence. The one is not temporarily prior to the other. But it is through the act of existing that the essence has being.

Talk about essence and existence admittedly gives rise to all sorts of problems. The main point, however, is that, for Aquinas, no finite thing exists necessarily in virtue of its essence. Every existential proposition, the subject of which is a finite thing, is a contingent proposition. It is only in God that essence and existence are identical. Of God alone is it true to say that he cannot not exist. All finite things are distinct from God through their existential instability.

The essence–existence distinction is a basic form of the potentiality–act relation which, for Aquinas, is found in all finite things.[2] Any finite thing is necessarily something, but it can change. A material thing is capable of changing substantially. An animal, for instance, can die, disintegrate and become a multitude of substances. An angel cannot change substantially; but it has the potentiality of, say, eliciting acts of love. It is only that which is pure act, without any limitation, which is changeless and undergoes no change or becoming. This is God.

A relation which is found only in corporeal or bodily substances is that between matter and form, matter in this sense being pure potentiality, form being the act which makes a substance the kind of thing which it is. Matter in itself, as pure potentiality, cannot exist by itself. 'Matter

---

include the notion of being extinct. For if this notion is included, the statement that there are no dinosaurs becomes analytically true.

[1] If it is asked whether Aquinas regards existence as a perfection, a distinction has to be made. It is not a perfection in the same sense in which being wise, for example, is a perfection. For Peter could not be wise unless he exists. But as the foundation of all other perfections, the act of existence is described by Aquinas as 'the perfection of all perfections' (De potentia, 7, 2, Reply 9).

[2] That is to say, essence can be regarded as potentiality in relation to the act of existence.

cannot be said to be; it is the substance itself which exists.'[1] At the same time Aquinas regards matter in this sense as having some 'demand' for quantity, for being, so to speak, quantified.[2] He cannot, therefore, accept the theory, derived from Ibn Gabirol and adopted, for example, by Bonaventure, of hylomorphic composition in purely spiritual finite substances. Angels, according to Aquinas, are pure forms without any so-called spiritual matter. Further, as Aquinas accepts the Aristotelian theory of matter as the principle of individuation within a species, he has to hold that each angel constitutes a species by itself. That is to say, there are as many angelic species as there are angels.

Obviously we have here a hierarchic conception of the universe, ranging, if one may so express it, from matter as pure potentiality at the bottom of the scale up to God, who is pure act, at the top.[3] But it is not a static conception of the universe. For Thomas looks on all finite things or substances as tending naturally to the actualization of their potentialities.[4] Each substance is a centre of activity, the principle of activity being the thing's substantial form, the immanent constitutive principle which makes a thing the kind of thing that it is and determines it to act in specified ways. For example, in the case of a beech tree it is its substantial form which makes it this particular kind of living organism and determines it to act as a totality in certain ways.

Like Aristotle before him, Aquinas uses the word 'soul' (anima, Aristotle's psyche) in a very broad sense, as meaning, that is to say, 'the first principle of life in living things about us'.[5] In this sense of the word, the beech tree has a soul, its substantial form. But its functions are obviously very limited. Animals possess sensitive souls, while human beings possess rational souls. This does not mean, however, that man has three souls, one vegetative, one sensitive and one rational. For Aquinas, there is in man only one soul, one substantial form,

---

[1] Summa contra Gentiles, Bk II, Chapter 54.

[2] If 'first matter' is regarded as pure potentiality, it is difficult to see how it can have any intrinsic relation to or demand for quantity.

[3] This is, it is true, an unfortunate way of putting things. For Thomas looks on God as transcendent and infinite, not as simply the first member of a graded hierarchy. However, he certainly speaks of God as the first or supreme unmoved mover. And Duns Scotus was to object that this Aristotelian concept tended to make God the highest member of a hierarchy, bringing him within the world.

[4] Considered precisely as definable, substance is 'essence', while considered as active, it is 'nature'. But these technicalities are not always observed.

[5] Summa Theologiae, Pt 1, Qu. 75, Art. 1.

which is the principle of life, reproduction, sensation, all intellectual activities and free choice. It is the one soul of man which performs the functions of Aristotle's active and potential intellects, and which is the form of the body. Indeed, it is the soul which makes the body a human body. At death the body disintegrates and ceases to be a unified living organism.

As Thomas accepts the Aristotelian theory of the soul as the form of the body, he naturally rejects any account of the relation between them which is based on the analogy of a pilot's relation to his ship or an agent's relation to the instrument which he employs. Soul and body constitute one living, sensing, feeling, desiring, willing and thinking organism. And the natural conclusion might well seem to be that the human soul, no less than other kinds of soul, perishes when the organism dies. Aquinas, however, wishes to combine a psychology based on Aristotle with belief in personal immortality. Thus he argues that some of the activities of the human soul transcend the power of matter, that this fact reveals the spiritual nature of the human soul, and that therefore the soul does not perish when the organism dies. This may appear to constitute an attempt to have things both ways at once, to insist, that is to say, that the human being is one substance, not two, and yet at the same time to maintain a position which implies that the soul is a substance in its own right. Thomas does, however, take his theory of the soul as the form of the body seriously enough to argue that the soul, when separated from the body, is not, properly speaking, a human person and that it is not in its natural state, inasmuch as it is, by its nature, the form of a body. As he himself explicitly admits, 'the immortality of souls seems then to demand the future resurrection of bodies'.[1] That is to say, resurrection seems to be demanded if we presuppose a universe in which human souls will not be left in a state which is contrary to their natures.

From the dynamic point of view man, like all other living things, strives after the actualization of his potentialities. Aquinas follows Aristotle in maintaining that by his nature man seeks 'happiness' (*beatitudo*). And this may seem to be a different point of view from saying that man strives to actualize the potentialities of his nature. But Aquinas thinks of man's potentialities as fully actualized only in the possession of a final good. 'Beatitude' or happiness, taken objectively, means that good the possession of which actualizes a man's potentialities, rendering him happy or satisfied. Taken in a subjective sense, it

[1] *Summa contra Gentiles*, Bk IV, Chapter 79.

means basically the activity of enjoying the possession of the good which perfects man's potentialities.

For Aquinas, as a Christian, man's supreme or final good is the possession of God, the vision of God in heaven. It by no means follows, however, that everyone understands this. People can form different ideas of what constitutes the final good of man. Moreover, even if someone does believe that the possession of God is his final end, he does not see God in such a way that his will is compelled to seek him consciously and deliberately. Again, God can appear to the mind as repugnant, from certain points of view, as prohibiting certain acts, for example, which appear attractive. Though, therefore, all men can be said, interpretatively, to be seeking God, this does not prevent them from fixing their conscious desires elsewhere. In other words, even though the possession of God is in fact man's final good, he is free to pursue other aims in life, pleasure, for instance, or power.

Given this teleological ethic, Aquinas naturally holds that good actions are those which are compatible with man's attainment of his final end, bad actions those which are incompatible with this attainment.[1] Morally obligatory acts are a subdivision of morally good acts. That is to say, an action is obligatory only when not to do it or to do something else would be morally bad. As with Aristotle, and indeed with every teleological system of ethics, the concept of the good is primary. In Kantian language, the moral imperative becomes an assertoric hypothetical imperative, commanding the taking of the means to attain a good which is necessarily willed and prohibiting the performance of actions incompatible with the attainment of this good.[2] We cannot discuss here the merits and demerits of a teleological interpretation of ethics. But it is important to notice that by taking over the Aristotelian ethics as the foundation for a Christian ethical point of view Aquinas is asserting the possibility of an ethical system based on rational reflection. If he relies heavily on Aristotle, this is because, in his view, the Greek philosopher makes sense of man's moral life. Aquinas has, of course, to interpret Aristotle in such a way as to leave philosophical ethics open to a Christian supernatural outlook. At the

[1] Aquinas is not, of course, thinking only of actions considered exteriorily or 'materially'. One might, for instance, give a poor man a sum of money with a bad intention. A morally good 'human act' demands the fulfilment of certain conditions which include intention.

[2] It is not a case of the technical imperative or imperative of skill, such as 'if you wish to be a successful burglar, wear gloves'. Rather it is a case of 'you necessarily seek X; therefore you ought to do a and not do b'.

same time he recognizes the existence of an ethics which is developed through reflection on human nature and which is, in principle at any rate,[1] knowable by the non-Christian philosopher.

As has already been noted, Aquinas looks on man as striving to actualize his potentialities. Man has certain basic tendencies or inclinations, grounded in his nature. For example, as a living organism man naturally strives to preserve himself in life, while as a rational being he has the capacity for apprehending truth. Reflecting on such basic tendencies the reason can promulgate such precepts as 'life is to be preserved' and 'truth should be sought after'. Most people, of course, do not explicitly formulate such precepts to themselves. But they can be formulated and used as premises in the deduction of more particular precepts. The totality of such precepts is the 'natural law'.

The concept of a natural moral law has given rise to a considerable amount of discussion, into which we cannot enter here. It is worth remarking, however, that such discussion can hardly be profitable unless there is agreement about what is being discussed. As far as Aquinas is concerned, it should be clear that the term 'natural law', as used in the present context, has not got the same sense as 'law of nature' when the law of gravitation, for example, is described as a law of nature or a natural law. If we talk about irrational things, such as stones, obeying a natural law, the word 'law', Thomas insists, is used analogically. For he regards law as a rule conceived by reason and promulgated with a view to the common good. And it hardly needs saying that stones neither promulgate any law to themselves nor recognize and consciously obey any law promulgated by a lawgiver. They can be described analogically as fulfilling laws of nature; but the ethical natural law is the totality of moral precepts promulgated by the human reason as a result of reflection on the nature of man in society.

According to Aquinas the natural law is a 'participation of the eternal law in a rational creature'.[2] To speak anthropomorphically, God sees eternally in human nature the activities which constitute its objective development or unfolding and the acts which are incompatible with this development. When the human reason promulgates to itself the natural law, it participates in God's eternal law, in the divine plan for

---

[1] Aquinas thought that though certain very broad ethical precepts can easily be recognized by all, there is room for doubt and ignorance in regard to more concrete and particular precepts. Hence the moral need for revelation, if men in general are to live as they ought.

[2] *Summa Theologiae*, Pt 1 of Pt 2 (1a 11ae), Qu. 91, Art. 2.

human beings, a plan which is not arbitrarily determined by the divine will but logically presupposes God's vision of himself as imitable in a certain way in creation. If the moral law depended simply on God's arbitrary choice, it could be known only by revelation. As, however, the divine will for man logically presupposes the idea of human nature, it can be known by the human reason, even without any explicit thought of God. That is to say, it can in principle be recognized by the human reason, in so far as it presupposes simply the idea of human nature and does not involve God's free vocation of man to a super-natural end. In spite, therefore, of the relation which Thomas asserts between the natural law and the eternal divine law or plan, there is still room for a philosophical ethics. It is only later in the Middle Ages that a theological authoritarianism in ethics comes to the fore.

As for the relation between the natural moral law and the positive law of the State, Thomas argued, as one would expect, that legislation must be compatible with the natural moral law. That is to say, if a given law is incompatible with the natural moral law, 'it will not be law but a perversion of law'.[1] Such laws should not be obeyed, not at any rate if they contradict the moral law.[2] The relation between the positive law of the State and the moral law is not, however, adequately described by saying that the former must be compatible with the latter. For Thomas looks on positive law as having the function of clearly defining the natural law and providing the temporal sanctions which are otherwise lacking. For example, if we assume that there is a natural right to own property and that it is wrong to violate another's right, what constitutes stealing needs to be clearly defined by positive law, and penalties for stealing have to be determined. It does not necessarily follow, however, that every kind of infringement of the moral law should be prohibited and punished by the State. For the legislator should have in view the common good. And the common good is not always best served by legal enactments. Though, therefore, Thomas clearly envisages a much closer relationship between ethics and positive legislation than many people would favour today, it does not follow from his position that every moral precept must be made the

[1] Ibid., Qu., 95, Art. 2.
[2] There may be laws which, basically, do not contradict the moral law but possess some feature which makes them unjust. Taxation, for example, is not in itself contrary to the moral law, but it can be unjust. In this case the citizens affected are not bound in conscience to obey the relevant law of the State, unless the common good demands it.

subject of legislation by the State. In his view the interest of the common good constitutes the criterion. It would thus be open to Aquinas, if he lived in a pluralist society, to accept a more liberal view of the extent to which a Christian could reasonably demand that his moral convictions should be reflected in the law of the State.

Thomas's Christian adaptation of the Aristotelian ethics, according to which man attains his ultimate end or final good in the vision of God in heaven, obviously presupposes a theistic interpretation of reality. The question arises therefore whether, in Thomas's view, philosophy is able to prove the existence of God. Indeed, the question whether God's existence can be demonstrated is one of the first questions raised in both *Summas*.[1] When treating of this matter Thomas obviously writes as a Christian believer, or as one whose world-vision is theocentric. That is to say, he does not suspend his personal belief while reflecting on the evidence for the existence of God and then take it up again as a result of his proofs. It by no means follows, however, that he does not regard his arguments as genuine proofs and as sufficient to convince an open-minded and well-disposed atheist or agnostic. It is indeed open to anyone to say that, as far as he is concerned, Thomas's proofs of the existence of God are simply illustrations of ways in which a religious believer can see the world. But it would be unhistorical to ascribe this view of the matter to Thomas himself.

Thomas rejects the Anselmian argument from the concept of God as absolute perfection to God's existence, on the ground that it involves an illicit transition from the conceptual to the existential order. Inasmuch as he maintains that in God essence and existence are identical, it may seem that this should be for him the one case in which the transition is not illicit. His point, however, is that man in this life does not enjoy that insight into the divine essence which would be required from the proposition 'God exists' to be for him an analytic or self-evidently true proposition. Man can come to know by philosophical reasoning which takes the existence of the finite things given in experience as its point of departure that there is in fact a being in which

[1] If we follow Thomas's order of treatment in the *Summas*, the proofs of the existence of God should obviously be considered at an early stage. His ethics, for instance, as distinct from mere exposition of Aristotle's ethics, clearly presupposes the existence of God. At the same time the part of metaphysics which treats of God presupposes a number of general metaphysical principles and concepts, and Thomas thinks of the mind of the philosopher as moving from the material world to spiritual reality, and from physics or natural philosophy to metaphysics. Cf. *In Boethium de Trinitate*, 5, 1.

essence and existence are identical. We can say, therefore, that the proposition 'God exists' is 'in itself' analytically or self-evidently true. But it is not so 'for us'.[1]

It has been argued that Aquinas does not do justice to Anselm's argument. We cannot, however, devote further time to this theme. Whether justifiably or not, Aquinas refuses to accept the argument. Instead he starts with what he believes to be empirical facts and argues that they require a cause which explains them. In the case of the first three 'Ways'[2] most people would not find any difficulty in admitting that what Aquinas believes to be empirical facts are empirical facts. It is evident that there are things which 'move' or change. It is also evident enough that some things act on other things, and that there are things which come into being and pass away. The statements that we find in things objective degrees of perfection and that there are natural bodies which act 'for an end'[3] obviously cause more difficulty. But, by and large, it can hardly be denied that Aquinas starts with his feet on the ground. Difficulty arises in regard to the processes of reasoning rather than in regard to the empirical points of departure.

In the first proof Aquinas argues from the existence of things which are 'moved'[4] to the existence of a supreme 'unmoved mover'; in the second from the existence of an order or hierarchy of efficient causes to the existence of an ultimate uncaused cause; in the third from the existence of things which are capable of coming into being and passing away ('possible' things) to the existence of an absolutely necessary being; in the fourth from the existence of degrees of perfection in finite things to the existence of a being which is the cause of all finite perfections; and in the fifth from final causality in the corporeal world to the existence of a mind which is responsible for finality and order in

[1] Duns Scotus was later to object that a proposition is either analytic or not analytic, and that the number of people who see or do not see that a given proposition is analytic is irrelevant from the logical point of view.

[2] The 'Five Ways' are succinctly expressed in the *Summa Theologiae*, Pt 1, Qu. 2, Art. 3. In the *Summa Contra Gentiles* (Bk I, Chapter 13) Aquinas gives versions of the first, second, fourth and fifth ways, the first being developed at greater length than in the *Summa Theologiae*.

[3] Thomas does not believe, of course, that natural bodies act deliberately with a view to an end. His thesis is rather that they do in fact act in such a way as to produce a relatively stable and ordered world, and that this demands an intelligent agent which is external to the visible world.

[4] It is as well to remind the reader that though local motion is included, 'movement' has a much broader sense for Aquinas, comprising all reduction of potentiality to act.

the world. The arguments were by no means entirely new. Nor did Aquinas think that they were. Indeed, some writers have maintained that when he says that the existence of God is proved in five ways, he means that he has found in the writings of philosophers and theologians five lines of argument which he can himself accept and restate. Others have agreed that Aquinas means to claim more, namely that there are five classes, and five classes only, of empirical facts which form points of departure for *a posteriori* proofs [1] of God's existence. However this may be, the precise number does not seem to be of any great importance. The main point is that according to Aquinas the world reveals itself to the reflective mind as dependent on an ultimate reality which he calls 'God'.

In several of the proofs Aquinas argues that it is not possible to proceed to infinity. As has already been remarked, he is referring, for example, to a hierarchy of causes acting here and now, as, for instance, the pen or pencil moving over the paper depends here and now on the writer, while the existence of the writer depends here and now on the presence of air, and so on. The argument, in this case, is that unless there is a supreme cause which is itself uncaused, there is no explanation of the existence and activity of any subordinate cause. It is not, of course, the intention of the present writer to suggest that the idea of a hierarchy of causes, which was common enough in Hellenistic, Islamic and medieval philosophy and astronomy, seems as natural now as it did in the thirteenth century. The point is rather that in discussion of the Five Ways we should not complicate matters by attributing to Aquinas a thesis which he did not in fact hold, namely that it was clearly impossible for there to be a series stretching back indefinitely into the past.

There are indeed plenty of other problems which arise in connection with the Five Ways.[2] Instead, however, of attempting to discuss them

[1] This term refers to an argument for God's existence which proceeds not from the essence or definition of God to his existence but from existing facts of experience to a cause which transcends them. To say that an *a posteriori* proof proceeds from effect to cause is true in a sense; but it can be misleading. For what such a proof purports to do is to show that the 'effects' *are* effects.

[2] There are, for example, problems in regard to the use made of the idea of causation and in regard to the term 'necessary being'. Then there is the general question whether the proofs, or most of them at any rate, do not tacitly presuppose that the world is intelligible, when to be intelligible means precisely to be explicable in terms of one ultimate explanation. As Aquinas will obviously not be satisfied until he has arrived at one ultimate ontological explanation, does he not tacitly

in what would be inevitably an extremely inadequate manner, it is preferable to draw attention to the fact that Thomas treats of the existence of God (the question *Utrum Deus sit*) before proceeding to discuss the divine nature and attributes (the question *quid Deus sit*). This is the traditional procedure; and to most people it doubtless seems to be the natural one. But in modern philosophy it has been urged that clarification of the concept of God is the primary task. For we cannot profitably discuss the question whether there is an X, unless we first know what X signifies and what we are talking about. In other words, the problem of meaning should be considered before the existential question. For if analysis of the concept of God revealed that the concept was self-contradictory, it would be as much a waste of time to discuss the existence of God as it would be to discuss the question whether there is a round square. If, however, the concept of God proves to be logically viable, we can then inquire into the evidence for the concept being instantiated.

It is clear that a case can be made out on behalf of this contention, advanced mainly by philosophers of the so-called 'linguistic analysis' or 'logical analysis' current of thought. How Aquinas would react to it, it is impossible to say. It should be remembered, however, that Aquinas does not assume that everyone has the same idea of the divine. When referring to Anselm's argument (though without mentioning its author's name) he makes the point that it is not everyone who understands the term 'God' in the way in which Anselm understands it. Aquinas does indeed end each of his proofs by some such phrase as 'and all call this *God*'. But he has been arguing that various aspects of the world or sets of empirical facts require an ultimate ontological explanatory cause. And in each case he takes it that the conclusion of the argument relates to what Christian theologians call 'God', when considered in relation to the facts which constitute the point of departure. As already remarked, we cannot be certain what Aquinas would say if he was to be faced by the contention referred to above. Given, however, his view that we know of the divine nature what it is not rather than what it is, it seems essential for him to have the point of anchorage provided by arguments which cumulatively show, or purport to show, that finite things depend on a being which transcends

---

assume that there *must* be one? If so, can the assumption be justified philosophically? Discussion of this problem seems to be a more important task than that of refurbishing the proofs, cutting out references to outdated scientific ideas, and so on.

them. On the whole, therefore, it seems probable that Aquinas would maintain the primacy of the problem of reference, and that there is not much point in discussing how we ought to think of God, unless we are first assured that there is a being which can reasonably be described as divine.

When treating of God's attributes, of the ways in which we ought to think of the divine reality, Thomas remains convinced of the fact that the divine essence in itself transcends the grasp of the human mind. He therefore employs the traditional negative way or approach. He argues, for example, that the supreme cause, absolutely necessary being and so on cannot be finite or mutable. We express this by employing what may seem to be positive terms, 'infinite' and 'immutable'. But they are equivalent to not-finite and not-mutable. To be sure, the divine infinity in itself is a positive reality. But we do not apprehend it in itself. We simply see that finitude cannot be legitimately predicated of God.

An exclusive adherence, however, to the negative approach would seem to lead in the direction of agnosticism.[1] So Aquinas employs also the affirmative way, attributing to God perfections which, in his opinion, are not intrinsically bound up with corporeality or with finitude. Wisdom is an example. But here a major difficulty arises. For according to Thomas's own account of human knowledge we derive an idea of wisdom through experience of human wisdom. If we attribute this to God, do we not turn God into a kind of superman? If, however, we attribute wisdom to God in an entirely different sense from that in which it is attributed to human beings, and if at the same time the divine nature transcends our experience, it seems to follow that the term 'wise', when predicated of God, has no assignable meaning. To meet this sort of difficulty Aquinas insists that such terms as 'wise', when predicated of God, are used neither univocally nor equivocally but analogically.

The word 'analogy', however, does not constitute a magic wand, the waving of which is sufficient to clear up all outstanding problems. For it is always possible to ask, 'Yes, but what does this term mean when it is used analogically?' Thomas makes a gallant attempt to cope by distinguishing between 'mode of signification' and 'that which is signified' (reference). If we consider terms such as 'wise', 'as regards the mode of signification, they are not properly predicated of God. For they have a

[1] 'Unless the human intellect knew something positively about God, it could not deny anything of him': *De potentia*, 7, 5.

mode of signification which belongs to creatures.'[1] That is to say, we cannot help conceiving wisdom in terms of our experience of human wisdom. And human wisdom cannot be predicated of God. But the term is used to signify something in God, the divine wisdom. And this is a positive reality, identical with the divine essence. The fact remains, however, that we cannot say what the divine essence is in itself. So it is hardly surprising if Thomas asserts roundly that 'we cannot understand of God what he is: but (we understand of him) what he is not and how other things are related to him'.[2]

Thomas certainly makes a contribution to discussion of language about God. But unless we look on use of the word 'analogy' as solving all problems, it can hardly be claimed that he left us with no problems to discuss. Some theologians seem to think that the trouble with Thomas is that he persists in introducing metaphysics, and that if we would only keep to biblical language and concepts, everything would be simple. But this is patently not the case. For problems certainly arise in regard to biblical talk about God. It does not necessarily follow, of course, that they have to be solved in terms of theories advanced by Thomas Aquinas. But they at any rate require philosophical reflection, or reflection which will inevitably involve, or at least tacitly assume, a metaphysics of some sort.[3] The discussion of religious language continues.

In 1277, three years after Thomas's death, a large number of propositions, derived from a variety of sources, were condemned by the bishop of Paris, Stephen Tempier. The condemnation was aimed in large measure at teachers in the Faculty of Arts in Paris; and further reference will be made to it in the next chapter. The point which is relevant here is that some propositions which had been held by Thomas were included in the condemnation, though his name was not mentioned. An example was the Aristotelian theory of matter as the principle of individuation. Very shortly afterwards, in the same year, the Dominican Robert Kilwardby, archbishop of Canterbury, visited Oxford and censured a number of propositions which included Thomas's theory of the unicity of the substantial form in any sub-

[1] *Summa theologiae*, Pt 1, Qu. 13, Art. 3.
[2] *Summa contra Gentiles*, Bk I, Chapter 30
[3] Even if it is claimed that talk about God consists of a set of stories, for which no truth-claims need be made but which form a psychological background for and stimulus to a life of Christian love, it will be found that the reasons for adopting such a thesis presuppose an implicit metaphysics, in the sense of a theory of being.

stance.[1] In 1284 Kilwardby's successor in the see of Canterbury, John Peckham (or Pecham), followed his predecessor's example, describing the offending propositions as heretical.

Apart from their general significance, which will be briefly discussed in the next chapter, the condemnations are of interest as showing that to the more conservatively minded theologians Thomas appeared as an innovator, and a dangerous one at that. As one would expect, however, hostile attack diminished after Thomas's canonization in 1323. And meanwhile the Dominican order had, in general, rallied to Thomas's defence and adopted him as their official Doctor. But though in the fourteenth century Thomism was regarded as a highly respectable form of the 'ancient way' (via antiqua), as distinct from the 'modern way' associated with Ockham and his followers, it never enjoyed in the Middle Ages that position in the Catholic Church which was accorded it by the encyclical Aeterni Partis issued in 1879 by Pope Leo XIII and by subsequent documents such as the code of canon law which came into force in 1918.[2]

The position accorded in the Catholic Church to the teaching of Aquinas has naturally produced in recent years a notable degree of revulsion among students in Catholic educational institutions. One can only hope that this will be succeeded not by a return to the previous attitude but by a genuine appreciation both of the qualities of Thomas himself and of the challenge which he represents to develop, as far as this is possible in the modern world, an open-minded but overall Christian vision and interpretation of reality as it is known today. We cannot return to the Middle Ages. But leading medieval thinkers such as Aquinas can be the source of creative stimulus and inspiration. Literal-minded though well-meaning discipleship misses the point and converts a creative thinker into a hindrance to original reflection.

[1] It appears that the theories of Aquinas were making some headway among the younger members of the Dominican house of studies at Oxford, of which Kilwardby had once been in charge. As for the particular theory mentioned above, one reason why the conservatives objected to it was that, in their opinion, if the soul of Christ was the one substantial form of Christ's body and there was no 'form of corporeity', it would logically follow that between Christ's death and resurrection this body was not his body at all. Further, it was thought that on Thomas's theory the veneration of the bodies and relics of saints could not be justified.
[2] Canon 1366, Section 2.

13

Aristotelianism and the Faculty of Arts at Paris

I

As we have seen, the teachers of the Faculty of Arts at Paris were debarred for a time from lecturing on the physical and metaphysical works of Aristotle. So in a sense the theologians enjoyed what might be described as an unfair advantage. The fact remains, however, that it was theologians such as St Albert the Great and St Thomas Aquinas who first made use of the metaphysical works of Aristotle and who saw the importance of the newly received philosophical literature. At the same time it was not to be expected that the lecturers of the Faculty of Arts would long remain content with grammar and logic, when a much wider field had been opened up before their eyes. In 1252 the statutes of the English nation[1] imposed on candidates for the licence to teach the obligation of commenting on Aristotle's *De anima*, and in 1255 the Faculty of Arts in general promulgated a statute requiring study of all the known works of Aristotle. The prohibition of lectures on the physical and metaphysical writings of the Greek philosopher had already become a dead letter; and it seems probable that the statute of 1255 was more of a systematization of the programme of studies than a revolutionary act. In any case Aristotle was being freely lectured on in the Faculty of Arts about the middle of the thirteenth century.

[1] The students and staff of the Faculty of Arts at Paris were grouped according to four 'nations': the Picards, the French, the Normans and the English. Those who did not come literally from any of these regions (the French 'nation' represented the *Île de France*) joined one or other of them.

It has been pointed out by historians that after Bonaventure had been elected minister general of the Franciscans in 1257 and Aquinas had left Paris in 1259 or 1260 there was nobody of comparable stature left in the Faculty of Theology (Albert the Great was in Germany). It was thus easier for the teachers in the Faculty of Arts to take the bit between their teeth. The theologians had been careful either to reject and argue against Aristotelian theories which they considered incompatible with Christian orthodoxy or to interpret Aristotle's thought in such a way as not to entail the offending theories. Soon after 1260, however, a number of teachers in the Faculty of Arts began expounding Aristotle, whom they regarded as the embodiment of philosophical wisdom, with scant attention to the demands of theological orthodoxy. When they took stock of the situation, the theologians and ecclesiastical authorities saw in this movement the invasion of naturalism and rationalism and a menace to Christian faith. In the end this reaction led to the famous condemnation of 1277, of which something more will be said later in this chapter.

In the past the lecturers and writers at Paris who aroused the opposition which led to the condemnations have commonly been described as Latin Averroists.[1] One obvious reason for this description was the fact that some teachers expounded Averroes's theory of the unicity of the potential intellect in man. It has already been noted that Avicenna's theory of the unicity of the active intellect aroused no vehement opposition. For it was compatible with belief in personal immortality. And some Christian thinkers identified the one active intellect with God, ascribing to it the functions fulfilled by Augustine's divine illumination. The doctrine of the unicity of the potential intellect, however, seemed to the theologians to remove any basis in psychology or anthropology for belief in personal immortality and thus to undermine belief in reward and punishment in another life. It was the occasion for the publication of polemical writings such as Aquinas's *On the Unity of the Intellect against the Averroists*, and it constituted a controversial feature

---

[1] In the last century E. Renan, in his *Averroès et l'averroisme*, defended the view that the Faculty of Arts at Paris in the thirteenth century was the centre of an Averroist school. For good measure he added the Franciscans. As far as the existence of 'Latin Averroism' in the Faculty of Arts was concerned, Renan's view was continued by P. Mandonnet in his *Siger de Brabant et l'averroisme latin au XIIIe siècle*, though without Renan's failure to distinguish between two questions: that of the unicity of the active intellect and that of the unicity of the potential intellect.

of such prominence that historians of the period have found it natural to describe as Averroists the whole group of teachers in the Faculty of Arts at Paris who expounded the philosophy of Aristotle in a manner which seemed objectionable to the theologians.

Use of the term 'Latin Averroists' as a general description has been sharply criticized, notably by Van Steenberghen. To be sure, the writings of Averroes were available and well enough known by 1260; and Averroes was called 'the Commentator'. But the very fact that Averroes was known as 'the Commentator', while Aristotle was known as 'the Philosopher', shows that the Paris professors and lecturers were concerned much more with the latter than with the former. Averroes set out to rediscover the genuine thought of Aristotle; and when Averroes's interpretations were accepted, this was because they were thought to represent the mind of the Greek philosopher. What the teachers of the Faculty of Arts were concerned with expounding was an integral Aristotelianism rather than a specifically Averroist system. It is indeed true that some of them embraced the specifically Averroist theory of the unicity of the potential intellect in all men. And when Aquinas, for example, wrote against the 'Averroists', he was referring to those who accepted this theory. Hence there is ground for describing these particular teachers as Averroists. At the same time it must be remembered that they embraced the theory because they thought that Averroes had given the correct interpretation of Aristotle.[1]

What Van Steenberghen has argued at considerable length seems to the present writer to be substantially correct. He likes to speak of the current of thought which gave rise to the condemnations of 1277 as 'heterodox Aristotelianism'. And though this description may pass muster from the theological point of view, 'integral Aristotelianism' seems to be preferable. In any case, however, it seems to be true that the teachers of the Faculty of Arts were concerned more with Aristotle than with Averroes, and that though some of them did indeed embrace Averroes's theory of the unicity of the potential intellect, the term 'Averroism' cannot legitimately be used to cover all the propositions which were condemned in 1277. For example, the theory of the eternity of the world was censured; and this theory had been held by Avicenna no less than by Averroes, while both attributed it to Aris-

[1] Besides arguing against the theory of the unicity of the intellect in all men (a theory which has been described as monopsychism) Aquinas argued that the theory represented a misinterpretation of Aristotle.

totle.[1] Moreover, some condemned propositions had nothing to do with Averroes.

Having agreed, however, with Van Steenberghen that the term 'Latin Averroism' is unsatisfactory and misleading as a general description of the movement which led to the condemnation of 1277, let us turn our attention to the most famous of the professors of the Faculty of Arts in the relevant period, namely Siger of Brabant.

2

Siger was born, doubtless in Brabant, about the year 1240.[2] He seems to have been a canon at Liège; but sometime between 1255 and 1260 he went to Paris to study in the Faculty of Arts, taking his final degree some time between 1260 and 1265. In 1266 he was mentioned by Simon de Brion, the papal legate, as one of the chief disturbers of peace in the Faculty. His *Questions on the Third Book of the De Anima* (*Questiones in tertium de anima*, about 1268) gave expression to the theory of the unicity of the intellect in all men. That is to say, the lowermost intelligence in the hierarchy of separate intelligences, which emanate successively from God, is the intellect of the human race; and it has two distinguishable factors, the active and the potential intellects. It functions indeed in individual human beings; but they are perishable and mortal.

The doctrine of Siger of Brabant was the principal object of attack in St Thomas Aquinas's little work *On the Unity of the Intellect against the Averroists* (1270). Thomas argued, for example, that if the theory were true, it would be false to say that Tom or Jack understands, whereas it is an evident fact that understanding is a function of this or that individual human being.[3] Besides being attacked by theologians such as Bonaventure and Thomas, monopsychism was also among some doctrines condemned by the bishop of Paris in 1270.[4]

[1] There was, of course, an important difference. Aristotle had no theory of divine creation, whereas both Avicenna and Averroes regarded the world as ontologically dependent on God. However, none of them regarded the world as having had a temporal beginning.

[2] The actual date is unknown.

[3] We have seen that Averroes anticipated this line of objection and tried to cope with it, even if without conspicuous success.

[4] The eternity of the world was included; also denial of human freedom and of God's universal providence. For good measure the bishop excommunicated those who knowingly asserted and taught the condemned doctrines.

It seems that Siger made a reply to Aquinas's treatise. If so, the work has been lost; but passages from Siger are quoted by Agostino Nifo[1] as coming from a treatise *On the Intellect* (*De intellectu*). And as the passages do not appear to be derived from Siger's *On the Intellectual Soul* (*De anima intellectiva*), the conclusion has been drawn that the *De intellectu* was a different work and an immediate reply to St Thomas. In it Siger continued to defend his doctrine of the unicity of the intellect in all men, while trying to answer the objections raised by St Thomas. In the *De anima intellectiva*, however, which was written later, though before Thomas's death,[2] Siger modified his position to some extent. At the same time it seems unlikely that he altered his teaching in any notable degree, as towards the end of 1276 he was summoned to appear before the tribunal of the inquisition of France. Siger left France and was no longer in the country when in March of 1277 the bishop of Paris took it upon himself (in response to an invitation from Pope John XXI to inquire into and report on errors disseminated in the University) to condemn a mixed bag of 219 propositions.

Siger went to Italy and apparently appealed to the tribunal of the Holy See. What happened is obscure, though it seems that he was acquitted of heresy. He died at Orvieto. The story is that he was assassinated by his mad secretary. As his death is referred to in a letter written by John Peckham towards the end of 1284, it probably took place earlier in that year.

Van Steenberghen has made much of Siger's conversion to Christian belief. And unless he was or became a Christian believer, it is certainly very difficult to explain the fact that Dante not only places him in Paradise, but also puts praise of him into the mouth of St Thomas Aquinas.[3] The problem, however, is that of ascertaining to what extent Siger himself ever maintained personally the doctrines associated with his name. For in the *De anima intellectiva* he said roundly that the principal business of philosophy is to expound the opinion of the philosophers rather than the truth, while in his work on some of the

---

[1] Agostino Nifo (*c*. 1473–*c*. 1546) wrote copiously on Aristotle and attacked Pietro Pomponazzi, who denied the immortality of the soul.

[2] Thomas is referred to in the work as a living man.

[3] Various explanations have been given by, for example, Mandonnet, Gilson, Bruno, Nardi and Van Steenberghen. To be plausible, any explanation must be consistent with the fact that Dante, while consigning the prophet Mohammed to Hell, places Avicenna and Averroes in Limbo (as though doing the best for them that he can) and Siger in heaven.

books of Aristotle's *Metaphysics* he remarked that Aristotle's opinions should not be concealed, even if they were contrary to the truth. Obviously, if Siger seriously equated philosophy with reporting and explaining the theories of past thinkers, we would be no more justified in attributing to him personally the views which he mentioned than we would be in concluding that a historian who gave an objective account of Nietzsche's ideas was himself a Nietzschean. At the same time it is clear that Aquinas did not take such protestations by teachers in the Faculty of Arts very seriously. He referred not so much to writings as to what was actually taught to students, in holes and corners as he put it. Moreover, the inquisitor of France presumably had some reason for supposing that Siger had been expounding certain theories, such as the unicity of the intellect, the eternity of the world and the direct emanation from God of only one being,[1] as being true and not simply as having been held by philosophers in the past. The inquisitor must at any rate have suspected that this was the case, and that further inquiry was needed. It may, of course, have been Siger's firm conviction that his job was simply that of elucidating the opinions of past philosophers, especially of Aristotle. But his expression of this idea may equally well have been an act of prudence. We really do not know. However, he seems to have allowed, or have come to allow, that in the case of a clash between philosophy and revelation, the truth lay with revelation.

3

Another interesting figure is a Dane, Boetius of Dacia. Unfortunately we know very little of his life. As, however, he was not only involved in the condemnation of 1277 but also described as the principal defender of some of the offending propositions, he must obviously have been teaching in the Faculty of Arts before the year mentioned. Among his writings are a small work *On the Supreme Good* or *On the Life of the Philosopher* (*De summo bono sive de vita philosophi*) and one *On the Eternity of the World* (*De aeternitate mundi*).

The propositions condemned in 1277 included the statements that

---

[1] Siger's thought was not entirely Aristotelian, in the sense of representing simply Aristotle's ideas or views which could reasonably be attributed to him. Siger seems to have held for a time that the first intelligence proceeded directly from God, but that the other separate intelligences and the world proceeded in a hierarchical sequence.

the philosophers are the only wise people in the world and that the highest or most excellent activity of man is to devote himself to philosophy. The target here is Boetius of Dacia, who certainly made these statements. At the beginning of his *De summo bono*, however, he had made it clear that he was prescinding from the supernatural order and from revelation and that he was writing simply and solely from the point of view of a philosopher, concerned with truths accessible to the human reason working without the light of faith. In other words, his question was this, 'What is the highest life which can be led by man in the world, so far as we can discover it by the use of reason alone?' And the answer which he gives is, substantially, the answer given by Aristotle.

In his little treatise on the eternity of the world Boetius makes some distinctions which show his idea of the limits of philosophical knowledge. The natural philosopher or physicist is concerned with generation within the world but knows nothing of creation. It does not follow that he must deny creation. It is rather that divine creation is a subject which lies altogether outside his field. The metaphysician can prove that the world is created, in the sense that it depends ontologically on a cause which transcends it; but he is unable to prove whether or not the world had a temporal beginning. The reason for this is that it depended entirely on God's free choice whether or not he created the world in such a way that there was an ideally assignable first moment of time. And what depends entirely on God's free choice in this manner cannot be known by man without revelation. Given a world, it must be a created world; but the metaphysician cannot go any further.

Needless to say, we do not know what Boetius said in writings which are lost. But if we go by what we have, we are faced with a difficulty analogous to that which has been mentioned in connection with Siger of Brabant. In the case of Siger, it may have been a poor idea of philosophy to reduce it to elucidation of the theories of Aristotle, Averroes and other writers; but it was hardly a heretical idea. In the case of Boetius of Dacia, it may have been an act of self-flattery for a philosopher to extol philosophizing as the highest activity of man which can be discovered by reason unenlightened by faith; but the notion was hardly heretical. Why then, we may ask, all the fuss? Was the bishop of Paris so stupid as not to be able to understand what people such as Siger and Boetius said or wrote? Or was he so impetuous that he did not take the trouble to examine the matter? Or was there some other reason which contributed to the condemnation of 1277?

4

Soon after the beginning of the year 1277 Pope John XXI,[1] having been informed that errors were being propagated in the University of Paris, asked Stephen Tempier, the bishop, to inquire into the matter and to report to him. The bishop quickly assembled a commission of theologians[2] which must have done its work in a pretty hurried manner. For on 27 March the bishop, instead of reporting to the Holy See, condemned 219 propositions. These were arranged without any attempt at systemization; and the condemnation affected not only philosophers, such as Aristotle, Avicenna, Averroes and Boetius of Dacia, but also writings which were judged immoral and works on magic and necromancy. For good measure, the teachers of the Faculty of Arts were accused of holding the double-truth theory, namely that a proposition could be true in philosophy and false in theology. Those who had taught or listened to the errors mentioned were excommunicated, unless they presented themselves for penance within seven days to the bishop or his chancellor.

It is indeed clear both that the inquiry was carried out in a hurried and slovenly manner and that the bishop acted impetuously and precipitately. But it is also obvious that the inquiry and condemnation would not have taken place in this way unless there was a sense of urgency, unless it was felt that there was a menacing situation in the University, and probably not unless there was growing pressure from conservative forces. In a sense discussion of the statements made by Siger of Brabant and Boetius of Dacia borders on the irrelevant. For it is clear that a general impression must have been created that in the Faculty of Arts there was a growing and spreading current of naturalism which set Christian belief aside or rejected it. For example, Boetius of Dacia may have said that he was speaking simply as a philosopher when he asserted that man's supreme good lay in this life and in philosophy, and that he prescinded from, but did not deny, theological teaching about man's supernatural end in the next life. But even if he spoke sincerely, it is not unreasonable to suppose that the impression

---

[1] He was the same man as Peter of Spain, the logician who will be mentioned again later.

[2] The commission included Henry of Ghent (d. 1293).

was conveyed that the rational man finds happiness in the philosophical contemplation of truth, and that if there is something more, it is, so to speak, a gratuitous extra. It is significant that the condemned propositions included such statements as that Christianity is a hindrance to education, that there are fables in Christianity as much as in other religions, that theology is not the source of any knowledge, and that what the theologians say rests on fables. We have indeed no warrant for attributing such opinions to Siger of Brabant or Boetius of Dacia. But they presumably represent an impression of the sort of ideas which were gaining ground. And if this was the impression made on people such as the bishop of Paris, one can hardly be altogether surprised at his action.

To be sure, it was a misrepresentation to attribute to the teachers of the Faculty of Arts the absurd idea that a proposition could be true in philosophy and at the same time false in theology. Siger of Brabant, for example, maintained that if certain philosophical premises were accepted, certain conclusions were inevitable. But he added that if these conclusions clashed with Christian beliefs, truth lay with the latter. There is no warrant for saying that he seriously held that two contradictory propositions can be true at the same time. But a good deal depends on how things are said. A man might say that philosophical reasoning led to conclusion X, but that as X clashed with theological doctrine, it could not be true; but he might say it in such a way as to give a quite different impression, namely that it was the philosophical proposition which should really be accepted.

The point is therefore that, however open to criticism the condemnation of 1277 may be, it must have been the result of a general impression that a non-Christian philosophical naturalism was making headway at Paris. It was also the result of an increasing pressure. In the latter part of his life Bonaventure frequently drew attention in strong terms to the shortcomings of Aristotle. Both he and Aquinas fulminated against certain doctrines (especially the unicity of the intellect) expounded in the Faculty of Arts. Nor did Albert the Great fail to take a hand. Giles of Rome, an Augustinian and theologian, wrote his *Errors of the Philosophers* (*Errores philosophorum*) about 1270, in which he enumerated the errors of Aristotle, Avicenna, Averroes, Maimonides and other thinkers. Conservatives such as John Peckham were out for blood. Stephen Tempier's intemperate act was doubtless the culmination of a growing movement among conservative theologians of hostility towards the radical Aristotelianism of the Faculty of Arts and the Faculty's tendency to ignore their theological colleagues.[1]

In the event the condemnation did not affect only the philosophers of the Faculty of Arts, nor even only the University of Paris. As we have already noted, some propositions which had been held by Aquinas were included in the list. In other words, the condemnation was not simply a victory for the Faculty of Theology over that of Arts. It was a victory for the conservative theologians. Even Giles of Rome was affected and had to leave Paris until he had retracted his alleged errors. Moreover, at the end of April Pope John XXI told Tempier to extend his investigation to the Faculty of Theology, with a view to purging the Theological Faculty too of doctrinal errors.[2] Meanwhile, a few days after the Paris condemnation, Robert Kilwardby, the Dominican archbishop of Canterbury, visited Oxford and censured a number of propositions asserted by Aquinas. As has already been mentioned, these censures were confirmed by Kilwardby's successor in the see of Canterbury, the Franciscan John Peckham, in 1284 and again in 1286.

The situation in 1277 seems to have been the occasion for Albert the Great making a special visit from Cologne to Paris to defend the orthodoxy of his onetime pupil, Thomas Aquinas. And although Kilwardby was himself a member of the order, the Dominicans in general were becoming more Thomist-minded and prepared to rally to the defence of their illustrious colleague's reputation. Hence, they were not pleased when William de la Mare, a Franciscan, published his criticism of Thomas, the *Correctorium fratris Thomae*, in which he objected to a considerable number of opinions held by Aquinas. According to the Dominicans, this *Correction* really amounted to a *Corruption* (or distortion) and a number of *Corrections of the Corruption* (*Correctoria corruptorii*) were published.

It would, however, be a great mistake to interpret the Paris and Oxford condemnations simply in terms of rivalry between two religious orders. Basically they were the result of apprehension about what was, or seemed to be, a growing spirit of pagan rationalism which paid little more than lip service to Christian belief and theology. As,

[1] The teachers of the Faculty of Arts could, of course, appeal to the fact that they were not supposed to treat of theological matters.
[2] John XXI died in May 1277. And in the interval between this event and the election of Nicholas III in late November the cardinals at Rome seem to have told Tempier to stay his hand and await further instructions.

however, is apt to happen in cases of this kind, when panic measures are taken, signs of heresy or at any rate of dangerous teaching are found in all sorts of unexpected places. When the modernist crisis occurred in the Roman Catholic Church early in this century, it was by no means only writers such as Loisy who suffered. Many quite inoffensive fish were caught in the net of suspicion and denunciation. Analogously, Thomas Aquinas, who had fulminated against 'Averroism' and denounced a group of teachers in the Faculty of Arts for disseminating error among the students outside the regular lecture-programme, was himself posthumously affected by the Paris and Oxford censures. In the minds of the conservatives the Christian Aristotelianism of Aquinas was contaminated by the poison which was more evidently doing its deadly work in the Faculty of Arts.

5

The effects of the condemnations should not, of course, be exaggerated. Both at Paris and at Oxford they were acts of local ecclesiastics and had local application. Besides, in the Middle Ages such condemnations were not taken with the degree of seriousness with which they were taken in the highly centralized and authoritarian Church of a later date. Some theologians doubtless availed themselves of the opportunity offered of bringing accusations against rivals. But there was nothing like the reign of terror which prevailed in the aftermath of the modernist crisis, even if the academic careers of a few individuals, such as Siger of Brabant and Boetius of Dacia, came to an end.

The reaction against the spread of Greco-Islamic philosophy in general and of Aristotelianism in particular, a reaction which resulted in the condemnations, had, however, one effect which should be mentioned, namely a kind of 'back to Augustine' movement, especially among Franciscan thinkers. True, appeal was made not only to Augustine himself but also to such thinkers as Alexander of Hales and Bonaventure. But their thought was regarded as a faithful development of Augustine's.

John Peckham, of course, was an adherent of the Augustinian tradition and an opponent of Thomism. So was William de la Mare. So was Matthew of Aquasparta, though in a less polemical manner. Matthew taught at Paris from 1275 until 1276 or 1277 and then in Italy. In 1287 he was elected minister general of the Franciscans, and in the following year he was nominated a cardinal. He died in 1302. He looked on Augustine as the source of wisdom and maintained the Augustinian theory of sensation, namely that while sensation demands that a sense organ should be affected by a physical object, the act of sensation must be attributed to the soul alone.[1] That is to say, in sensation the soul acts on the occasion of a sense organ being affected by a physical object. Again, Matthew continued Augustine's theory of divine illumination, maintaining that the archetypal ideas or *rationes aeternae* exercise a regulative action on the human intellect, enabling it to perceive the relation between an object and its eternal exemplar, though the archetypal ideas are not themselves perceived. Matthew also upheld Augustine's theory of seminal forms (*rationes seminales*), while from Bonaventure he derived the theory of hylomorphic composition in all creatures, including angels. As against Aquinas, he maintained that the human mind knows the individual thing directly and in itself.[2] Sense intuition apprehends a thing as 'there', as existing, while intellectual intuition apprehends the individual essence. If this were not the case, the formation of universal concepts would be left unexplained. Again, while the soul certainly does not start with an intuition of itself but can come to knowledge of itself only through reflection, it is none the less capable of achieving a direct intuition of itself, which was denied by Aquinas, who thought that in this life at least self-consciousness never amounts to a direct vision of the soul by itself.

A more robust Augustinian, who found Matthew of Aquasparta too given to accommodation and compromise, was the English Franciscan Roger Marston, who died in 1303 after having taught at Oxford and Cambridge and being provincial of his order. In Marston's opinion the 'saints', such as Augustine and Anselm, are to be preferred to those 'infernal men' the pagan philosophers. What Marston means, however, is that in the case of a clash the 'saints' are to be preferred to the philosophers. It does not follow that he is not prepared to defend the opinions of the former by argument. For example, he argues with Bonaventure that it is impossible that the world should not have had a beginning. Nor does it follow that he obstinately refuses to recognize any truth in non-Christian philosophy. For instance, though he in-

[1] See Matthew's *Quaestio disputata de cognitione* (*On Knowledge*).
[2] Aquinas maintained that while sense apprehension is of individual things, what the mind first grasps is not the individual essence as such but rather the form or nature considered in its common or universal aspect: I *see* Peter and *conceive* him as 'a man'.

sists that Augustine's theory of divine illumination is necessary to explain human certainty and that it should not be accepted in word and then whittled down to the point of disappearance, he identifies the separate active intellect of Avicenna with God, considered as illuminating the human mind.

Among other thinkers who accepted the condemnations of 1277 we can mention the Franciscan Richard of Middleton (Ricardus de Mediavilla), who was teaching philosophy at Paris about 1284–6 and subsequently became tutor of Louis, son of Charles II of Sicily. Richard seems to have finished his commentary on Peter Lombard's *Sentences* in about the year 1295; and he probably died about the turn of the century, though the date is not known.

Richard of Middleton accepted the condemnation of 1277 and clearly thought that it was necessary to develop a theology and a philosophy to counterbalance the condemned theses. But he was notably more inclined than was, say, John Peckham or Roger Marston to sympathize with certain Aristotelian and Thomist positions. He retained indeed a number of theories which were characteristic of the Franciscan tradition as developed by Alexander of Hales and Bonaventure, such as the impossibility of creation from eternity, hylomorphic composition in all creatures and the primacy of the will.[1] But he rejected the Augustinian theory of divine illumination – that is to say, he considered that in order to explain human knowledge there was no need to postulate any special illumination by God in addition to the divine activity of sustaining all creatures in being and concurring with their operations. Provided that we do not regard the mind as a purely passive recipient of sense-impressions, we can quite well explain man's limited knowledge of spiritual reality in terms of abstraction and reflection. Nor is there any need to regard the active intellect as a separate entity and then identify it with God. In other words, in regard to human knowledge Richard approximated to the position of Aquinas, though he insisted that the intellect can know the individual thing directly. At the same time he rejected Aquinas's doctrine of the unicity of the substantial form in every material substance, while characteristically modifying this rejection by speaking of different 'grades' of the same form in, for instance, man rather than of separate biological or vegetative and sensitive forms.

[1] The Franciscans, generally speaking, emphasized the primacy of love, and so the will, whereas Aquinas was more intellectualist, emphasizing knowledge, and so the intellect. In this matter the Franciscans were Augustinian, Aquinas Aristotelian.

Though, therefore, the reaction to the spread of non-Christian philosophy took the form of a recall to the teaching of the 'saints', it was hardly possible for intelligent men to confine themselves to repetition of the views of past theologians. Those who considered that the line of thought developed by Thomas Aquinas represented unwarrantable concessions to Aristotle and, in general, a contamination of Christian belief by non-Christian rationalism had to work out their own harmonization of Christian theology with philosophical reflection. The greatest among such thinkers was the Franciscan John Duns Scotus.

14

Duns Scotus

I

THE term 'scholastic philosopher' tends to suggest the idea of a thinker dealing with arid abstractions and developing closely reasoned but involved logical arguments, subtle no doubt but pedantic, his thought redolent of the schools, of the academic world of classrooms and formal disputations. Most people who dipped into the pages of Duns Scotus would probably think that this sort of idea was verified in his case. They might see why he became known as the Subtle Doctor; but they might very well wonder why the poet Gerard Manley Hopkins had such a regard for him. Though, however, his writings can hardly be called exciting, at any rate according to most people's standard of what constitutes excitement, Duns Scotus was one of the most able and acute thinkers Britain has produced. Of a critical turn of mind and gifted with an ability to discover fine distinctions and shades of meaning, he possessed at the same time a power of constructive systematization. As a Franciscan he was naturally influenced by the philosophical traditions of his order; but he was also strongly influenced by Aristotelianism and by Islamic thought, particularly that of Avicenna. However, he brought to bear on the various elements which helped to form his philosophy the power of an original, constructive and yet critical mind.

Duns was the philosopher's family name. It seems probable that he was born near the end of the year 1265 or early in 1266. As for his place of birth, this is uncertain. According to one tradition he was born not far from Maxton in Roxburghshire, his father being Ninian Duns, while according to another tradition he was born in Berwickshire. He entered the Franciscan order as a novice at an early age; and we know that he was ordained priest at Northampton by the bishop of Lincoln on 17 March 1291. Where he was in the meantime we do not know with certainty, but he seems to have been at Oxford for a period, and it is possible that he was also at Cambridge and at Paris. He acquired the name Scotus or the Scot to distinguish him from other Johns in the Franciscan order.

In 1300 Scotus was lecturing at Oxford on the *Sentences* of Peter Lombard. He then seems to have been sent to Paris in 1302 for studies in theology and continued lecturing on the *Sentences*. When a dispute broke out between Philip the Fair of France and Pope Boniface VIII, Scotus sided with the pope; and in consequence he had to leave Paris for a short while. But he must have completed the requisite lectures on the *Sentences* by the end of 1304, as he received the doctorate or mastership in theology early in 1305.

Scotus's subsequent career is obscure. But it seems that he was lecturing in Cologne from 1307 to 1308. The traditional date of his death is 8 November 1308. He was buried in the church of the Franciscans at Cologne. He would thus have been forty-two years old at the time of his death.

After Scotus's early death his disciples set about editing his writings and made a fine hash of the work. Various versions of lectures were simply put together, deletions and corrections and marginal notes all being incorporated in the text. To complicate matters still further, a number of spurious works were later attributed to Scotus and appeared in the collected works published by Luke Wadding in the seventeenth century. The editors of the critical edition of Scotus's writings, publication of which began in 1950 after a good many years of hard work, were faced with no easy task.[1]

Scotus's lectures on the *Sentences* are represented mainly in two works, known traditionally as the *Opus Oxoniense* (*Oxford Work*) and the *Opus Parisiense* or *Reportata Parisiensia* (*Paris Work* or *Paris Reports*). The former, as handed down, contains, but does not consist exclusively of, the *Ordinatio* (a draft finally approved for publication by the author), which the editors of the critical edition have been labouring to restore in its purity. The latter, the Paris work that is to say, consists of notes taken down by students or scribes, though part was examined by Scotus himself (*Reportata examinata*). We also have a number of *Questiones quodlibetales*, representing Scotus's teaching at

[1] References to *Opera*, with volume and page, are to this edition.

Paris, and of *Collationes* which may represent disputations in the Franciscan house of studies. The *Tractatus de Primo Principio* (*Treatise on the First Principle*) is a compendium of Scotus's 'natural' or philosophical theology.[1] This work is certainly authentic, and so is the main part, though not all, of the *Quaestiones subtilissimae in Metaphysicam Aristotelis* (*Most subtle Questions on Aristotle's Metaphysics*). There are a number of other writings on the Aristotelian logic, and one on Porphyry, which are generally regarded as authentic.

Among the works falsely attributed to Scotus in the old collected editions of his writings are the *Grammatica speculativa* (*Speculative Grammar*) and the *De rerum principio* (*On the Principle of Things*), which have been now ascribed respectively to Thomas of Erfurt and Vital du Four. A special difficulty is created by the *Theoremata* (*Theorems*). External evidence favours its authenticity, but as the author asserts that a good many propositions cannot be proved which Scotus undertakes to prove in the certainly authentic writings, those who accept the authenticity of the little work have a problem of interpretation on their hands. It is not surprising that E. Longpré refused to accept the work as authentic, though since he published his work on Scotus in 1924 some historians have insisted that we have no real warrant for disregarding the external evidence in favour of authenticity.

Considered simply as an intellectual power, the human mind, Scotus insists, is capable of knowing all that is intelligible. This means that its natural object is being as being; for all being is intelligible. To define the primary object of the human intellect in the way that Aquinas does is like claiming that the primary object of human vision is what can be seen by candlelight.[2] It is indeed true that the range of the human mind in this life is limited.[3] But in other conditions, as in the next life, the

---

[1] There are two English translations. See Bibliography.

[2] *Opus Oxoniense* (*Ordinatio*), Book I, Distinction 3, Question 3, No. 186 (*Opera*, III, p. 112).

[3] Scotus suggests several reasons for the limitation of the scope of the human intellect in this life. One is theological, namely that the limitation may be an effect of the Fall, of original sin that is to say. Another suggested cause is natural, namely that the harmony of man's powers requires this limitation. Aquinas's thesis was based on his conviction that the human soul is by nature the form of the body, so that the limitation of the range of the mind, which is consequent upon the intimate union of soul and body, is 'for the good' of the soul and natural to it. Aquinas did not deny that intellect as such is the capacity of knowing the intelligible and so all being. But he would insist that what he was talking about in the context was the human intellect, not intellect in a purely abstract sense.

intellect can know spiritual realities directly, though the nature of the intellect in itself remains what it was. If, therefore, it is a question of defining the basic object of the mind, we should follow Avicenna in asserting that it is being as such. If the statement were untrue, we should have to conclude that metaphysics is impossible or that it is simply part of natural philosophy or physics. Indeed, it is no matter for surprise if those who regard the natural object of the human mind as being the form or nature of the material thing or physical object prove the existence of God by means of an argument which implies that God is the highest being within the universe rather than as transcendent.

When, however, it is a question of the way in which man actually arrives at knowledge in this life, Scotus is perfectly prepared to accept the Aristotelian doctrine that all our knowledge arises from or is based on sensation and that the mind is, at the start, simply a capacity to know, without any innate ideas or principles. Further, he roundly denies the theory, which had been so dear to Bonaventure and most Franciscan thinkers, that any special divine illumination is required for the attainment of certainty. What, he pertinently asks, is this divine illumination supposed to do? If it is postulated on the ground that physical objects are always changing,[1] is the divine illumination supposed to alter their nature? If so, we do not know them as they are; and in this case we cannot be said to acquire certain knowledge. If not, the illumination seems superfluous. Similarly, if the fact that our minds and ideas can change are considered to be an obstacle to certainty, we can hardly seriously suppose that divine illumination remedies this alleged defect.

Scotus's arguments against the theory of divine illumination are directed mainly against Henry of Ghent. As for Augustine, Scotus is careful not to contradict him but to argue that Henry has misinterpreted the saint's meaning. Scotus's interpretation of Augustine is ingenious but perhaps not very convincing. He argues in precisely the way which Roger Marston condemned, namely by minimizing Augustine's claim that divine illumination is required to grasp 'eternal truths'. However, Augustine's doctrine is none too clear; and Scotus makes out an at any rate plausible case for his interpretation.

In any case Scotus's attempt to undermine Henry of Ghent's interpretation of Augustine is a minor point. His own position is made clear enough. The so-called 'eternal truths' are analytic propositions; and the

[1] Scotus refuses to admit that things are always changing in a sense which excludes all stability.

mind does not require any special illumination to see their truth. 'The terms of self-evident principles have such an identity that it is evident that the one necessarily includes the other.'[1] The concepts of whole and part, for instance, are derived by abstraction from sense-experience. Once they have been formed, however, the mind assents to the proposition that every whole is greater than any of its parts 'in virtue of the terms'.[2] No verification is required. That is to say, the proposition cannot be construed as an empirical hypothesis, which might turn out to be false. Its truth depends on the meaning of the terms; and the mind sees the relation between them without requiring any other illumination than the general illumination provided by God's conserving activity.[3]

We can thus get on quite well without postulating any special divine illumination to account for human certainty. It is, therefore, not required in metaphysics. But what is metaphysics? What does it study? Averroes said that God and the pure spirits or separate intelligences constitute the subject-matter of metaphysics; and he found fault with Avicenna for having denied this. Scotus sides with Avicenna. God is the subject-matter of theology, but not of metaphysics. For no science proves the existence of its own subject-matter. Physics does not prove the existence of bodies; it assumes their existence and studies them and their movements. The botanist does not undertake to prove the existence of plants. The metaphysician, however, proves the existence of God. Hence we cannot legitimately say that God is the primary subject-matter of metaphysics, even though it culminates in the assertion of God's existence. The subject-matter of metaphysics is, as Aristotle claimed, being as being.

Very well, but what is being as being? It is not a thing. Rather is it the universal concept of being which applies to infinite and finite being, to spiritual and material being, to existent and possible being. Being as being is, in other words, the most abstract of all concepts, considered prior to all determination. It is opposed simply to notbeing.

Professor Gilson likes to make a sharp distinction, in this connection, between Aquinas and Scotus. Aquinas is primarily concerned

---

[1] *Opus Oxoniense*, Bk I, Dist. 3, Pt 1, Qu. 4, No. 229 (*Opera*, III, p. 138).
[2] Ibid., No. 234 (*Opera*, III, p. 141).
[3] When Augustine says that the 'eternal truths' are above the mind, all he means, according to Scotus, is that they are necessarily true, and that the human mind cannot alter them.

with being in the sense of existence (*esse*) and always focuses his attention on existing things. Scotus's point of departure is an abstract concept, to which is opposed bare not-being or nothingness. Aquinas is thus the true existentialist, not indeed in the modern sense of the term, but in the sense that he is concerned with existing beings. Scotus, as starting with an abstract concept, can be seen as looking forward to a philosopher such as Hegel, who begins his dialectic with the concept of being as such.

However this may be, how can we get any further if we start with the abstract concept of being? In Scotus's opinion we can study the attributes of being as such. These are transcendental in the sense that they transcend the Aristotelian categories (substance, quality and so on). Indeed, metaphysics can be said to be the science of the transcendentals.[1]

The transcendental attributes of being are of two kinds. There are attributes which are coextensive with being itself, the *passiones convertibles*. Thus every being is one, true and good. Then there are the disjunctive attributes (the *passiones disiunctae*). They fall into pairs, each pair being convertible with being, though neither member, taken by itself, is convertible with being. Thus a being must be either infinite, either necessary or contingent, and so on. We cannot, of course, deduce the *existence* of, say, necessary or contingent being from the abstract idea of being. The point is that if there is a being, it must be either infinite or finite, contingent or necessary, and so on. All that we can say *a priori* is that any being must be one or the other.

The general scheme comes from Avicenna. But whereas for Avicenna exemplification of the disjunctive attributes was really necessary throughout, inasmuch as he regarded creation as necessary, Scotus insists that we cannot deduce the existence of the less perfect from the existence of the more perfect. We can argue, for example, that if there is contingent being, there must be necessary being; but we cannot argue that if there is necessary being, there must be contingent being. Scotus thus leaves room for free creation by God, though it is not very clear how his thesis can be proved *a priori*.

Given Scotus's position, it follows that man's natural knowledge of God must be inferential. To be sure, if the object of the human mind is being in all its amplitude, then, if there is a God, he can in principle be known by man. In point of fact, however, the human mind in its present state is dependent for its knowledge on sense-experience. It

[1] *Quaestiones subtilissimae in Metaphysican Aristotelis*, Prologue, No. 5.

enjoys no intuitive knowledge of a transcendent reality. Apart, therefore, from revelation or mysticism, our knowledge of God in this life is inferential.

At this point Scotus adopts a point of view which should win him some good marks from modern philosophers. For he maintains that if we are going to discuss whether there is a God, we must first know what we are talking about. That is to say we must have some concept of God. 'For I never know anything to exist unless I first have some concept of that of which existence is asserted.'[1] Further, this concept must be positive, not purely negative. We do not assert existence of not-being. Provided, however, that the concept is positive and that it is the concept of a being which could properly be called God, there is no need to analyse the meaning of all the terms which Christians predicate of God. That is to say, a minimal concept is all that is required for proving God's existence.

For Scotus at any rate the concept required is that of an actually infinite being. Nothing less than infinite being can properly be described as God. The basic question, therefore, is whether there is such a being. In dealing with this question we have to argue inferentially. In Scotus's opinion we cannot do so, unless there is some fundamental sense in which the concept of being is univocal and can thus serve to bridge the gap, as it were, between the finite and the infinite. A concept is said to be univocal when it possesses sufficient unity for a contradiction to result if it is both affirmed and denied of the same thing, and for it to serve as the middle term in a syllogism.[2] The concept of being is univocal in this sense, if it is taken as signifying simply opposition to not-being.[3] God and creatures are both opposed to not-being, and they can be thought of in this way, in spite of the gulf which actually separates the infinite from the finite.

At first sight the obvious way of proceeding is to take the actual

---

[1] *Opus Oxoniense*, Bk I, Dist. 3, Pt 1, Qu. 1, No. 11 (*Opera*, III, p. 6).

[2] Ibid., Bk I, Dist. 3, Pt 1, Qu. 2, No. 26 (*Opera*, III, p. 18).

[3] It is not only the concept of being which, according to Scotus, is univocal in this sense. The concepts of all 'pure perfections' (perfections which are not intrinsically bound up with corporeal reality or with finite beings in general) can be used univocally. For example, the divine wisdom is actually very different from human wisdom. But, in Scotus's view, there can be a concept of wisdom as such, which prescinds from such differences and is therefore univocal. In other words, analogical predication presupposes a basis of univocal predication. Otherwise we could not argue from creatures to God. And no assignable meaning could be given to statements about God.

existence of finite things as our point of departure and to argue that they require a cause of an unmoved mover or something of the kind. But this way of arguing seems to Scotus unsatisfactory. If we assume with Avicenna that creation is necessary and that necessity reigns throughout the world, all existential propositions relating to finite things become necessary propositions and so capable of forming the basis of a demonstration which will satisfy Aristotle's demands for a strict demonstration. But Scotus refuses to admit that all factual propositions relating to finite things are necessary. For him, existential propositions asserting the existence of finite things are all contingent. They can indeed form the basis for an argument to God's existence; but the conclusion will then be contingently true. If there are finite things, there is a God.

Scotus prefers, therefore, to argue from the *possibility* of there being any finite thing at all. He wishes to show that the existence of God is the ultimate and necessary condition of the possibility of any contingent being. To put the matter in another way, he wishes to show that God's existence is the ultimate and necessary condition of all contingent truths. God is the ground of possibility of there being a world.

There is another consideration to bear in mind. Avicenna held that the existence of God can be proved only in metaphysics, whereas Averroes thought that it could be proved in physics. Scotus asserts that Avicenna was right, as it is questionable whether a physical proof would be a proof of the existence of *God*. In regard, for instance, to the argument from motion Scotus remarks that the truth of the principle on which the argument rests, namely that whatever is moved is moved by something else, is none too clear.[1] In any case, the argument, if valid, would prove the existence of a supreme mover in the hierarchy of movers rather than that of the unique transcendent God. We can infer, therefore, that Scotus would have little use for arguments based on scientific theories, arguments which would conclude to God's existence as an empirical hypothesis. Nor would he look on such a concept as Whitehead's highest actual entity as an adequate concept of God. Scotus insists on what he considers to be a proper metaphysical approach; and the God whose existence he wishes to prove is the actually infinite Being.

Scotus's line of argument, as given in the Oxford commentary on the *Sentences* and summarized in *On the First Principle*, is complex, involved and difficult to follow. He starts by asserting that something

[1] It is not clear, for example, that the soul cannot initiate its own movements.

is producible (which he regards as necessarily true) and argues that therefore something can be productive. The producible cannot be produced by itself. If produced, it must be produced by something else. And in the long run the possibility of production entails the possibility of an ultimate productive agent or first efficient cause (the *primum effectivum*).[1] Again, that which is producible can be ordered to an end, exemplifying final causality; and Scotus argues that for final causality to be possible an ultimate final cause must be possible, the *primum finitivum*. Similarly, the order of 'eminence' or perfection requires a *primum eminens*, a supremely perfect being.

Now the ultimate condition of all possibility cannot itself be producible. It cannot, therefore, be simply possible but exists actually and necessarily. Similarly, the ultimate final cause and the ultimate source of the possibility of perfection or of degrees of perfection must exist in actuality. Further, Scotus argues, the *primum effectivum*, the *primum finitivum* and the *primum eminens* are one and the same necessarily existing being, the condition or ground of all possibility, which has been considered under three aspects.

The way then lies open to proving the infinity of the necessarily existing being. Scotus does this in a long series of arguments. For example, he argues that the necessarily existing being must know the infinity of possible effects, and so must be infinite in itself. In the course of his series of proofs he makes use of the Anselmian argument, though, he tells his readers, it must be 'coloured' or retouched by addition of the words 'without contradiction'.[2] God is the being which, conceived without contradiction, is so great that a greater being cannot be conceived without contradiction. According to Scotus, the mind perceives no repugnance or contradiction in the concept of infinite being; and no greater being than the actual infinite can be conceived. God must therefore be infinite.

Infinity is for Scotus the basic 'absolute' property or attribute of God.[3] He is not, however, prepared to claim that all the attributes of the divine nature can be proved in metaphysics. For example, the philosopher cannot prove that God is omnipotent: divine omni-

[1] Scotus is talking about causes which must coexist for the effect under consideration to be produced and continue in being, not of a series of causes in which the effects can continue to exist in the absence of their causes (as in the case of children which can continue in being when their parents are dead).

[2] *Opus Oxoniense*, Bk I, Dist. 2, Pt 1, Qu. 2, No. 137 (*Opera*, II, pp. 208–9).

[3] To be, for instance, first efficient or productive cause is a 'relative' attribute, in the sense that a relation to creatures is implied.

potence is a matter of faith. This statement may sound very odd, in view of the fact that Scotus has already proved to his satisfaction the existence of the infinite ground of all possibility. But what he appears to mean is this. It can indeed be proved that God is omnipotent in the sense of being able to do all that is logically possible; but the philosopher cannot prove that it is possible for God to produce all those effects immediately which are actually produced through secondary causes. If one may be permitted to use an illustration from modern thought, in the process of evolution the emergence of animal organisms presupposes certain conditions, such as a world capable of producing and sustaining them. Could God produce and sustain these organisms without any material environment, without a world? The philosopher cannot prove that this would be possible, though the theologians may assert, as a matter of faith, that whatever God does through secondary causes he can do without them.[1]

In general, the specifically Christian concept of God is left by Scotus to the sphere of faith. In his view, for example, the philosopher is unable to prove that God is either just or merciful. As Scotus does not believe that the philosopher can do more than produce persuasive arguments in favour of immortality, he obviously cannot maintain that philosophy can demonstrate the divine justice, in the sense of showing that God rewards and punishes human beings in another life. As for mercy, Scotus probably means that the philosopher cannot prove that God forgives sins. The whole question of salvation belongs to theology, not to philosophy. The philosopher can prove that there is an actually infinite being, but the concept of the Father–God is a matter of revelation.

Perhaps a brief mention should be made of the distinction which Scotus asserts between the divine attributes. Aquinas maintained that it is only from our human point of view that there is any distinction between the divine attributes. We experience only the perfections of creatures, and in creatures we obviously find objective distinctions. One man may be kind but not notable for intelligence, while another may be described as just but as not given to showing mercy. Again, willing and understanding are distinct. Though, however, we form

---

[1] Professor Gilson has suggested that behind Scotus's reservations in regard to the philosopher's capacity to prove that God is omnipotent there lies the Avicennian picture of the world in which God produces immediately only the first subordinate separate intelligence. In other words, the philosopher, in Scotus's mind, is represented by Avicenna.

distinct ideas of different qualities, capacities and activities and predicate of God those which are compatible with infinite spiritual being,
that to which the different terms refer is one and the same reality.[1]
God's intellect and will, for example, are identical with the divine
essence. Scotus, however, is not satisfied with this point of view.
Whereas for Aquinas the ground in God of the distinctions which we
make is simply the infinite divine perfection which cannot be grasped
by the finite mind in a simple concept, Scotus claims that the distinctions which we make between the divine attributes reflect distinctions
in God himself. The distinction in question is not, of course, a real
distinction between two separate entities. But neither is it simply a
mental distinction in the sense of being due solely to the limitations
and approach of the finite human mind. It is a distinction between
different 'formalities' of one and the same reality. There is, for instance, a formal but objective distinction (*distinctio formalis a parte rei*)
between the divine intellect and will.

Scotus did not confine the application of his 'formal distinction' to
the divine attributes. He found such a distinction, for example, between the human nature of Tom and his 'thisness', his Tom-ness as
one might put it.[2] It is indeed rather difficult to see precisely what the
distinctio formalis a parte rei is supposed to be, but the general principle
on which Scotus works is clear enough. In regard to the divine attributes Henry of Ghent, with whom Scotus, as is his wont, is much more
concerned than with Thomas Aquinas, maintained that the distinction
between them is purely mental. Scotus, however, considers that this
theory endangers the objectivity of our statements about God. He
therefore tries to find an objective basis in God for the distinctions
which we make[3] and asserts a distinction which is less than a real distinction but more than a purely mental distinction. There are distinct
'formalities' in God, such as intellect and will, though they are neither

[1] Aquinas admitted no distinctions in God except the distinctions between
the divine Persons. This, however, is a theological matter outside the field of
philosophy.
[2] Scotus's doctrine of universals and of the common nature influenced the American philosopher C. S. Peirce. See, for instance, *Charles Peirce and Scholastic
Realism: A Study of Peirce's Relation to John Duns Scotus* by J. E. Boler (Seattle,
1963).
[3] For Aquinas there is indeed a foundation in God of the distinctions which we
make. But this is simply the infinite divine perfection which can be grasped by
the human mind only in, so to speak, a piecemeal fashion and by means of concepts derived from experience of the things of this world.

separate nor separable entities. It is difficult to see how objective distinctions in the divine nature can be reconciled with assertion of the divine simplicity; but it is at any rate clear that Scotus is concerned with providing a language about God with an objective basis.

Turning from God to man, we can note that according to Scotus the philosopher can prove that the rational or intellectual soul of man is the substantial form of the human organism, the intrinsic principle of life, movement, sensation, understanding and willing. For theological reasons Scotus does indeed retain the old theory of a distinct 'form of corporeity'.[1] But he will have nothing to do with the idea of the rational or intellectual 'part' of man as a separate substance which in some mysterious way cooperates in or makes possible human understanding. This theory, attributed to 'that accursed Averroes' (*ille maledictus Averroes*) is said by Scotus to be intelligible neither to Averroes himself nor to any of his followers.[2] If it were true, we could not speak of this or that man understanding. For man as such would be nothing more than a kind of superior irrational animal.

Scotus is not, however, prepared to admit that the philosopher can demonstrate that the human soul is immortal. It is no good appealing to Aristotle. For his opinion is in any case obscure. 'He speaks in different ways, in different places, and he held different principles, from some of which one conclusion seems to follow, whereas from others the very opposite conclusion can be drawn.'[3] As for the argument that the operation of the intellect transcends the power of sense and does not depend on any organ in the way in which vision depends on the eyes, it is not conclusive. If it is true that intellectual activity does not depend on the condition of a particular organ, it follows that the rational soul cannot perish in the same way as a power of sense perishes, namely through the destruction of a particular organ. But this would not prove that when the composite organism disintegrates at death, the form of the composite substance does not cease to exist. It may be more probable that it does not perish. Persuasive probable arguments can be advanced in favour of immortality. But they do not amount to a demonstrative proof. In any case persuasive arguments can be advanced against immortality.

[1] We have already referred to the contention that if there were no 'form of corporeity' the body of Christ in the tomb would not have been *his* body, with the consequence that at the resurrection it was not Christ's body which rose.
[2] *Opus Oxoniense*, Book IV, Dist. 43, Qu. 1, No. 5 (Vivès edition, XX, p. 37).
[3] Ibid., Qu. 2, No. 16 (Vivès, p. 46).

As for arguments based on a natural desire not to die or to continue in life, they have little probative force. If we are talking about a biological intuitive tendency, animals can shun things which threaten their existence. But it does not follow that they are immortal. If, however, we are talking about a conscious desire not to die or to survive death, this might be a disordered or vain desire. Human beings can, after all, desire things which cannot be attained. In order to show that the desire is well ordered and will be fulfilled, we must first show that survival is *possible*. For the same reason no argument based on the need for sanctions in another life can be demonstrative, even if it has some persuasive force. For we have first to prove that there is another life in which sanctions could be realized.

Scotus is not denying immortality. What he maintains is that there is no philosophical proof of it. It belongs to the *credibilia*, to those truths which are believed on faith in a manner analogous to that in which certain divine attributes are matters of faith. It may be the case that Scotus tends to restrict the scope of philosophical proof to that which non-Christian philosophy has, in his opinion, succeeded in proving. But when he states that immortality cannot be philosophically demonstrated, he is not simply saying that as a matter of historical fact this or that Greek or Islamic philosopher has not proved it or has not believed in it. For he gives reasons for claiming that the philosophical arguments offered by previous Christian thinkers do not amount to demonstrative proofs.

There is an aspect of man on which Scotus insists strongly: his freedom. In his opinion the will is essentially a free power. The intellect is not. For it cannot but assent to the truth of a proposition when the truth is perceived, whereas the will always remains free, even in heaven. As, therefore, Scotus attaches great value to freedom, in the scholastic controversy about the respective ranks of intellect and will he regards the will as the nobler power. Besides, the will is the seat of love. And love of God takes precedence of knowledge of him. After all, which is worse, to hate God or not to know him?

Dispute about the comparative nobility of intellect and will is hardly likely to arouse much enthusiasm nowadays, not at any rate if it is expressed in these terms. But the matter can, of course, be put in another way. Scotus, we can say, emphasizes the volitional and affective aspect of man. He sees freedom as man's most striking characteristic and love as his highest activity. Aristotle, the great pagan philosopher, emphasized above all man's intellectual activity; and the highest achievement of the human race was for him the philosopher and scientist. For Scotus, the man who loves most genuinely and deeply is the man who exhibits human excellence in its highest degree. By 'love' he means love of the good for its own sake. He agrees with Aristotle that man has a natural inclination to seek his own happiness or self-perfection. But he does not look on man as restricted to loving either other people or God simply as means to his own self-perfection. God, as conceived by Christian faith, does not love other beings as means to his own advantage. He loves them altruistically. God's love is the measure of love. And the man who loves God freely because God is what he is, absolute goodness, is, so to speak, the Christian man. Scotus is not, of course, one to belittle intellectual activity and achievement. But in his awarding of the palm to will rather than to intellect we can see, underlying the scholastic dispute about powers or faculties, the drawing of a contrast between Christian love and philosophical rationalism.

Scotus's emphasis on love comes out in his ethics. God is infinite goodness and the supreme object of love. Hence the fundamental ethical norm is that God is to be loved for his own sake and above all things. And the basic prohibition is that God ought never to be hated or dishonoured. These precepts are immutable. God could never command anyone to hate him, nor forbid anyone to love him, as such commands would be incompatible with the divine nature. Love of God can never be wrong; and hatred of God can never be right.

If love of God is the fundamental and immutable moral precept, it follows, according to Scotus, that a human act cannot be morally good unless it is motivated, actually or virtually, by the love of God.[1] It does not follow, however, that a human act which is not so motivated is necessarily evil. If it is incompatible with the love of God, it is evil. But an act may be compatible with the love of God without being referred to God either actually or virtually. For example, someone who does not believe in God at all may give an alms to a poor man out of pity. His action is certainly not evil. Though, however, it has a certain natural goodness, it is, from the moral point of view, 'indifferent', neither morally good nor morally evil.[2] It stands outside the moral order, which is based on the norm of loving God.

[1] A man need not consciously say to himself, on the occasion of every act, that he is doing it for the love of God. But, for Scotus, it must at any rate be virtually informed by the love of God.
[2] Aquinas did not admit a class of morally indifferent 'human acts' (as distinct

Now Scotus asserts that 'the divine will is the cause of good, and so by the fact that he wills something it is good'.[1] Taken by itself, this statement need not mean more than the whole of creation depends on the divine will,[2] and that as God is infinite goodness whatever he wills is the effect of an infinitely good creative will and so itself good. But it is a notorious fact that according to Scotus certain precepts of the moral law depend on the divine will, and that they ought to be obeyed because God commands us to do so. If he meant simply that there would be no moral precepts unless there were a world with human beings and that creation depends on the divine will, there would be nothing odd in his statement, given his basic theistic belief. Again, if he meant simply that the Christian conscience is motivated by the desire to do God's will rather than by motives suggested by a purely utilitarian ethics or one of human self-realization or self-perfection, this point of view would be hardly surprising in the case of a man who regarded the basic moral norm as the love of God above all things. In point of fact, however, Scotus makes certain precepts of the moral law dependent on the divine will in respect of their content. This does not apply, of course, to the precepts of loving God above all things and of never hating or dishonouring him. For, as we have seen, not even God himself could change these precepts. But it applies to precepts relating to the neighbour or, as Scotus puts it, to the commandments of the second table of the Decalogue. It has, therefore, been maintained that with Scotus we can see the beginning of the first stage of the theological authoritarianism in ethics which was to become much more marked in the thought of William of Ockham.

What Scotus has in mind is partly a matter of logic. In his view God could not command anyone to hate him without self-contradiction. For the command would be to hate the infinitely lovable, the supreme

from, say, reflex actions). A human act is either compatible or incompatible with man's attainment of his final end, and it is thus either good or bad. Scotus, however, conceives the moral order in such a way that room is left for a class of human acts which fall outside this order.

[1] *Reportata Parisiensia*, Bk I, Dist. 48, Qu. 1. (Vivès, XXII, p. 512).

[2] Scotus maintained that if we ask why God created this or that, the only answer available is that God willed it. What he meant was that for contingent truths (that X or Y exists, when X and Y are finite things) no necessary reasons can be given. Hence the philosopher is unable to prove why God created this or that. God, being absolute goodness, must create with a view to the realization of goodness. But it does not follow that we can discover by philosophical reasoning why God created this sort of world rather than another.

object of the human will. But as far as logic is concerned, God could have commanded human beings to have all things in common. In this case there would have been no private property, and the precept of not stealing would be deprived of any moral force. Further, in adopting this point of view Scotus is influenced by accounts in the Old Testament in which God is depicted as ordering actions which are normally forbidden (the command to Abraham to sacrifice his son Isaac is an example) or can be interpreted as dispensing from some precept or as permitting its infringement (as in the case of polygamy on the part of the patriarchs). God, Scotus argues, could not command Abraham to sacrifice his son, if such a command would be self-contradictory in the sense in which a command to hate God would be self-contradictory. As for polygamy, divine permission to practise it involved no contradiction, when it was a question of the need for increasing the Israelite population. If the earth became depopulated through war or disease, God could permit it again.

If Scotus were looking at ethics simply and solely from the point of view of a logician, we would know where we were. The relevant questions would be logical ones. The whole matter is complicated, however, by Scotus's clear admission of the idea of a natural law. He distinguishes between actions which are wrong simply because they are forbidden and actions which are forbidden because they are evil. For example, to eat meat on a Friday is, in itself, no more wrong than to eat meat on a Monday. It is wrong, for a member of the Catholic Church, only if, and so long as, the Church forbids it, and provided that none of the recognized excusing conditions are present. Other actions, however, such as adultery, are forbidden because they are evil. And Scotus roundly asserts that 'all sins which concern the ten commandments are formally evil not merely because they are forbidden but because they are evil'.[1] They are forbidden by God because they are against the law of nature; and man's reason can see that the relevant precepts ought to be obeyed. How, we may well ask, is this point of view compatible with the statement that the precepts of the second table of the Decalogue depend on the divine will?

The answer seems to be on these lines. Reason can see that certain types of action are normally injurious to man in society. It therefore dictates that they should not be performed. If God forbids them because they are contrary to 'right reason', it becomes morally obligatory in the full sense not to perform them. For the supreme ethical norm is

[1] *Reportata Parisiensia*, Bk II, Dist. 22, Qu. 1, No. 3 (Vivès XXIII, p. 104).

to love God; and love is shown in obedience. If, however, it is logically possible (that is to say, without contradiction being involved) for the opposite of a certain precept to be commanded or for a dispensation to be given, it is in the power of God (though of nobody else) to do so. Take the case of polygamy. The precept of loving God does not logically entail having only one wife. Hence it is in God's 'absolute' power to command polygamy. That is to say, as far as logic is concerned, God could command it. If, however, we leave the field of pure logic and assume a world in which polygamy is normally injurious to man in society, it is clear that, whatever God may be able to do according to his 'absolute' power, he will in fact permit polygamy only in circumstances such as the threatened extinction of the human race, when it becomes more beneficial than injurious.

Scotus's ethical outlook is not such as to be acceptable to most moral philosophers today. But perhaps we can understand it better if we connect it with his view of the Incarnation as providing the key to history, and not as an event which would not have taken place, were it not for the Fall. Man is in any case called to incorporation in Christ. Christian ethics demands the fulfilment of God's will, acting out of obedience to the Father, as Christ did. True, God does not in fact issue commands and prohibitions in a purely arbitrary manner. There can be an ethics of 'right reason', a secular or philosophical ethics. But acts performed for prudential or utilitarian reasons are not moral acts in the strict sense. In the moral life, as Scotus conceives it, love of God, and so obedience to God, is the supreme norm.

From one point of view Scotus's thought can be seen as part of the Christian reaction against the spread of philosophical rationalism, which led to the condemnations of 1277. It is evident, however, that he made a far greater use of philosophical reflection, especially perhaps of the philosophy of Avicenna, than the diehard conservatives such as John Peckham. Scotus developed a system of a complex and original character. And it is really no matter of surprise that the Franciscans came to regard him as their principal Doctor and intellectual luminary, even if Bonaventure stood closer, both in time and spirit, to St Francis of Assisi. It is, of course, regrettable that Scotus died at a comparatively early age. But such regrets are useless.

15

The Fourteenth Century [1]
William of Ockham

1

THE leading medieval thinkers who combined theological and philosophical speculation belonged mainly to the thirteenth century, though some, such as Duns Scotus, died early in the fourteenth century. The systems of some of these thinkers lived on as bodies of doctrine characteristic of definite schools. As these schools tended to be associated with religious orders, they were assured of longevity. Aquinas became the official doctor of the Dominican order before the end of the thirteenth century. At a later date the Franciscans came to regard Duns Scotus as their particular intellectual luminary.[1] And the Hermits of St Augustine adopted Giles of Rome. In the course of time the schools were to produce learned expositions of end commentaries on the works and ideas of their patrons. The first outstanding commentator on Aquinas was John Capreolus (c. 1380–1444), who was succeeded by the famous Cajetan (Thomes de Vio, 1468–1534). But in the fourteenth century these schools did not produce much creative work. Together they represented the 'ancient way' (*via antiqua*) in contrast with the 'modern way' (*via moderna*), which is associated with the name of Ockham in particular.

The new movement is commonly described as the nominalist or terminist movement. It was characterized in part by the development of a logic, beginning in the thirteenth century and representing pretty

[1] The doctrine of Scotus was not imposed at any rate on the order until towards the end of the sixteenth century.

well the original medieval contribution to logical studies, in which great attention was devoted to analysing the functions of terms in propositions. Indeed, when the word 'terminism' is used to signify a certain logical development rather than as a synonym for nominalism in general, it is associated principally with the theory of *suppositio*, namely the theory of the substantive term's function of standing for things in the proposition. We shall return presently to this theme.

Another characteristic of the new movement was the interest shown in the analytical treatment of particular problems rather than in the creation of comprehensive syntheses. The approach to philosophical problems was predominantly analytical, critical and sometimes empiricist. Moreover, there was a strong tendency to regard as probable arguments previously regarded as demonstrative. We have already had occasion to notice this tendency in connection with Scotus on immortality. With fourteenth-century thinkers such as Ockham and, still more, Nicholas of Autrecourt we can find a thoroughgoing criticism of traditional metaphysical arguments.

One result of this was a growing separation between theology and philosophy. A good deal of the traditional metaphysics, which had formed a bridge between the two disciplines, was relegated to the sphere of faith; and logic and what we may describe as analysis tended to form the occupations of philosophers. It does not follow, of course, that the two disciplines were pursued by different sets of people in completely watertight compartments. William of Ockham, for example, was theologian, philosopher and logician, not to speak of his activities in political controversy. But this does not alter the fact that the close links between philosophy and theology which had seemed natural to most thirteenth-century thinkers[1] were breaking under the pressure of criticism. This is apparent in the metaphysical field, where doubt about the validity of traditional arguments was accompanied by a strong dosage of theological fideism.[2] And it is also apparent in the ethical field, where, with some thinkers at any rate, there is a strong tendency to make the moral law dependent on the divine will, intensifying and carrying further a tendency already discernible in Duns Scotus.

[1] The separation between philosophy and theology had already begun, of course, in the Faculty of Arts at Paris during the second half of the thirteenth century, in the decades preceding the condemnation of 1277.
[2] If, for instance, a man refuses to admit that there is or can be any proof of the existence of God but asserts God's existence on faith, his attitude can be said to express a 'fideist' point of view.

Aquinas's attempt to synthesize Aristotelian and Christian ethics shows distinct signs of floundering.

How one regards fourteenth-century thought obviously depends very largely on one's personal convictions in the areas of theology and philosophy. Followers of Aquinas have naturally been inclined to look on the fourteenth century as the period in which the medieval synthesis (syntheses would be more accurate) broke down under the pressure of misguided criticism. They have, of course, differed in their estimates of the situation. Some have regarded the nominalist movement as frankly deplorable. Others, while prepared to reject the nominalist criticisms of traditional metaphysics, have shown no hankering after a fossilized society or changeless cultural situation. In general, however, Thomists have regarded the thirteenth century as representing the high peak of philosophical thought in the Middle Ages and the fourteenth century as representing a critical and even destructive phase of thought, which doubtless occurred in accordance with a general pattern (speculative and constructive thought followed by criticism of presuppositions) but which failed to come up to the level of the preceding phase. At the opposite pole are those who for various reasons regard the new movement of thought in the fourteenth century with warm approval. For some it represents a struggle to liberate Christian faith from the contamination of Greek and Islamic metaphysics. For others it gives expression to a concept of philosophy which is much more like their own, namely the concept of philosophy as consisting mainly in logical studies, analysis and the criticism of presuppositions. It is perfectly understandable that a good many modern philosophers should feel themselves in a strange land when they study the writings of the great theologians of the thirteenth century and much more at home when they turn to the logical studies of the fourteenth century. One may receive the impression that William of Ockham, for example, in spite of his strong theological convictions, would have felt more or less at ease in a discussion group of present-day analytical philosophers.

Needless to say, from the philosophical point the relevant question in regard to, say, fourteenth-century criticism of traditional metaphysical arguments is whether the criticism is valid or invalid. To describe it as 'destructive', if it is in fact well grounded, is unhelpful. Again, though some people may be inclined to deplore the shifting of interest in university or academic philosophy to logical and analytic inquiries, the relevant question is whether these inquiries achieved anything. A waxing enthusiasm for speculative metaphysics may well have been accompanied by logical developments of value. Theories about separate intelligences, active intellects, divine ideas and so on are by no means to everybody's taste. Nor, of course, are inquiries into logical paradoxes, the nature of implication or the propositional functions of terms. But it is not unreasonable to suggest that in inquiries of the second type there is a good hope of getting somewhere, whereas in regard to the movements of the heavenly bodies there was not much hope of developing anything but picturesque speculations before the rise of astronomy as a science. It may be objected, and with justice, that thirteenth-century metaphysics was very far from consisting simply of airy speculation which was destined to give way in the course of time to scientific investigation. This is quite true. But medieval metaphysics included of course a great deal of conceptual analysis.

In the course of time the new movement came itself to be embodied in a school, the so-called nominalist school. But as far as the fourteenth century is concerned it is preferable to speak of a movement of thought rather than of a school. The movement was not confined to one place or to any particular corporation or religious order. Its influence became strong in some of the new universities founded towards the end of the fourteenth century; but it also penetrated older universities, such as Oxford. As for religious orders, reference has been made to the association of the schools with definite orders; but this does not mean that the orders were immune from influence by the new movement. Ockham was a Franciscan; and his influence was felt not only in his own but also in other religious institutes.

Moreover, if the influence of the new movement was not confined to any particular centre or corporation, nor was it always uniform in character. Some philosophers were attracted by the terminist logic and concentrated particularly on logical studies, while others might be more interested in the critical analysis of philosophical ideas and arguments. Again, while some of those who criticized the traditional metaphysics adversely seem to have concerned themselves very little with the theological implications of this criticism, others regarded such criticism as effecting a welcome liberation of faith from the tyranny of rationalist metaphysics of non-Christian origin. In short, the new movement was complex in character and influence.

2

It would, of course, be absurd to describe the spirit of the thirteenth century as theological and metaphysical and that of the fourteenth century as logical, as though the theologians and metaphysicians had paid no attention to logic. Apart from the fact that theological and philosophical thinking was set in a severely logical mould, it was the theologians, as we have already noted, who first made real use of what, at the time, was known as the 'new' logic, the logic, that is to say, contained in the books of Aristotle's *Organon* which the translations had made available in addition to the already known books comprising the 'old' logic. Further, the logical developments of the 'modern' or 'new' logic in the sense in which the 'new' logic came to be distinguished from the 'old' and 'new' logics in the sense mentioned above, had their origins in the thirteenth century. In other words, the Aristotelian logic, comprising both the 'old' and 'new' in the first mentioned sense of these terms, formed the springboard or point of departure for the logical inquiries which represented original work and constituted the 'modern' or 'new' logic in the second sense of the term. To put the matter simply, what had previously been described as the new logic came to be lumped together with the old logic as constituting together logic which was 'old' in comparison with the fresh inquiries which began in the thirteenth century and flourished in the fourteenth.

A thirteenth-century logician who should be mentioned is the Englishman William of Sherwood or Shyreswood, who was born early in the century and died between 1266 and 1271. For a time he taught at Oxford. In his *Syncategoremata*[1] he examined the properties and use of syncategorematic terms (logical constants), such as 'not', 'if' and 'or'. The word 'syncategorematic' seems to go back to the Stoics, who used it for words which cannot function as subject or predicate in a proposition, have no referential function and signify only in virtue of their logical functions in propositions. William of Sherwood also wrote *Introductions to Logic* (*Introductiones in Logicam*) in six parts.[2] In the fifth treatise, on the properties of terms, he included the topic of *suppositio*, of the substantive term's function of standing for an object or

---

[1] This treatise, edited by J. R. O'Donnell, has been published in *Medieval Studies*, Vol. 3 (1941), pp. 46–93.

[2] A translation has been published by N. Kretzmann (Minneapolis, 1965).

objects, as the noun 'man' stands for men.[1] Among William's other treatises there was one *De insolubilibus*, on paradoxes such as the paradox arising from the sentence 'what I am saying is false', when this sentence is my only utterance, so that the sentence is self-referring. By the term 'insoluble', as used in this connection, medieval logicians did not mean literally insoluble but rather very difficult to solve.

One of the most influential logical treatises of the thirteenth century was the *Summulae Logicales* of Peter of Spain. A native of Lisbon, Peter studied at Paris, his teachers including Albert the Great and (probably) William of Sherwood. In 1245 or 1246 he left Paris and taught and practised medicine for a time at Siena. Eventually he was elected pope as John XXI, and it was in this capacity that he asked Tempier, bishop of Paris, to investigate the teaching in the Paris Faculty of Arts. He died in 1277.

It is generally agreed that as a logician Peter of Spain was inferior to William of Sherwood. But his *Summulae Logicales* became a favourite text book. Logic, the author insists, is the art of arts and science of sciences, in the sense that it is a preparation for all the other sciences. It is the art of reasoning; but reasoning has to be conducted through the instrumentality of language. Hence the study of logic must begin with an examination of terms and their functions. Peter discusses a variety of topics; but we must restrict ourselves to noting a few points in regard to his treatment of *suppositio*. One form of this is what he calls *suppositio discreta*. This phrase refers to the function of a term in standing for one individual, as in 'Socrates is a man'. Discrete supposition is thus to be distinguished from common supposition (*suppositio communis*), which occurs when, for instance, the subject of a proposition is a universal term, as in 'man is mortal'.

Common supposition is subdivided into natural and accidental supposition. A term such as 'man' is a sign with a certain sign-function or meaning (its *significatio*). Because of this meaning it is capable of standing in a proposition for those things of which it can be predicated.[2] Thus 'man', because of the meaning of the term, can be used to stand for all men, including those who have existed in the past or will exist in the future. Accidental supposition, which can itself be of different kinds, is found when the kind of 'standing for' which a term has is

---

[1] Obviously, in Latin *homo* may mean 'the man' or 'man' (as in 'man is a rational animal'). In English 'man' would normally be understood as referring to men in general, as we have the definite article for use in referring to a particular man.

[2] In other words, *significatio* is presupposed by *suppositio*.

determined by something added (*adiunctum*). If we say, for instance, that every animal except man is irrational, we restrict the supposition of the term 'animal'.

In the statement that every man is an animal, the term 'animal', in Peter's view, stands only for the nature of the genus animal and not for individual animals.[1] This is a case of simple accidental supposition. In the statement that some man is running the word 'man' stands for any individual human being, so far as language is concerned. This is a case of personal accidental supposition.

3

William of Ockham was born at Ockham in Surrey about the year 1285. (at any rate between 1280 and 1290). Becoming a Franciscan, he began his theological studies at Oxford in 1309 or 1310, lectured on the Bible from 1315–17 and on the *Sentences* of Peter Lombard from 1317–19. Normally he would in due course have received his licence to teach as a doctor of theology; but in 1323 John Lutterell, chancellor of Oxford, went to Avignon to prefer charges of erroneous teaching against him.[2] The result was that early in 1324 Ockham was summoned to Avignon to answer the accusations. Lutterell had debated fifty-six propositions from Ockham's commentary on the *Sentences*; and a commission was chosen to investigate the matter. The members of the commission selected for consideration some thirty-three propositions, mainly theological, and added some others. The inquiry remained unfinished, but Ockham never received the licence to teach. Hence the descriptive title *Venerabilis inceptor*, the word *inceptor* or 'beginner' indicating that though Ockham had fulfilled the requirements for the doctorate, he never became an actual professor, a *magister actu regens*.

While Ockham was at Avignon, Michael of Cesena, minister general of the Franciscans, arrived at the papal court there to answer for his attacks on the papal decisions about evangelical poverty in the Franciscan order. The minister general unfortunately succeeded in interesting Ockham in the dispute;[3] and when in May 1328 he fled from Avignon,

---

[1] Peter remarks that it would be false to claim that every man is *this* animal.
[2] In 1322 Edward II forbade Lutterell to go to Avignon, telling him not to endanger the University's reputation by referring domestic issues to the pope. But in 1323 the king gave his consent to the journey.
[3] 'Unfortunately' because it is unlikely that anything terrible would have happened to Ockham on account of the charges made by that zealous Thomist John

he took Ockham along with him. They found refuge with Ludwig of Bavaria at Pisa and then accompanied him to Munich. Ludwig was involved in his own quarrels with the pope over papal temporal power; and Ockham defended the anti-papal point of view in a series of political writings.

Ockham had been excommunicated along with Michael of Cesena when they fled from Avignon. And at Ludwig's death in 1349 he apparently took steps to reconcile himself with the Holy See, making an act of submission. But he died in 1349, probably of the Black Death; and it is not known if a formal reconciliation ever took place.

Ockham's main work is his commentary on the *Sentences* of Peter Lombard. The first book was revised by the author and so constitutes the *Ordinatio*. The other three books consist of *reportata*, probably unrevised reports of Ockham's lectures. In addition we have seven *Quodlibeta*, which also seem to be reports. We have also some small treatises on theological topics such as the eucharist and divine knowledge of future contingent events. In the field of logic Ockham wrote an explanation of Porphyry's *Isagoge*, expositions of Aristotle's work on the categories, of his *On Interpretation*, and of his work on fallacies, besides a *Summary of the Whole of Logic* (*Summa totius logicae*) and two other shorter treatises. In the area of physics Ockham wrote a commentary on Aristotle's *Physics*, besides *Questions* on this work and a summary of it. As for the writings on politics, we have a considerable number of tracts, such as *The Work of Ninety Days* (*Opus nonaginta dierum*) and the *Dialogue* (*Dialogus*).

Publication of a critical edition of Ockham's political writings was begun by the Manchester University Press in 1940 under the editorship of J. G. Sikes.[1] A critical edition of his philosophical and theological works is being published under the auspices of the Franciscan Institute at St Bonaventure, New York.[2]

When we study Ockham's thought it is important to bear in mind his theological convictions and his theologically based vision of the

---

Lutterell. If he had not got mixed up in the poverty dispute, he would probably have been able to pursue his academic career and publish writings which, from the philosophical point of view at any rate, would have been of more interest and value than his anti-papal polemics.

[1] Vol. III edited by H. S. Offler, 1956.

[2] *Guillelmi de Ockham opera philosophica et theologica ad fidem codicum manuscriptorum edita*, edited by S. Brown, O.F.M., with the collaboration of G. Gál, O.F.M., and others (first two volumes of the *Ordinatio*, 1967 and 1970).

world. On the one hand he sees God as omnipotent and free, able to do anything at all which does not involve a logical contradiction. On the other hand he sees the world as contingent through and through, or, if preferred, he sees true statements about finite things as contingent truths, dependent on the divine will. It does not follow that Ockham thinks of the divine omnipotence and freedom as philosophically demonstrable. The point is rather that his theological vision of reality, the Christian vision as he conceives it, predisposes him to think in certain ways. For example, Ockham's firm belief in the divine omnipotence and freedom predisposes him to reject any elements of Greek or Islamic necessitarianism. To accept the theory of the world as necessarily emanating from God by successive stages would be to him unthinkable. Even the doctrine of eternal divine ideas as exemplars or patterns of creation seems to him to smack of Greek necessitarianism, at any rate if it is interpreted as meaning that the divine will is constricted by eternal archetypes. Again, Ockham's vision of the world as contingent through and through predisposes him to insist that the only way to discover how things are is to look and see (or by deduction from already ascertained truths). For things are not necessarily as they are. They could be otherwise. The true statements which we make about them are contingent truths.

It is, of course, often difficult to assess how much Ockham was influenced by purely logical and philosophical considerations in asserting a given opinion or theory, and how much by theological considerations. The theological background of his thought is not, however, a matter of unimportance or a mere extra. When criticizing metaphysical arguments or theories advanced by his predecessors, he may appeal simply to logical criteria. Rightly so, as he is dealing with matters of logic. At the same time Ockham is far from trying to debunk metaphysics with the covert aim of implying that Christian faith is irrational. In addition to his logical preoccupations he has in mind the liberation of Christian faith from what he regards, rightly or wrongly, as the alien yoke of Greek and Islamic ways of thinking, which have contaminated its purity. It is possible, for example, to criticize proofs of God's existence with a view to showing that belief in God is unwarrantable. It is also possible for a man to criticize the traditional proofs not only because he thinks them invalid on logical grounds but also with the conviction that a God whose existence had been philosophically demonstrated would not be the transcendent God of Christian faith. It is doubtless an exaggeration to depict Ockham as a Barthian before Barth; but if he restricts the scope of philosophy on logical grounds, he also thinks that this is in the interest of faith and theology.

To put the matter succinctly, Ockham is not two personalities but one. Divine omnipotence and freedom are for him matters of faith, but it by no means follows that the beliefs which he accepts as a Christian are without any influence on his mind and thinking as a philosopher.

The foundation of all our knowledge of the world is for Ockham immediate awareness of individual things. It is only individual things which exist.[1] The notion that universals are substances existing outside the mind is absurd. This can be easily seen. If the human nature of Tom were really a common nature or universal essence ontologically common to all members of the human species, the annihilation of Tom would entail the annihilation of the species, of all men. But this is obviously not the case. As for Scotus's doctrine that there is a formal distinction in Tom between the common nature and his 'thisness', the theory is clearly an attempt to have things both ways. There is not, and cannot be, any universal nature which needs to be 'contracted' by some individualizing factor. By the very fact that anything exists it is an individual or singular thing. And all knowledge of reality presupposes immediate apprehension of individual existents.

Immediate intuitive apprehension of a thing is not indeed the same as judgement. But it is naturally expressed in the judgement that the thing in question exists. And Ockham defines intuitive knowledge (notitia intuitiva) of a thing as knowledge of such a kind that 'one can know by means of it whether a thing is or not; and if it is, the intellect immediately judges that the thing exists . . . '.[2] Intuitive knowledge thus enables the mind to enunciate a contingent proposition about the existence of the thing apprehended.

Ockham is not, however, prepared to allow that intuitive apprehension of a singular or individual object is an infallible guarantee that the object exists. He rather complicates matters by talking about 'intuitive knowledge' of a non-existing object. That is to say, a critic might wish to raise questions about the appropriateness of the word 'knowledge' in this context. This point apart, however, Ockham's position seems

---

[1] Ockham remarks that by a singular or individual thing he does not mean simply a thing which is numerically one. For a word is a singular thing in this sense. He therefore defines a singular thing as a thing which is not only numerically one but also 'not a natural or conventional sign belonging in common to many things signified' (Quodlibeta, I, Question 13, No. 3).

[2] Ordinatio, Prologue, Question I, Article 1 (critical edition, I, p. 31).

to be clear enough. We have to make a distinction between the act of seeing, for example, and the judgement that the thing seen exists as an extramental reality. The judgement is a contingent proposition; and the act of seeing does not guarantee its truth. On this matter Ockham appeals to the divine omnipotence, when this is taken to mean that whatever God does by means of secondary causes he can do without them. Normally vision of an object is caused by the presence of the object; but God *could* produce the physico-psychological act without the object existing, provided that the object has existed, will exist or is at any rate a possible object. It is true that according to Ockham the divine omnipotence is a truth of faith which cannot be proved in philosophy. But the reason why he believes that God could cause intuitive apprehension of a non-existing object is that there is, in his view, no logical contradiction between, say, the statement 'I see a star' and the statement 'the star does not exist' or 'there is no star there'. And this logical point can obviously be made without reference to God. The reason why Ockham brings God into the matter is his view that 'naturally speaking, intuitive knowledge cannot be caused or perceived unless the object exists'.[1] It is only God who can actually bring about such a situation. But he could not do so if it was a case of logical impossibility. And the philosopher can see that there is in fact no logical contradiction involved, even if he has to admit that in the natural order of things intuitive knowledge of an object is always an effect produced by an existing object.

This thesis was one of those to which Ockham's theological critics took exception. Presumably they thought that it was tantamount to claiming that God could be a deceiver. But though Ockham did say that God could produce in us assent to the proposition that a star (as object of vision) existed, when in fact it did not exist, he added that this assent would be a creditive act rather than evident knowledge.[2] And if he had not been diverted to the dispute about evangelical poverty, he should have been able to satisfy more temperate judges than Lutterell that what he had said was not so horrifying after all. As for the thesis in itself, profitable discussion would demand some careful analysis. For instance, according to our ordinary way of speaking, we can see a star, when, as

[1] *Quodlibeta*, VI, Qu. 6, No. 2.
[2] In other words, God could produce in us physico-psychological conditions which would naturally lead us to make a certain judgement, believing it to be true, though our belief would not amount to real knowledge. This was doubtless the line of thought which scandalized Lutterell.

the astronomers tell us, the star no longer exists. And if we are ignorant of what the astronomers say, we naturally judge that the star does exist. But, given some knowledge of the astronomical facts, what is the proper way of speaking? Can I properly say 'I perceive a star'? If so, what precisely is meant? Talk about my having 'intuitive knowledge' (*cognitio intuitiva*) seems to be open to criticism,[1] though it is clear enough that even in the natural course of events we can think that we perceive an actually existing object, when in point of fact it does not actually exist.[2]

In any case the foundation of all our knowledge of reality is intuitive apprehension of singular or individual objects. This is not to say that intuitive knowledge is the only form of knowledge. There is also abstractive knowledge. At this level universal concepts appear. Ockham seems first to have understood abstractive knowledge as any knowledge in virtue of which it cannot be known whether an object exists. For instance, I can know that John is white or that he is an Englishman. But even if the judgement that John is white implies that he exists, I cannot infer from my knowledge of his being white that he exists.[3] By the time, however, that Ockham came to write his *Quodlibeta* he had clearly linked abstractive knowledge with universal concepts. 'Man is mortal' would express abstractive knowledge. But this kind of knowledge presupposes *cognitio intuitiva*, intuitive knowledge. Indeed, however one understands abstractive knowledge, it always presupposes immediate awareness of individual objects.

Such objects need not be external material things, the objects of sense-perception. We can have intuitive knowledge of our interior acts, such as an act of desire or of willing. So we can say that for Ockham sense-

[1] It should be remembered, however, that Ockham explicitly asserts that the word 'knowledge' can have a variety of meanings (prologue to Ockham's exposition of the eight books of the *Physics* of Aristotle). For instance, we can say that we 'know' that Rome is a big city, even if we have never seen Rome but accept the fact on testimony. Again, I can properly say that I 'know' that X is my father. But such cases are not cases of 'evident knowledge'. Cf. *Summa totius logicae*, III, 2.
[2] Ockham might comment that even if his statement that in the natural order we cannot have 'intuitive knowledge' unless the object exists was inaccurate, the cause of the intuitive apprehension would be natural. In the case of the star which has ceased to exist, the cause of our perception was the star when still existing. The gap between our perception and the star's actual existence is easily explicable in terms of the scientific theory of the transmission of light.
[3] John is *ex hypothesi* absent and not an immediate object of my perception. I can reasonably be said to know that he is white and not some other colour. But it is conceivable that he has just died.

perception and introspection are the sources of our natural knowledge of reality. And the principle of economy or parsimony[1] can be employed to eliminate entities the existence of which is neither verifiable in experience nor deducible with the aid of self-evident principles nor guaranteed by revelation.

Well, what sort of things exist in the world? Substances and their qualities. All other categories are connotative terms. A table, for example, is identical with its quantity. If we say that the table has or possesses quantity, quantity is not an entity distinct from the table. The word 'quantity', in this case, signifies the table itself and connotes its having parts. If it had no parts, it would not be a table. As for relations, there are no such entities distinct from the things which are said to be related and the activity of the mind which compares them. It is quite correct to say, for example, that two blades of grass are alike in certain respects. But it by no means follows that there is any relation of similarity distinct from the two objects and the comparing activity of the mind. If we apply the principle of economy or parsimony, we can get rid of all alleged distinct entities called relations.[2] The world is then seen to consist of distinct substances with their various qualities.

Each of these substances or things could exist by itself – not, of course, in the natural order but through the divine power. For there is no logical contradiction between the statement that Tom exists and the statement that no other finite thing exists. In other words, there are no necessary relations between things. It follows that if A is the cause of B, this is simply a matter of contingent fact. And such facts cannot be ascertained purely *a priori*, but only through recourse to experience. To intuit B is not to untuit A. The idea of the one does not contain in itself the idea of the other, except perhaps by the force of association. If we wish to discover the cause of an event X, we have to ascertain the factor which always precedes X and in the absence of which X never occurs. 'It is proved that fire is the cause of heat, since, when fire is there and all other things (that is, all other possible causal factors) have been removed, heat follows in a heatable object which has been brought near (the fire). . . . Similarly, it is proved that the object is the cause of intuitive knowledge, for when all other factors are present and the

[1] The principle, as stated by Ockham, asserts that plurality is not to be postulated without necessity or that what can be explained by postulating fewer things is vainly explained by postulating a greater number of things.
[2] Ockham admits 'real' relations in the Trinity; but this topic lies outside the philosopher's range.

object alone has been removed, intuitive knowledge does not follow.'[1]

Ockham does not deny the principle of causality in the sense of claiming that a thing can come into being without any cause. Nor does he reduce the idea of causality to that of regular sequence. What he says is that we cannot discover the cause of an event except through experience. And the method of presence and absence, or of exclusion, is offered by Ockham as a way of discovering the cause of a particular event. In point of fact he expounds Aristotle's doctrine of the four types of causation; and he himself argues in a manner which clearly implies the belief that an event must have *some* cause. After all, if God were to create a single human being, without any other finite thing existing, this human being would still have a cause, though not an empirical one.

Use of abstract terms, Ockham maintains, inclines people to think that there must be entities corresponding to these terms. For example, we talk about things being in time. And we may therefore be disposed to think that there must be some mysterious entity called 'time' in which events occur. The word 'time', however, signifies the same as 'motion', though it connotes an act of the mind, distinguishing between before and after in motion. As for motion, to say that a body is moved locally is to say that it occupies several places successively. There is no entity or quality called 'locomotion', an entity distinct, that is to say, from things. 'It would be astonishing, if my hand caused some power in a stone through coming into contact with it by local motion.'[2] We need not invent entities or powers or special qualities to explain motion. The question is what stops a thing moving, once it has started, rather than why it continues to move.

Motion is thus analysed in terms of things and places. And place itself is defined in terms of the surface or surfaces of bodies in regard to which a certain thing is said to be in a certain place. So in the long run we arrive at a world consisting of things and their absolute accidents.

Ockham can certainly not be described as an empiricist, if by empiricism we mean the philosophy of Hume or if we understand it as involving the rejection of metaphysics. At the same time we can justifiably speak of empiricist elements in his thought. We have considered some of them. And we can now turn to some logical topics.

In the first place Ockham distinguishes between 'real' science and

[1] *Ordinatio*, Bk I, Qu. 1 and Qu. 3 (critical edition, I, p. 416).
[2] *Reportata*, Bk II, Qu. 26.

'rational' science. These are technical terms and need some explanation. All sciences, Ockham insists, are concerned with propositions. It is of propositions that we predicate truth or falsity. Though, however, all sciences are propositional, there are different types of science. In physics, for example, the physicist or natural philosopher is concerned with common concepts which stand immediately for things.[1] In ordinary language we would be inclined to say that physics treats of things. This is, however, a loose way of talking. If the physicist or natural philosopher makes a general statement about, say, moving bodies, he is immediately concerned with the concept of 'the moving body', which is said to stand for individual moving bodies. Physics is a real science. And while all real sciences treat of things, they do so mediately, in the sense that they are concerned with common concepts which stand directly for things. Logic, however, treats of concepts which stand for other concepts. If, for example, the logician makes the statement that species are subdivisions of genuses, the term 'species' stands for the concepts of 'man', 'lion', 'horse' and so on. Logic, therefore, as being concerned with concepts which stand for other concepts, is described as a rational science. To put the matter in another way, the real sciences treat of terms of first intention, signifying things, while rational science treats of terms of second intention, signifying other terms.[2]

It may seem perhaps that the statement that logic is concerned with terms is incompatible with the statement that it is concerned with concepts standing for other concepts. For is not a term a word and not a concept? To answer this difficulty, reference must be made to some important distinctions, a grasp of which is essential for an understanding of Ockham's position.

The word 'term', Ockham remarks, can be used in several senses.[3] In the first place it can be used in a broad sense to include, for example, everything which can be the subject of a sentence. In this case even a

[1] Ockham refers to Aristotle's doctrine that science is concerned with universals, but not with individual things. There can be no science of the individual thing as such.
[2] The distinction between terms of first and second intention is not identical with names of first and second imposition. 'Species' is a term of second intention inasmuch as it signifies other concepts (terms of first intention). But it is a name of first imposition, in so far as it is used to signify natural signs (concepts) and not conventional signs (words as such). 'Noun', as used by the grammarian, would be a name of second imposition.
[3] See *Summa totius logicae*, I, Chapter 2.

proposition can be described as a term. For if we say ' "man is mortal" is a true proposition', the sentence 'man is mortal' functions as the subject of which truth is predicated. Secondly, terms can be contrasted with sentences in such a way that every non-complex expression is described as a term. In this case syncategorematic words (such as 'every', 'or' and 'not') count as terms. Thirdly, the word 'term' can be taken to designate everything which *in its significative function* can be either subject or predicate in a proposition.[1] This, according to Ockham, is the more precise use of 'term'.

Now if we consider categorematic terms according to their significative function, we have to make further distinctions. When we speak of terms, we may be referring to the written term (*terminus scriptus*) or the spoken term (*terminus prolatus*). Considered in this way, terms are conventional signs. In the English language we use 'man' to signify men, in French *homme*, in Italian *uomo*. This is a matter of linguistic convention. The mental content or concept is the same, however, whichever conventional sign is used. The *terminus conceptus* (the conceptual term or mental concept, *intentio animae*) is thus what Ockham describes as a natural sign. It is expressed, of course, by means of a conventional sign; but it is not itself a conventional sign. Provided therefore that 'term' is understood in the sense of conceptual term, there is no incompatibility between the statement that real science is concerned with concepts and the statement that it is concerned with terms.

Terms such as 'man' and 'white', which can stand as subject or as predicate in a proposition, are meaningful by themselves. They possess a significative function. But it is only in a proposition that a term acquires the function of 'standing for' something else, the function of *suppositio*.[2] Thus in the sentence 'man is mortal' the term 'man' acquires the function of standing for all individual men, while in the sentence 'some man is running' it acquires the function of standing indeterminately for a man.

There are several kinds of *suppositio*. First, there is what Ockham calls 'personal supposition' (*suppositio personalis*). By definition this is said to obtain 'when a term stands for what it signifies and is used in its

---

[1] 'From', for instance, cannot be used, in its significant function, as subject or predicate. For it is a syncategorematic word and has what may be described as a co-signifying function. It can of course function as subject in the grammatical statement '*from* is a proposition'; but it is not then used as a sign of something other than itself.

[2] See *Summa totius logicae*, I, Chapter 62.

significative function'.[1] If we say, for example, that every man is mortal, the term 'man' stands for what it signifies, namely men, and is used to signify them. Secondly there is 'simple supposition' (*suppositio simplex*), which obtains when a term stands for a concept (*intentio animae*) but is *not* used in its significative function. For example, if we say that man is a species, the term 'man' stands for a concept but it is not used in its significative function. We are obviously not claiming that individual men are species. Thirdly there is 'material supposition' (*suppositio materialis*), which obtains when a term stands not for what it signifies but for a written word or vocal sound. For instance, if we say that 'man' is a noun, the term 'man' stands for itself as a conventional sign and not for what it signifies. Men are not nouns.[2]

It is in terms of the notion of supposition that Ockham develops his theory of truth, the truth of propositions that is to say. In his view a necessary and sufficient condition for a proposition being true is that 'subject and predicate should stand for the same thing'.[3] If we take as an example the singular proposition 'Socrates is a man', this is true if what the predicate stands for is the same as Socrates. If we assume, for instance, that the predicate stands for 'humanity', the proposition is false. If the proposition is true, 'a man' must stand for Socrates. And it states that he is truly a man. In other words, in true propositions predicates do not designate entities distinct from the entities signified by absolute terms. If they do, the propositions in question are false.

Ockham insists that 'Socrates is a man' would be false, if it were interpreted as meaning that humanity is 'in' or 'a part of' Socrates. There is no common nature, humanity, which can be in or a part of anything or which requires individualizing by matter (Aquinas) or by a 'thisness' (Scotus).[4] It cannot therefore be predicated of Socrates. Nor, of course, can we say that Socrates is a universal concept.

---

[1] *Summa totius logicae*, Chapter 63.
[2] It should be clear enough from this summary account that, as Ockham warns his readers, the words 'personal', 'simple' and 'material', as used to describe different types of supposition, are employed in technical senses. Personal supposition, for example, should not be taken as implying that it necessarily stands for a person or persons.
[3] *Summa totius logicae*, II, Chapter 2.
[4] The question, therefore (How is the common nature contracted to individuals or how is it individualized?), is for Ockham a pseudo-question. The only answer which one can give is to show that the question rests on a false assumption, namely that there is an extramentally existing universal or common nature which stands in need of individualization.

The question of the way in which the universal concept arises belongs to psychology rather than to logic. Ockham's general view is that it arises through comparison of abstractive concepts or acts of knowledge of particulars. What it represents is not a common nature but similar individuals, their similarity consisting in the fact that they are what they are, not in their sharing in any common entity. As for the nature of the universal concept in itself, Ockham does not appear to have any very strongly felt conviction. In his commentary on the *Sentences* he mentions three possible views. The view which he himself finally adopts is, as one might expect, the most economical view, namely that the concept is identical with the act of understanding individual objects in a certain way. This enables him to eliminate the idea of the universal as a distinct mental reality functioning as a representation of objects. But what Ockham insists on is not so much the nature of the concept as the fact that, whatever its precise nature may be, there is no universal whatsoever outside the mind.

In the arrangement of the matter in his *Summa totius logicae* Ockham follows a traditional pattern by treating first of the logic of terms, then of the logic of propositions and finally of the logic of reasoning or inference. Further, though he certainly shows awareness of the fact that syllogistic inference is not coextensive with the whole field of inference or reasoning, he adopts a traditional position of treating syllogistics as central and giving his rules for consequences only after dealing with the various types of syllogism, whereas Walter Burleigh and Albert of Saxony arrange the matter in their respective treatises in such a way as to exhibit more clearly their recognition of the fact that the general theory of consequences is presupposed by syllogistics.

It by no means follows, however, that Ockham's theory of consequences is devoid of interest. For example, discovery of 'laws' for the negation of conjunctions and disjunctions used to be attributed to the nineteenth-century logician Augustus De Morgan. Though, however, De Morgan did state the laws in question, we can find something of the kind in Ockham's writings. He asserts, for example, that 'the contradictory opposite of a copulative proposition is a disjunctive proposition composed of the contradictory opposites of the parts of the copulative proposition.'[1] He adds that there is always a valid consequence from a copulative proposition to either part, but that, except in certain circumstances, inference from a part to the whole is not valid. Ockham also states that 'the contradictory opposite of a disjunctive proposition

[1] *Summa totius logicae*, II, Chapter 32.

is a copulative proposition composed of the contradictory opposites of the parts of the disjunctive proposition.'[1]

By 'consequences' (*consequentiae*) the medieval logicians meant conditional propositions (if *p*, then *q*). Ockham divides them into 'formal' and 'material' consequences. By formal consequences he understands implication which is governed, immediately or mediately, by a logical rule that is concerned simply with the logical form or structure of the relevant propositions, and not with the content of the propositions. By material consequences he understands implication which holds 'precisely by reason of the terms',[2] in virtue, that is to say, of the content specified by the descriptive terms of the relevant propositions. It is under the heading of material consequences that Ockham includes such odd utterances as 'if a man is running, God exists' and 'man is a donkey, therefore God does not exist'. In the first case it is assumed that a true proposition 'follows' from any proposition, in the second that from an impossibility anything 'follows'. Elsewhere Ockham mentions 'you are white, therefore God is three in one' and 'you are a donkey, therefore you are God'.[3] He remarks that these consequences are not formal ones and that they neither should be nor are much used.

To turn to metaphysics. If we ask, 'What is for Ockham the subject-matter of metaphysics?', we are asking a question which, in his opinion, is like asking 'Who is the king of all Christendom?'[4] In both cases the presupposition is false – in the second case that there is a king of all Christendom, in the first that metaphysics has one subject-matter. Avicenna claimed that the subject-matter of metaphysics was being, Averroes that it was God. According to Ockham, if the two Islamic philosophers are understood as claiming that metaphysics has one single subject-matter, then they are both wrong. If, however, they are understood as talking about priorities, both theses are defensible. As far as priority of perfection is concerned, God is the primary subject-matter of metaphysics. As far as priority of predication is concerned, being is the primary theme. For we cannot conceive or speak of God except in terms of being and its attributes.

It is, of course, only beings which exist. But it is possible to form a

---

[1] *Summa totius logicae*, Chapter 33.
[2] Ibid., III, Chapter 1.
[3] Ibid., III, Chapter 36.
[4] *Ordinatio*, Prologue, Qu. 9 (critical edition, I, p. 259). Cf. the prologue to Ockham's commentary on the eight books of Aristotle's *Physics*.

common concept of being which is predicable of all beings, whether finite or infinite. As so predicable, 'being' simply means 'something', in so far as something is opposed to nothing. Understood in this sense, the word 'being' is univocal. We can say of both God and creatures that they are not nothing. It by no means follows, however, that God and creatures are opposed to nothing in the same ways, or that the actual being of God is of the same kind as that of creatures. It is not. If, therefore, we use the term 'being' to signify the actual being of God and the actual being of a creature, the term is used equivocally, in different senses.

Ockham is therefore no pantheist. Nor does he bring down God to the level of creatures. 'Nothing real is univocal to God and the creatures'.[1] At the same time he lays stress upon our ability to form univocal concepts. As we enjoy no intuitive knowledge of God in this life, we cannot have a concept of him which expresses a vision of the divine reality in itself. Our idea of God must be dependent on our ideas of finite things and their qualities. But we cannot predicate, for example, creaturely being or wisdom as such of God. If we are able, therefore, to have any valid idea of God at all, we must be able to strip away the finite limitations by forming univocal concepts. We are then in a position to develop a composite concept which is predicable of God alone. Univocal concepts provide, as it were, a bridge; and without them we would be condemned, in Ockham's view, to agnosticism.

It is worth remarking that Ockham refuses to allow that essence and existence are really distinct. It is obviously absurd to suppose that existence is added to a 'pre-existing' essence. As for the existing thing itself, 'existence' does not signify anything different from the thing. It is perfectly true that 'thing' (res) signifies in the manner of a noun, while 'to be' (esse) signifies in the manner of a verb, and that we cannot simply substitute the one for the other, 'as they do not have the same functions'.[2] But to imagine that such linguistic distinctions justify the theory of a real extramental distinction between essence and existence is, for Ockham, to be misled by language. Nor is the theory necessary in order to safeguard the difference between God and creatures. To say that in God essence and existence are identical is simply to say that he exists necessarily and not as the result of a cause. The creature does not exist necessarily. And the distinction between it and its cause is quite sufficient to distinguish it from God.

[1] *Ordinato*, Dist. 2, Qu. 9 (critical edition, II, p. 317).
[2] *Summa totius logicae*, III, 2, Chapter 27.

Similarly, Ockham interprets the distinction between possibility and act as a distinction between two modalities of statement. The statement that Socrates is white is of a different type from the statement that Socrates can sit. But this is no good reason for developing a theory of 'possibles' and maintaining that 'something which is not in the universe, but can be, is truly a being'.[1]

Once more, therefore, the world consists simply of substances with their absolute accidents. The existence of one of these substances does not logically entail the existence of any other. And faith sees all finite substances as ontologically dependent on God. Can the philosopher, however, prove the existence of God? We have seen that according to Ockham we could not have any valid idea of God unless we could form univocal concepts. But is there any philosophical proof that the idea of God is instantiated, that there is a God of whom we can have an idea?

Some writers have maintained that for Ockham there is no philosophical proof of God's existence, and that belief in his existence is simply a matter of faith. Others have flatly denied this and have pointed to the fact that Ockham supplies us with a proof. He says explicitly, for example, that the existence of a first efficient cause can be proved, provided that we concern ourselves with the order of actually conserving causes rather than with that of productive causes. If we consider the production of things, it is clear that a thing, once produced, may continue to exist even though its productive cause no longer exists. Hence we cannot argue that if an infinite series of productive causes is postulated, we are committed to defending the possibility of an actual infinity of finite beings (which for Ockham is impossible). But this is not the case in regard to the order of actually conserving causes. For if this series, of causes actually conserving here and now, is prolonged to infinity, we are committed to the notion that there can be an actually infinite number of things existing simultaneously. Hence 'we must stop at some being which conserves without being conserved by another in any way'.[2]

If by 'God' we mean a first conserving cause in the hierarchy of conserving causes, then Ockham certainly admits a proof of God's existence. He says himself that we can prove that God exists, if by 'God' we mean 'that than which nothing is more noble and more perfect'.[3] But he adds that it does not follow that it can be demonstrated

[1] Summa totius logicae, I, Chapter 38.
[2] Quaestiones in librum I Physicorum, Qu. 136.
[3] Quodlibeta, I, Qu. 1.

that there is only one God. For there might be another being (perhaps another first conserver in another world) which, though not *more* perfect than the first conserver of this world, would not be *less* perfect. We can indeed understand by 'God' 'some being more noble and more perfect than anything other than itself'.[1] Though, however, there could not be more than one such being, 'it cannot be evidently known that God, understood in this sense, exists'.[2]

The answer to the question whether Ockham holds that the existence of God can be proved depends therefore on the sense which we attach to the word 'God'. If we understand by the word simply a first con-serving cause of this world and a being which has no superior in per-fection (even though there might conceivably be an equal or equals), he certainly admits that God's existence can be proved in metaphysics. If, however, we understand by 'God' an absolutely supreme, perfect, unique and infinite being, omniscient and omnipotent, he does not think that God's existence can be philosophically proved. At the same time Ockham might perhaps comment that though, in his opinion, the divine unicity, infinity, omniscience and omnipotence are known, with certainty at least, only by faith, the God of Christian faith is in fact the first conserving cause of this world. In other words, he could argue that the being whose existence can be philosophically proved is not a *different* being from the God of Christian faith, though the philosopher can attain only a very inadequate concept of God. Presumably this is how Ockham thought of the matter.

However attained, our knowledge of God is conceptual. Some con-cepts are connotative, like the concept of infinity which connotes the finite negatively (by denying finitude), while others, such as goodness, are common concepts, predicable of both God and creatures. Using these concepts, we can form a composite concept which is proper to God, in the sense that it is predicable only of him. And it is this com-posite concept which is the immediate object of our knowledge, not God himself. 'What we know immediately are concepts which are not really God but which we use in propositions to stand for God.'[3] The theologian, we may say, is concerned with the proper ways of thinking and speaking about God. He cannot increase our immediate knowledge of God. We have not got any to increase. Nor could the theologian increase it, if we had. But Ockham does not deny that we can have

[1] Ibid.
[2] Ibid.
[3] *Ordinatio*, Dist. 3, Qu. 2 (critical edition, II, p. 413).

mediate knowledge of God. And the theologian can help us to increase it.[1]

In psychology Ockham wields his razor to get rid of really distinct faculties. We certainly experience in ourselves both acts of understanding and acts of volition or willing. But this is no reason for postulating distinct faculties. The words 'intellect' and 'will' signify the same rational soul; but 'intellect' connotes acts of understanding, while 'will' connotes acts of willing. Both kinds of acts proceed from the same source. It by no means follows, however, that the philosopher can give a strict proof that the rational or intellectual soul is the form of the body, even if it is more probable that it is than that it is not. Moreover, even if we assume that it is, the philosopher cannot demonstrate that it is spiritual and incorruptible or immortal. Experience and natural reason would suggest that the human soul perishes with the body. That there is in the human being a rational soul which is at the same time the form of the body, spiritual and immortal, is known only by faith, by revelation that is to say.[2]

Ockham does not believe that human freedom, freedom of the will that is to say, can be demonstrated. It is, however, known by experience, by our experiencing in ourselves the fact that a judgement of the intellect about the rightness of an act does not entail our performance of the fact, and that a judgement about the badness of an act does not entail our refraining from this act. In the language of faculties, Ockham appeals to experience against the theory that the intellect determines the will. Man may know that *a* is the action which he ought to perform and yet not do it.

As free, the created will is subject to obligation. The ontological foundation of obligation is the dependence of the creature on the holy, good and omnipotent divine will. But while all creatures depend on God, there is obviously no sense in talking about obligation in the case of creatures which act purely intuitively and without freedom. Obligation arises in the encounter between a created free will and the divine will. Ockham speaks plainly enough on this point. 'By the very fact that God wills something , it is right for it to be done. . . .'[3] Obviously

[1] Some writers may tend to write off as low-down 'nominalism' Ockham's view that the immediate object of knowledge of God in metaphysics and theology is concepts (*quid nominis* rather than *quid rei*). But it was common doctrine among medieval theologians that we enjoy no natural intuitive knowledge of God. So he does not seem to be saying anything exceptional.

[2] *Quodlibeta*, I, Qu. 10.

[3] *Reportata*, Bk IV, Qu. 9, E-F.

Ockham does not think of the divine will as expressing simply power. For God, as conceived by faith, is not only infinite power but also infinite goodness and holiness. If, therefore, God is conceived as faith conceives him, it follows by definition that whatever God wills is good, and that whatever God commands is right. At the same time Ockham wishes to avoid giving any impression of holding that the divine will is in any way determined, by for example eternal norms to which God is bound to conform his will. 'Obligation does not fall on God, since he is not under any obligation to do anything.'[1] Ockham therefore represents the divine will as the ultimate source of norms rather than as subject to norms which hold good independently.

Ockham's ethical authoritarianism presupposes a concept of God which, in his view, goes beyond the range of philosophical proof. And presumably he thinks that it fits in with the Christian moral consciousness, as this is more concerned with doing the will of God than with pursuing some end such as self-realization or happiness. If the Christian does seek eternal happiness, he does so because God wills its attainment. The divine will is thus the ultimate norm for the Christian.

Now if Ockham were claiming that moral precepts depended simply and solely on the arbitrary choice of God, he would have to hold that it is only through divine revelation that man can know what he ought and ought not to do. In point of fact, however, he often appeals to 'right reason' as the norm of morality. True, a man may mistakenly think that an action is right when in fact it is wrong. And though he may be responsible for his ignorance, he may also be ignorant through no fault of his own. He is then morally bound to follow his conscience. 'A created will which follows an invincibly erroneous conscience is a right will.'[2] But if a man can be mistaken, he can also make a correct judgement. In other words the human reason is capable of discriminating between what is right and what is wrong. And the question arises, how can this belief be reconciled with the view that the divine will is the ultimate norm of morality?

We have to make a distinction which is of some importance for an understanding of Ockham's theory. Like Scotus, he maintains that by his 'absolute' power God can do anything which does not involve a contradiction. As Ockham sees no contradiction in God's ordering one man to kill another or someone to commit fornication or adultery, he maintains that by his absolute power (*potentia absoluta*) God could

[1] Ibid., Bk II, Qu. 5, H.
[2] *Reportata*, Bk III, Qu. 13, O.

command what he has in fact forbidden. And if he did so, the relevant acts would be good and meritorious. In actual fact, however, God has created man in such a way that certain acts are harmful to human nature and human society. A rational ethics is thus possible. And by his *potentia ordinata* (his power considered in relation to his actual creative activity) God wills that man should follow the dictates of 'right reason'. Although, absolutely speaking, God could command actions which we know to be prohibited, he has in fact established a certain moral order; and reason can discern something of its content.

It is not the intention of the present writer to suggest that Ockham's position is satisfactory. If the human reason, unaided by revelation, can discern a natural moral law, it is very difficult to see how God could order anything else, unless we think of God simply and solely as absolute power. Ockham seems to be trying to reconcile the evident fact that pagan philosophers expounded moral precepts and ideals with a theologically based authoritarianism; and the two elements do not appear to fit together. Perhaps he would answer, however, that while natural reason can develop a prudential or utilitarian code of ethics or an ethics of self-realization or self-perfection, moral obligation in the strict sense arises only because God commands observance of the natural moral law. We can see by reason that certain actions are 'in-expedient', in the sense that they are harmful to man in society. But that such actions are in fact forbidden by God (even if, by his absolute power, he could command them) is known only through revelation. It is not surprising, therefore, that in Aristotle we find no idea of obliga-tion as Ockham understands it, an obligation imposed by the divine will on the free will of man.

Ockham evidently wishes to free ethics from any elements of Greco-Islamic necessitarianism, which would represent the divine will as sub-ject to norms in a manner analogous to that in which the created free will is subject to norms and to obligation. He sets the concept of an absolutely free and omnipotent divine will over against the concept of a God who is bound to act in certain ways. But he shows little sign of being clearly aware of the difficulties to which his ethical authoritarian-ism gives rise. Besides, while he is evidently opposed to the idea of a secular or purely humanistic ethics, it is arguable that he in fact, and contrary to his intentions, tends to promote this idea by insisting on reason as the norm of morality in such a way that his theologically based authoritarianism appears as a superstructure which does not fit in with the substructure. Ockham doubtless thinks of reason as 'right' when it dictates what God has in fact commanded and forbids what God has in fact prohibited. But God's commands and prohibitions can be known only by revelation. And if a man does not share Ockham's concept of God and faith in revelation, he is likely to think that reason by itself is a sufficient guide.

There is a particular point which is worth drawing attention to. Ockham, like Scotus, interprets the divine omnipotence as meaning that whatever God does through secondary causes, he could do immediately, without any secondary cause. And, unlike Scotus, he draws the conclusion that by his absolute power God could cause in a man an act of hatred of himself (of God that is to say).[1] In this case the man would not sin. At the same time we have to be careful about saying that Ockham contradicts Scotus by asserting that God could command a man not to love him, on the ground that, whatever Scotus may have thought, such a command would involve no contradiction. For Ockham points out that if God ordered a man not to love him, and the man obeyed, the man would be doing the will of God and therefore loving him. By obeying the divine command not to love the man would in fact be showing love, while if the man disobeyed and persisted in loving God he would not in fact be loving God, as disobedience to God and love of God are incompatible. Though, therefore, Ockham suggests that God could, without contradiction, command a man not to love him, he goes on to add that 'the will in this situation cannot perform such an act'.[2]

Ockham's political writings were prompted more by particular issues than by systematic reflection on political theory. For example, the *Opus nonaginta dierum* was composed with the aim of defending his views on Franciscan poverty against the pronouncements made on this matter by Pope John XXII in his bull *Quia vir reprobus* (1329), while a later work (*An princeps pro suo succursu*) was written to defend the action of Edward III of England in demanding money from the clergy for his war against France. As, however, Ockham was a philosopher and theologian and not simply a polemical pamphleteer, he naturally discussed broader issues than the particular controversy under consideration. Thus in the *Opus nonaginta dierum* he is immediately concerned with the pope's contention that it was absurd for the Franciscan enthusiasts of the party of Michael of Cesena to claim that they had no

[1] It seems that, for this claim to be intelligible, God must be conceived simply as absolute power.
[2] *Quodlibeta*, III, Qu. 13.

right of use in regard to things such as food and clothing, the ownership of which was vested in the Holy See. The pope argued, not
unreasonably, that if the Franciscans had no right to use temporal
things, they ought not to use them, but that as in fact they were justified
in using them, they must have a right to do so. In treating of this
question Ockham goes back to the theory of natural rights, explaining
in what sense he regards private property as a natural right. It is in this
context that he discusses the distinction between which rights can be
renounced and which cannot. And he is then in a position to argue that
it is possible to renounce even the right of use, while at the same time
a precarious 'use of fact' remains.[1]

Similarly, Ockham's defence of his patron, Ludwig of Bavaria, led to
a series of writings in which he made clear not only his firm conviction
that temporal rulers were in no sense nominees or vicars of the pope,
but also his dislike of absolutism both in Church and State. Though,
however, he advocated a limiting of papal power by means of general
councils, he did not deny that the pope was St Peter's successor; nor
did he depict a general council as an organ for issuing dogmatic pronouncements quite independently of the pope. He was concerned with
applying to the papacy his dislike of absolutism in general and with
proposals for constitutionalizing papal government, not with abolishing
the papacy, nor with questions of dogma. He was not a revolutionary.
And when he insisted that the power of the temporal sovereign was
derived, immediately or mediately, from the people, and that if the
ruler abused his trust the political community was entitled to depose
him, he was not proposing a view hitherto unheard of in the Middle
Ages. Obviously, if we look back on Ockham's ideas from a great
distance in time, we naturally tend to see in them the seeds of later
developments. But if we are seeking a revolutionary in political theory,
Ockham is not a very suitable candidate for the post.

[1] Thus, according to Ockham, the Franciscans renounced not only the right of
ownership or possession but also the right of use over goods, the ownership of
which was vested in the Holy See. What they had was a mere 'use of fact', permitted by the Holy See but revocable at any moment.

16

The Fourteenth Century [2]

I

THE attitudes and ideas characteristic of the 'modern way' spread far and wide in the course of the fourteenth century. At first they were more or less concentrated in England and France. At Oxford lecturers such as the Franciscan John of Rodington (d. 1348) and Adam Wodham or Woodham or Goddam (d. 1358) promoted the separation of philosophy from theology by questioning the provability of God's existence, unicity and omnipotence. At Cambridge the Dominican Robert Holcot or Holkot (d. 1349) maintained that only analytic propositions (when the predicate is contained in the concept of the subject) are certain, and that as our concepts are derived from sense-experience it is not possible to prove the existence of any incorporeal being. Theology must thus stand on its own feet without help from philosophy. Indeed, ordinary logic is not applicable in the sphere of faith. The doctrine of the Trinity, for instance, is incompatible with the logical principles of Aristotle. This does not matter, however, provided that we recognize that there is a 'logic of faith' which transcends even the principles of identity and non-contradiction.

It is of course sometimes difficult to assess the extent of Ockhamist influence on a given thinker. For example, Gregory of Rimini (d. 1358), who taught for a time at Paris and became superior general of the Hermits of St Augustine, held certain views which had in fact been expounded by Ockham. But in defending them Gregory was wont to appeal to Augustine. However, thinkers such as those mentioned above, to whom we may add the Oxford scholar Thomas Buckingham (d. 1351), were clearly adherents of the new movement. As for the Frenchmen John of Mirecourt and Nicholas of Autrecourt, something will be said about them in the next section.

Needless to say, the spread of Ockhamist lines of thought did not proceed without any opposition being aroused.[1] Let us take a particular example. The traditional theological teaching was that divine grace was required for man to perform acts which were meritorious in God's eyes and to achieve salvation. Nor did Ockham deny that God had actually arranged things in this way. But as he maintained that whatever God can do through secondary causes he can do without them (by his 'absolute' power, that is to say), Ockham inferred that God could, if he so chose, dispense with the need for supernatural grace and accept as meritorious human acts performed without grace. Further, Ockham was convinced that no human act can be meritorious unless it is a free act, proceeding from the human will as its cause.[2] It is true that he himself, speaking as a theologian, maintained that God knows all future contingent facts; but some of his followers safeguarded human freedom either by claiming that contingent propositions relating to the future were neither true nor false and therefore not known by God or by suggesting that God did know future contingent facts but not with certainty. The result of this insistence on human freedom, coupled with Ockham's admission of the theoretical possibility of man's performing meritorious acts and achieving salvation without the intervention of grace as a secondary cause, was the impression in certain quarters that a new form of Pelagianism had arisen, concerned with emphasizing human freedom and self-sufficiency at the expense of the universal divine causality and the divine omniscience. Hence the sharp attack made by Bradwardine in his *De causa Dei contra Pelagium*.[3]

Thomas Bradwardine (d. 1349) was a mathematician, scientist and

[1] Talk about 'Ockhamist lines of thought' should not be taken to imply that whenever these lines of thought are encountered in the fourteenth century, they are derived directly from Ockham himself. Ockham was the chief, though by no means the most extreme, representative of a movement. His thought certainly exercised a wide influence; but the movement, though conveniently labelled Ockhamist, was wider than Ockhamism in the sense of a school of disciples.
[2] Ockham also wished to hold, or rather held, that God is at any rate the partial cause of all human free acts. And he found difficulty, as we can appreciate, in reconciling this claim, together with his assertion that God knows all future contingent events, with his insistence on human freedom. His solution was to say that for the finite mind in this life no solution is possible.
[3] The traditional date of this work is 1344. But some writers have favoured an earlier date.

theologian of Merton College, Oxford, who became chaplain to Edward III and was eventually nominated archbishop of Canterbury a few months before he fell victim, as so many others did (including probably Ockham) to the Black Death. As he regarded the Ockhamists as the 'new Pelagians', one might have expected him to argue as a theologian, as Augustine had argued against Pelagius. In point of fact Bradwardine argues more as a metaphysician. From the concept of God as first cause he deduces that the divine causality operates throughout the universe, and that human acts are caused by God. There is then, of course, no difficulty either in asserting that God knows future contingent facts or in explaining how this is possible. The explanation is that God wills and causes man's future acts. The difficulty lies obviously in reconciling this view with human freedom, if, that is to say, one wishes to preserve belief in it. Bradwardine's policy is to maintain that God causes the human will to act predictably but freely. The divine will is both neces- sary (as one with the divine essence) and free, as being subject to no constraint. Similarly, the human will acts necessarily, inasmuch as its choices are infallibly predictable, but also freely, inasmuch as it is not effectively moved by any factor save God. Though, however, Brad- wardine does not deny human freedom, his retention of it naturally appears to simple minds as being purely nominal. And it is not al- together unreasonable to see his doctrine, some features of which recur with John Wyclif (d. 1384), as looking forward to the philosophy of Spinoza.

As both Ockham and Bradwardine exalt the divine will and omni- potence, it may seem that their positions are not really very different. And it has been maintained that Bradwardine simply draws the deter- ministic conclusions which follow from the doctrine of divine omni- potence, even if he objects to Ockhamist suggestion that man could perform meritorious acts and achieve salvation without grace. But the approaches of the two men seem to be pretty different. Ockham, as a theologian, is concerned with liberating the divine will from any con- straint and insists on God's power to alter the order of things, whether supernatural or natural, which he has actually established. As a philos- opher he is concerned with safeguarding the reality of human freedom. And, as we have seen, he is prepared to say that the finite mind is unable to solve the problems which arise out of the attempts to recon- cile human freedom with divine knowledge of future contingent events. We just have to hold on to human freedom as a datum of consciousness and to accept the divine foreknowledge as faith. This is an instance of how philosophy and theology tend to fall apart in the 'new way'. Bradwardine, however, is really carrying to its logical conclusion the traditional metaphysics with its principle that whatever is moved is moved by something else, the something else being ultimately God. He is more concerned with what God *does* than with what he *could* do by his 'absolute' power.

2

In addition to Oxford, the other main centre in the first half of the fourteenth century of what can loosely be described as Ockhamist ideas was Paris. The University of Paris provides us with two interesting examples of the strong tendency within the new movement to limit certain knowledge to the area of analytical propositions.

John of Mirecourt, known as the *monachus albus* (white monk), seems to have been a Cistercian and to have lectured on the *Sentences* of Peter Lombard at the Cistercian college of St Bernard at Paris. In his view there are some propositions which are reducible by analysis to the principle of non-contradiction. Their truth is evident in the highest degree. There is, however, only one empirical proposition of this kind, namely the proposition asserting the existence of the thinker or speaker. As St Augustine showed, this proposition cannot be denied without self-contradiction. Its truth, therefore, is certain. What John of Mirecourt calls evident assent (*assensus evidens*) in the strict sense is given only to those propositions which rest upon the principle of non-contradiction and in the case of which we have the highest degree of evidence (*evidentia potissima*) of their truth.

Apart from the proposition asserting the existence of the thinker or speaker, no empirical proposition is absolutely certain. John's lectures, which were apparently given in 1399–45, gave rise to criticism; and he wrote an explanatory defence of his views, in which he made a distinction. With the exception mentioned, no empirical proposition (no proposition which reflects an experience of reality) is reducible to the principle of non-contradiction or merits unqualified assent to its truth. At the same time there are propositions which are not self-evidently true but which none the less merit 'evident assent' (*assensus evidens*) rather than 'inevident assent' (*assensus inevidens*). We cannot attribute to them *evidentia potissima* (evidence in the highest degree); but we can attribute to them 'natural evidence' (*evidentia naturalis*).

What John means seems to be this. Suppose that I see an object in the far distance and judge that it is a man. Not only is it possible that I am mistaken but I am also well aware of the fact. The object may turn out to be a tree trunk. Hence it is with 'fear of error' that I assent to the statement that the object is a man. The statement is not 'evidently' true. Suppose, however, that I say that there are material things or that heat is caused by fire. In both I could be mistaken, as far as the principle of non-contradiction is concerned. For John of Mirecourt holds, with Ockham, that by his absolute power God *could* produce in me all those physico-psychological conditions which lead to my judging that there are material objects out there, without these objects actually being there. Similarly, God *could* produce cases of heat immediately without employing any secondary cause such as fire. The propositions in question therefore do not enjoy *evidentia potissima*. At the same time I have no reason for thinking that God is using his 'absolute' power to alter the course of events which he has actually established. The situation is such that I give a 'natural' assent to the statement that there are material things. And the statement can be said to be 'evidently' true, even though the evidence does not amount to evidence in the highest degree (*evidentia potissima*), inasmuch as no contradiction is involved by denial of the truth of the statement.

Unless the principle of causality is transformed into a tautology (for example, there is no effect without a cause) it cannot be shown to depend upon the principle of non-contradiction in such a way that denial of the principle involves one in contradiction. It follows, therefore, that no causal agreement for God's existence can be an absolutely certain proof. In his first apology John does indeed assert that the opposite of 'God exists' involves a contradiction. But he goes on to say that a proposition of this kind does not enjoy the evidence possessed by the principle of non-contradiction. Presumably he means that while 'God exists' is in itself a necessary proposition, in the sense that it is objectively impossible for God not to exist, no philosophical *a posteriori* proof of God's existence can be absolutely certain.

We have noticed that John of Mirecourt, like Ockham, appeals to the absolute power of God. But it is possible of course to express his doctrine, as outlined above, as a theory about the logical status of different classes of propositions, without bringing in any theological themes. We may thus be inclined to look on the theological aspect of his doctrine as a superfluity, significant enough in the context of medieval thought but at the same time dispensable. In the area of ethics, however, the theological aspect of John's thought becomes more prominent.

According to John of Mirecourt, God could, absolutely speaking, cause any act in the human will, even hatred of himself. Again, to hate one's neighbour is sinful only because it is prohibited of God. When subjected to attack, John explained that it was not his intention to deny that hatred of the neighbour was contrary to the moral law. At the same time the man who does hate his neighbour was contrary to the moral law. At the same time the man who does hate his neighbour runs the risk of bringing divine punishment upon himself only because God has forbidden such hatred. Reference to divine sanctions, however, does nothing to alter the fact that John subjects moral precepts to the absolute power of God.

In addition John of Mirecourt appears to have held a theory of the divine causality which resembled that defended by Bradwardine. God, that is to say, is the cause of all human acts, even the sinner's. It does not follow, he insists, that God sins. For sin can be committed only through a human will. But by willing that there should be no moral rectitude in the sinner's will God causes his act, even though he himself does not sin.

In his exaltation of the absolute power of God John inclined to the view proposed by St Peter Damian in the early Middle Ages that God could bring it about, retrospectively as it were, that the past should not have happened. However, he is careful not to assert that this *would be* possible. What he says is rather that its impossibility is not clear to him. From the logical point of view John confines certainty in the full sense to analytic propositions, reducible to the principle of non-contradiction. From the theological point of view he clearly strains at the leash, as Robert Holcot did in England with his 'logic of faith'.

In 1347 the chancellor of Paris condemned a number of propositions taken from John's teaching. These included the statements that God could cause a man to hate him, that God is the cause of the sinner's act, and that, as far as natural reason is concerned, it is not clear that there are any accidents distinct from substance itself. Obviously the authorities were more concerned with the theological aspects and implications of John's teaching than with his logical theory as such.

Another lecturer at Paris whose opinions were subjected to censure was Nicholas of Autrecourt. After lecturing on the *Sentences* of Peter Lombard he was summoned to Avignon in 1340 for an inquiry into his teaching; but the death of Pope Benedict XII resulted in the proceedings being postponed. They were resumed under Clement VI, Nicholas being given the opportunity of defending himself in the pope's presence. In 1346 Nicholas was sentenced to burn his writings publicly at Paris and to recant the condemned propositions. He was also expelled from the teaching body of the University. In 1347 he complied with the provisions of the sentence. In 1350 he obtained a post at the cathedral of Metz; but the date of his death is unknown. Of his writings we possess two letters, plus some fragments, of a series written to the Franciscan Bernard of Arezzo, one of his critics, part of a letter written to a certain Giles,[1] a treatise which opens with the words *Exigit ordo executionis*, and a theological work. We also have a list of the condemned propositions and some remarks by John of Mirecourt about Nicholas's doctrine on causality.

Writing to Bernard of Arezzo, Nicholas explains that the principle of non-contradiction is the primary principle, both in the sense that there is no more ultimate principle and in the sense that all other principles presuppose it. Every proposition which is reducible, either immediately or mediately, to this principle is certain. A proposition is immediately reducible if the predicate is contained in the concept of the subject. It is mediately reducible if the conclusion of an argument is identical with part of the premise or antecedent.[2]

Nicholas is thus at one with John of Mirecourt in maintaining that all analytic propositions are certain. But Nicholas also regards immediate perception as a source of certain knowledge. If, for example, I perceive a colour, say a patch of green, my act of perceiving is not a premise from which I infer the presence of green. For to say that I perceive a colour is to say that the colour appears to me. And in perceiving it I am aware that it appears. So long, therefore, as I restrict my judgement to the assertion that I perceive a patch of green, the truth of the judgement is certain. I might perhaps use the wrong word, according to the conventions of the language which I am using, to describe the colour; but to say that I perceive a colour and that the colour does not exist (does not appear to me) would involve me in a contradiction.

Nicholas will not, however, allow that from the fact that A exists I can infer with certainty the existence of B, if A and B are distinct things. For there is no logical contradiction in asserting the existence of one thing and denying the existence of another, when the two things in

---

[1] We also have a reply from Giles to Nicholas.

[2] If, for example, all Xs are Ys, the statement that this X is Y is said to be identical with part of the premise. To assert the premise and deny the conclusion would involve a contradiction.

question are separate or really distinct. 'From the fact that something is known to exist it cannot be inferred evidently, with, that is, evidence reducible to the first principle or to the certitude of the first principle, that another thing exists.'[1] It is all very well, says Nicholas, to argue with Bernard of Arezzo that because there is whiteness, there is a substance. If we assume that whiteness is an accident and that an accident necessarily inheres in a substance, it certainly follows from the existence of whiteness that there is a substance. To assert the premise and deny the conclusion would involve one in contradiction. But there is no compelling reason why one should accept the assumption or presupposition in question. And in point of fact Nicholas will not allow that from the existence of phenomena, the immediate objects, whether internal or external, of perception we can infer with certainty the existence of any substance.[2]

This line of thought is applicable of course to the causal relation. Nicholas admits that if I have had immediate evidence in the past that when I put my hand near the fire it becomes warm, it is probable that if I do the same in the future, the result will be the same. But he seems to be speaking of one's expectations rather than attempting to develop any theory of probability. Repeated experience of a relation of regular sequence between A and B leads one to expect that in the future too A will be followed by B. But there is no proof that this must be the case. Bernard of Arezzo argued that if fire is applied to tow, and if there is no obstacle to combustion, one can infer with certainty that there will be heat. Nicholas denies this. For the propositions 'fire is applied to tow and there is no obstacle' and 'there will not be heat' are not contradictory.

Given this point of view, any causal argument for God's existence obviously falls to the ground. For in this case we cannot even appeal to past immediate perception of a conjunction or sequence. As for the argument from degrees of perception, Nicholas denies that we can prove any objective hierarchy of levels of perfection. Nor can we prove that anything is the final cause of anything else. So all the traditional demonstrations of God's existence go overboard. As far as certainty at any rate is concerned, we are left with analytic propositions (or

[1] See documents edited by J. Lappe in *Beiträge*,VI, 2 (1908), 9*, 15–20.
[2] Nicholas certainly held that we cannot prove the existence of any material substance. But there is some dispute about the right interpretation of his apparently divergent statements about inferring the existence of one's soul from acts of understanding and willing.

'tautologies') and immediate judgements of perception which do not involve any inference from what appears (the phenomena) to anything distinct from it.

The upshot is that we really know very little, and that we certainly do not know all that Aristotle and his followers have claimed to know. In the *Exigit* therefore Nicholas says how astonished he is to find people studying Aristotle and Averroes up to a decrepit old age instead of attending to moral matters and care for the common good.[1] Ockham had a great respect for Aristotle; but Nicholas of Autrecourt takes a very dim view of Aristotelianism.

Though Nicholas is best known for the critical and empiricist aspects of his thought, he offered a positive philosophy of his own. He did not claim anything more than probability on its behalf, but he evidently thought that his hypotheses were more probable than those of Aristotle. That is to say, while he did not claim that his arguments were conclusive and allowed that his conclusions might be false, he thought that an impartial mind would prefer his arguments to those with which he disagreed.

As we have seen, Nicholas rejected any claim that an objective hierarchy of degrees of perfection can be philosophically demonstrated. At the same time he agreed that if we assume as probably true both that we have an idea of the good as a standard or criterion for judging about the relations between things and that the universe is such as to satisfy this criterion, we can conclude as probably true that all things are so interconnected that every one of them exists for the good of the whole, and that the universe is perfect.[2] In a perfect universe, however, nothing perishes, for it is required for the good of the whole. It is true that this idea flies in the face of appearances. But the fact that a given thing no longer appears does not constitute any proof that it no longer exists. We have no right to assume that to be perceived and to exist are the same thing. As for the phenomena of change, these can be explained much better in terms of a theory of eternal atoms than by means of Aristotle's concepts of substantial and accidental change.

[1] *Exigit ordo executionis*, edited by J. R. O'Donnell and published in *Medieval Studies*, Vol. 1. (1939), pp. 179–280. See pages 181–2. We know little of Nicholas's ethical ideas. But from a condemned proposition it seems clear that he accepted Ockhamist ideas about God's 'absolute' power in regard to moral precepts. As for political theory, he seems to have lectured on Aristotle's *Politics* and relevant questions.

[2] In this context Nicholas accepts the existence of a final end, the supreme good or God, as a probable hypothesis.

Some of Nicholas's ideas scandalized the ecclesiastical authorities. For example, his interpretation of reward in the next life in terms of the soul's conjunction with better collections of atoms (as objects of knowledge) seemed to them quite unsatisfactory. And when he remarked that he was only proposing probable hypotheses and that if they clashed with revealed truth they should be rejected, he was accused of indulging in 'foxy' excuses. But his positive philosophy does not seem to be of much importance in comparison with his doctrines about analytic propositions, immediate perception and the causal relation and his criticism of traditional metaphysics. He has been described as the medieval Hume. And whether one thinks the description appropriate or inappropriate, it is obvious that Nicholas's thought is a standing refutation of any notion that radical criticism was unknown in the Middle Ages.

3

Logical theories can obviously have a bearing on philosophy. Nicholas of Autrecourt provides us with an example. If we assume with him that we can never argue with certainty from the existence of one thing to the existence of another, it does not follow that there is no God; but it does follow that there can be no causal demonstration of his existence. Further, if we take it that Nicholas's position implies that the word 'cause' signifies that which is found in experience to be regularly followed by a certain event which we call its 'effect', it is difficult to see how God could be appropriately described as 'first cause'. For we can hardly be said to have experience of relations of sequence between God and the world.

Though, however, logical theories can have a bearing on philosophical theories, studies in logic can be pursued more or less independently. And the more logic undergoes formalization, the greater is the degree of independence likely to become. It is no matter of surprise, therefore, if the terminist logic was developed by people of rather different philosophical outlooks.

A case in point is the English Franciscan Walter Burleigh (d. *c.* 1345). He was a realist on the subject of universals and a critic of the 'moderns'. Moreover, his realism affected his theory of supposition.[1] At the same

[1] In what Burleigh calls 'absolute supposition' (a subdivision of 'simple supposition') the subject term is said to stand for a universal in so far as it is present in a plurality of things. An example given by Burleigh is 'man is the most dignified of creatures'.

time the fact that he begins his work *On the Purity of the Art of Logic*[1] by giving general rules for consequences has some importance. For it expresses a recognition both of the basic role played in logic by inferential operations and of the subordination of syllogistics to a general theory of inference.

Again, though the Frenchman John Buridan (c. 1295–c. 1358), who was twice rector of the University of Paris, was not without nominalist tendencies, he was a critic of extremists such as Nicholas of Autrecourt. At the same time his logical treatise on *Consequences* (*Consequentiae*) has been acclaimed as the first attempt in the Middle Ages to supply a deductive derivation of the laws of deductive inference.[2] Among other logical topics, he wrote on sophisms (*Sophismata*). In the psychological field he is well known for maintaining that the will must choose what reason presents as the greater good. Hence the problem of 'Buridan's ass' which is faced by two equally appetizing bundles of hay and, unable to choose between them, dies of starvation. This particular illustration of the sort of problem referred to does not seem to occur in the extant writings of Buridan himself; but he uses a similar illustration, relating to a dog, based on Aristotle.

It has already been noted that treatises on sophisms[3] were written from the twelfth century onwards. In the fourteenth century this number was added to by, for example, William Heytesbury (d. c. 1380), a scientist and logician of Merton College, Oxford, and Buridan. In his *Sophismata* Buridan mentions a large number of puzzles, such as negative existential statements ('there is no chimera', for instance), the inference 'no proposition is negative, therefore some proposition is negative'[4] and variations on the liar paradox. Suppose that someone asserts 'what I am saying is false', and that no other proposition whatsoever is enunciated. The proposition seems to be self-referring, predicating falsity, that is to say, of 'what I am saying is false', in which case it seems to follow that what I am saying is true. Ockham's way of dealing with this sort of paradox was to claim that such a proposition as 'every

[1] *De puritate artis logicae*, edited by P. Boehner (New York, 1951).
[2] See *Truth and Consequence in Medieval Logic* by E. A. Moody (Amsterdam, (1953), p. 8.
[3] The term *Sophismata* was used to cover a wide variety of logical puzzles, paradoxes and 'misleading' utterances which stood in need of analysis. Sometimes, however, there were separate treatments of certain paradoxes. Thus the liar paradox might be treated under the heading of *De insolubili,*
[4] If the antecedent is true, there is at least one negative proposition, namely the antecedent itself.

proposition is false' could not be self-referring, as the subject term 'every proposition' must stand for *other* propositions. Buridan, however, is not satisfied with this solution. What can be thought can be said. I can think about the proposition which I am enunciating; therefore I can intend reference to it in the proposition itself. One of the solutions which Buridan himself offers is to claim that any proposition, by its very form as a proposition, implies its truth.[1] If, therefore, a proposition is such that it both asserts and denies its own truth, it must be false.[2]

Buridan seems to have influenced Albert of Saxony (*c.* 1316–90), who became rector of the University of Paris in 1357, first rector of Vienna in 1365 and bishop of Halberstadt in 1366. In his *Perutilis logica* (*A Very Useful Logic*) a great deal of the matter is derived from Ockham and Buridan, perhaps also from Burleigh. Albert gives elaborate rules of supposition and inquires into the truth-conditions of modal propositions. In his treatment of consequences he distinguishes between formal and material consequences. By formal consequences he means an implication which holds because of the syncategorematic terms, while by material consequences he means an implication which holds because of the meanings of categorematic terms. 'A man is running, therefore an animal is running' is, for Albert of Saxony a case of material consequence; but if we include 'every man is an animal' and transform the inference into a syllogism, it becomes an example of formal consequence.

Medieval logic became increasingly a logic of terms and of propositions and the relations between them. That is to say, it became clear to the medieval logicians that they were dealing not with extramental substances, nor even with concepts as psychical realities, but with terms and propositions. There was obviously a close connection between logic and language. This is clear, for example, in the case of the theory of supposition which played such a prominent role in the new or modern logic of the thirteenth and fourteenth centuries. It is clear, too, from the treatment of semantic topics such as 'exponibles', propositions which were ambiguous or 'systematically misleading' and stood in need of analysis. At the same time there was in medieval logic a movement of increasing formalization, though the logicians laboured of course under a handicap, the lack of an adequate notation.

---

[1] That is to say, every proposition implies another proposition in which truth is predicated of the first.
[2] Buridan had second thoughts about the claim that every proposition implies, by its very form, that it is true. And he offered a variant solution of the liar paradox.

4

What is known as 'speculative grammar' was really something distinct. To say this is not to deny the influence of grammar on medieval logic. It is to say that whatever overlapping there may have been, the speculative grammarian had a distinguishable aim, the creation of a science of grammar. Needless to say the medievals were well aware that grammar differed with different languages. But some of them believed that the study of grammar, which they had inherited from the ancient world, could be made to fit the Aristotelian concept of a science. This aim could obviously not be achieved as long as grammar was regarded as identical with the study of the grammar of different actual languages, such as Latin, Greek and Arabic. It would be necessary to discover an essential structure underlying differences which could be looked on as 'accidental'. Thus in the thirteenth century Robert Kilwardby, commenting on Priscian, remarked that the subject-matter of a science must be the same for all men, and that for this reason the subject-matter of grammar could not be identical with a study of the grammars of different languages. Similarly, in his Greek grammar Roger Bacon asserted that in its substance grammar is one and the same in all languages. If this premise is accepted, there can, of course, be a science of grammar in the sense intended.

In the development of this science, or alleged science, there obviously had to be a shift of attention from grammatical differences to a conceptual structure which was considered to be the same for all men and which found expression in discourse. This conceptual structure was, for the speculative grammarians, pretty well the basic concepts or categories envisaged by Aristotle. The conceptual structure was regarded as reflecting an ontological structure and as being in turn expressed in discourse, this expression converting a *vox* (a word considered as a mere sound or physical entity) into a *dictio* (word).

The characteristic feature of speculative grammar was its attempt to deduce the parts of speech from the forms of thought, from basic concepts, that is to say, which were themselves expressions of the ontological studies of reality. For example, the noun was thought to express the concept of that which is stable, of substance, while the verb expressed the concept of becoming and, in the infinitive at least, the concept of 'matter'. A word becomes a definitive part of speech through its 'mode of signifying' (*modus significandi*), these modes being concepts of the understanding which bind the word, as it were, to some mode of being. While metaphysics studies the modes of being (for instance, substance as an objective mode of being of things) and logic the modes of understanding, speculative grammar studies the modes of signification, deducing and justifying, so to speak, the parts of speech. Hence the treatise *De modis significandi* (*On the Modes of Signification*) written by the speculative grammarians.

Syncategorematic words were obviously not capable of being linked to modes of being in the same way as nouns and adjectives. Nor were they capable of undergoing the inflections of which verbs were capable.[1] They were regarded as ornaments of speech, as pertaining to its *bene esse* rather than to its *esse*. And there was a tendency to look on them as pretty inferior parts of speech, whereas the logicians came to pay serious attention to them.

Peter of Elia, who was a professor of grammar at Paris about the middle of the twelfth century and who commented on Priscian, is traditionally regarded as the fountainhead of the movement which produced speculative grammar. Among the edited texts of representatives of the movement is the *Summa modorum significandi*[2] of Siger of Courtrai (d. 1341). Another example is the *Tractatus de modis significanda seu Grammatica speculativa* of Thomas of Erfurt, who taught logic and grammar at Enfurt in the first half of the fourteenth century.[3] Speculative grammar seems to have faded away in the second half of the fourteenth century, giving way before the terminist logic. The two should not be confused. Speculative grammar was what its name implies. The formal logic of the thirteenth and fourteenth centuries represented the culmination of logical studies until the nineteenth century.

5

Reference has already been made to the interest shown in scientific topics by thinkers such as Robert Grosseteste and Roger Bacon. In the fourteenth century we can find other remote precursors of the rise of natural science which took place at a later date. To label such men as

[1] There was some rather fanciful speculation on this point, an analogy being drawn between the way in which other parts of speech are subordinate or submissive to the inflections of the verb and the way in which other animals are submissive to man.

[2] Edited by G. Wallerand in *Les philosophes belges*, Vol. 8 (Louvain, 1913).

[3] This work was formerly attributed to Duns Scotus and is included in the Vivès edition of Scotus's works.

Ockhamists simply because of their scientific interests would be a mistake. It is doubtless possible to regard the Ockhamist philosophy as potentially favouring the growth of empirical science. For if the way in which things are is a purely contingent fact, the only way of discovering how they are is to investigate the matter empirically.[1] It is true, of course, that observation, or what Ockham calls 'intuitive knowledge', would not, by itself, get us very far in science. Hypothesis and deduction are required. But if connections between things are purely contingent, any hypothesis which is constructed stands in need of empirical testing, whenever possible. Though, however, it is arguable that the general attitude of the Ockhamists militates against the acceptance of traditional scientific theories either on authority or on the ground that they represent what *must* be the case, it by no means follows that any given nominalist made any personal contribution to scientific theory, nor that those who did make personal contributions of this nature subscribed to Ockhamist theses in philosophy.

To say this is not to deny factual connections. In the fourteenth century Albert of Saxony was both a terminist logician and a physicist, while Marsilius of Inghen had been a pupil of Buridan. But an enlightened scientific attitude was not peculiar to Ockhamists. In the thirteenth century Robert Grosseteste, who was certainly no Ockhamist before Ockham, was well aware that the more economical hypothesis is to be preferred to the less economical. He also understood that a mathematical explanation in astronomy does not provide a knowledge of causes in a metaphysical sense. Roger Bacon was no nominalist. And Dietrich (Theodoric) of Freiberg in Saxony, a Dominican who studied, among other things, the rainbow and colours[2] and who died after 1310,[3] was concerned, as a philosopher, with reconciling Aristotelianism and Neoplatonism. In the fourteenth century Masilius of Inghen, though he certainly held some Ockhamist theses, did not accept the more radical criticism of metaphysics.

[1] It might also be argued perhaps that insistence on God's 'absolute' power to alter at any moment the course of Nature would tend to discourage rather than to encourage scientific inquiry. But Ockham envisaged natural philosophers or physicists as proceeding on the hypothesis of the uniformity of Nature, an hypothesis which could not of course be demonstrated but which was required for their work.

[2] Dietrich's explanation of the rainbow, which was in part correct, was adopted by Descartes. His theory of colours was also not without value.

[3] The date of Dietrich's death is unknown. But in 1310 he was elected to a position in his order; and he appears to have died not long after that year.

One of the physical problems to which attention was given in the fourteenth century was that of motion. Aristotle had made a distinction between natural and violent motion. Fire, for example, has a natural tendency to upward motion: it is naturally light and tends towards its natural place. A stone, however, is naturally heavy and has a natural tendency to downward motion. But if someone throws a stone upwards, it moves for a time with an unnatural or violent motion, until its natural tendency to rejoin its natural place reasserts itself. What is the explanation of this unnatural movement? It cannot be due to the stone, which, left to itself, moves downward to the earth. Nor can it be due simply to the person who throws the stone, for he is no longer in contact with it once it has left his hand. According to Aristotle, the man who throws the stone also moves the surrounding air, and this air moves the air further on, each portion of the air moving the stone with it, until the successive movements of air become so weak that the stone's natural movement reasserts itself and the stone starts to move towards its natural place.

Ockham rejected this explanation of 'violent motion'. Suppose that two archers shoot at one another at the same time and the arrows meet in flight. It is absurd to suppose that the same air moves in opposite directions. It is quite sufficient to say that a moving body moves simply because it is in motion. We may require an explanation of the cessation of the stone's motion, but not of the motion itself.

The leading fourteenth-century physicists agreed with Ockham's rejection of the Aristotelian theory; but his explanation of a projectile's movement seemed to them to be no explanation at all. They preferred a theory which had been advanced by Philoponus in the sixth century and adopted in the thirteenth century by the Franciscan Peter John Olivi.[1] According to this theory the moving agent impresses on the projectile a certain quality or energy which they called *impetus* (Olivi had spoken of 'impulse'), in virtue of which the projectile continues to move until the impetus is overcome by the resistance of the air and the natural weight of the projectile. This was, of course, the sort of theory which Ockham wished to avoid, as it introduced an entity (impetus) of the kind which he was determined to eliminate. Indeed, the upholders of the impetus theory found themselves driven to ask how they should classify impetus in terms of the Aristotelian theory of

[1] Olivi, who died in 1298, anticipated Scotus's theory of the 'formal' distinction. He also maintained that the intellectual 'part' of the soul does not inform the body directly, a doctrine which was condemned by the council of Vienna in 1311.

categories or *praedicamenta*. Albert of Saxony said that it was the meta-physician's business to answer this question, though he himself thought that impetus should be classified as a quality.

The impetus theory was adopted by a number of thinkers, including Buridan, Albert of Saxony, Marsilius of Inghen and Nicholas Oresme. Buridan remarked that the Aristotelian theory of motion was unable to explain the motion of a spinning top, whereas the impetus theory could easily explain it. Albert of Saxony also tried to give an account of gravity. He made a distinction between the centre of gravity in a body and the centre of its volume, maintaining that the two do not neces-sarily coincide. It is the earth's centre of gravity which is really the centre of the world; and the tendency of each body possessing weight to unite its centre of gravity with the centre of the world is in effect what we mean by gravity.

The theory of impetus had wide implications. For example, Buridan suggested that if we conceive God as impressing a certain impetus on the heavenly bodies at creation no further explanation of their move-ment is required, as they encounter no resistance. There is no need to believe that they are composed of some special element; and there is no need to postulate the existence of intelligences or angels which move them. In other words, the explanation of the movements of the heavenly bodies is basically the same as that of movements on earth. True, Buridan proposed this theory in a tentative manner, saying that he would like to know what the theologians had to say about it. But it had a considerable success, being adopted by thinkers such as Albert of Saxony, Marsilius of Inghen and Nicholas Oresme. The theory obviously paves the way for a mechanical view of the world, in which the world is conceived as a system of bodies in motion, motion or energy being transmitted from one body to another.

One of the most remarkable Paris scientists was Nicholas Oresme (d. 1382). He seems to have entered the University of Paris, in the college of Navarre, in 1348. In 1356 he became master of the college; but after having been tutor to the future king Charles V he received ecclesiastical preferment, and in 1377 he was nominated bishop of Lisieux. He wrote commentaries on Aristotle's *Ethics*, *Politics*, *Eco-nomics* and *De Caelo*, questions on some other Aristotelian writings, a number of treatises on mathematical topics and on dynamics and attacks on astrology. In addition he wrote on theology, but his com-mentary on the *Sentences* has been lost.

Nicholas Oresme refused to allow that strict demonstrations are possible in physical science. In other words, scientific theories are hypotheses. To prove his point Nicholas tried to show how appearances can be saved (phenomena explained) by different hypotheses. The best-known example of this procedure is his treatment of the question of the earth's movement in relation to the sun in his treatise *On the Heaven and the World* (*Du ciel et du monde*). It was impossible, he argued, to prove by observation that the heaven rotates daily, while the earth remains stationary. For the appearances or phenomena would be precisely what they are even if it were the earth which rotated. As for other objections against the possibility of the earth's rotation, replies can be made to them all. And in regard to the Scriptures, we have to remember that the Bible uses the common ways of speaking and should not be looked on as a set of scientific treatises. In fine, the theory that it is the earth and not the sun which rotates daily can be disproved neither by observation nor by abstract reasoning nor by appeals to the Scriptures. Further, the hypothesis of the earth's rotation is more economical than the hypothesis that it is the heaven and not the earth which rotates. That is to say, on the first hypothesis one has to make a smaller number of postulates than in the second hypothesis.

The possibility of the earth's rotation had been discussed before. And it had been seen that observation alone was unable to decide the issue. While, however, Buridan and Albert of Saxony discussed the hypothesis of the earth's daily rotation on its axis quite sympathetically, they both rejected it. Albert seems to have thought, for example, that if the earth were conceived as rotating, this idea involved eliminating all the movements of the heavenly bodies; and he remarked that the movements of the planets could not be simply denied. Nicholas Oresme, however, saw that the hypothesis of the earth's rotation would not entail elimination of the movements of the planets, but only the alleged rotation of the 'fixed' stars.

In the end Nicholas opts for the common opinion of his time, the traditional hypothesis, on the ground that the reasons for accepting the hypothesis of the earth's daily rotation are not conclusive. It is pretty clear, however, that he considers that his hypothesis is more economical than and therefore preferable to the alternative hypothesis, even if its truth cannot be demonstrated.

A similar cautious spirit is shown in Nicholas's discussion (in the same treatise) of the possibility of there being other worlds than this one. The arguments, whether theological, philosophical or scientific, to prove that there could not possibly be a plurality of worlds are not cogent. At the same time we must take it that in point of fact this is the only world.

In his treatise *On the Configurations of Qualities* (*De configurationibus qualitatum*) Nicholas discussed the problem of the variation of qualities in intensity [1] and developed a geometrical treatment by means of graphs. This method was also proposed as a means of exhibiting variations in velocity. Nicholas discovered, for example, that the distance travelled by a body moving with a uniformly increasing velocity is equal to the distance travelled in the same time by a body moving with a uniform velocity equal to that attained by the first body in the middle instant of its course. To express these and similar successive variations in a way which would facilitate understanding and comparison, Nicholas conceived the idea of representing them by rectangular coordinates. Space or time, for instance, was represented by a straight base line, on which vertical lines were erected, their lengths corresponding to the position or the intensity of the variable. By connecting the ends of the vertical lines Nicholas obtained a curve representing fluctuations in intensity.

In his work on proportions of proportions (*De Proportionibus proportionum*) or ratios of ratios Nicholas made significant contributions to mathematics. In his writings against the astrologers he included the argument that on the assumption that planetary velocities are incommensurable it is not possible to predict the precise positions of planets.

When we think of the achievements of science, we are inclined to think of the fruits of applied science and technology. And in this field the Middle Ages have, of course, little to offer. There were, for example, some inventions in optics. And there were the unrealized dreams of Roger Bacon. But if we consider the history of science from the Renaissance onwards, it is obvious that advances in theoretical science preceded the age of striking inventions and the development of a technological era. And in the field of theory the Middle Ages were not so 'dark' and obscurantist as has sometimes been supposed. Nicholas Oresme, for instance, anticipated certain theorems of Galileo. The beginnings of science in the medieval period have had, however, to be rediscovered. They were in a sense abortive. Why this should have been the case is not easy to explain. But plague, war, the great schism, the sense of impending disaster which stimulated the growth of religious fanaticism of one kind and another, did not contribute to the spread of scientific research in the fourteenth century.

[1] This problem (that of the *intensio et remissio qualitatum*) had already been discussed, for example at Oxford by the scientists of Merton College.

6

To return to the diffusion of the 'modern way' in philosophy. We have seen that in the first half of the fourteenth century Ockhamist influence tended to be concentrated at Oxford and Paris. But in the second half of the century it spread far and wide. In 1389 a statute was enacted in the University of Vienna requiring students in the Faculty of Arts to attend lectures on the logical works of Peter of Spain, while later statutes imposed a similar obligation in regard to works on logic by William Heytesbury and others. Ockhamist tendencies were strongly represented in the Universities of Heidelberg (founded in 1386), Enfurt (1392), Leipzig (1409) and Cracow (1397). Indeed, the University of Leipzig is said to have owed its origin to the exodus of Ockhamists from Prague, when John Hus and Jerome of Prague taught the realism which they had learned from John Wyclif.

Some universities stuck to older traditions. Thus at Cologne (1389) the doctrine of Albert the Great and Thomas Aquinas held the field, in spite of some efforts made to induce the university authorities to discard realism in favour of nominalism. These efforts were made on the rather odd ground that the theological errors of John Hus followed from his philosophical realism. But the University of Cologne maintained that this was untrue. Louvain, founded in 1425, was also a stronghold of the older tradition. By and large, however, nominalism had extended itself pretty firmly in the universities of Europe by the end of the fourteenth century, in spite of occasional attacks, such as condemnations at Paris in 1339 and 1340. Needless to say, the more that the *via moderna* made itself felt and won recognition and acceptance, the more did it tend to become a scholastic tradition like the older schools. Indeed, given the concentration on logical studies it was capable of assuming a peculiar aridity of its own.

17

Speculative Mysticism

THERE were, of course, mystics throughout the Middle Ages. As for mystical theology, we have only to think of the writings of St Bernard and Richard of St Victor in the twelfth and of St Bonaventure in the thirteenth century. In the fourteenth century, however, there was a current of philosophical speculation which was clearly influenced by reflection on mystical experience. Two themes especially are prominent, the relation of finite being in general to God and that of the human soul in particular to God.

It is doubtless tempting to see in the flowering of speculative mysticism in the fourteenth century a reaction against the disputes and wranglings of the schools. What could be more natural, we may be inclined to ask, than that the religious consciousness should turn in disgust from the arid and inconclusive discussions of Thomists, Scotists and nominalists to a line of thought which emphasized the 'one thing needful'? Thomas-à-Kempis was not indeed a philosopher; and he wrote in the fifteenth century, not the fourteenth. But he surely gave expression, someone may claim, to the natural reaction of a religious man to the disputes and speculations of theologians and philosophers. 'What do genuses and species matter to us?' he asks. Again, 'A humble rustic who serves God is certainly better than a proud philosopher who, neglecting himself, considers the movement of the heavens.' Or, 'I desire to feel compunction rather than to know its definition.' And if appeal to Thomas-à-Kempis is disallowed, what about John Gerson (1363–1429) who became chancellor of the University of Paris in 1395? Did he not inveigh against 'vain curiosity in the matter of faith', insist on the primacy of mystical theology and show his conviction that the real remedy of his time lay in a deepening of the religious life and spirit?

That there was some religiously inspired reaction against the wrangling of the schools is doubtless true. Gerson, for example, refers to the spirit of contention and envy, of pride and vanity and contempt for the uneducated which, in his opinion, showed itself in scholastic disputes. But it would be a mistake to suppose that Gerson was an enemy either of theology or of philosophy. It would have been rather odd if he had been, given the fact that he was a Paris theologian and became chancellor of the University. What he objected to was not scholastic theology and philosophy as such but rather the overstepping of limits (logicians deciding metaphysical issues, metaphysicians making incursions into theology) and the contamination of Christian theology by a strong dosage of Greco-Islamic necessitarianism. He was concerned with the preservation of Christian faith in its purity, but he was not an anti-intellectualist.

In any case the wranglings of the schools took place in universities, whereas mystical tendencies were widely diffused and expressed a general striving after immediate communion with God rather than a particular reaction against the talk of academics. Some of these tendencies kept within the confines of religious orthodoxy, but others could and did take the form of movements which embodied a protest against the hierarchic Church.[1] Again, there were religious movements which were closely associated with the conviction that the end of the world was imminent. In all these movements, however, whether within or overstepping the bounds of what was considered orthodoxy, there was the belief that the regeneration of society could be attained only through a religious renewal and a deepening of the religious life. Obviously, speculative mysticism is not the same thing as a life of prayer, and still less can it be equated with the goings-on of, say, the Flagellants. The point is, however, that it has a much wider background than reaction against the aridities of academic discussion.

It has been suggested that Ockhamist criticism of traditional metaphysics may have contributed to the growth of speculative mysticism. For if the human reason is unable to prove the existence of God or to tell us much about him, the conclusion may be drawn that the only way of approaching God is experimentally, through knowledge of

[1] See, for example, *Heresy in the Later Middle Ages* by Gordon Leff (Manchester University Press; N.Y., Barnes and Noble, 2 vols, 1967).

acquaintance that is to say. This suggestion seems, however, to be a case of detecting a possible connection more than the result of detailed research. Gerson thought that the best way of finding God is through the cooperation of the cognitive and affective powers. But this is not the same as claiming that reason is incapable of attaining any knowledge about God. As for Eckhart, the foremost and most influential representative of speculative mysticism, he was born some twenty-five years before Ockham. And he was in any case no nominalist.

2

John Eckhart (c. 1260–1327), commonly known as Meister Eckhart, was born at Hochheim near Gotha. After entering the Dominican order he studied at Cologne and Paris. He seems to have taken the doctorate in theology at Paris in 1302 and to have taught there for a while, until he was appointed to a succession of high offices in his order in Germany. He wrote a number of treatises, some in Latin, others in German. He was also a noted preacher; and we have texts of both Latin and German sermons which he delivered.[1] He was given to making provocative statements, especially in his sermons. And towards the end of his life he came under suspicion of heresy. The archbishop of Cologne started an inquiry in 1326. Eckhart defended himself, admitting some exaggerated language but complaining of misrepresentation and giving orthodox explanations of his remarks. He also appealed to the Holy See.[2] He died in 1327, two years before Pope John XXII condemned twenty-eight propositions culled from or based on Eckhart's writings, seventeen as heretical, eleven as savouring of heresy.

In a real sense Eckhart's mind was steeped in the thought and categories of the past. He was familiar with and influenced by the theological and philosophical ideas of Albert the Great and Thomas Aquinas; but he was also strongly influenced by the Neoplatonist tradition. He had a speculative mind and thought deeply about the relation between the world and God and about that between the human soul and God. But he was also profoundly concerned with the deepen-

[1] In 1936 publication of a collection of Eckhart's German and Latin works, *Meister Eckhart: Die deutschen und lateinischen Werke*, was begun at Stuttgart under the auspices of the *Deutsche Forschungsgemeinschaft*.
[2] Eckhart is not the only religious writer who has made arresting and provocative remarks and who then, in face of criticism, has provided explanations which made the statements less interesting but more acceptable by common standards of orthodoxy.

ing of religious life and with an immediate approach by the soul to God. Though he was doubtless sincere in claiming to be orthodox in his thought, he certainly laid much more emphasis on interiority and on mysical union with God than on any outward observances of piety. This is of course only what one would expect of a mystical writer. But he was of a speculative turn of mind; and he expressed his mystical insights not in autobiography nor in poetry but in theological and philosophical language which already had a range of determinate meaning. At the same time he was evidently concerned with drawing attention in a forcible way to truths which he believed to have great religious importance. The result was a number of bold antinomies, paradoxical utterances and provocative statements which scandalized ecclesiastical authority. And his apologia was unable to disarm his adversaries, who were doubtless more concerned with his assertions as they stood than with his intentions.

In his *Opus Tripartitum (Work in Three Parts)* Eckhart asserts that God and existence are the same.[1] If someone asks, 'what is God?', the proper reply is 'existence' (*esse*). Again, in his exposition of the book of Exodus Eckhart states that in God essence and existence are identical, whereas in creatures they are distinct. He is the plenitude of being, the One, beyond plurality and distinction. God himself has told us, 'I am who am'.

Elsewhere, however, Eckhart makes the Neoplatonist statement that God is higher than or above being.[2] As cause of being God transcends being. He is intellect or understanding (*intelligere*). This is not a Neoplatonist statement, as for Plotinus the One transcended understanding. But Eckhart appeals to the fourth Gospel. St John does not say that in the beginning was being. He says that in the beginning was the Word. And Christ said of himself that he was the truth.

Some historians have maintained that, after having held the view that God was above being and that his essence is to understand, Eckhart changed his mind and adopted the Thomist view that God is existence itself (*ipsum esse*). But as Eckhart's different ways of speaking cannot be really separated as succeeding one another, this is a difficult interpretation to defend. It is much simpler to refer to Eckhart's statement that in God *esse* and *intelligere* are identical, and that God is because he is intellect or understanding.[3] God is 'the purity of being', and this is

---

[1] *Opus Tripartitum*, prologue, *Die lateinischen Werke* (Stuttgart), I, pp. 42-3.
[2] *Quaestiones parisienses, Die lateinischen Werke*, V, pp. 41 f.
[3] Ibid., p. 40. The same idea is found elsewhere too.

understanding. If we think of God simply statically, as it were, or simply in himself, we must describe him as existence. If we consider God as active, we see that the being of God is to understand.

The word 'understand' is admittedly inadequate. For in an ordinary language to understand is to understand what somebody says or an already existing situation or the solution of a problem, and so on, whereas *intelligere*, as used by Eckhart with reference to God, is creative. When speaking of the Trinity, he describes the Father as *intelligere*, the intellectual act which generates the Son and in the Son or Word the archetypes of creation. Again, it is by thinking them, in a creative sense, that God brings creatures into being.

Among the condemned propositions we find the statements that God created the world together with the generation of the Son, and that the world existed from eternity. Eckhart had indeed asserted explicitly that God did not exist before the world, and that the world was created by God at the generation of the eternal Son or Word.[1] But the first of these assertions was in no way a novelty. St Augustine, for example, had drawn attention to the impropriety of talking about God existing 'before' the world, as though he was involved in the temporal sense of events. As for the 'simultaneous' generation of the Son and the creation of the world, this idea naturally gave the impression that according to Eckhart the world existed from eternity. In his apologia, however, he explained that he was referring to the creative act in God himself and the creation of what one might describe as the archetypal world, its idea in God. The creative act, as it is in God himself, must be eternal, inasmuch as it is identical with the divine essence; and the archetypal ideas or essences in the Word must also be eternal. But it does not necessarily follow, Eckhart argues, that creation in a 'passive' sense, the multiplicity of creatures, had no beginning. In other words, Eckhart claimed that he had been saying no more than what Albert the Great and Thomas Aquinas had said before him.[2]

However this may be, let us take it that God's creative act is the act of creative thought. 'The (divine) intellect is the principle of the whole of Nature.'[3] The question arises, what is the status of creatures and their relation to God? Here we encounter one of Eckhart's more

---

[1] *Exposition of the Book of Genesis, Die lateinischen Werke*, I, p. 190.
[2] For example, in his commentary on the *Celestial Hierarchy* (4) of the Pseudo-Dionysius, Albert the Great remarked that 'God created from eternity, but the created is not from eternity'.
[3] *Exposition of the Book of Genesis, Die lateinischen Werke*, I, p. 50.

notorious statements, namely that creatures are nothing. In the fourth German sermon we read that 'all creatures are a pure nothing. I do not say that they are little or something; they are pure nothing.'[1] At first sight at any rate this seems to be a case of preaching pantheism from the pulpit. Elsewhere Eckhart says that 'outside God there is nothing'.[2] It may appear therefore that in his view God is the one and only reality, and that creatures are 'part' of God, within the divine being. For Eckhart obviously does not mean to say that they have no existence at all, whether inside or outside God. If this was the case, he would not be in a position to make any statement about the matter.

It does not require any very extensive knowledge of the philosophical theology or metaphysics of the Middle Ages to see that Eckhart would have no great difficulty in giving his statements meanings compatible with prevailing standards of orthodoxy. His explanation of the assertion that creatures are nothing is that they have no being of their own. If God was to turn away from them, as Eckhart puts it, or to cease thinking of them, they would cease to exist. As for the assertion that 'outside' God there is nothing, this was the ordinary traditional teaching. If God is infinite, omnipresent and holding all creatures in being by his creation and conserving activity, there cannot possibly be anything 'outside' him. The statement might, of course, be taken to mean that creatures are 'inside' God in the sense of being part of him. But while Eckhart says that nothing is so indistinct or so little distant from the creature as God is (in the sense that God is 'in' the creature, giving it being), he also says that nothing is so distinct or distant from the creature as God is. For God and creatures are 'opposed' as the One and the Many, the infinite and the finite.

Our ordinary experience is of the finite things about us, which in their interrelations constitute our material environment. They naturally seem to be the really solid datum, things existing in their own right. If we believe in God, we believe that finite things do in fact depend on him. But the natural tendency is to picture God as a kind of additional being. By provocative statements and bold antinomies Eckhart tries to arrest the attention of his hearers and to shock them into a better understanding of the implications of their professed religious beliefs and instead of seeing creatures as the solid reality and God as a shadowy figure in the background to see God as the one self-subsistent reality and creatures as nothing apart from him. Of course, if we accept

[1] *Die deutschen Werke* (Stuttgart), pp. 69–70.
[2] *Opus Tripartitum, Die lateinischen Werke*, I, p. 41.

Eckhart's own explanations of his statements, it may seem that we are making his thought less exciting than it would be, were we to assume that the medieval Dominican intended to expound pantheism from the pulpit. But it is not a case of trying to force Eckhart's thought into a more or less orthodox mould despite his statements. We must presumably give some credit to his own explanations. At the same time we need not try to render his provocative statements and antinomies 'innocuous'. For they clearly have a function. He employed them as a means of conveying more effectively a deeply religious vision of the world.

If Eckhart is concerned in general with the divine omnipresence and God's creative and sustaining activity in all things, he is concerned in particular with the relation between the human soul and God. In his view the soul comes near to God in proportion as it grows in detachment from the multiple objects of sense-experience and of thought and will and retreats inwards to what he regards as the essence or citadel or 'spark' (scintilla, vünkelin) or ground of the soul. This essence of the soul, its innermost ground, is described as intellect or understanding (intelligere). It is the likeness of God, who is himself intelligere; and it is only by the inward retreat into it that the Word can be born in the soul and mystical union with God achieved.

The general idea of the need for detachment, for interior recollection and for retreat into the interior of the soul as a condition for union with God was not of course in any way new. It is indeed arguable that in his insistence on intellect rather than on will as the means of coming to union with God, Eckhart shows an affinity with Neoplatonism rather than with the affective mysticism of the Middle Ages, even if he does Christianize the Neoplatonist line of thought by emphasizing the idea of the birth of the Word or Son in the soul.[1] But Neoplatonism was not precisely a novelty. The features of Eckhart's mystical doctrine which arrest attention are his statements about the total transformation of the soul into God and his assertion that there is in the soul something 'uncreated', namely the soul's innermost essence, the intellect. Thus in a German sermon he says that in mystical union the soul is changed into God in the way that in the eucharist the bread is changed into the Body of Christ.[2] It becomes one with God. Unless man ceases to be a

---

[1] It may be appropriate to recall that Aquinas laid emphasis on the intellectual 'vision' of God as the essence of beatitude, whereas the Franciscan tradition tended to stress the will and love.

[2] Die deutschen Werke, I, pp. 110–11. See also the following sermon, p. 119.

creature, he cannot live wholly in God. And he cannot cease to be a creature except through self-identification with the image of God, the 'uncreated' spark of the soul.

In regard to his statements about total transformation into God and man's identification with the divine Son, Eckhart subsequently admitted that he had been guilty of exaggeration. In regard to his description of the divine image as an 'uncreated' light in the soul, he drew attention to the fact that he had not identified this uncreated light with the created soul. What he had said was that *if* the soul was identical with the eternal image of God, it would be itself uncreated. In point of fact the human soul cannot be identified with God's eternal image. But it is only by becoming one with this image that the created soul puts off its creatureliness and is united with the divine being.

Eckhart's doctrine on this matter seems obscure. It is, however, clear that the tendency of his thought is well represented by Plotinus's idea of 'the flight of the alone to the Alone', provided that we allow for Eckhart's emphasis on regeneration through the birth of the Word or Son in the soul. Just as Eckhart finds in the soul a unitary centre or ground, beyond, as it were, the plurality of powers or faculties, so he tends to find in God a simple ground of the divine being beyond the distinction of Persons.[1] Mystical union thus tends to be conceived as the uniting of the ground of the soul with the divine One, the return of the soul to its true centre.

Some writers have seen Eckhart's thought as looking forward to German transcendentalism. His identification of the divine *esse* with *intelligere* can, if we so wish, be seen as an anticipation of the post-Kantian identification of ultimate reality or the Absolute with thought. For the matter of that, so can Aristotle's description of God as the thought which thinks itself. But unless we feel inspired to follow Hegel in regarding the whole of European thought as leading up to absolute idealism, it seems more appropriate to see Eckhart in his historical context, as a man who was concerned with a deepening of the religious spirit and with promotion of an immediate approach to and union with God. It was because of this concern that his thought could exercise an influence on medieval religious movements which in their hostility towards the official Church went far beyond Eckhart's own attitude. As for the attempts of certain Nazi writers to annex the eminent medieval Dominican, these can be dismissed as absurd. Employment of the

[1] In face of criticism Eckhart protested that it was only orthodox doctrine that there is one divine nature or essence, identical in each of the three divine Persons.

vernacular and appeals to interiority do not entail theories of blood and race.

3

Eckhart had a warm defender of his orthodoxy in a fellow Dominican, the mystical writer Blessed Henry Suso (c. 1295–1366), who was born at Constance. Like Eckhart, Suso was a preacher; but he was much less speculatively inclined. We find indeed in his writings the idea of the mystical union with God as taking place in the unifying centre of the soul, which is the image of God. And we also find the idea of the actualization of God's image in the soul through divinely infused knowledge and love resulting in 'the birth of God' or 'the birth of Christ' in the soul. But Suso's mystical doctrine is less Neoplatonist than Eckhart's and more in line with the affective and Christocentric spirituality of writers such as St Bernard. Suso does indeed use phrases such as sinking into God; but his thought is clearly not pantheistic. He was beatified in 1831.

Another fourteenth-century Dominican mystic is the famous preacher John Tauler (c. 1300–61). In man Tauler distinguishes three levels, man as sensing, man as rational and man considered in regard to the highest part of his soul, das Gemüt. This is said to be both higher and deeper than the powers or faculties of the soul, which are rooted in it. It is created, but it has an inborn and constant orientation to God. Sometimes Tauler seems to use Gemüt as synonymous with Grund, the ground of the soul. But it has been argued,[1] probably correctly, that the two concepts, though closely related, should be distinguished. The ground of the soul is the perpetual dwelling place of God, while the Gemüt is an active power, emerging from the ground, penetrating reason and will and drawing back the powers of the soul into itself and thence into the ground or dwelling place of God.

The foundation or presupposition of union with God is the soul's likeness to him, its bearing of his image. And as Tauler lays stress on conforming the powers of the soul to God and on willing and doing what God wills, it may seem that for him the actualization of the soul's likeness to God consists in conformity of will and conduct to God rather than in any mystical retreat into absorption in the divine being.

[1] See, for example, Homo Spiritualis: A Comparative Study of the Anthropology of Johannes Tauler, Jean Gerson and Martin Luther (1509–16) in the Context of Their Theological Thought by Steven E. Ozment (Leiden, 1969), pp. 22 f.

It is clear, however, that Tauler does in fact envisage a union of the human spirit with the divine in which man loses consciousness of his own distinctiveness. At the same time it is not clear whether he is speaking simply of a psychological state in which awareness of distinction is suspended or whether he is speaking of an ontological absorption. The former seems to be the case; but this is not a matter on which all writers are agreed. The general view is that Tauler insists on the need for grace in order to come close to God, and that in mystical experience God conforms the human will to his own and penetrates, as it were, the human soul, without any ontological identification of the finite with the infinite. With mystical writers, however, we can easily find phrases which lend themselves to a monistic interpretation, if that is what we wish to find.

4

Suso was a friend of Eckhart and defended his orthodoxy. Tauler was influenced by Eckhart, though by a good many other writers as well. Eckhart's influence was also felt by the Flemish mystic John Ruysbroeck (1293–1381). Ruysbroeck, like Suso, attacked those representatives of the widespread movement of 'the Free Spirit' who claimed to have become one with God, so that all their actions, however sinful by customary standards, were divine actions, and who rejected the Church and its sacraments. In other words, he opposed what he believed to be a false, dangerous and heretical mysticism. Instead he emphasized the necessity of self-purification and of the performance of good works as a preparation for an interior life of virtue in which the powers of the soul, intellect and will, can turn themselves, under the attracting influence of grace, to the indwelling God. The higher stage of mystical contemplation and union with God, which can be attained only through divine grace and not simply by human effort, expresses itself in a life of good works which flow from this union and are informed by it.

At the same time Ruysbroeck made use of expressions, reminiscent of Eckhart, which were to arouse criticism by Gerson. For example, Ruysbroeck spoke of a superessential unity in God beyond the distinction of Persons;[1] and he also wrote of a union of the soul with God without difference or distinction.[2] Whatever Gerson may have thought

[1] *The Adornment of the Spiritual Marriage*, III, 4.
[2] Ibid., III, 1.

about the matter, it is clear that the Flemish mystic was no pantheist. He was influenced by the writings of the Pseudo-Dionysius and made use of his language; but writings such as *The Mirror of Eternal Salvation* and *The Book of the Twelve Beguines* show Ruysbroeck's concern with avoiding any pantheistic identification of creatures with God. When he speaks of a union without distinction he is referring to an experience of total absorption in God from a psychological point of view, not to an ontological merging of natures. The soul, that is to say, is caught up into a state in which it is conscious of God alone; but it still exists.

5

John Gerson (1363–1429) who, as already mentioned, lectured on theology at Paris and became chancellor of the University in 1365, was well aware of the aridity of a theology divorced from religion and spirituality. At the same time he was acutely conscious of the dangers of uncontrolled mystical propensities, divorced from a sound philosophical and theological framework. He was in full agreement with Ruysbroeck's attack on the extravagant ideas and ways of the more heterodox representatives of the Free Spirit movement and praised him for it. At the same time he believed that some of Ruysbroeck's utterances showed pantheistic tendencies; and he criticized the Flemish mystic's *Adornment of the Spiritual Marriage*. John van Schoonhoven, a mystic who belonged to the same monastery of which Ruysbroeck had been a member, came to the latter's defence. But he took the unfortunate line, as far as Gerson was concerned, of arguing that mystical doctrine could not properly be discussed in the language of the schools. Van Schoonhoven certainly had a point. For criticism of the utterances of mystics by professional theologians is not infrequently apt to give the impression that they have taken paradoxical statements too literally and have failed to understand the difficulty encountered by mystics in using ordinary language to express unusual experiences. But Gerson too had a point, namely that mystical theology needed serious development, and that unless it occupied a prominent position in the theological teaching of the schools, theology would remain in an arid and impoverished state. A real deepening of the religious life could not be achieved by divorcing mysticism from theological reflection.

Gerson's own mystical teaching in his work *On Speculative Mystical Theology* (*De mystica theologia speculativa*) has a psychological basis. In his view the soul has three cognitive powers and three affective powers. In descending order, so to speak, in each case, the former are pure intelligence, discursive reason and sensibility, while the latter are *synderesis*, the rational appetite and the sensual appetite. Pure intelligence, which corresponds to the 'spark' (*scintilla*), is that power of the soul which, through a natural light from God, apprehends first principles with certainty. Synderesis is an appetitive power endowed by God with a natural inclination to the good. According to Gerson the actions or operations of the cognitive and appetitive powers are reciprocal, there being action and interaction between each member of a pair. 'Perhaps we cannot find a cognition which is not formally or virtually a certain affect, just as we do not seem to be able to find an affect without its being a certain experimental cognition.'[1] Knowledge of an object is accompanied by or involves a certain affective disposition in regard to it; and an affect or feeling involves some cognitive element.

In mysticism it is the two highest powers, pure intelligence and, on the affective side, or the side of the will, synderesis, which in their mutual interaction become the vehicle of the experimental knowledge of God. The mystical experience affects also the lower powers, inasmuch as man is a unity, but it is centred in the highest powers. Gerson emphasizes the role of synderesis, of love; but though mystical experience is for him not simply a matter of knowledge, knowledge is essentially involved, a knowledge by acquaintance rather than knowledge about. Given the due ascetic preparation and given the infusion of supernatural grace, the human spirit can be drawn to God in ecstasy or rapture and united to God in a conformity of will which, unlike ecstasy, can be permanent and which actualizes the soul's likeness to God.

Throughout his account of mystical experience Gerson is careful to make it clear that he does not postulate any merging of the soul with God. Mystical union of the soul with God is for him an actualization of the soul's potential likeness to its ideal standard, so to speak, in the divine mind. But likeness is a relation between ontologically distinct beings, a distinction which remains even when the intellect is enlightened by God and the human will united with the divine will. Gerson is also careful to insist on the role of the sacraments in the purification of the soul and its approach to God.

The term 'mystical theology' is ambiguous. It can mean the theory of mysticism, an analysis, for example, of the typical successive stages of the mystical life. But the term can also be used to mean the actual

[1] *De theologia mystica speculativa*, 17, 39.

experimental knowledge of God, as distinct from thought and discourse about God and his operations. Gerson tends to use the term in the second sense. But his work *On Speculative Mystical Theology* is, of course, concerned with reflection on mystical experience, its conditions, nature and implications. The precise sense in which the term 'mystical theology' is being used on a given occasion can be seen from the context.

In his general philosophical–theological outlook, apart from mystical theology, Gerson shows an affinity with the Ockhamists in his concern with eliminating those elements of Greco-Islamic thought which appear to limit the power and freedom of God. This is the real motive of his attack on realism. In their desire to bring God and his activity within the scope of human understanding Platonizing philosophers and theologians had, in Gerson's opinion, developed a theory of divine ideas which governed the divine will and so restricted God's liberty. They wished to understand creation and, whether they intended it or not, they tended to represent it as a necessary expression of the divine nature. Similarly, they were inclined to speak as though God were constrained or obliged to promulgate a certain moral law, whereas in point of fact actions are good because willed by God and bad because he prohibits them. In other words, realism exhibits a spirit of intellectual pride; and it is not surprising if John Hus and Jerome of Prague were realists. Theologians should pay more attention to the Bible and less to pagan and Moslem philosophers.

In view of his Ockhamist affinities Gerson's esteem for the Pseudo-Dionysius and for St Bonaventure may seem rather odd. He believed, however, that the former's writings were the work of St Paul's Athenian convert and that they must therefore contain sound doctrine, provided that they were interpreted correctly. As for Bonaventure, it was the saint's mystical doctrine, as expressed in the *Journey of the Mind to God*, and his criticism of pagan philosophy which attracted Gerson, rather than the saint's enthusiasm for the theory of divine ideas. In any case it would be misleading to describe Gerson as an Ockhamist. The lines of thought which he shared with the Ockhamists were subordinate to his religious aims; and he was prepared to see truth in other traditions besides that of the 'new way'. He was not concerned, for example, with criticizing traditional metaphysics in the way in which Nicholas of Autrecourt had criticized it. His concern was rather that the metaphysician should not attempt to usurp the position of the theologian.

6

In the thirteenth and fourteenth centuries the search for immediate contact with God showed itself in a variety of ways. It could and did show
itself in a mysticism which kept within the framework of the Church's
teaching and which did not deny the role of the Church and the sacraments in Christian life, even if emphasis was placed, very naturally, on
interiority. It was a question of priorities rather than of rejection of the
Church as an institution. At the same time the search for immediate
contact with God could and did show itself in popular movements
which either began by being or tended to become hostile to the Church
and indifferent to or even contemptuous of the official practices of piety.
At their worst such movements could involve a kind of reduction of
God to the level of man, in the sense that identification of the soul with
God was taken as a sanction of any sort of conduct.

Basically, the mystical writers whom we have considered belonged
to the first group. Eckhart, as we have seen, made provocative statements which led to a condemnation by ecclesiastical authority. And
Gerson criticized Ruysbroeck. But Eckhart was no enemy of the
Church; and Ruysbroeck was vehement in his denunciation of those
whom he looked on as pseudo-mystics. They all looked to mysticism
as a means of renewing the life of the Christian Church. They differed,
to be sure, in their speculative interpretations of mystical experience,
Eckhart, for instance, being more influenced by Neoplatonism than
were Suso or Gerson. But their religious concern was paramount. And
when Ockhamist influence is clear, as in the case of Gerson, it has to be
seen in the light of this religious concern. In fine, the speculative
mysticism of the fourteenth century was not part of the 'modern way'.
It continued the tradition of Richard of St Victor and Bonaventure,
though it showed a stronger sense of urgency in regard to the spiritual
regeneration of society. In a real sense the speculative mystics were
reformers. And with Gerson, in the University of Paris, the idea of
reformation was extended to the study of philosophy and theology with
a view to placing the Christian life in the foreground.

Obviously, the writers whom we have been considering interpreted
mystical experience in the light of pre-existing religious belief. At the
same time there are certainly differences in the extent to which the influence of specifically Christian beliefs manifests itself. With Gerson it
is clear enough. With Eckhart, however, the case is somewhat different.
He speaks indeed of the birth of the Word in the soul. And it would be

absurd to suggest that the Dominican preacher was not really a Christian at all. But though Eckhart was undoubtedly a Christian believer, the metaphysical element in his thought is much more prominent than in that of Gerson. Moreover, his metaphysics was strongly impregnated with Neoplatonist elements. It is therefore easy to understand why those who are interested in comparative mysticism and who are not committed to Christianity tend to single out Eckhart for special consideration and for comparison with oriental mystics. If we concentrate on his more provocative statements, they seem to break the limits of Christian belief; and his more speculative and metaphysical turn of mind naturally seems to give him a much greater degree of affinity with Hindu and Buddhist mystical writers than we would associate with the more obviously affective and Christocentric spirituality of the Middle Ages. The historical Eckhart lived and worked within the Christian religion; but it can hardly be denied that those who see in him a representative of a mysticism which transcends the bounds between different religions have some ground in his thought for their interpretation. This ground is mainly provided by a metaphysics of a type which Gerson deplored and which an Ockhamist would have questioned.

18

Political Philosophy:
Marsilius of Padua

I

POLITICAL philosophy obviously involved reflection on concrete political institutions and issues; and it is inevitably coloured to a greater or lesser extent by the political and social circumstances of the time.[1] In medieval Europe the existence of two types of society, the State on the one hand and a supranational Church on the other,[2] was the historical datum which formed the concrete point of departure for the political reflections of the medieval thinker. Obviously, there were a number of other factors which exercised varying degrees of influence on these reflections; the social-political thought of St Augustine,[3] concepts derived from Roman and canon law and, from the period of the translations, Greek political theory. But it scarcely needs saying that medieval political theory centred round the actual social and political life of the Middle Ages. It was in a sense this life

[1] It is indeed possible to confine political philosophy to an analysis of the language of politics. But political concepts and terms are used to talk about political institutions and issues. And one aim of analysis is presumably to facilitate a better understanding of the phenomena.

[2] 'Supranational' may seem to be a loaded or tendentious term. But it helps to emphasize the fact that whereas today the Church would commonly be thought of as one of a large number of societies existing within a pluralist political society, the medieval thinker did not conceive the Church in quite this way.

[3] The political theory of St Augustine has been briefly discussed in Chapter 3. And though it contributed to laying the foundations of medieval political theory, it is unnecessary to repeat what has already been said.

becoming conscious of itself and trying to settle its problems in a theoretical manner.

In the Frankish kingdom in the early Middle Ages the concept of royal rule was theocratic. The king ruled over a Christian people, and he received his power from God at his anointing and coronation. The situation was of course complicated by the claims of the papacy, backed by the forged Donation of Constantine, to dispose of the imperial crown. Thus in 816 Louis I, son of Charlemagne, was anointed and crowned by Pope Stephen IV at Rheims, while in 823 Lothar, son of Louis I, was crowned emperor at Rome. Again, in 850 Louis II was anointed and crowned emperor of the Romans by the pope. Though, however, the position of emperor of the Romans, which involved, theoretically, rule over the whole Christian world,[1] was claimed to be a papal appointment, kings were otherwise regarded as ruling by the grace of God bestowed on them at their anointing and coronation. They were also regarded as the fount of law. The monarch was doubt-less expected to show respect for the customs and folk-lore of his people; but his will was the source of positive law.

It by no means follows that the king was regarded as entitled to make any laws that happened to suit his interests. The concept of society was theocratic. The monarch, deriving his power and authority from God, had the task of interpreting and enforcing the divine law. In the ninth century, Hincmar, archbishop of Rheims, wrote of the bishops as electing the king on condition that he observed the laws. Though, however, the monarch was certainly expected to respect the enact-ments of his predecessors and though in making laws he might be expected to consult with others, it was his will which was actually the source of the authority of law. And provided that a law was not incompatible with divine law, the king's subjects, including the clergy, were morally obliged to obey. If, however, law was manifestly con-trary to or incompatible with divine law, there was no moral obligation to obey. The theocratic concept of society entailed the view that the king had a trust to fulfil, a trust from God that is to say, and that he could abuse this trust. If he did so, it was the duty of the bishops to call him to order.

What if the monarch degenerated into a tyrant? The theocratic

---

[1] Charlemagne may have regarded himself simply as emperor of Latin Christen-dom; but the papal policy was to claim that the emperor of the Romans, deriving his power from the Vicar of Christ, took the place of the Byzantine emperor and was, by right if not in fact, supreme temporal ruler of the whole Christian world.

concept of society obviously allowed for a distinction between the office of king and the man who held the office. Just as a king of Judah or Israel in Old Testament times could prove himself unworthy of his office, so could a monarch in the early Middle Ages. But if he refused to listen to the admonitions of the bishops, there was no way of deposing him. Hence the debates about tyrannicide. While some writers, such as Isidore of Seville in the Visigothic kingdom, thought that a tyrant should be endured, to avoid bringing about greater evils, others believed that he could justifiably be assassinated.[1]

The Frankish empire disintegrated. But in 962 Otto I was crowned emperor by Pope John XII. The position of emperor of the Romans was, of course, without practical significance in a country such as England; but a good deal of medieval political theorizing concerned the relations between the empire and the Holy See. It may appear that the German emperor's acceptance of coronation by the pope signified a subordination of imperial power to the papacy. This was certainly not the case at first, as far as practice was concerned. On the contrary, for some time it was the emperors who controlled election to and dismissal from the papacy. At the same time acceptance of coronation by the pope preserved, on the theoretical level, the papal view of the emperor as an instrument for the temporal government of Christendom. And it needed only a succession of strong popes for attempts to be made to implement the papal policy. Thus, during his pontificate 1073–85), Gregory VII made it quite clear that in his opinion the Holy See had the right to judge of temporal matters as well as spiritual, while Pope Innocent III (1198–1216) insisted that while the papacy was not concerned with feudal arrangements, the successor of St Peter possessed jurisdiction over temporal rulers in all matters where sin was involved. Innocent III also made it clear that the imperial crown had been transferred from Byzantium to the western emperors by the Holy See, and that the German emperor held his position by favour of the pope. The actual power exercised by Innocent III was hardly to be surpassed. But in the field of theory at any rate the classic expression of the more extreme papal claims was the Bull *Unam Sanctam* promulgated by Pope Boniface VIII in 1302.

It would be a mistake to suppose that the claims made on behalf

---

[1] It was all very well to say, in theory, that tyrants could be deposed. When there was no constitutional means of deposing tyrants, recourse could be had only to armed resistance and, if necessary, tyrannicide. Obviously, success was in practice the main criterion for justifying such measures.

of the papacy and the Church were motivated simply and solely by ambition and desire for power. Obviously it would be idle to deny that such motives played a part. At the same time we have to allow for sincerely held theological beliefs. Quite apart from forgeries such as the Donation of Constantine, it was believed that God had created man for a supernatural end, eternal life or eternal salvation, and that this was man's only final end or goal. Man had not got a temporal final end, catered for by the State, but a supernatural end, attainment of which was cared for by the Church. Man had one ultimate vocation, and this could be fulfilled only in and through the Church. It was natural, therefore, that the Church should be regarded as being in a real sense of superior dignity and value to any temporal society. It was also natural that theologians and canon lawyers should stress the duty of temporal rulers to facilitate man's attainment of his eternal goal by giving to legislation a moral basis and by assisting the Church in her work. Of course, it by no means followed from this that kings were pretty well delegates of the pope, nor that the imperial crown was for the pope to bestow. The point is, however, that behind or underlying even the more extreme claims of the papacy there lay a theologically based view of man and his destiny which went back to St Augustine and which made the making of such claims possible, though it did not entail them.

Papal claims or, more generally, claims on behalf of the Church were not, of course, made without being contested or without any opposition. For example, Pope Gregory VII first suspended and then deposed from his office the German king Henry IV.[1] Towards the end of the eleventh century a work was written, the *Book Concerning the Preservation of the Unity of the Church (Liber de unitate ecclesiae conservanda)* in which the author argued that God gave imperial power to such undesirable emperors as Nero and Julian the Apostate, that peace should be preserved, and that this meant submission even to unsuitable rulers, who received their power from God and not from the pope.

It can hardly be claimed that the polemical writings produced by this sort of controversy were of much philosophical profundity. But there is at any rate one writer who merits its mention here, namely Manegold of Lautenbach. In his *Book for Gebehardt (Liber ad Gebehardum)* he

[1] Henry protested that he was the Lord's anointed and therefore inviolable. The pope agreed that Henry was the Lord's anointed but for this very reason considered that the king was subject to papal jurisdiction.

intervened on the pope's side in the controversy aroused by the deposition of Henry IV. In Manegold's view unworthy kings could rightly be excommunicated and deposed; and he made it abundantly clear that he regarded Henry IV as one of them. The interesting point, however, is that he represented the king as entering into a covenant or pact with the people. If a king failed to observe the conditions of the covenant, he forfeited any right to continue in office and could be deposed. Manegold was engaged in defending the pope's right to depose; but the fact remains that he postulated a covenant or pact between the temporal ruler and his people.[1]

This theory of government as resting on a covenant between king and people hardly fitted in very well with the claims being put forward by the papacy Nor did it fit in with a completely theocratic concept of society. At the same time there is no great difficulty in seeing how it could arise. For it is obvious that the community did in fact have certain expectations in regard to the monarch and his conduct. True, the community could be represented as expecting that the king would fulfil the trust confided in him by God. And if he failed to fulfil it, the Vicar of Christ could be represented as having the right to admonish him and, if necessary, to depose him. But given the fact that the community had certain expectations – for example, that the king would not ride roughshod over the customary law of the land or the enactments of his predecessors – it is really not surprising if at any rate one writer started talking about a pact between king and people.

The general conviction was that all legitimate power, including, for instance, that of the father as head of the family, came from God. And the theocratic concept of kingship was symbolized and preserved by the ceremony of anointing, reminiscent of the Old Testament. But it by no means follows, of course, that the theocratic concept of kingship corresponded fully with the actual historical situation. Consider England, for example. The theocratic concept was present. Theoretically at any rate the monarch was the fount of law rather than subject to the law.[2] But there was also the feudal system. And as we all know,

[1] The existence of organized society is assumed as a datum by Manegold. He does not introduce any theory of society itself resting on a social compact or contract. He is concerned simply with the idea of a covenant whereby the monarch undertakes to fulfil certain duties and the people assume the obligation to obey him, provided that he fulfils his trust.

[2] The idea can be seen clearly in the thought of John of Salisbury which was briefly considered in Chapter 7. John made use of Ulpian's dictum that what pleases the prince has the force of law. He did not, however, intend to sanction any and

in 1215 the king was dramatically recalled to his feudal obligations. In practice the royal will was not the only factor in the law-making process. And the thirteenth-century lawyer Henry Bracton spoke of the king as being subject to the law. The feudal system, with its inbuilt checks on royal power, could indeed coexist with a formal recognition of the theocratic concept, especially if the idea of 'the Crown' was widened. But, formal reconciliation apart, the concept of the monarch as part of the feudal system, with obligations arising from his place in the system, was different from the concept of the king as the viceregent of God and the personal source of law. According to the purely theocratic concept the monarch's contractual obligations, so to speak, were to God. According to the feudal concept he was linked by contractual bonds to the community, at any rate as represented by the feudal lords. Moreover, as even in the theocratic concept the right of resistance to a tyrant had to be recognized, the concept was bound to undergo modification.

2

The translation into Latin of works such as Aristotle's *Politics*, changed the character of political theory in the Middle Ages. To say that before the rediscovery of Aristotle there was no basis for political theorizing which went beyond participation in polemics over concrete issues such as the relation of the emperor to the Holy See or of temporal rulers in general to the Church would be inaccurate. For there was the doctrine of St Augustine, helped out by ideas based on Roman and ecclesiastical law. At the same time it is clear that a better acquaintance with a political philosophy which went back to basic principles and which knew nothing of theocratic concepts of society and government was likely to exercise a powerful influence on medieval political theory, especially as Aristotle was looked on as the Philosopher in a pre-eminent sense. Given this estimate of Aristotle, a theologian such as Thomas Aquinas was faced with the task of adjusting the Aristotelian theory of the State to harmonize with Christian belief.

At first sight this was no easy task. For Aristotle knew nothing of any Church; nor had he any concept of revelation or of supernatural

---

every kind of legislation. For he thought of the king as obliged to make laws which would define, interpret or supplement but not impinge the moral law. If the monarch disregarded the moral law and natural justice and acted tyrannically, he could be resisted and, if necessary, killed.

life and salvation. He thought of man as a social being by nature and of political society as a natural institution, in the sense that it was demanded by and was a necessary condition for the fulfilment of man's nature and the actualization of his powers. As Aristotle put it, the man who had no need of society was either a beast or a god, either infra-human or supra-human. And by society he meant primarily political society as he knew it in ancient Greece, a society which was not irreligious but which was coterminous with the Greek *polis* or city-state. For him, it was in this society that man developed and fulfilled his potentialities as man. At first sight, therefore, it would seem that Aristotle's concept of society left no room at all for medieval convic-tions about man's supernatural destiny and the role of the Church, and that the two could not be reconciled. In other words, it might well appear, at first sight, that to accept Aristotle's political theory was to accept a naturalistic concept of the State, and that one could not at the same time look on man as having a supernatural end or goal and on the Church as superior to the State.

In some respects Aquinas found himself able to endorse whole-heartedly the doctrine of Aristotle. He was quite prepared to maintain with the Greek philosopher not only that society in general was natural to man but also that organized political society was a natural society. Even if man had never sinned, there would still have to be government. 'Man is by nature a social animal. Hence, in a state of innocence (if there had been no Fall, that is to say) man would have lived in society. But a common social life of many individuals could not exist unless there was someone in control to attend to the common good.'[1] Obviously, if nobody ever transgressed the law, the punitive power of the State would not be exercised. But there would still have to be some regulations, and so some person or body of persons to make the regulations.[2] Whatever St Augustine may have tended to think about the matter, there is no essential connection between the State and sin. Civil society and civil government are required for the fulfilment of man's natural needs and for the leading of a full human life. And as natural institutions in this sense they are willed by God, the creator of man.

Aquinas also accepts the Aristotelian idea of the State as a self-sufficing community, in the sense that it has at its disposal all the means

---

[1] *Summa theologica*, Part I, Question 96, Article 4.
[2] A simple example in modern times. The common good requires that there shall be traffic regulations, even if nobody ever transgresses them.

required for the attainment of its end, namely the common good. In the language used by the canon lawyers, the State is a 'perfect' society. But so is the Church. And Aquinas cannot simply juxtapose the concepts of State and Church, claiming that the former exists to secure to man the attainment of his natural final end, while the latter exists to help man to attain his supernatural final end. For Aquinas believes that man has only one final end, a supernatural one. At the same time he must attribute to the State a sphere and purpose of its own.

The obvious way of coping with the difficulty was to represent the State as caring for man's temporal welfare by preserving peace and by seeing that there was a sufficient supply of the necessities of life. But though Aquinas does say this, it is not all that he says.[1] The State's function is to promote the common good. And Aquinas, like Aristotle, looks on the common good as involving not only material welfare but also the good life defined as a life in accordance with virtue. If human virtue and moral action are involved, is not the State trespassing on the territory of the Church? Not in Aquinas's view. Nor in that of medieval theorists generally. For, as we have seen, the ruler was expected to enact laws which would define, interpret and supplement the natural moral law, and to attach sanctions for transgressions of the law. The State's business was not so much to impart virtue as to facilitate its acquisition and retention and to punish evildoers.[2] In general we can say that Aquinas looks on the State as concerned with man's temporal welfare and with creating and maintaining conditions which facilitate and safeguard the good life. The Christian State is expected to assist the work of the Church by creating and maintaining the conditions in which the Church can help man to attain his supernatural end.

Perhaps we can put the matter in this way. As a Christian theologian, Aquinas believes that man has a supernatural end, and that the Church exists to enable him to attain it. He therefore thinks of the Church as superior in value to the State; and he is convinced that in the event of a clash between man's supernatural interest and what appear to be his temporal interests the latter must be subordinated to the former. As a philosopher, however, Aquinas is concerned with political society in general. This is a natural institution, antedates the Church and has

---

[1] See *De regimine principum* (*On the Rule of Princes*), I, 15.
[2] It must be remembered that for Aquinas, as for Aristotle, 'virtue' includes the intellectual virtues. It is not simply a case of 'morality' as the term is often understood today.

foundations of its own. It follows therefore that even the Christian State is supreme in its own sphere, and that its ruler is not simply an employee of the Church or a delegate of the papacy. In matters which are connected with man's salvation, however, the State must defer to the Church's judgement and assist her.[1]

The interweaving of the points of view of the theologian and the philosopher shows itself in other ways too. For example, as a philosopher Aquinas is inclined to regard the State as a whole and the individual as a part, and to stress the State's function of aiming at the common good and the individual's obligation to subordinate his private interests to the common good. Even apart, however, from his belief in a natural moral law and natural rights, which any State should respect, Aquinas's theological conviction that man has a vocation which transcends political society obviously prevents him from looking on the individual as nothing more than a member of a temporal society.

It may appear that Aquinas simply adds a theological superstructure to Aristotle's political theory. There is obviously some truth in this. Aristotle knew nothing of Christian theology: Aquinas adds it. At the same time Aquinas tries to find what we might describe as points of insertion. For instance, Aristotle remarked that a good citizen does not necessarily possess the qualities of a good man. And this remark can be used by Aquinas as authorizing a distinction between the good citizen and the genuine Christian. Again, though Aristotle emphasized man's social nature, it is a notorious fact that he found man's highest activities in those which, while presupposing society, can most easily be pursued in solitude and make a man relatively self-dependent. Aquinas has only to transform Aristotle's purely intellectual and theoretical activities into Christian ideas of religious contemplation and personal union with God. This is, of course, a considerable transformation. But from Aquinas's point of view there is a point of insertion.

When Aquinas is thinking as a philosopher who draws inspiration from Aristotle and who is concerned with the concept of political society in general, his treatment of government is on broad lines. There are various possible types of government, and no one form is divinely appointed for all men. Aquinas prefers a 'mixed' constitution, a monarchy, that is to say, which is limited not only by conscience and

[1] This view can of course be made the basis for a claim that the Christian State should assist in repressing heresy.

respect for established custom and existing laws, but also by elements of aristocracy (the rule of the best) and democracy.[1] The really important point, however, is that government should be conducted with a view to the common good. We probably ought not to press remarks to the effect that legislation pertains 'to the whole multitude or to the public person who has care of the whole multitude'[2] or that the prince 'has no legislative power except as representing the multitude'.[3] Some writers have seen in these remarks the assertion of a doctrine of popular sovereignty, namely that sovereignty is given by God to the whole community which can either exercise it itself, through legislating as a community, or delegate it to a person or group of persons. But in interpreting such remarks we obviously have to refer to the context. And it can be argued that in the case of the second remark Aquinas is talking about elected princes rather than enunciating an abstract theory about government in general. In any case Aquinas sees that it is preferable to try to prevent the monarch degenerating into a tyrant by incorporating into the constitution some aristocratic and popular checks on his activity than to be faced with a situation in which tyrannicide appears to be the only practicable solution.

The treatise *De regimine principum* or *De regno* (*On Kingship*) was addressed to Hugh III of Cyprus.[4] And some writers make a good deal of the fact that in his desire to deter Hugh from yielding to any temptation to rule tyrannically Aquinas appeals to the self-interest of the monarch. By seeking their own advantage rather than the common good tyrants alienate actual and potential friends; they involve themselves in the expense of self-protection; and they sacrifice an eternal reward for the sake of some transitory gains. Though, however, Aquinas certainly does write at length in this way, it is understandable, given the medieval monarch's opportunities, that he should try to persuade the prince that good and just rule is to his personal advantage. And in the same work he says explicitly that the government of a kingdom should be so arranged that the opportunity for the king to become a tyrant should be as far as possible removed. In spite, there-

---

[1] Monarchy, for Aquinas, represents the principle of unity, and it seems to him to be commended by analogies, such as divine rule of the universe. But he has, of course, the sense to see that whereas the divine will is by definition good or holy, the temporal ruler's will is not. Hence the need for checks.

[2] *Summa theologica*, first part of Part II, Qu. 90, Art. 3.

[3] Ibid., Qu. 97, Art. 3. Reply 3.

[4] It has been argued that Hugh II was the prince addressed.

fore, of all appeals to motives of prudent self-interest, which presuppose that the opportunity of becoming a tyrant is present, Aquinas clearly prefers that there should be constitutional limitations of the monarch's power.

3

Aquinas's idea of the two spheres of Church and State and of the balance of the two powers was shared substantially by the great poet Dante (1265–1321). There were indeed differences of outlook. Aquinas was primarily concerned with the medieval king, the feudal monarch, whereas Dante was much more concerned with the idea of the empire. But this difference is easily explicable in terms of the conditions of the poet's life. For he was a witness to the effects of the quarrels between papacy and empire; and he was involved in the factions between the papal and imperial parties. He therefore naturally tended to think in terms of Church and empire; and in his book *On Monarchy* (*De monarchia*) he defended the imperial cause. In his view temporal monarchy, in the sense of a universal empire, was necessary to the wellbeing of man. If peace and freedom are to be attained and preserved there must be a supreme temporal judge and ruler. Dante tended to idealize the empire and to disregard the fact that the medieval empire, which had never really been a universal monarchy, even within Christendom, was becoming less and less of an effective reality. Dante also tried to show that imperial authority was derived immediately from God, and that the emperor had no human superior.

At the same time, even if Dante's sympathies were with the emperor, whereas Aquinas's had been with the pope, the poet made no attempt to deny the spiritual jurisdiction of the papacy; and his philosophical principles were more or less those of Aquinas. He shared the latter's view of man and his destiny; he recognized the two powers and the two spheres of jurisdiction; and his idealization of the empire and his derivation of the emperor's authority directly from God were not designed to promote monarchic despotism or tyranny. The practical reason why he espoused the imperial cause was his belief that only through the empire as he conceived it could peace be attained. In his opinion realization of this peace was prevented by the papacy's insistence on temporal as well as spiritual jurisdiction and by its political policy. From the theoretical point of view he subscribed to the teaching of Pope Gelasius I that neither the spiritual nor the temporal power should attempt to usurp the function of the other. And this was, of course, also the view of Thomas Aquinas.

4

Popes such as Innocent III and Innocent IV had exalted the papal sovereignty and position in both theory and practice. As we have noticed, however, the extreme statement of the papal claims was that of Boniface VIII in his bull *Unam Sanctam* (1302). Boniface did not indeed deny the theory of the two powers; but he insisted that though the temporal sword should not actually be wielded by the Church, it was wielded by temporal monarchs, Christian monarchs that is to say, only in subordination to the Church. The spiritual power is judge of the temporal; but the spiritual power itself can be judged only by God.

At the end of the bull Boniface asserted that it was necessary for the salvation of 'every human creature' that it should be subject to the Roman pontiff. It may therefore seem that the pope is claiming that all monarchs, whether Christian or not, are subject to his jurisdiction. But it is obvious that he does not expect a Moslem sovereign, while remaining Moslem, to recognize papal jurisdiction, though he doubtless believes that if the Moslem ruler wishes to be saved he must be converted to Christianity, in which case he should recognize papal supremacy. So we can take it that Boniface is actually addressing himself to Christian rulers, whom indeed he probably considers to be the only temporal rulers possessing legitimate authority.

King Philip IV of France objected strongly to the content of the papal bull. And the pope explained that he had no intention of trying to usurp the king's power and jurisdiction. What he had said was common doctrine, namely that all the faithful, including Christian kings, were subject to the pope *ratione peccati* (*by reason of sin*). That is to say, if a temporal ruler pursued a sinful course, he could be judged by the pope; but if the pope acted in a similar way, God alone would be his judge, as the pope had no earthly superior. Though, however, it is perfectly true that Boniface had said this in his bull, he had also asserted that both swords, spiritual and material, belong to the Church, and that kings wield the material sword on the consent and sufferance of the priest (*ad nutum et patientiam sacerdotis*). The pope had in mind Christ's saying that all power has been given to him in heaven and on earth, and he concludes that this plenitude of power has been vested in the Vicar of Christ, though it would be unsuitable for him actually to wield the material sword as well as the spiritual. But the king of France was understandably incensed at being represented as a kind of delegate of the pope, exercising his power *ad nutum*.

Boniface had read and utilized the treatise *On Ecclesiastical Power* (*De potestate ecclesiastica*) by Giles of Rome (d. 1302). In this work[1] Giles argues that just as Christ possessed all power, spiritual and temporal, so does the Church, and especially the pope. Christ, however, did not make use of his temporal sovereignty; and the Church, following his example, leaves the management of temporal affairs in the hands of kings. Sovereignty (*dominium*) in the full sense of the word therefore remains with the Church, though the use of temporal power has been committed by the Church to secular monarchs. Further, just as all human beings are subject to Christ *de iure*, so are all men subject *de iure* to the Roman pontiff. Obviously they are not all subject *de facto*. Non-Christian monarchs, however, not having received their temporal jurisdiction from the Church, are more usurpers than legitimate monarchs.[2]

5

Giles of Rome's *On Ecclesiastical Power* was written in support of the claims of the papacy in its quarrel with the French king, though it obviously went beyond this particular issue. Needless to say, treatises were also written in support of the royal side of the quarrel. One of the more interesting is the work *On Royal and Papal Power* (*De potestate regia et papali*) by the Dominican John of Paris or John Quidort (d. 1306).

In this work John of Paris follows to a considerable extent the teaching of Aristotle and St Thomas Aquinas. The political community has its roots in human nature, created by God; and it existed long before Christ's institution of the Church. It is a natural institution, and it does not stand in need of the Church for a justification of its existence. Civil government, too, as essential for the maintenance and well-being of political society, is a natural institution. It owes neither its

---

[1] In his *De regimine principum* Giles of Rome wrote more under the influence of Aristotle and St Thomas Aquinas than he did in the work under consideration here.

[2] The realistic view of the kingdoms of this world as developing through conquest, violence and usurpation comes, of course, from St Augustine. For Giles of Rome it is only in Christendom that states can be, as it were, redeemed.

existence nor its justification to the Church. Though, therefore, the king, considered as a Christian man with a Christian's obligations, is subject to the spiritual authority of the pope, as a king he is independent. The State as such is not concerned with man's supernatural end, as revealed by Christ. It pursues natural goals. And in this sphere it is autonomous. Neither by abstract nor by historical argument can it be shown that the king of France is, as king, subject to the pope.

The interesting feature of John of Paris's work is the particular way in which he represents the nature of Church and State. It will be remembered that one of the ideas put forward by the papacy and the defenders of its claims was that the unity of Christendom requires one temporal head, the emperor, just as there is one spiritual head, the pope. This view was linked with papal claims to temporal jurisdiction by the thesis that though the Church does not actually wield the material sword, the emperor receives his jurisdiction from the pope. The question of whether or not the king of France was subject to the emperor as temporal head of Christendom was, of course, an academic or theoretical rather than a practical question. The immediate issue for John of Paris was the relation between the French monarch and the papacy. But the unity of Christendom theme gave him an opportunity of developing some ideas about the nature of Church and State.

As far as the Church is concerned, universality in principle belongs to its essence. Man has one final and supernatural end; and the Church, concerned with man's attainment of this end, has a universal mission. The revealed truth is the same for all and does not differ with differences between peoples. In the case of the State, however, the situation is not like this. The State is a natural, not a supernatural institution. And natural differences, geographical, climatic and ethnic, demand a variety of political societies, adapted to different circumstances. There is no valid argument from the spiritual unity of Christendom under one head to the need for a temporal unity under one emperor. To argue in this way is to confuse the supernatural and natural levels.

Further, precisely because the Church is a supernatural and supranational institution it must not be confused with the State. It is the channel by which divine grace is communicated; and its instruments are preaching and persuasion. It does not possess, or ought not to possess, any coercive power such as the State possesses. And it is only by confusing Church and State and by regarding the Church as a kind of super-State that one can argue, for instance, that the papacy has the right of levying taxation or of disposing of laymen's property. In its own natural sphere the State is autonomous; and the monarch, as monarch, is not a subject of the pope. The pope can indeed excommunicate, when there is good cause; but this is a spiritual penalty, and it should not be regarded as having civil effects.

Another interesting feature of the position of John of Paris is his view of the status of the king within the State. Ultimately all legitimate power is indeed derived from God the creator. But it by no means follows that because the royal power does not come from God through the pope it comes to him directly from God. On the contrary, the royal power comes through election by the people. For John of Paris, therefore, sovereignty, under God, rests with the people. True, once he has assumed office, the king has a right to the obedience of his subjects. But this is conditional on his trying to fulfil his mandate to create, maintain and promote the conditions for a good life in the natural order. If the king abuses his trust, the people has a right to depose him. John of Paris extends this idea even to the pope. The pope is elected; and an unworthy pope can be deposed by a general council or by the cardinals, representing 'the people', the community of Christians. John of Paris thus takes his place in the conciliar movement.

6

In the early Middle Ages it may indeed have been the case that people thought in terms of 'Christendom', without making any very clear distinction between the spheres of Church and State. The pope–emperor controversy can be regarded as representing a prolongation of the unitary concept of Christendom. But by the fourteenth century the concept had evidently become strained and in some obvious respects anachronistic in view, that is to say, of the development of national states. It is significant that Dante, an upholder of the idea of the empire and a supporter of the imperial cause, was a native of a divided country, one which knew no national unity such as could be found in England or Spain or France.

Nationalistic motives certainly played a part in resistance to papal claims to the possession of temporal sovereignty over states outside the territories directly governed by the Holy See. Such motives were obviously operative in France. On the level of theory, however, the spread of Aristotelianism was a factor which contributed powerfully to insistence on the autonomy of the State. We have indeed to avoid the temptation to exaggerate the effective influence of philosophy in the political arena. It is also possible, however, to underestimate it. With the gradual development of national states within Christendom resistance to the more extreme papal claims was doubtless inevitable. But Aristotelian political theory provided a theoretical foundation for such resistance, a line of thought for clarifying, expressing and justifying attitudes which were not themselves simply due to philosophical reflection. In other words, Aristotelianism provided upholders of the autonomy of the State with a theory in terms of which their practical attitudes could be expressed and defended, and which in turn influenced these attitudes.

Thomas Aquinas and Giles of Rome tried to combine Aristotelian political theory with recognition of the superiority of the Church to the State and with acknowledgment of papal jurisdiction over temporal rulers *ratione peccati* (by reason of sin or in matters where sin was involved). Given their theological convictions, this attempt at harmonization is perfectly understandable and reasonable. At the same time it is clear that Aristotelian political theory could be used in such a way as to exalt the State at the expense of the Church and to subordinate the latter to the former. This could hardly be done so long as Church and State were interpreted with the aid of the same categories and regarded as two 'perfect' societies in the same or strictly analogous senses. In this framework of thought emphasis on the unity of Christendom naturally led to the attempt to combine a recognition of the State's autonomy in its own sphere with recognition of the superiority and indeed supremacy of the Church, while emphasis on the status of the political community as a self-sufficing or perfect society led to insistence on its independence of the Church, though without any subordination of Church to State, inasmuch as the Church too was regarded as a self-sufficing or perfect society. Once, however, theorists ceased to think of the Church in terms which suggested a kind of super-State or supra-national State and to emphasize differences between the types of society exemplified in Church and State, the way lay open to some pretty revolutionary points of view.

With John of Paris we can see this process of differentiating between the types of society exemplified in Church and State making some headway. For in spite of his Aristotelian background John tends to represent the Church as a society of a peculiar kind rather than to fit it into Aristotelian categories and depict it as a kind of super-State. And the process is carried further by Marsilius of Padua, to whom we can now turn. Ockham's attack on papal absolutism may have contributed to heralding the abortive conciliar movement. But though he indulged in sharp polemics on behalf of his patron Ludwig of Bavaria and in defence of various causes, his political theory was not in itself particularly startling. For something more revolutionary we have to turn to Marsilius.

Marsilius (or Marsiglio) of Padua seems to have studied medicine at the University of Padua. Subsequently he was rector of the University of Paris (1312–13). He may then have returned to Italy for a couple of years; but in any case he had completed his famous work *Defensor pacis* (*The Defender of the Peace*) by 1324. The book was denounced to ecclesiastical authority; and when in 1326 it became known that Marsilius was the author, he fled from Paris with his friend John of Jandun and took refuge at the court of Ludwig of Bavaria. Pope John XXII described him as a heretic. Marsilius's ideas were congenial to Ludwig, but they aroused criticism from Ockham, who was also enjoying Ludwig's protection, in his *Dialogue*. Marsilius replied in his *Defensor minor*. He also wrote a tract to show that the emperor had the power to dissolve an existing marriage on his own authority and to dispense from the impediment of consanguinity.[1] The date of Marsilius's death is unknown; but as Pope Clement VI, writing in April 1343, refers to the 'heresiarch' as dead, it is probable that he died in 1342.

When we consider the political theory of Marsilius of Padua, it is doubtless advisable to bear in mind the historical conditions in his native land. The principalities and city-republics of northern Italy were racked by factions and wars, with all their accompanying evils. As Marsilius saw the situation, this condition of affairs was primarily due to papal policy and claims and to disturbances of the peace through the interference of ecclesiastical authorities in matters of state, wielding the arms of excommunication and interdict. Whether his interpretation was adequate or inadequate, it at any rate helps us to understand his vehement opposition to papal claims to jurisdiction in the temporal sphere. His enthusiasm for the autonomous State and his comparative disregard of the empire express a passionate devotion to the cause of the small city-republic of northern Italy. And his enmity towards the papacy is due in large part to his interpretation of the afflictions of his native land.

It will not do, however, to lay exclusive emphasis on this aspect of Marsilius's thought. For his theoretical treatment of the issues in-

[1] The occasion was a projected marriage of Ludwig's son.

volved possesses an importance which extends well beyond a mere interpretation of the contemporary scene. It is true that reference to the historical factors which influenced the direction of his thought helps to prevent over-modernization of his ideas. At the same time such reference can be overdone. The *Defensor pacis*, condemned in 1327 and again in 1378, was printed in 1517 and was apparently utilized by Cranmer and Hooker. It is not necessary to turn Marsilius into a modern political philosopher in order to see that his thought looks forward to later political theory and to the development of the post-medieval State. Marsilius himself naturally focused his attention on contemporary issues as he saw them; but his general attitude has a wider significance.

Marsilius follows Aristotle in his general view of the State as a self-sufficing community which originally came into being for the sake of life but which has as its end the promotion of the good life. He then goes on to show the direction of his thought by including the priesthood as a 'part' of the State.[1] In the course of his book it becomes clear enough that he is not content simply with rejecting ecclesiastical interference in temporal affairs but that he is intent on subordinating the Church to the State. His position can thus be described as frankly 'Erastian', provided that this term is not understood as meaning that Marsilius was a Protestant before Protestantism. He begins the *Defensor pacis* by quoting Cassiodorus in praise of peace and goes on to remark that while Aristotle mentioned most of the causes of strife in human society, there is another cause which neither Aristotle nor any of his predecessors or contemporaries saw or could see. The reference is obviously to the Church's claims and activities which, in the opinion of Marsilius, disturb the peace. In other words, if Marsilius subordinates the priestly order to the State, he is doing so in what he believes to be the State's interest and the cause of peace rather than as a result of religious or theological convictions.

Marsilius thus finds the solution to his problem, that of the restoration and preservation of peace, in the Aristotelian idea of the autonomous State, interpreted as involving the subordination of the Church to the State. This may well strike us as a pretty naïve idea. For we are hardly likely to think of subordination of Church to State as in any way a guarantee of peace. In this respect Marsilius shows his preoccupation with certain particular issues. At the same time his development of the Aristotelian side of medieval political theory in such a way

[1] *Defensor pacis*, I, 5–6.

as to undermine or destroy the other side, the insistence on the independent spiritual power, has a wider significance and importance.[1]

In defence of his main aim Marsilius develops the philosophy of law in a direction which differs from that taken by the thought of, say, Thomas Aquinas. In the thought of Aquinas the various types of law are, as we have seen, closely linked together. For the positive law of the State is based on the natural moral law, while the natural law is an expression of the eternal law of God, who is the ultimate source of all law. Marsilius, however, tends to divorce human positive law, in the sense of the law of the State, from its relation to the natural law. He does not indeed deny that there is such a thing as natural law; but he distinguishes two types of it. In the first place the term 'natural law' may refer to those laws which are enacted in all nations and the obligatory character of which is practically taken for granted. In the second place 'there are certain people who call "natural law" the dictate of right reason in regard to human acts, and natural law in this sense they subsume under divine law'.[2] In these two descriptions of natural law the term 'natural law' is used equivocally. Why? The reason brings us to the heart of the matter. Marsilius defines law in the strict sense as a preceptive and coercive rule, fortified by sanctions applicable in this life. In this case, however, it is human positive law, in the sense of the law of the State, which is law in the strict sense. Natural law, in the second sense mentioned above, is not law in the strict sense. True, a dictate of right reason becomes law if it is embodied in the legal code of a State and if definite temporal sanctions are fixed for transgressions. But if natural law is considered simply as a moral law, the sanctions being applicable only in the next life, it is law in an equivocal sense.

It follows from this thesis that the law of Christ is not law in the strict sense. It is more akin, Marsilius remarks, to the prescriptions of a doctor. Nor is the law of the Church law in the strict sense. For, in itself, it is furnished only with spiritual sanctions. It may, of course, be furnished with temporal sanctions, fully applicable in this life. But if so, the fact is due to the permission and will of the State. And the law in question becomes State law.

Marsilius does sometimes say, in a rather conventional manner, that in the event of a clash between divine and human law, it is the former

---

[1] There does not seem to be any very good reason for speaking of Marsilius's use of Aristotle as specifically 'Averroist'.

[2] *Defensor pacis*, II, 12.

which should be obeyed. But it is also pretty clear that in his view it is within the competence of the State to judge whether a given law or projected law is consonant with the divine law or not. Those writers who wish to make out that Marsilius is not nearly so revolutionary as he is sometimes said to have been can appeal, of course, to the fact that he does not actually reject the Thomist concept of natural law but simply points out that it does not exemplify a certain definition of law. They can also appeal to the fact that Marsilius allows that the Christian ought to obey God rather than man. But if there is no such thing as sacerdotal jurisdiction in the proper sense of the term, and if it is the State which judges whether a projected law or an existing law is compatible with morality, conventionally pious assertions about obeying divine rather than human law do not amount to more than recognition of the fact that a Christian may feel bound in conscience to disregard the orders of the State and, if necessary, to suffer for his disobedience.

The fact of the matter is that for Marsilius the preservation of unity and peace within the State requires rejection of the theory that the Church is a 'perfect' society, superior to the State and possessing jurisdiction in a sense which might involve a clash between Church and State. Marsilius is perfectly ready to admit that the clergy can perform a useful function within the political community through their spiritual and moral teaching. He does not seek the abolition of the Church in the sense of doing away with the clergy and the administration of the sacraments. What he insists on is that if canon law has any coercive force (in terms of temporal sanctions), it possesses this force only by permission of the State, and that in this case it becomes State law. Marsilius gives the example of heresy. If it wishes, the State can make heresy a crime with a view to the temporal welfare of the political community, to secure, for example, a greater degree of solidarity. But the Church has no right to inflict any other than purely spiritual penalties. Nor is it entitled to give orders to the State in regard to coercive action against heretics. Marsilius does indeed appeal to the Scriptures to disprove papal claims and the concept of the Church as a self-sufficing society distinct from and even against the State. But what he is really interested in is not theological discussion but rather the complete autonomy of the State, an autonomy which can be effectively realized only by rejecting the concept of the Church as an independent and law-making supranational society and by reducing it, to all intents and purposes, to the status of a department of the State. Marsilius certainly makes use of theological arguments. But he writes from the point of view of a political philosopher and a defender of the autonomy of the State, not from that of a theologian who is primarily interested in exhibiting Gospel truth. His references to the behaviour of Christ and the apostles are arguments *ad hominem* rather than manifestations of a profound interest in theology.

Laws in the strict sense, therefore, can be enacted only by the temporal legislator. But who is the temporal legislator? According to Marsilius, the primary efficient cause of law is the people, or at least the more weighty part (*pars valentior*) of the people.[1] This more weighty part need not be a numerical majority; but it must be legitimately representative of the people. It is indeed difficult for the whole body of citizens to draw up laws. But a committee or commission can formulate projected laws and propose them to the legislator for acceptance or rejection. As for the prince, his office is to apply and enforce the laws. The executive power is thus subordinated by Marsilius to the legislature. And in his opinion this subordination is best expressed in practice if each prince or government is elected. This is not a necessity; but election is, in itself, preferable to hereditary succession.

In these views we can see the expression of Marsilius's attachment to the small city-republic of his native land, an attachment which reflects that of Aristotle for the Greek *polis* and which puts us in mind of some of Rousseau's ideas in the future. Apart, however, from this point, the interesting feature of Marsilius's thought is his distinction between the legislative and executive powers. The claim that he envisaged a clear separation of powers in the State stands in need of qualification. For he subordinated the judiciary power to the executive. However, he certainly advocated the subordination of the executive power to the legislative body.

Though Marsilius recognizes in a sense the sovereignty of the people, he makes no explicit statement of a social contract theory.[2] His subordination of the executive to the legislature was dictated by practical considerations rather than by any philosophical theory of a social contract. He was concerned above all with peace; and he saw that despotism and tyranny were not conducive to peace within the State.

---

[1] *Defensor pacis*, I, 12, 3.
[2] The theory that political society originated in a compact of some sort between the members had been implied by John of Paris. As for the theory of a pact between citizens and ruler, this, as has been seen, can be found as early as the eleventh century in Manegold of Lautenbach.

Attention has been drawn above to Marsilius's preoccupation with problems of contemporary Italy. At the same time it can hardly be denied that his political theory, when seen in the light of subsequent history, foreshadows the growth of the State of a later age. In the period of transition and formation between the fall of the Roman empire and the establishment of the western medieval civilization the Church had been the great unifying factor. In the early Middle Ages the idea of the empire, if not the reality, was strong. And in any case the concept of the two powers, whether conceived in terms of empire and Church or of kingdom and Church, won general acceptance. During the Middle Ages, however, strong states were growing up, as the effective power of monarchs such as the king of France gradually increased. True, the period of the great absolute monarchies lay still in the future. But the gradual emergence of national self-consciousness was a historical fact which corresponded, on the plane of theory, to that development of the Aristotelian element in medieval political philosophy which we find in the writings of a thinker such as Marsilius of Padua. Marsilius, of course, concentrated on attacking the papacy and ecclesiastical jurisdiction within the medieval context. And it was in this light that he was understood in the fourteenth century. But it is not unreasonable to see his thought as looking forward to the political theory of Hobbes and the historic growth of the modern State. For him it was only the State which was truly a 'perfect' society. The Church's task, as far as this world was concerned, was little more than that of serving the community by creating the moral and spiritual conditions which would facilitate the work of the State.

19

Nicholas of Cusa

I

IN histories of medieval thought we can often read about the break-down or disintegration of the medieval synthesis. This way of talking suggests the idea of an organic synthesis of different elements – philosophy and theology, Church and State – having first been successfully achieved and of its then being broken up by people who did not properly appreciate its value and principles. In this account of the matter William of Ockham and kindred thinkers are regarded as having contributed to the disintegration of the synthesis by driving a wedge between philosophy and theology through their criticism of previous metaphysics and by the emphasis which they placed on God's 'absolute' power, while John of Paris and, still more, Marsilius of Padua are regarded as contributing to the breakdown of the political-ecclesiastical unity of Christendom. In brief, such thinkers are given bad marks for having helped to wreck a great achievement.

This is indeed one possible way of looking at the matter. But there are other ways. One can see, for example, philosophy being reborn and growing up under the shadow and care of theology, reaching a more or less adult age and then tending to go its own way and assert its independence. As for Ockhamist criticism of previous metaphysical arguments, some would obviously claim that the criticism was fully justified from a logical point of view, and that if traditional metaphysics was undermined, this was because it had no firm foundations. As for the political-ecclesiastical unity of Christendom, it can obviously be argued that this unity was inherently precarious, that the historical development of the feudal states was bound to upset it on the political side at least and to produce a reaction to papal claims, and that thinkers such as Marsilius of Padua were not responsible for the historical tendencies at work, even if they expressed and to some extent intensified them. In other words, it can be maintained that the so-called breakdown or disintegration of the medieval synthesis was simply a phase in the general development of European culture and civilization, and that to deplore it is to express a nostalgia for a state of affairs which could not last.

However this may be, it is easy to understand the powerful attraction which can be exercised by the ideal of unity, of a harmonious accord between faith and reason, between theology and philosophy and science, and between Church and State. Needless to say, if a man thinks that theology is nonsense or that there is no good reason whatsoever to believe that there is a God capable of revealing himself, and if he thinks that the Church is superfluous or even harmful to human interests, he will not feel this attraction. At any rate he will feel that the ideal of unity would be more appropriately realized through elimination of the supernatural interpretation of the world. In fact, he might see in the Middle Ages a radical dualism which needed to be overcome. If, however, we presuppose retention of religious faith and of a supernatural interpretation of the world, we can understand attempts to reassert the ideal of synthesis in a rather different setting and way. And we can find something of this kind in the thought of Nicholas of Cusa (1401–64).

The propriety of including a treatment of Nicholas of Cusa in a book on medieval philosophy is indeed open to question. The traditional element in his thought is certainly marked, and this fact provides some justification for pushing him back, as it were, into the Middle Ages, even though his dates overlap those of an early Renaissance figure such as Marsilius Ficinus (1433–99). It is possible, however, to emphasize the forward-looking elements in his thought and to associate him with the beginnings of 'modern' philosophy. Better still perhaps one can take note of the combination of elements in his thought and assign him to the Renaissance. None the less there seems to be some justification for giving a sketch of his philosophy in a book on medieval philosophy, precisely because of his character as a transition-thinker, a philosopher who has one foot, so to speak, in the medieval and the other in the post-medieval world. After all, it is useful to remind oneself of the element of continuity in the history of philosophy, and of the fact that there was no sudden and abrupt transition from medieval to modern philosophy.

Given the spread of the terminist logic in the fourteenth century and the beginnings of empirical science in the thirteenth and fourteenth centuries, one might perhaps have expected that in the field of philosophy logical studies would have become more and more prominent and that the scientific work of such men as Nicholas Oresme would have borne immediate fruit in a more widely diffused scientific movement. But this is not what actually happened. The philosophy of the fourteenth century was succeeded by the philosophies of Nature of the Renaissance; and logical studies did not flourish again in any remarkable manner until the nineteenth century. Further, the literary or humanistic Renaissance preceded the scientific development associated with such names as Galileo.

In some respects the philosophical speculation of Nicholas of Cusa belongs to the thought of the Renaissance. And there are links between Nicholas in the fifteenth century and Giordano Bruno in the following century. In other respects, however, especially in its unambiguously Christian and theocratic character, Nicholas's thought appears as a prolongation of medieval thought, not indeed of the Ockhamist movement but of the Neoplatonist tradition.[1] So once again he can be represented as a transition-thinker, combining medieval lines of thought with ideas which were to become prominent at a later date.

2

Nicholas Kryfts or Krebs was born at Kues (Cusa) on the Moselle and was educated as a boy by the Brethren of the Common Life at Deventer. After studying at the universities of Heidelberg, Padua and Cologne he took the doctorate in canon law in 1423. His interest in reform[2] led him to support the conciliar party and he took part in the council of Basel as a moderate adherent of the conciliar point of view. Disappointment at the council's failure to carry out any real reform of the Church led him later to change his position. He became a supporter of the papacy and fulfilled various missions on behalf of the Holy See. For example, he was sent to Byzantium in connection with the reunion

[1] The influence of Neoplatonism also links Nicholas with the Renaissance.
[2] A private interest or hobby was the collection of manuscripts. He discovered, for example, a number of lost comedies of Plautus. In this respect Nicholas was very much a Renaissance figure.

of the eastern Church with Rome, which was accomplished, though only temporarily, at the Council of Florence in 1439. In 1448 he was created a cardinal, and in 1450 he was appointed bishop of Brixen. He died at Todi in Umbria in 1464.

Nicholas wrote on a variety of topics. His first important work was the *De concordantia catholica* (*On Catholic Unity*, 1433-4), which represented his earlier ideas on Church reform. His philosophical writings include the well known *De docta ignorantia* (*On Learned Ignorance*, 1440), *De Deo Abscondito* (*On the Hidden God*, 1444), *Idiotae Libri* (*The Books of the Idiot*, 1450) and *De venatione sapientiae* (*On the Pursuit of Wisdom*, 1463). Among his writings on mathematical subjects are *De transmutationibus geometricis* (*On Geometrical Transformations*, 1450) and *De mathematica perfectione* (*On Mathematical Perfection*, 1458).

3

Like Leibniz (1646-1714), Nicholas of Cusa was inspired by the idea of synthesis, of the reconciliation of differences and oppositions. At the time when he assisted at the council of Basel he saw the unity of Christendom threatened; and he was determined to do what he could to preserve it. Unity, however, did not mean for him the elimination or crushing of all differences. Nor did he aim at the attainment of unity by means of absolutism or despotism, whether in State or Church. In Nicholas's view the monarch did not receive his authority directly from God but rather from or through the people. And while he supported the old idea of the empire, he thought of it in terms of a federation rather than in terms of an emperor overriding the rights of national monarch or princes. In regard to the Church, Nicholas believed that a general council, representing the whole body of the faithful, was superior to the pope and could, if necessary, depose him.[1] He believed also that the work of reform, which was essential for the preservation of unity within the Church, could best be carried out through a general council. If he later changed his attitude, this was because he had come to see in the papacy the expression of the essential unity of the Church and, on the practical level, because he had become convinced that the task of reform was more likely to be fulfilled by the

[1] Nicholas was impressed by the role played by the council of Constance (1414-18) in putting an end to the Great Schism which had divided Christendom and caused so much scandal.

central authority than by a general council, the deliberations of which might tend to promote anarchy rather than unity.

The central idea of Nicholas of Cusa's speculative philosophy is that of the synthesis or identity of opposites (*coincidentia oppositorum*). In finite beings we find distinctions and oppositions. For example, in all finite beings essence and existence are distinct, whereas in infinite being, God, they coincide. This is, of course, a familiar Thomist idea. But for Nicholas it is a general principle that the oppositions and distinctions of creatures coincide in God. This theory may remind one of Schelling's 'philosophy of identity', that is, of the phase in which Schelling looked on the Absolute as the vanishing point of all differences. While, however, there are resemblances between the thought of the fifteenth-century cardinal and the philosophy of the nineteenth-century German idealist, Nicholas's thought is definitely theistic in character.[1]

By asserting the identity of opposites in God Nicholas does not intend to imply that by juggling with terms and simply stating the identity of opposed or distinct predicates we can achieve an adequate positive understanding of God. His thesis is more or less this. We come to know a finite thing by relating it to what is already known; we compare it with the already known, noting similarities and dissimilarities. Finite things differ, and must differ, from one another in various ways. And through experience of these differences we come to have distinct concepts. No one of these concepts can express adequately the nature of the infinite. As all finite things mirror the infinite, their distinct attributes must be found identified in the infinite. At the same time, as all our concepts are derived from experience of creatures and reflect this experience, no one concept is applicable to God in a univocal sense. What, therefore, the identity of opposites in the infinite actually is cannot be positively apprehended by the discursive reason, which can only approach this apprehension as the ideal term of a process, a term which is never reached.

Nicholas thus asserts the primacy of the 'negative way'. But if we wish to describe this as agnosticism, we have to add that it is not an agnosticism which results from refusal to make an intellectual effort but rather one which results from increasing understanding of God's infinity and transcendence. 'Ignorance' it may be; but it is, in Nicholas's phrase, 'learned' or 'instructed ignorance'. It is only by the sustained

[1] Schelling went on later to expound a speculative theism. But the 'philosophy of identity' has seemed to most readers to involve a pantheistic point of view.

effort to understand God that we come to realize that God transcends our understanding. The infinite is not an object which is proportionate to the discursive reason. The discursive reason feeds on the similarities and dissimilarities found in creatures; and it is governed by the principle of the incompatibility or mutual exclusion of opposites. It is therefore not the discursive reason (*ratio*) which grasps the truth of 'coincidence of opposites' but intellect (*intellectus*).

To a certain extent what Nicholas of Cusa says is reasserted by Hegel in the nineteenth century. According to Hegel traditional formal logic, resting on the principle of non-contradiction, freezes concepts, as it were, in sharp opposition to one another. If X, then not Y. If Y, then not X. The understanding (*Verstand*), operating with traditional logic, cannot grasp the inner life of the Absolute. Though, however, Nicholas certainly believes that reason (in the sense of understanding or *Verstand*) cannot grasp the divine Absolute, he is not prepared to maintain, as Hegel later maintained, that by means of *intellectus* (or *Vernunft*), operating with dialectical logic, the human mind can penetrate the essence of God. For Nicholas the intellect can grasp the fact that God is the *coincidentia oppositorum*, but it cannot penetrate the divine identity of opposites and lay it bare to view.

Nicholas does indeed try to make use of language to suggest at any rate what he is getting at. For example, God is rightly described as the supreme and absolutely greatest being. He could not be greater than he is. But we can also say that God could not be smaller than he is. If he is the *maximum*, he is also the *minimum*. He is both in a perfect 'coincidence of opposites'.[1] But we can also say that God is neither, neither great nor small that is to say. He is neither and both. It depends on what you mean. But though conceptual analysis can help us to understand that God both transcends and confines in himself all distinctions and oppositions, it cannot give us a vision of the divine identity in itself. Nicholas likes using mathematical analogies. For instance, if one goes on adding sides to a polygon in a circle, the polygon may approximate more and more to coinciding with the circle: but it will never achieve this coincidence, however many sides we may add. Similarly, the human reason can approach the infinite in many ways and approximate to a positive understanding; but it will never actually achieve it. Again, if the diameter of a circle is extended to infinity, the circumference will coincide in the end with the diameter. We can then say that the infinite straight line is both a triangle and a circle. But the

[1] Cf. *De docta ignorantia*, I, 5 f.

mathematical analogy is simply a symbol which is an aid to the mind but not an explanation of the divine reality. The mathematical infinite can symbolize the divine infinity; but it is not the same thing.[1]

As we have noted in the course of this book, one of the stock objections against exclusive use of the negative approach to knowledge of God is that we cannot significantly deny anything of God unless we have some positive knowledge of him. We must at least have a positive idea of what we are denying something or other. Nicholas seems to have come to much the same conclusion. At any rate he remarks in his last work (*De apice theoriae*, 1464) that he had once thought that the truth about God is found in darkness and obscurity more than in light or clarity, a remark which implies that he sees the need of counterbalancing his negative theology in some way. He adds that even a boy can understand what it means to be able to do something – to run, for example, or to eat. God is absolute power or *posse*, in the sense that he is eternally what he can be.

In point of fact Nicholas had said this before. In the *De possest* (1460) and again in the *De venatione sapientiae* (1463) he had stated in his own way the traditional doctrine that God is infinite act, that there is in him no gap between what he can be (*posse esse*) and what he is. Further, Nicholas continues to insist that the divine power to be at once all that he can be is incomprehensible to the finite mind, and that there is no common measure which can be applied both to creaturely power or potentiality and to the infinite divine power. So even if Nicholas does take note of the difficulty in maintaining a purely negative theology, it is going much too far to suggest that he changed his mind in his last years and abandoned the 'negative way'. He calls attention indeed to the actuality of God, identical with his power; but he continues to insist on the divine transcendence.

Though for Nicholas God in himself is incomprehensible, he shows himself in the world, which is a theophany, a sensible appearance of God. In Nicholas's language, the world is the 'contraction' of God. It is a 'contracted infinite' and a 'contracted unity'.[2] That is to say, in creation, which is the 'unfolding of God' (*explicatio Dei*), infinity is 'contracted' into finitude, absolute unity into plurality, eternity into time (the moving image of eternity, as Plato said). In his *Compendium* he depicts the incomprehensible infinite as manifesting or showing

---

[1] *De venatione sapientiae*, 14.
[2] *De docta ignorantia*, II, 4.

itself in a variety of signs, as one face can appear in several mirrors, the face in itself remaining the same while the appearance or reflections are distinct. Each reflection is a 'contraction'. And every creature is, 'as it were a created God'.[1]

It is obvious that Nicholas's thought is heavily impregnated with Neoplatonism; and it recalls in some important respects the philosophy of John Scotus Erigena. But he develops his world-vision in a fresh way. Though the world consists of finite beings, there is a sense in which it can be called infinite. In regard to time, the world's duration is potentially endless. It does not exist, so to speak, all at once; but there are no intrinsic limits to duration, which can be likened to an infinite line. In regard to space, the world can have no fixed limits. For there is nothing to limit. Nor does it make any sense to speak of 'up' or 'down' or 'the centre' in an absolute sense. We can, of course, fix a point or points, in reference to which we can use such terms. But then we are making relative judgements. It is a mistake to suppose, for example, that the earth is the stationary centre of the universe. All the heavenly bodies move, including the earth;[2] and the fact that we do not actually perceive the earth's movement is no good argument against its motion. If we were on Mars or the moon, we would be inclined to think the same of Mars or the moon, namely that it was stationary. For us, of course, the earth has a privileged position; but in itself it has no such position. Nor has the sun. There are no fixed points in the created infinite, independently, that is to say, of a human decision to select certain points for definite purposes of reference.

Nicholas's idea of the infinite system of Nature as the 'explication' of God was developed by Giordano Bruno and kindred thinkers, though Bruno, and after him Spinoza, developed it in a manner which was alien to Nicholas's fundamentally orthodox Christian standpoint. His idea of the self-unfolding system of Nature as a progressive manifestation of God links him also with Leibniz. So too does the emphasis which he lays on individual things as particular 'contractions' of the infinite. Each individual thing mirrors the whole universe. The universe thus exists in a 'contracted' manner in every individual thing. And as the world is itself the mirror of God, each individual thing must be a reflection of God in its own way. From this point of view it

[1] (quasi Deus creatus), Ibid., II, 2.
[2] Nicholas does not appear to assert explicitly that the earth rotates round the sun. But he certainly maintains that the sun, moon, earth and all other such bodies are in motion, though their velocities differ.

follows that no individual things are exactly alike. There are indeed levels of being, and there are specific similarities; but no two things are in every respect alike. At the same time all things are interrelated in the one universe. These two ideas of the unique character of each individual thing and of the relation of each thing to every other member of the universe, so that each member mirrors the whole, are found again in the philosophy of Leibniz.

Though every single individual thing can be said to mirror the universe, this is particularly true of man, who combines in himself matter, organic life, sensitive animal life and spiritual intelligence. Man is thus the microcosm, the universe in miniature.[1] He also reflects in an imperfect way the divine identity of opposites. For example, spirit and matter are united in man. The supreme expression of the *coincidentia oppositorum* is, however, Christ, God and Man, who unites in himself the infinite and the finite, the uncreated and the created, the divine and the human. Christ is also the *medium absolutum*. the absolute means or mediator, in the sense that he is the unique and necessary means of man's union with God.

4

After the logical studies and rather critical philosophy of the fourteenth century it may seem odd to find in the fifteenth century a world-vision so obviously inspired by the Neoplatonist tradition as that of Nicholas of Cusa. It is indeed a Neoplatonism recast or rethought in a Christian mould or framework. But the combination of Neoplatonism and Christianity may incline one to regard Nicholas's thought not only as essentially medieval but also as a throwback to the pre-Ockhamist era. This would be a mistake. We can of course regard Nicholas's philosophy as a prolongation of medieval thought. The Neoplatonist tradition did not simply disappear with the spread of Aristotelianism in the thirteenth century. Nor was it totally eclipsed by the terminist or nominalist movement in the fourteenth century.[2] And Nicholas of Cusa was evidently convinced that what he wanted to

[1] Nicholas finds a further expression of man's status as the microcosm in the fact that both the world and man are ensouled (cf. *De ludo globi*, I), He is well aware that the idea of a soul of the world comes from Plato; but he seems to use the phrase as signifying the immanent divine activity in the world, and not a distinct intermediary being.

[2] In point of fact Platonism received a new lease of life with the Italian Renaissance.

say could best be said in terms of Neoplatonist ways of thought. At the same time his insistence on 'infinite' Nature as the manifestation of the infinite which transcends our understanding, his sense of the divine in Nature, his rejection of geocentricism and his openness to fresh ideas link his thought clearly enough with the philosophies of Nature of the Renaissance, especially with that of Giordano Bruno. True, Nicholas's thought was theistic whereas Bruno has at any rate generally been thought of as a pantheist.[1] But some of Nicholas's leading ideas reappear with Bruno; and the distinction between *Natura naturans* and *Natura naturata*, to be found later in Spinoza, expresses Nicholas's concept of the relation between the absolute infinite and the 'contracted' infinite.

Attention has already been drawn to features of Nicholas's thought which link it with that of Leibniz. Nicholas's ideals of harmony and unity, as shown not only in his theoretical work but also, for example, in his work for unity within the Church and for the reunion of eastern and western Christendom, were strongly influential on the mind of Leibniz. Again, Nicholas's ideas of each individual thing as mirroring the whole universe and of no two things as being altogether alike, reappear in the monadology of Leibniz. To look further afield, we can find some links, if we look for them, between the philosophy of Nicholas of Cusa and German metaphysical idealism in the first half of the nineteenth century.

Nicholas of Cusa tried, of course, to contribute to the preservation of medieval ideals of the unity of Christendom. In this respect he belongs to the Middle Ages. To say this is not to depreciate the ideals in question. When, however, we look back with our knowledge of the divisions which were to come between Christians and of the growth of political divisions and of nationalism in later years, we naturally tend to think of Nicholas as trying to swim against the incoming tide and to preserve the past, even if we do justice to his adaptation of the old ideals to new circumstances and to his realization of the fact that without internal reform in the Church unity could hardly be preserved. As we have indicated, however, Nicholas's insistence on the concept of Nature as the created infinite, and his idea of the world as an intelligible and harmonious system, the self-unfolding of God on

---

[1] Bruno did not in fact deny the divine transcendence; but there was, of course, a notable tendency towards monism in his thought. However, neat classifications of thinkers as theists or pantheists are difficult, for reasons which become clear to anyone who gives any serious thought to the matter.

the plane of created existence, link his thought with the philosophies of the Renaissance. And it was these philosophies, rather than terminist logic, which actually formed the mental background of the age in which the great scientists of the Renaissance lived and worked.

20

Epilogue

I

By definition the past no longer exists.[1] Every account of it is a reconstruction. There are doubtless historical propositions about the truth of which everyone is agreed and which, though from the philosopher's point of view they may be interpretations, can be said, for all practical purposes, to express bare facts. That is to say, in the field of historiography we can make a distinction between the facts which are presupposed in common by the different interpretations of a course of events given by different historians and the interpretations.[2] That Julius Caesar crossed the Rubicon in a certain year may be an interpretation from the point of view of the philosopher who questions the concept of 'bare facts';[3] but it is obviously taken as a basic fact by historians who concern themselves with the historical significance of Caesar's action. Agreement about the fact does not entail agreement about its historical significance. It is only the naïve or people who have never thought about the matter who assume that the general interpretation of, say, the history of a given period which they read in a certain

[1] It may be said that the past is subsumed in the present or that the present presupposes the past and, being partly at any rate its result, comprises it within itself. In this case, however, the past as existing would be the present.

[2] Ordinary language and common sense thought obviously allow for a distinction between fact and interpretation. Philosophers are quite justified in examining the assumptions of ordinary language and raising questions about them. But this need not affect the utility of the distinctions which we make.

[3] Some philosophers might wish to refer to the interpretation of 'sense-data'. The problem of whose sense-data are being interpreted can be left to their ingenuity to solve.

textbook at school must be on the same level as the facts about which all historians of the period agree.

The same sort of rather banal remarks can be made about the history of medieval philosophy. That St Thomas Aquinas died in 1274, that he wrote, for instance, the *De ente et essentia*, and that he asserted a distinction between essence and existence are statements of which we can say with a high degree of confidence that they are true or false.[1] But if it is a question of a general estimate of the significance of Aquinas's achievements, the situation is rather different. This is still more the case if a general picture of medieval philosophy is attempted. Provided, however, that one does not foolishly claim to be giving the only possible general picture, a general summary may be useful for the reader, even if it inevitably involves some repetition of what has been said already.

2

Within Christianity 'philosophy' was originally and basically an attempt to articulate and express a Christian vision of the world and of man. It was Christian wisdom, regarded as subsuming in itself, transcending and succeeding the wisdom of the Platonists, the Stoics and other philosophers of the pagan world. It was not, of course, looked on as something given once and for all in a completed state. The Christian revelation, received in faith, had to be appreciated and understood, and its implications worked out. In the process categories of thought taken from non-Christian philosophy could be and were employed. And themes were discussed which could be described as philosophical even in terms of a later use of the word 'philosophy'. But for the Christians of the ancient world philosophy was really the saving wisdom, developed in the process of faith understanding its content and implications.

As we have seen, some logical treatises were preserved in the period following the fall of the Roman empire and were studied among the liberal arts, giving rise to some philosophical problems, notably that of universals. Though, however, some of the dialecticians were men of high intellectual calibre, and though the development of theology itself led to the discussion of some philosophical problems, by and large

---

[1] That Aquinas asserted some sort of distinction between essence and existence is clear enough. The precise nature of the distinction and the proper way of stating it are further questions.

the growth of philosophy as a distinct group of disciplines or branches of study ranging over a wide area had to await the translation of works from Greek and Arabic into Latin. With the new vistas opened up by these translations a clearer recognition of philosophy (in a wider sense than logical studies) as a distinct and autonomous discipline became pretty well inevitable. Greek philosophy had obviously preceded Christianity and developed independently. In the forms given it by the Islamic philosophers it had coexisted with another religion. With the exception of some branches of study, such as medicine and law,[1] 'philosophy' came to mean, to all intents and purposes, secular knowledge as distinct from theology based on revealed premises.

The influx of ideas from outside Christendom created a problem. To some it seemed that a naturalistic world-outlook, represented chiefly by Aristotle, was clashing with the supernatural world-vision of Christianity, and that its spread should be checked. The attitude of theologians such as St Albert the Great and St Thomas Aquinas was, of course, different. They did not believe that everything said by a Greek or Islamic philosopher was true. In view of the variety of things which had been said this could not in any case be a reasonable belief. But they were convinced that the literature which had been made available contained a great deal of truth which, as true, must necessarily be compatible with Christian revelation. As for the philosophy of Aristotle, Aquinas in particular believed that it was, by and large, true in itself and that, though it could be presented as a naturalistic world-view, it could also be used as a powerful instrument in the development of an overall Christian vision of reality. He was fully aware, of course, that the thought of Greek and Islamic philosophers was not a deduction from specifically Christian premises, and that philosophy had to be recognized as a distinct and autonomous discipline. But in so far as he aimed at synthesizing without confusing Aristotelian philosophy with Christian theology, he can be said to have prolonged or continued to some extent the attitude of St Augustine. That is to say, while he made a clear distinction between theology or 'sacred doctrine' on the one hand and philosophy on the other, a distinction which Augustine did not and indeed could not make,[2] Aquinas clearly thought in terms of an overall Christian vision of reality, enriched by the thought of men who had worked without the Christian faith.

[1] We can add literature, of course, which belonged to the liberal arts.
[2] 'Could not' because the word 'philosophy' was understood by Augustine in a sense which prevented any clear distinction between philosophy and theology.

Indeed, the development of philosophy in the thirteenth century was the work of theologians rather than of the professors of the Faculty of Arts who, according to their own account at any rate, were more concerned with history of philosophy.

Philosophy, however, cannot be kept at heel like a well-trained dog, unless indeed at the cost of depriving it of life and vigour. In spite of the heroic efforts of enlightened theologians such as Albert the Great and Thomas Aquinas to show the basic compatibility of Aristotelianism and Christianity, it is pretty clear that within the Faculty of Arts philosophy was sometimes being pursued without much regard for theological orthodoxy. If we fix our attention on the open-minded attitude of Aquinas, we naturally think of the condemnations of 1277 as an expression of ultra-conservatism and obscurantism. In spite, however, of the precipitate haste shown by Stephen Tempier and his associates, in spite of the prejudices of a man such as Kilwardby and in spite of misunderstanding of particular issues,[1] the promoters and applauders of the condemnations presumably had a real fear that autonomous philosophy, paying little but lip service to Christian theology, was invading the Faculty of Arts and spreading among teachers and students, and a sincere belief that there was a real risk of the growth of a naturalistic outlook. The conservative authorities were clearly not much impressed by protestations that offending or suspected teachers were simply expounding Aristotle or Averroes and not giving their own opinions. Obviously the condemnations must have been the expression of a mixture of attitudes and motives, as indeed the ragbag of condemned propositions suggests. There are always people to whom anything which sounds novel smacks of heresy. And there were doubtless those who felt that to substitute new-fangled Aristotelian theories for the ideas of past and venerated Christian worthies was a scandalous proceeding. But some at any rate seem to have felt that pagan philosophy was getting the upper hand and threatening faith.[2]

However this may be, the fourteenth century did not in fact see the

---

[1] This is particularly true in regard to the propositions which had been held by Aquinas and which came in for censure at Paris or Oxford.

[2] Even if Stephen Tempier and Company were no great intellects, they were presumably in a better position than we are to know what was being said in holes and corners, as Aquinas put it. True, reports of what teachers have said are by no means always reliable. At the same time it is difficult to suppose that there was no foundation at all for the fears of the pope and the Paris theologians.

spread of a world-view which was a rival to or incompatible with a Christian interpretation of reality. What it saw was rather an attempt to dehellenize Christian thought, in the sense of eliminating elements of necessitarianism derived from Greco-Islamic philosophy. The general approaches and interests of Ockham in the earlier part of the century and of Gerson at the end of it showed very considerable differences; but both men were intent on overcoming what they considered to be the infiltration of philosophical necessitarianism into Christian thought. Each man was concerned with bringing Christian theology and the Christian world-vision closer to what he believed they ought to be.

Needless to say, we cannot be sure what might have happened in a completely free arena. However much Ockham may have attacked the papacy on particular issues such as Franciscan poverty and on broader issues such as papal claims to authority over temporal rulers or absolutism in the Church, he was and remained a Christian theologian. We would hardly expect him, therefore, to propose a world-view at odds with Christian theology. It may be, however, that if it had not been for the watchful eye of ecclesiastical authorities and the activities of inquisitors, stormy petrels such as Nicholas of Autrecourt would have developed rival systems to the prevailing Christian interpretation of reality. We cannot tell. We only know that in point of fact the 'modern way' did not produce any notable world-view of this kind.

It may be said that while on the theological side the 'modern way' showed the influence of the movement of reaction which had led to the condemnations of 1277, on the philosophical side it so concentrated on logical studies and on critical and analytic thought that the question of its producing a philosophical world-view hardly arose. Ockham, for example, would not allow that the arguments advanced by some of his predecessors to prove that man possesses a spiritual and immortal soul amounted to logical demonstrations. But he had no intention of denying human immortality or asserting that the human soul perishes when the body dies. He simply said that immortality could not be proved by the philosopher. He was concerned with the logical status of arguments, not with calling Christian doctrines in question. It was common doctrine that the Trinity could not be proved in philosophy; but the doctrine was none the less accepted as a revealed truth. Ockham simply extended the number of propositions the truth of which could be known only by revelation.

This is true enough as far as it goes. Though, however, the terminist logicians were obviously not concerned with producing world-views, the effect of the *via moderna* was to simplify the existing ones. With Ockham, for example, the 'common nature' of Scotus's philosophy disappears. So do relations as extramental entities. We are left with an omnipotent transcendent God on the one hand and individual finite substances with their absolute accidents on the other. With the upholders of the impetus theory of motion the paraphernalia of movers of the spheres becomes superfluous, even if it is not formally and expressly rejected. And the way lies open for a view of the world as a mechanical system of bodies in motion.

There is a further point to remember. Divine omnipotence meant for Ockham (as indeed it had for Scotus) that whatever God can do or does through secondary causes he can do without them. He could, if he so chose, maintain an elephant in life even though the whole of the rest of the universe had been annihilated. He could create a human being and maintain him in life as a human being,[1] even though nothing else had been created. Ockham maintained, however, that it is only by faith that we know that this is so. It cannot be proved philosophically. In this case, we may be inclined to conclude, the pure philosopher will assume that the activity of secondary causes is necessary. In other words, a purely philosophical view of the world will include seeing things as linked by necessary causal relations. And such a view will be incompatible with the theological view of the matter. In point of fact, however, Ockham avoids this situation by rejecting, on purely logical and philosophical grounds, all necessary causal relations between distinct finite substances. Hence even if the philosopher not only cannot prove but is also ignorant of the divine omnipotence, his world (the world of the Ockhamist philosopher, that is to say) can fit in, without the need for adjustment, with the theologically based view of the world as subject to God's absolute power.

In other words, there is such a thing as an Ockhamist world-view. And its structure can exercise a powerful attraction on some minds. On the one hand we have a picture of the world as consisting of distinct substances, no one of which exists necessarily and between which there

---

[1] According to Ockham, God could, for example, cause immediately the effects normally produced by the atmosphere. He could himself cause directly those modifications of the sense organs which provide the basic data for the activity of imagination and mind. Obviously, Ockham does not think that God actually behaves in this way. But what is under discussion is what God *could* do, not what he does.

are no necessary connections. On the other hand, we have the complementary picture of these substances and the connections between them depending on the omnipotent divine will. That is to say, if we ask why things are and why things are as they are, the answer in both cases is that God so wills it. The first half of the world-picture, so to speak, stands on its own feet. That is to say, its correctness can be shown without reference to the divine will. All existential propositions relating to finite things and all propositions asserting causal connections between finite things are contingent. The second half of the world-picture, the view of the world as depending on the divine will, in regard not only to its *that* but also to its *how*,[1] is a matter of faith. Its truth cannot be philosophically proved, and it does not depend on philosophical reasoning. Hence belief in its validity cannot be undermined by criticism of arguments purporting to demonstrate its truth. Each half of the picture is in a real sense independently based. At the same time they fit admirably together. What could be more satisfactory? One can argue with the unbeliever about the correct philosophical view of the world; and one may be able to convince him of the truth of the kind of world-view which he would have if he believed in the omnipotent and free God. But one is not committed to maintaining that the existence of God can be proved by traditional metaphysical arguments.

This account of the matter is indeed somewhat of an exaggeration. As we have seen, Ockham admitted a proof of the existence of a first conserving cause of the world. He did not simply reject philosophical theology, even if he subjected some of his predecessor's arguments to trenchant criticism. At the same time it is clear that a wedge was being driven between the area of philosophically provable truths and the area of religious faith. To say this, however, is insufficient. If the divine omnipotence, as understood by Ockham and those who shared his views, cannot be proved by the philosopher, it follows of course that the philosophical half of the picture does not logically entail the theological half. But it seems that the converse is not true. For divine omnipotence means for Ockham that God can produce without a secondary cause any effect which, in the established or natural order of things (*de potentia Dei ordinata*), he produces through a secondary cause. This, however, would not be possible if the causal connections between finite things were logically necessary. It seems, therefore, that religious belief in an omnipotent God entails a certain view of the world,

---

[1] In regard, that is to say, both to the existence of things (*that* they are) and the arrangement, so to speak, of the world (*how* they are).

the sort of view proposed by Ockham and stated in modern times by Ludwig Wittgenstein in the *Tractatus*. In other words, the religious belief affects one's view of the world. It is not irrelevant to it. At the same time one is not committed to maintaining that the existence of a transcendent and omnipotent God can be philosophically proved.

It hardly needs saying that this sort of attitude has proved attractive in modern times to a number of theologians. They are well aware of the criticism to which metaphysical proofs of the existence of God have been subjected. And they understandably do not wish to make assent to statements of religious belief dependent on acceptance of traditional metaphysics. They are also aware of the way in which metaphysical philosophy can invade, as it were, the theological spheres and influence the representation of God and of the world's relation to him. In other words, they are aware of the problems which faced Ockham, the transformation, under the influence of philosophy, of the biblical God into the God of the philosophers. They are also acutely conscious, as Ockham, needless to say, was not, of the series of metaphysical systems and world-views which have appeared since the Middle Ages, which have differed from one another, and some of which at any rate have been incompatible with Christianity. It is understandable, therefore, if a number of theologians welcome any rejection of speculative metaphysics by the philosophers themselves and a limiting of the scope of serious philosophy to logical or conceptual analysis. Coexistence between Christian faith and freely ranging metaphysical speculation is difficult, especially when ecclesiastical authorities no longer have the power, and perhaps not the will, to keep the philosopher in check. But coexistence between Christian faith and a philosophizing which limits itself by its own decision and abstains from the construction of metaphysical systems and world-views seems to be made easier, especially if it is a question of a form of philosophy which leaves room for Christian faith.

This attitude is obviously understandable. And it is in no way surprising if modern fideism has a sympathy with the fideist tendencies of the fourteenth century. The question has to be faced, however, has faith any rational foundation or justification or has it not? Ockham himself provided some sort of rational justification, even if it was a pretty meagre one. But what about his modern successors? Is 'encounter', for example, the justification of faith? If so, how do we know that we have encountered what we believe that we have encountered? Or do we not know? Again, is it sufficient justification of the use of a language-game (in this case the religious one) to note that it is actually played by a number of people? If, for example, a considerable number of people used the language of necromancy, would there be nothing more to be said? Would all criticism from outside be impertinent, irrelevant and illegitimate?

If these questions are taken to imply that the path taken by the Ockhamists should be retraced and that there should be a return to traditional metaphysics, the question arises whether the criticism which has been levelled, whether in the fourteenth century or in subsequent centuries, against the arguments of philosophical theology can be successfully met. If it is a question of refurbishing old arguments, such as those of Aquinas, it has to be shown that the assumptions which they make are either unquestionable or defensible. Modern 'transcendental Thomism' has given some attention at any rate to this matter.[1] If it is a question of looking for new arguments, this activity suggests the idea of searching for apologetic arguments to defend a belief which one continues to hold meanwhile on other grounds. What grounds?

These rather obvious queries are not raised in order to discuss them and offer solutions. Rather is it a question of indicating, in regard to a specific area of philosophical thought, that medieval philosophy is not so entirely remote from contemporary problems as one might be inclined to think. There are obviously differences in historical context. In the case of Ockham, for example, we have one man who is both theologian and philosopher, a theologian of the divine omnipotence and freedom and, in some respects, an empiricist philosopher. Nowadays we are more likely to find the theologian on the one side and the philosopher on the other, even if an Ockham-like mixture is by no means unknown even today. But there is continuity in the dialogue, whether it is carried on within a single individual or between several distinct individuals. In fine, reflection on fourteenth-century developments in regard to the relation between philosophy and the area of religious belief can give us food for thought even today, though we are likely, of course, to conceive the area of religious belief in a broader way than a fourteenth-century theologian would have conceived it.

[1] I refer to the line of thought represented by, for example, J. Maréchal, A. Marc, J. B. Lotz, E. Coreth and B. Lonergan.

3

In his stimulating article on medieval philosophy in *The Encyclopedia of Philosophy* [1] Dr D. P. Henry draws attention to what he describes as a breakdown of communication in the philosophy of the Middle Ages. The medieval thinkers developed a semi-artificial language, neither purely natural nor wholly artificial. That is to say, they enriched (or, as John of Salisbury would claim, disfigured) ordinary language [2] with technical terms and used a number of ordinary words in technical senses. The semi-artificial language perhaps found its highest degree of development with Duns Scotus. With Ockham, however, a reaction set in. He tended to see in ordinary language a criterion of linguistic propriety; and he was given to understanding in terms of ordinary language statements and distinctions made by his predecessors and which had been intended in technical senses. He then proceeded to criticize the statements of his predecessors on the basis of this misunderstanding, or at any rate misinterpretation, with the result that the criticism was misplaced or beside the point. The definitional control provided by a wholly artificial language might have prevented this state of affairs. As it was, the ambiguities of the semi-artificial language facilitated a breakdown in communication or understanding.

One of the examples referred to by Dr Henry is Ockham's denial of a real distinction between essence and existence. If, says Ockham, there was such a distinction, essence and existence would be distinct entities. In this case they would be separable in principle. God therefore could create Tom's essence without his existence or his existence without his essence. But this is an absurd notion. Therefore essence and existence are not really distinct. Is not Ockham assuming, as it would doubtless be assumed in the area of ordinary language, that a real distinction, as contrasted with a purely mental distinction, [3] can be found only between distinct things? If so, he fails to appreciate the fact that the upholders of the theory of a real distinction between essence and existence did not understand the term 'real distinction' exclusively in this sense. For Aquinas, for example, there was of course a real distinction between

[1] Edited by Paul Edwards (N.Y., Macmillan and The Free Press; London, Collier-Macmillan, 1967), Vol. V. pp. 252–8.
[2] As far as the Christian medieval thinker was concerned, the 'ordinary language' was, of course, Latin.
[3] A mental distinction is one freely made by the mind, as one might distinguish parts in an undivided apple. One can designate the parts as one likes.

distinct things. But there could be a real distinction, in the sense that it was not a mental fiction but had an objective basis, between two ontological co-principles in any created thing, ontological component elements which could not be separated[1] but which the mind was forced to distinguished when it adverted to the substance's basic metaphysical structure. Ockham, it may be said, was attacking a man of straw. Either he had not done his homework and taken the trouble to find out what his predecessors really meant, or he was hypnotized by ordinary usage, according to which real distinctions exist only between distinct entities.

If we ask whether Ockham misunderstood his predecessors, we have first to ascertain whom he had in mind. If he imagined that Aquinas had regarded essence and existence as distinct *things*, he would certainly have been mistaken. For according to Aquinas essence and existence were basic ontological components in the metaphysical structure of any created thing: they were not themselves things. Giles of Rome, however, had spoken of essence and existence as distinct things (*res*) and thus played straight into the hands of William of Ockham. And not only into Ockham's hands. For Scotus, too, denied that there was any real distinction between essence and existence, understanding by 'real distinction' a distinction between different entities. Although Ockham had little use for Scotus's formal objective distinction, he was at one with him in rejecting the sort of view advanced by Giles of Rome. It must be added, however, that the polemics of Scotus and Ockham were directed not so much against Aquinas, nor even against Giles of Rome, as against Henry of Ghent who had complicated matters by distinguishing between the being of essence (*esse essentiae*) and the being of existence (*esse existentiae*). Thus when Ockham treats of essence and existence in the *Summa totius logicae*,[2] he refers to the term *esse existere*.

It must be admitted that the language used was in a real sense systematically misleading. It is true that the word used by Aquinas and others for existence was generally a verb (*esse*). And Thomists are able to draw attention to this point and maintain that for Aquinas 'existence' is an act, the created act of a created essence, the two being distinguishable but not separable. At the same time in the phrase 'essence and

---

[1] Obviously, when an animal dies, its existence (if one wishes to use noun-language) disappears; but its essence does not continue either. The component ontological elements or principles come into being together and perish together.
[2] III, 2, Chapter 27.

existence' *esse* functions as a verbal noun, and the two words tend to suggest two entities. That is to say, there is a temptation to regard 'essence' and 'existence' as names which stand for distinct entities. And anyone who, like Ockham, is intent on eliminating any superfluous multiplication of entities is likely to deny that there is any real distinction.

It may indeed be the case, as Dr Henry suggests in his article, that the temptation to think that distinct entities are being referred to could be diminished by the substitution of verb-like for abstract nouns.[1] But some philosophers would probably be inclined to maintain that all metaphysical talk should be changed into talk about propositions. Instead of saying that Aquinas asserted an objective distinction between essence and existence, we would do better to say that he drew attention to the difference between descriptive and existential propositions. This, however, would be an inadequate account of what Aquinas actually thought. For he clearly believed that he was making a distinction not simply between types of proposition but between ontological components in the metaphysical structure of things. At the same time it is open to anyone to claim that Aquinas's view of the matter was wrong, and that he was misled by language. This is the point of view which Ockham might well take. Indeed, he says explicitly that 'essence' and 'existence' signify the same thing, the one in the manner of a noun (*nominaliter*), the other in the manner of a verb (*verbaliter*). As the words do not have the same functions in speech, they cannot with propriety (*convenienter*) be used interchangeably. But it by no means follows that essence and existence are distinct entities.

In other words, Ockham thought that in a number of cases his predecessors had been misled by language, and that their metaphysics was to this extent the fruit of linguistic or logical confusion. To say this

[1] Dr Henry is here referring to Scotus's distinction between, say, the common nature (the humanity) of Tom and the individuating principle, the thisness of Tom. For Scotus there is a formal objective distinction, but not a 'real' distinction. Ockham takes this denial of a 'real' distinction as equivalent to an assertion of identity. According to Dr Henry, Ockham is treating 'humanity' and 'Tom-ness' as names of entities. And it clear that if Bill and James are not really distinct, they are identical. Scotus, however, is talking about 'formalities' which are, for him, 'formally' distinct but not really distinct as separable entities. Confusion could be avoided, Dr Henry suggests, by substituting verb-like nouns such as 'humanizing' and 'Socratizing' for abstract nouns such as 'humanity' and 'Socrateity'. Possibly; but I doubt whether Ockham would be reduced to silence by this linguistic change.

is not, of course, to contradict Dr Henry. For he explicitly refers to the way in which, when it was a question of propriety of expression, Ockham gave the preference to ordinary language rather than to technical speech. It is, however, possible to doubt whether such adjustments in technical speech as substituting verbal for abstract nouns would have satisfied Ockham. It might have satisfied him if he had failed to understand the theory which one of his predecessors had been trying to express. For, given suitable verbal adjustment, he might then have said 'now I see what you mean, and I agree with you'. But I strongly suspect that to satisfy Ockham linguistic change would have to be carried to the point at which a metaphysical theory was transformed into a logical theory or, if preferred, talk about talk. It is true that Ockham cannot be properly described as an anti-metaphysician. He was not. But his world was a simplified world. And what he could get rid of, he got rid of. And one of the ways of getting rid of ontological components, distinct formalities and what not was to interpret the distinctions in question as linguistic distinctions.

Obviously, it is open to the Thomist or the Scotist to retort that we make this or that verbal distinction because things are such that we are driven to make it. It may also be the case that Ockham did sometimes misunderstand or misrepresent his predecessors. At the same time he knew quite well what he was about. He was depopulating the universe, purging it of what he regarded as fictitious entities. He may have tried to eliminate what cannot in fact be eliminated. But he was not simply acting like a bull in a china shop, smashing valuable crockery because he was unable to appreciate its value. Rightly or wrongly, he had come to a considered conclusion, that his predecessors had filled the universe with fictions, and that logical analysis was required to depopulate it.

4

Certain aspects at any rate of the cosmological speculation of the Middle Ages are apt to appear strange and bizarre to modern minds. We can, of course, understand the reasons why philosophers postulated movers of the spheres, even if the hypothesis in question seems to us superfluous. We can even understand why certain philosophers, such as Avicenna, should have postulated a hierarchy of separate intelligences, the lower emanating or proceeding from the higher. But the fact remains that the whole concept of a hierarchy of separate intelligences and corresponding spheres seems to us remote and alien. And it is unlikely that we are prepared to take very seriously the notion of the lowest separate intelligence performing the function of the 'active intellect' in human minds. As for Averroes's monopsychism, this is apt to appear as fantastic to us as it did to Aquinas.

It may be said that ideas of this sort seemed as real to people in the Middle Ages as the mythology of Freud or dialectical materialism or racial myths have appeared to people in modern times. True enough. But this does not alter the fact that the medieval cosmology is not ours. And we are likely to sympathize with the tendency in the late Middle Ages to jettison some of the metaphysical paraphernalia of preceding generations. Discussion of the question whether impetus is a substance or an accident may seem to us to depend on a questionable assumption.[1] But at any rate the impetus theory made it unnecessary to postulate any movers of the spheres beyond the original conferrer of impetus.

Medieval philosophy did not, however, consist simply of hypotheses which seem superfluous to us, because we think that the questions which they were supposed to answer can be answered better in other ways. There were serious logical studies which reached their peak point in the fourteenth century. And there was a great deal of serious conceptual analysis. For example, the medievals may not have solved all problems in regard to language about God in such a way that there is nothing left to discuss. Indeed it is evident that this was not the case. But the discussion, as carried on by Aquinas for instance, was not by any means devoid of value and can still serve as a very useful introduction to and point of departure for reflection on this subject.

When we read medieval philosophical discussions, care has to be taken to avoid misleading impressions. Consider, for example, the question how God knows future contingent events. At first sight it may seem that ability to answer this question would demand a personal acquaintance with divine psychology which even the most devout believer would hesitate to claim. Indeed, we might suppose that the more genuinely devout a man was, the less inclined he would be to claim an insight into the inner life of God. But the medieval philosopher or theologian who asked such a question was not, of course, expecting to be given a phenomenology of God's mental activity. The first question to be answered was whether there was anything to be known. That is, can we predicate truth or falsity of contingent propositions relating to the future? This is a perfectly respectable logical question.

[1] The assumption, that is to say, that the noun 'impetus' must signify an entity of some kind.

If it is answered affirmatively, then an infinite and omniscient God must know whether such propositions are true or false. How does he know? This is not a request for novel information about the working of the divine mind. It is really a question about the proper way of speaking within the framework of certain concepts and premises. If, for example, a philosopher believes that God, as the infinite transcendent being cannot be dependent on things outside him for his knowledge, he will probably say that God knows future contingent events by knowing his own essence. If he does say this, he will obviously be faced with problems in regard to human freedom. But he is not claiming that his assertion is the result of a privileged access to God.

Again, we have seen that some conservatives took umbrage at Aquinas's theory of the unicity of the substantial form in man. And as talk about 'forms', such as forms of corporeity, vegetative life, sensitive life and rational life, does not nowadays form part either of ordinary language or of the commonly accepted philosophical jargon, we may be inclined to think that the problem with which Aquinas was dealing is outdated and dead. So it may be, when expressed in the precise way in which it was discussed in the thirteenth century. Basically, however, the problem was that of the unity of man. And if we consider the frequency of discussion about the so-called mind-body problem, we can see that there is a sense in which the problem is by no means dead.

We can take another example. There was much talk in the Middle Ages about 'essences' and 'natures'. And it may appear that such talk belongs simply to a bygone pre-evolutionary era in which people believed in static or fixed species and natures. Jean-Paul Sartre has told us that existence precedes essence, and that there is no such thing as a human essence or nature which is present from the start in all men. But M. Sartre is presumably as well able as the next man to distinguish between the lions in Africa and the human beings in Africa. And we might well ask ourselves whether an insistence on the rights of un-developed nations and our rejection of any racialism which implies that members of a given race are pretty well subhuman do not presuppose some sort of belief in a human nature or entity. To be sure, we fight shy of any idea of an occult essence hidden away inside. But even if some medieval writers used language which suggests that this is the sort of idea which they had in mind, some of them at any rate were careful to avoid postulating an occult common nature, though they did not deny that human beings are similar in nature or essence. Obviously, there are a number of difficult problems which can be raised in regard to the language of essences or natures. The point is, however, that reflection on our ordinary language and our convictions might well make us think twice before dismissing the whole concept as so much medieval rubbish.

It is, of course, possible to recognize that during the Middle Ages sound work was done in the field of logic and that real philosophical problems were discussed, and at the same time to maintain that a good deal of intellectual ability and effort were devoted to reflection about questions which cannot be answered or which are of little, if any, importance or relevance. The problem of the reference of universal terms, for example, was a worthwhile topic for discussion; and if it was not settled once and for all in the Middle Ages, one reason was probably the fact that attention was concentrated on one particular area of discussion, such as abstract nouns 'standing for' species or genuses. The general question needed more breaking up into a number of different but related questions. But the questions actually treated were certainly answerable in principle. It is not so clear, however, that questions about the *universale ante rem* or ideas in the divine mind were answerable, except perhaps on the supposition (which the medievals themselves would exclude) that God is a kind of magnified human being. Again, the question whether reflection on our language and on the experience which it expresses forces us to postulate distinct rational faculties in man, intellect and will, or whether we can dispense with this hypothesis is a perfectly reasonable subject for discussion. But whereas there is hope of getting somewhere in the field of human psychology, it by no means necessarily follows that talk about the understanding and willing of a transcendent God is likely to be profitable. Again, while the medievals doubtless made some sound observations about different types of propositions, existential and descriptive, necessary and contingent and so on, what are we to make of such a statement as that God is subsistent existence itself (*ipsum esse subsistens*)? Has it any intelligible meaning, unless perhaps it is meant to imply what is obviously not intended, namely that 'God' is a name for the totality of existing things? In general, medieval philosophy seems to be a strange mixture of logical studies, acute philosophical discussion and analysis, and flights into a superterrestrial realm from which it is unlikely that any reliable news will be brought back.

This general impression is understandable. It is not, of course, a matter of discussion about, say, the status of the emperor in relation to the papacy. For it is obvious that particular political issues can be burning questions in a particular historical situation and then lose their contemporary relevance when the historical situation has changed. The general impression is covered rather by the combination of acute critical analysis with what may appear to be metaphysical excursions which border on the unintelligible. On the one hand we find medieval thinkers recognizing, for instance, the difference between the grammatical and logical forms of a proposition long before Bertrand Russell arrived on the scene, or interpreting statements about chimeras and so in such a way as not to imply that these must be entities corresponding to the subject-terms of the relevant propositions. On the other hand we find medieval thinkers making such statements as the one referred to above, namely that God is existence itself, a statement which to many people is frankly unintelligible.

A rather obvious comment is that a man's attitude to medieval philosophy depends partly on his own presuppositions. If, for example, he is a logical positivist and approaches medieval thought with the conviction that all talk about a transcendent God is so much nonsense, he will be, from the start, unsympathetically disposed to the philosophical theology of the Middle Ages. This need not prevent him from recognizing the achievements of medieval thinkers in certain areas, such as logic. But if he is aware of the intellectual status of the leading thinkers of the Middle Ages, he is likely to ascribe their metaphysics simply to the influence of pre-existing religious beliefs, just as they might ascribe his attitude to his pre-existing philosophical commitments.

We cannot embark here on a discussion of logical positivism. But it is worth pointing out that even a positivist should be capable of understanding how medieval thinkers came to make such odd statements as that God is existence itself. It is not a case of a medieval philosopher believing that he has privileged access to a transcendent reality, so that he can make a voyage of discovery and come back with news for his colleagues. Rather it is a case of his believing that within an assumed conceptual framework and language other ways of speaking are excluded. For instance, if one spoke of God as an essence which receives existence or is actuated by existence, one would make of God a limited thing, something within the universe as the member of a class with many members. For in the essence-existence language essence is said to limit existence, if, that is to say, we postulate a distinction between them. If we deny any distinction but assert identity, then that in regard to which this identity is asserted must be referred to as pure being or existence itself. We can, of course, question or reject the language. The point is, however, that, given the particular language and conceptual framework, certain things must be said and other statements excluded. In other words, a proposition can have a function within a given language, even though it may seem unintelligible to those who do not use the language in question.

The medieval thinkers did not suffer from schizophrenia. That is to say, they did not at one moment pursue careful and patient logical and conceptual analysis and then at another moment indulge in flights of unrestrained fantasy. They employed the same logical and conceptual tools when they were developing philosophical theology as when they were discussing the function and reference of universal terms. While, therefore, it is understandable if positivistically inclined minds tend to think of medieval philosophy as a mixture of careful analysis and cloudy metaphysics, it is also understandable if others tend to see it as an all-embracing rationalism which endeavoured to obtain conceptual mastery even over God. Hegel, who tried to lay bare the life of the Absolute by reconstructing it dialectically, regarded himself as carrying on and carrying further the programme of medieval theologians, the programme of 'faith seeking understanding'. And some modern theologians regard the philosophy of the Middle Ages as exhibiting a tendency to substitute Greek rationalism for biblical thinking.

Obviously, global impressions of a complex set of different lines of thought are open to criticism on the ground of oversimplification and of giving undue prominence to this or that particular aspect or phase of a complex whole. It is true that St Anselm spoke of proving Christian doctrines such as the Trinity by 'necessary reasons'; but he certainly did not intend to imply that he would cease to believe in the Trinity if he were unable to find a philosophical demonstration of this doctrine. The fact of the matter is that in the early Middle Ages, when there was no very clear demarcation between philosophy and theology, we can find a kind of youthful enthusiasm for applying dialectic or logic whenever possible. This led to the development of scholastic theology. St Anselm was himself one of the chief contributors to this development. When the field of philosophical reflection had been widened and enriched, a clearer distinction between philosophy and theology became, as we have seen, inevitable. This distinction brought with it a clearer recognition of the distinction between truths which could be proved by the philosopher and those which could not. And as the Middle Ages wore on, there was a marked tendency to increase the number of truths which belonged to the sphere of revelation and faith and could not be demonstrated philosophically. This tendency was accompanied by a reaction against what was regarded as the invasion of the rationalism and necessitarianism of Greco-Islamic philosophy, a reaction which is clearly seen with such writers as Ockham in the first decades of the fourteenth century and Gerson at the end of the century. Even if Hegel was able to claim with some show of plausibility that certain medieval thinkers had taken steps in the direction in which he himself tried to go, Ockham was not one of them. We have seen that in his opinion philosophy could establish very little about God. And though he did not deny that theology could form a composite concept which was 'proper' to God in the sense that it could be predicated of him alone, he insisted that the direct object of our knowledge is a web of concepts which 'stands for' God. Any idea of the philosopher being able to take God by storm, as it were, and penetrate the divine essence by dialectical thinking was foreign to his mind.

At the same time the medieval thinkers certainly had a profound confidence in reason, a confidence which lay behind and inspired the development of both scholastic theology and philosophy. They differed, of course, in their ideas of what reason could accomplish. Some of them at any rate recognized the role of empirical hypotheses in science and saw that a successful 'saving of the appearances' was not necessarily a proof of the relevant hypothesis. And Ockham's strict idea of what was required for a logical demonstration led him to regard as merely probable arguments which some of his predecessors seem to have looked on as demonstrative proofs. Besides, his emphatic rejection of all necessary causal connections between finite things and his belief that the *how* of the world, no less than its existence, depended on the free and omnipotent divine will obviously restricted the area in which, for him, demonstrative proof was possible. It is a mistake to suppose that the medieval philosophers imagined that the ideal of Aristotelian demonstration could be realized in all areas of inquiry. They were not, however, the men to appeal to 'reasons of the heart' or to make emotive appeals or edification do duty for close reasoning. If some of them greatly restricted the sphere of the demonstrable, they did not do so in order to make way for appeals to emotion or aesthetic satisfaction or anything of that sort.

Perhaps the point can be illustrated by reference to theology. When Duns Scotus said that theology was not a science, he did not mean that it was a matter of feeling. He meant two things. First, in so far as theology deals with God in himself, it is indeed treating of necessary truths, in the sense that God cannot be otherwise than he is. But as the premises are accepted by the human mind on faith and not as self-evident principles, theology is not for us a science in the strict Aristotelian sense. Secondly, in so far as theology treats of truths which depend on God's will and free choice, of contingent truths that is to say, it cannot for this reason exemplify the concept of a science in the strict sense. If, however, we mean by 'science' simply a body of propositions derived from certain premises, without regard to the question whether the ultimate premises are self-evidently true propositions or truths revealed by God and accepted on faith, then theology can indeed be described as a science. The fact that Scotus and Ockham describe theology as a practical rather than as a speculative science does not affect the issue. They are not suggesting that theological doctrines are true in a purely pragmatist sense. They are emphasizing the function of revelation and theology in relation to human conduct leading to salvation. Whereas astronomy has a purely theoretical function, to obtain knowledge for its own sake, God reveals truths to man not simply for the sake of imparting information but to enable man to attain his supernatural end or goal.

The mention of theology may seem irrelevant. But this is not really the case. The purely propositional theory of revelation has been challenged in modern times. But we can pass over this issue. The point is that the medieval thinkers employed a process of reasoning, based on certain premises, both in theology and in philosophy. Obviously, the philosopher did not imagine that he could manage simply with *a priori* deductions from self-evident principles. Aquinas, for example, had to introduce empirical premises, such as 'there is something which moves', into his proofs of the existence of God. But the Aristotelian ideal of science exercised a powerful influence on both theologians and philosophers, whatever modifications they had to make in practice. In the world of Ockham this ideal played a much more restricted role than in the world of Avicenna. But though Ockham's view of causal relations meant that emphasis had to be placed on the role of empirical observation, he had a great respect for reason and reasoning. One would hardly expect such an eminent logician to prefer appeals to the heart or the emotions. Nor did he.

Besides their devotion to reasoning, another characteristic of the medieval philosophers was their realism, in the sense in which realism is opposed to subjective idealism. Aquinas was careful to explain that the concept is that *by which* something is known or understood: it is not itself *that which* is known. Needless to say, Aquinas does not deny that we can make concepts the object of our attention. What he means is that when our attention is directed to an extramental thing, our concept is not the terminating object of our knowledge but that by which (the *medium quo*) we know the thing itself. Durandus (d. 1332), however, an independent minded Dominican, got rid of the cognitive *species*, in the sense of concepts as accidental forms or modifications of the mind. That is to say, he got rid of intermediary entities and represented knowing as simply a cognitive relation, a relation between the mind and the object. It is true that Pierre Auriol (d. 1322) asserted that the object of the act of the intellect is the mental concept. But by the mental object he meant simply the thing as known (as having 'intentional existence', *esse intentionale*). It was not a question of expounding subjective idealism but rather of eliminating the traditional theory of the 'means by which' (*medium quo*) and identifying the concept with the object when considered precisely as object of knowledge. As for Ockham's doctrine that God could produce in us the intuition of a star when there was no star in existence, he was talking about what God *could* do by his absolute power, not about what normally happens. He was not claiming that what we perceive are simply our own ideas.

In spite, therefore, of what some people would regard as unfortunate metaphysical excursions, the medieval philosophers were in certain respects indubitably sober-minded thinkers, given to logical reasoning and confident that we can know the real world and are not imprisoned in the circle of our own ideas. Indeed, what some students miss in medieval philosophy is a passionate concern with questions about the meaning of life and about human destiny. It all seems so arid and academic. It must be remembered, however, that in the Middle Ages people looked elsewhere than to philosophy for answers to such questions. To be sure, with St Augustine 'philosophy' was still the saving wisdom. But the more philosophy became separated from theology, the more arid (in the sense intended) it became. This was not due, of course, simply to the separation. When philosophy has gone off on its own, it is natural that there should arise some philosophers at any rate who devote attention to the sort of questions which have previously been answered in theological terms. But in the medieval context, in which, generally speaking, the philosophers were also Christian theologians, the driving of a wedge between philosophy and theology tended to involve the reduction of philosophy to logical studies and critical analysis, consideration of questions about the meaning of life and so on being relegated to the sphere of faith. Hence the philosophizing of the Ockhamist bears more resemblance to that of the present-day analytic movement than it does to the thought of, say, Nietzsche or Camus. Needless to say, medieval thinkers could and did feel strongly about certain issues. Aquinas, who was generally very moderate in his attitudes and criticism, reacted strongly to Averroistic monopsychism. Ockham felt strongly about the question of Franciscan poverty on the one hand and about the divine freedom and omnipotence on the other. But one could not reasonably expect Christian theologians such as Aquinas, Scotus and Ockham to look to philosophy for answers to questions which they believed to have been answered on the plane of revelation and theology. We have to see medieval philosophy in its historical context and not expect of it what it did not claim to provide.

Bibliography

I GENERAL

P. BOEHNER *Medieval Logic: An Outline of its Development from 1250–c. 1400* (Manchester, 1952).

E. BRÉHIER *The Middle Ages and the Renaissance* (Chicago, 1965).

M. A. CARRÉ *Realists and Nominalists* (Oxford, 1946).

F. C. COPLESTON *A History of Philosophy* (London): Vol. II, *Augustine to Scotus* (1950); Vol. III, *Ockham to Suarez* (1953).

C. S. J. CURTIS *A Short History of Western Philosophy in the Middle Ages* (London, 1950).

M. DE WULF *History of Medieval Philosophy* (London): Vol. I (1935); Vol. II (1938); Vol. III, *Après le treizième siècle* (Louvain, 1947, 6th ed.).

B. GEYER *Die Patristische und scholastische Philosophie* (Berlin, 1928; reprint, Basel, 1951).

E. GILSON *History of Christian Philosophy in the Middle Ages* (London, 1955). Highly recommended.

—— *The Spirit of Medieval Thought* (London, 1962).

M. GRABMANN *Mittelalterliches Geistesleben* (Munich, 1926 and 1936), 2 vols.

D. J. B. HAWKINS *A Sketch of Medieval Philosophy* (London, 1946).

D. KNOWLES *The Evolution of Medieval Thought* (London, 1962). Very readable account.

G. LEFF *Medieval Thought from Saint Augustine to Ockham* (Penguin Books, 1958).

G. LEFF *Heresy in the Later Middle Ages* (Manchester and New York, 1967), 2 vols.

A. MAURER *Medieval Philosophy* (New York, 1962).

B. SMALLEY (ed.) *Trends in Medieval Political Thought* (Oxford, 1965).

R. W. SOUTHERN *Medieval Humanism and Other Studies* (Oxford, 1970).

—— *The Making of the Middle Ages* (London, 1953).

W. ULLMAN *A History of Political Thought: The Middle Ages* (Penguin Books, 1965). Highly recommended.

P. VIGNAUX *La pensée au moyen âge* (Paris, 1938).

J. R. WEINBERG *A Short History of Medieval Philosophy* (Princeton, N.J., 1964).

2 EARLY CHRISTIAN PHILOSOPHY AND ST AUGUSTINE

TEXTS

J. P. MIGNE (ed.) *Patrologiae cursus completus*. Paris. This work contains two series, *Patrologia Graeca* (161 vols., comprising texts up to the Council of Florence) and *Patrologia Latina* (221 vols., comprising texts up to the early part of the thirteenth century). It is a non-critical work, but it is valuable for early medieval writers.

—— *Griechische Schriftsteller der ersten Jahrhunderte* (Berlin, 1897 f.). This is the *Corpus Berolinense* (*C.B.*) sponsored by the Prussian Academy and contains a critical edition of Greek texts of the first three centuries.

—— *Corpus Scriptorum Ecclesiasticorum Latinorum* (Vienna, 1886 f.). This is the *Corpus Vindebonense* (*C.V.*) and contains critical texts of the Latin Fathers.

There are several collections in English translation, such as:

Ante-Nicene Christian Library (Edinburgh, 1866 f.), 24 vols.

Select Library of Nicene and Post-Nicene Fathers (Oxford, 1886 f.), 28 vols.

Ancient Christian Writers: The Works of the Fathers in Translation, ed. J. Quasten and J. C. Plumpe (Westminster, Maryland, 1946 f.).

The Fathers of the Church (Washington, D.C., 1947 f.).

BOOKS ON ST AUGUSTINE

G. BONNER *St Augustine of Hippo: Life and Controversies* (London, 1963).

V. J. BOURKE *Augustine's Quest of Wisdom* (Milwaukee, 1945).

C. BOYER *Christianisme et néo-platonisme dans la formation de Saint Augustin* (Paris, 1920).

—— *L'idée de vérité dans la philosophie de saint Augustin* (Paris, 1920).

—— *Essai sur la doctrine de saint Augustin* (Paris, 1932).

P. BROWN *St Augustine of Hippo: A Biography* (London, 1967). Highly recommended, and contains extensive bibliography.

R. A. DEANE *The Political and Social Ideas of Saint Augustine* (New York, 1963).

J. N. FIGGIS *The Political Aspects of St Augustine's City of God* (London, 1921).

E. GILSON *The Christian Philosophy of Saint Augustine*, trans. L. E. M. Lynch (London, 1961). Highly recommended. Contains a bibliography.

J. M. LE BLOND *Les conversions de Saint Augustin* (Paris, 1948).

R. A. MARKUS *Saeculum: History and Society in the Theology of St. Augustine* (Cambridge, 1970).

—— 'Augustine', *Critical History of Western Philosophy*, ed. D. J. O'Connor (New York and London, 1964), pp. 79–97.

—— 'Augustine, St', *The Encyclopedia of Philosophy*, ed. P. Edwards (1967), vol. I., pp. 198–207.

—— *Marius Victorinus and Augustine*, Part V of *The Cambridge History of Later Greek and Early Medieval Philosophy*, ed. A. H. Armstrong (Cambridge, 1967), pp. 331–419.

The writings by Markus on St Augustine are highly recommended.

H. I. MARROU *Saint Augustin et la fin de la culture antique* (Paris, 1938; with *Retractio*, 1949).

—— *Saint Augustine and His Influence through the Ages* (London, 1957).

J. J. O'MEARA *The Young Augustine* (London, 1954).

E. PORTALIÉ 'Augustin, saint', *Dictionnaire de Théologie Catholique* (Paris 1902), Vol. I.

B. SWITALSKI *Neoplatonism and the Ethics of St Augustine* (New York, 1946).

F. VAN DEN MEER *Augustine the Bishop* (London, 1961).

There are several collections of articles, such as *Augustinus Magister: Congrès international augustinian* (Paris, 1954), 3 vols.

SOME BOOKS ON OTHER EARLY CHRISTIAN WRITERS

A. H. ARMSTRONG *An Introduction to Ancient Philosophy* (Methuen, 1947). Includes an outline of early Christian thought.

H. VON BALTASAR *Présence et pensée: Essai sur la philosophie religieuse de Grégoire de Nysse* (Paris, 1943).

L. W. BARNARD *Justin Martyr: His Life and Thought* (Cambridge, 1967).

H. M. BARRETT *Boethius, Some Aspects of His Times and Work* (Cambridge, 1940).

H. CHADWICK *Early Christian Thought and the Classical Tradition: Studies in Justin, Clement and Origen* (Oxford, 1966).

H. CRONZEL *Origène et la philosophie* (Paris, 1962).

J. DANIÉLOU *Platonisme et théologie mystique: Essai sur la doctrine spirituelle de saint Grégoire de Nysse* (Paris, 1944, 2nd ed. 1953).

—— *Philon d'Alexandrie* (Paris, 1958).

—— *Origen*, trans. W. Mitchell (London, 1955).

E. DE FAYE *Origène* (Paris, 1923–8), 3 vols.

C. MONDÉSERT *Clément d'Alexandrie: Introduction à l'étude de sa pensée religieuse à partir de l'Écriture* (Paris, 1944).

E. F. OSBORN *The Philosophy of Clement of Alexandria* (Cambridge, 1957).

E. K. RAND *Founders of the Middle Ages* (Cambridge, Mass., 1928). Includes Boethius.

A. ROQUES *L'univers dionysien* (Paris, 1954).

R. R. RUETHER *Gregory of Nazianzus, Rhetor and Philosopher* (Oxford, 1969).

W. VÖLKER *Der wahre Gnostiker nach Clemens Alexandrinus* (Berlin, 1952).

The Cambridge History of Later Greek and Early Medieval Philosophy contains 'Philo and the Beginnings of Christian Thought' (Part II) by H. Chadwick and 'The Greek Christian Platonist Tradition from the Cappadocians to Maximus and Eriugena' (Part VI) by I. P. Sheldon-Williams.

3 EARLY MIDDLE AGES

TEXTS
See Migne, *Patrologia Latina.*

Other works

H. BETT *Johannes Scotus Eriugena: A Study in Medieval Philosophy* (Cambridge, 1925).

E. M. W. BUXTON *Alcuin* (London, 1922).

M. CAPPUYNS *Jean Scot Erigène: sa vie, son œuvre, sa pensée* (Paris, 1933).

M. L. W. LAISTNER *Thought and Letters in Western Europe, A.D. 500–900* (London, 1931).

A. J. MACDONALD *Berengar and the Reforms of Sacramental Doctrine* (London, 1930).

P. MAZZANELLA *Il pensiero di Giovanni Scoto Eriugena* (Padua, 1957).

F. PICAVET *Roscelin, philosophe et théologien, d'après la légende et d'après l'histoire* (Paris, 1911).

J. REMIERS *Der Nominalismus in der Frühscholastik* (Münster, 1910; *Beiträge*, VIII, 5).

A. SCHNEIDER *Die Erkenntnislehre des Johannes Eriugena im Rahmen ihrer metaphysischen und anthropologischen Voraussetzungen* (Berlin, 1921–3), 2 vols.

W. SEUL *Die Gotteserkenntnis bei Johannes Skotus Eriugena unter Berücktsichtigung ihrer neo-platonischen und augustinischen Elemente* (Bonn, 1932).

P. G. THÉRY *Études dionysiennes* (Paris, 1932–7).

D. TURNAU *Rabanus Maurus praeceptor Germaniae* (Munich, 1900).

L. WALLACH *Alcuin and Charlemagne* (Ithaca, N.Y., 1959).

4 ANSELM AND ABELARD

TEXTS
Migne, *Patrologia Latina* (Anselm, Vols. 158–9; Abelard, Vol. 178).

S. Anselmi Cantuariensis Archiepiscopi Opera Omnia, ed. F. S. Schmitt, O.S.B. (Edinburgh, 1946–61), 6 vols. A critical edition.

St Anselm's Proslogion with a Reply on Behalf of the Fool by Gaunilo and the Author's Reply to Gaunilo, translated with an introduction and philosophical commentary by M. J. Charlesworth (Oxford, 1965).

The De Grammatico of Saint Anselm: The Theory of Paronymy, Latin and English text with discussion by D. P. Henry (Notre Dame, Ind., 1964).

Ouvrages inédits d'Abélard, ed. V. Cousin (Paris, 1836).

Opera Petri Abaelardi, ed. V. Cousin (Paris, 1849–59), 2 vols.

Peter Abaelards Philosophische Schriften, ed. B. Geyer (Münster, 1919–33; *Beiträge*, XXXI, 1–4).

Pietro Abelardo. Scritti filosofici, ed. M. Dal Pra (Rome and Milan, 1954).

Abaelardiana Inedita, ed. L. Minio-Paluello (Rome, 1959).

Peter Abaelards Theologia 'Summi Boni', ed. H. Ostlender (Münster, 1939; *Beiträge*, XXXV, 2–3).

Petrus Abaelardus. Dialectica, ed. by L. M. de Rijk (Assen, 1956).

Abelard's Christian Theology, trans. J. R. McCallum (Oxford, 1948).

Abelard's Ethics, trans. J. R. McCallum (Oxford, 1935).

The Story of Abelard's Adversities: A Translation with Notes of the Historia Calamitatum, trans. J. T. Muckle (Toronto, 1954).

STUDIES

Anselm

K. BARTH *Fides quaerens intellectum. Anselms Beweis der Existenz Gottes im Zusammenhang seines theologischen Programms* (Munich, 1931). Translation by J. W. Robertson (London, 1960).

J. FISCHER *Die Erkenntnislehre Anselms von Canterbury* (Münster, 1911, *Beiträge*, X, 3).

C. FILLIÂTRE *La philosophie de saint Anselme, ses principes, sa nature, son influence* (Paris, 1920).

A. KOYRÉ *L'idée de Dieu dans la philosophie de saint Anselme* (Paris, 1925).

J. MCINTYRE *St Anselm and his Critics: A Re-Interpretation of the Cui Deus Homo* (Edinburgh, 1954).

R. W. SOUTHERN *St Anselm and His Biographer* (London, 1962).

Abelard

R. DAHMEN *Darstellung der Abälardischen Ethik* (Münster, 1906).

M. T. FUMAGALLI *La Logica di Abelardo* (Florence, 1964).

E. HOMMEL *Nosce te ipsum: Die Ethik des Peter Abelard* (Wiesbaden, 1948).

O. LOTTIN: See under *Twelfth century schools*.

D. E. LUSCOMBE *The School of Peter Abelard* (Cambridge, 1969).

J. MCCABE *Peter Abelard* (London, 1901).

A. V. MURRAY *Abelard and St Bernard: A Study in Twelfth-century 'Modernism'* (Manchester, 1967).

C. OTTAVIANO *Pietro Abelardo: La vita, le opere, il pensiero* (Rome, 1931).

J. REIMERS *Der aristotelische Realismus in der Frühscholastik* (Bonn, 1907).

C. DE RÉMUSAT *Abélard: sa vie, sa philosophie, sa théologie* (Paris, 2nd ed. 1855), 2 vols.

J. G. SIKES *Peter Abailard* (Cambridge, 1932).

R. E. WEINGART *The Logic of Divine Love: A Critical Analysis of the Soteriology of Peter Abailard* (Oxford, 1970).

5 TWELFTH CENTURY SCHOOLS

TEXTS

Migne, *Patrologia Latina* (The *Philosophia mundi* of William of Conches is included among the writings of Honorius of Autun, Vol. 172).

John of Salisbury's *Metalogicon* and *Policraticus* (2 vols.) have been edited by C. C. J. Webb and published at Oxford in 1929 and 1909 respectively.

The *Metalogicon* has been translated by D. P. McGarry (Berkeley, Calif., 1955) and part of the *Policraticus* by J. B. Pike in *Frivolities of Courtiers and Footprints of Philosophers* (Minneapolis, 1938).

Peter Lombard's *Libri Sententiarum* has been published in a critical edition (Quaracchi, 1916), 2 vols.

STUDIES

M. D. CHENU *La théologie au XIIe siècle* (Paris, 1957).

A. CLERVAL *Les écoles de Chartres au moyen âge* (Paris, 1895).

J. DE GHELLINCK *L'essor de la littérature latine au XIIe siècle* (Brussels and Paris, 1946).

—— *Le movement théologique au XIIe siècle* (Paris, 1957).

J. EBNER *Die Erkenntnislehre Richards von Sankt Viktor* (Münster, 1917; *Beiträge*, XIX, 4).

A. M. ETHIER *Le De Trinitate de Richard de Saint-Victor* (Paris, 1939).

H. FLATTEN *Die Philosophie des Wilhelm von Conches* (Coblenz, 1929).

C. HASKINS *The Renaissance of the Twelfth Century* (Cambridge, Mass., 1927).

J. KILGENSTEIN *Die Gotteslehre des Hugo von Sankt Viktor* (Würzburg, 1897).

H. OSTLER *Die Psychologie des Hugo von Sankt Viktor* (Münster, 1906; *Beiträge*, VI, 1).

G. PARÉ, A. BRUNET and P. TREMBLAY *La renaissance du XIIe siècle: Les écoles et l'enseignement.* (Paris and Ottawa, 1933).

J. M. PARENT *La doctrine de la création dans l'école de Chartres* (Paris and Ottawa, 1938).

C. SCHAARSCHMIDT *Joanus Saresberiensis nach Leben und Studien, Schriften und Philosophie* (Leipzig, 1862).

F. VERNET 'Hughes de Saint-Victor', *Dictionnaire de Théologie Catholique*, Vol. 7.

C. C. J. WEBB *John of Salisbury* (London, 1932).

6 THE PHILOSOPHY OF ISLAM

TEXTS

Al-Fārābī

Der Musterstaat von al-Fārābī, trans. F. Dieterici (Leiden, 1900).

Idées des habitants de la cité vertueuse, trans. R. P. Jaussen, Y. Karam and J. Chlala (Cairo, 1949).

The two books just mentioned are translations of Al-Fārābī's work on the ideal State.

Al-Fārābī's Short Commentary on Aristotle's Prior Analytics, trans. N. Rescher (Pittsburgh, 1963).

Al-Fārābī's philosophische Abhandlungen, trans. F. Dieterici (Leiden, 1892).

The Fusul al-Madani: Aphorisms of the Statesman of Al-Fārābī, translated and edited with introduction and notes by P. M. Dunlop (Cambridge, 1961).

Compendium Legis Platonis, edited with a Latin translation and notes by F. Gabrieli (London, 1952; *Plato Arabus*, Vol. 3).

De Platonis philosophia, edited with a Latin translation and notes by F. Rosenthal and R. Walzer (London, 1943; *Plato Arabus*, Vol. 2.).

On the Philosophy of Plato, trans. Muhsin Mahdi (New York, 1962).

On the Philosophy of Aristotle, trans. Muhsin Mahdi (New York, 1962).

On Attaining Felicity, trans. Muhsin Mahdi (New York, 1962).

Al-Ghazzāli (Algazel)

Al-Ghazālīs Tahafut al-Falsifah (Incoherence of the Philosophers), trans. S. A. Kamali (Lahore, 1958).
Algazel's Metaphysics: A Mediaeval Translation (Toronto, 1933).

Avicenna

A critical edition of the *Al-Shifā* began appearing at Cairo in 1952 under the general editorship of I. Madkur.
Avicennae Metaphysices Compendium (Rome, 1926). Trans. into Latin and annotated by N. Carame
Avicenna on Theology, trans. A. J. Anberry (London, 1951).
Die Metaphysik Avicennas, trans. M. Horten (Halle, 1907).
Le livre de science, trans. M. Ackena and H. Massé (Paris, 1955), 2 vols.
Avicenna's Psychology, trans. F. Rahman (London, 1952).

Averroes

The Incoherence of the Incoherence, trans. S. Van den Bergh (Oxford, 1954).
Averroes' Commentary on Plato's Republic, trans. E. I. J. Rosenthal (Cambridge, 1956).
Averroes on the Harmony of Religion and Philosophy, trans. G. F. Hourani (London, 1961).
Aristotelis opera cum Averrois Commentariis (Venice, 1562–74).
Corpus Commentariorum Averrois in Aristotelem, published by the Medieval Academy of America (Cambridge, Mass., 1953).
The Philosophy and Theology of Averroes, trans. M. Jamil-Ur-Rehman (Baroda, 1921). Translation of the *Decisive Treatise* and several other writings. There is a Spanish translation by M. Alfonso (Madrid, 1947).

STUDIES

General
T. J. DE BOER *History of Philosophy in Islam,* trans. E. R. Jones (London, 1903).
B. CARRA DE VAUX *Les penseurs d'Islam* (Paris, 1921–6), 5 vols.
M. FAKHRY *A History of Islamic Philosophy* (New York and London, 1971).
L. GAUDET and M. M. ANAWATI *Introduction à la théologie musulmane* (Paris, 1948).

L. GAUTHIER *Introduction à l'étude de la philosophie musulmane* (Paris, 1923).

J. DE MENASCE *Arabische Philosophie* (Bern, 1948).

S. MUNK *Mélanges de philosophie juive et arabe* (Paris, 1927).

S. H. NASR *Islamic Cosmological Doctrines* (Cambridge, Mass., 1964).

F. RAHMAN *Prophecy in Islam* (London, 1958).

N. RESCHER *Studies in Arabic Logic* (Pittsburgh, Pa, 1963).

E. I. J. ROSENTHAL *Political Thought in Medieval Islam* (Cambridge, 1938).

M. M. SHARIF (ed.) *A History of Islamic Philosophy, I* (Wiesbaden, 1963).

R. WALZER *Greek into Arabic: Essays on Islamic Philosophy* (Oxford, 1962).

—— *Early Islamic Philosophy*, Part VIII of *The Cambridge History of Later Greek and Early Medieval Philosophy*.

W. MONTGOMERY WATT *Islamic Philosophy and Theology* (Edinburgh, 1962).

Particular

Al-Fārābī

N. RESCHER *Al-Fārābī: An Annotated Bibliography* (Pittsburgh, Pa, 1962).

Al-Ghazālī

B. CARRA DE VAUX *Gazali* (Paris, 1902).

M. SMITH *Al-Ghazālī, the Mystic* (London, 1949).

A. J. WENSINCK *La pensée de Ghazzālī* (Paris, 1940).

Avicenna

S. M. AFRAN *Avicenna: His Life and Works* (London, 1958).

B. CARRA DE VAUX *Avicenne* (Paris, 1900).

L. GARDET *La pensée religieuse d'Avicenne* (Paris, 1951).

A. M. GOICHON *Introduction à Avicenne* (Paris, 1933).

—— *La distinction de l'essence et de l'existence d'après Ibn Sina* (Paris, 1937).

—— *La philosophie d'Avicenne* (Paris, 1944).

W. KLEINE *Die Substanzlehre Avicennas bei Thomas von Aquin* (Fribourg, 1933).

Y. MEHDAWI *Bibliographie d'Ibu Sinā* (Tehran, 1954).

G. M. WICKENS (ed.) *Avicenna, Scientist and Philosopher: A Millenary Symposium* (London, 1952).

Averroes

T. ALLARD *Le rationalisme d'Averroès* (Paris, 1955).

M. FAKHRY *Islamic Occasionalism and Its Critique by Averroes and Aquinas* (London, 1958).

L. GAUTHIER *Ibu Rochd (Averroès)* (Paris, 1948).

E. RENAN *Averroès et l'averroisme* (Paris, 1869, 3rd ed.).

7 JEWISH PHILOSOPHY

TEXTS

Saadia

Les œuvres complètes de Saadia, ed. J. Derenbourg (Paris, 1893–6), 6 vols.

Book of Beliefs and Opinions, trans. S. Rosenblatt (New Haven, Conn., 1948).

Ibn Gabirol

Avencebrolis Fons Vitae, ex arabico in latinum translatus ab Johanne Hispano et Dominico Gundissalino, ed. C. Baeumker (Münster, 1892–5; *Beiträge*, I, 2–4).

The Fountain of Life, trans. H. E. Wedeck (New York, 1962).

The Improvement of the Moral Qualities, trans. S. S. Wise (New York, 1902).

The Kingly Crown, trans. B. Lewis (London, 1961).

Choice of Pearls, trans. A. Cohen (New York, 1925).

Paquda

Torath Hoboth Ha-Sebaboth (New York, 1925–47), 5 vols. Contains ibu Tibbon's Hebrew translation of the *Duties of the Heart* with an English translation by M. Hyamson.

Halevi

Book of the Kuẓari, translated with introduction and notes by H. Hirschfeld (New York, 1946).

Das Buch al-Chazari (Leipzig, 1887). Contains the Arabic text of the above, Ibn Tibbon's Hebrew translation and a German translation by H. Hirschfeld.

Maimonides

The Guide of the Perplexed, translated with introduction and notes by S. Pines (Chicago, 1963).
Le Guide des égarés, ed. S. Munck (Paris, 1856–66), 3 vols. Contains the Arabic text of the above and a French translation.

Gersonides

Milhamot Adonai ('*Wars of the Lord*') (Leipzig, 1866, reprint of 1560 edition).
Die Kämpfe Gottes von Lewi ben Gerson (Berlin, 1914). A partial German translation of the above by B. Kellerman.

Crescas

Or Adonai ('*Light of the Lord*') (Ferrara, 1555, and Johannesburg, 1861).
Two sections have been translated, one into English by H. A. Wolfson (*Crescas' Critique of Aristotle*, Cambridge, Mass., 1929), the other into German by P. Bloch (*Die Willensfreidheit von Chasdai Crescas*, Munich, 1879).

STUDIES

General

J. B. AGUS *The Evolution of Jewish Thought* (New York and London, 1959).
J. B. BLAU *The Story of Jewish Philosophy* (New York, 1962).
J. GUTTMANN *Philosophies of Judaism*, trans. D. W. Silverman (New York, 1964).
I. HUSIK *History of Medieval Jewish Philosophy* (New York, 1916).
S. MUNK *Mélanges de philosophie juive et arabe* (Paris, 1859).
G. VAJDA *Introduction à la pensée juive au moyen âge* (Paris, 1947).

Particular

Saadia

H. LEWY, A. ALTMAN and I. HEINEMANN (eds.) *Three Jewish Philosophers: Philo, Saadya Gaon, Jehuda Halevi* (Cleveland and New York, 1960). Selections with introductions.

H. MALTER *Life and Works of Saadia Gaon* (Philadelphia, 1921).

M. VENTURA *La philosophie de Saadia Gaon* (Paris, 1934).

Ibn Gabirol

J. GUTTMANN *Die Philosophie des Salomon ibn Gabirol* (Göttingen, 1889).

D. KAUFMANN *Studien über Salomon ibn Gabirol* (Budapest, 1899).

Paquda

G. VAJDA *La théologie ascétique de Bahja ibn Paquda* (Paris, 1947).

Halevi

D. DRUCK *Yehuda Halevy: His Life and Works*, trans. M. Z. R. Frank (New York, 1941).

R. KAYSER *The Life and Times of Jehudah Halevi*, trans. F. Gaynor (New York, 1949).

M. KÖNIG *Die Philosophie des Jehudah Halevi* (Giessen, 1929).

H. LEWY *et al.* (eds.) *Three Philosophers*. See above under *Saadia*.

Maimonides

S. BARON (ed.) *Essays on Maimonides: An Octocennial Volume* (New York, 1941).

I. EPSTEIN (ed.) *Moses Maimonides: 1135–1204* (London, 1935).

J. GUTTMANN *Der Einfluss der Maimonideschen Philosophie auf das christliche Abdendland* (Leipzig, 1908).

L. G. LEVY *Maïmonide* (Paris, 1932, 2nd ed.).

J. MUNZ *Moses ben Maimon: sein Leben und seine Werke* (Frankfurt am M., 1912).

A. ROHNER *Das Schöpfungsproblem bei Moses Maimonides, Albertus Magnus und Thomas von Aquin* (Münster, 1913; *Beiträge*, XI, 5).

L. ROTH *Spinoza, Descartes und Maimonides* (Oxford, 1924).

—— *The Guide for the Perplexed, Moses Maimonides* (London, 1948).

H. SEROUYA *Maimonides, sa vie, son œuvre, avec un exposé de sa philosophie* (Paris, 1951).

Gersonides

H. WOLFSON 'Maimonides and Gersonides on Divine Attributes as Ambiguous Terms', in Kaplan Jubilee Volume, ed. M. Davis (New York, 1953).

Crescas

M. JOEL Don Hasdae Crescas' religionsphilosophische Lehre in ihrem geschichtlichen Einflusse dangestellt (Breslau, 1966).

M. WAXMAN The Philosophy of Don Hasdai Crescas (New York, 1920). For Crescas's influence on Spinoza see essay by D. Newmark in Essays in Jewish Philosophy (Cincinnati, Ohio, 1929).

8 THIRTEENTH CENTURY: UNIVERSITIES AND TRANSLATIONS

J. BONNEROT La Sorbonne, sa vie, son rôle, son œuvre à travers les siècles (Paris, 1927).

M. D. CHENU La théologie comme science au XIIIe siècle (Paris, 1957, 3rd ed.).

L. J. DALY The Medieval University, 1200–1400 (New York, 1961).

H. DENIFLE and A. CHATELAIN Charterlarium Universitatis Parisiensis (Paris, 1889–97), 4 vols.

—— Les universités françaises au moyen âge (Paris, 1892).

A. B. EMDEN A Biographical Register of the University of Oxford to A.D. 1500 (Oxford, 1957–9), 3 vols.

P. GLORIEUX Répertoire des maîtres en théologie de Paris au XIIIe siècle (Paris, 1933–4), 2 vols.

M. GRABMANN Forschungen über die lateinischen Aristotlesüber setzungen des XIII Jahrhunderts (Münster, 1916; Beiträge, XVII, 5–6).

A. M. HAMELIN Pour l'histoire de la théologie morale: L'école franciscaine de ses débuts jusqu'à l'occamisme (Louvain, 1961).

A. JOURDAIN Recherches critiques sur l'âge et l'origine des traductions latines d'Aristote (Paris, 1843, 2nd ed. by C. Jourdain).

R. KLIBANSKY The Continuity of the Platonic Tradition during the Middle Ages: Outline of a Corpus Platonicum Medii Aevi (London, 1950, 2nd ed.).

A. G. LITTLE The Grey Friars in Oxford (Oxford, 1892).

O. LOTTIN Psychologie et morale aux XIIe et XIIIe siècles (Gembloux, 1942–60), 6 vols.

G. H. LUQUET *Aristote et l'université de Paris pendant le XIIIe siècle* (Paris, 1904).

A. MASNOVO *Da Guglielmo d'Auvergne a San Tommaso d'Aquino* (Milan, 1930–45), 3 vols.

H. RASHDALL *The Universities of Europe in the Middle Ages*, edited by F. M. Powicke and A. B. Emden (Oxford, 1936) 3 vols.

D. E. SHARP *Franciscan Philosophy at Oxford in the Thirteenth Century* (Oxford, 1936).

C. E. SMITH *The University of Toulouse in the Middle Ages* (Milwaukee, 1958).

F. VAN STEENBERGHEN *Aristote en Occident* (Louvain, 1946). Translated as *Aristotle in the West* (Louvain, 1955).

—— *The Philosophical Movement in the Thirteenth Century* (Edinburgh, 1955).

—— *La philosophie au XIIIe siècle* (Louvain and Paris, 1966).

9 ST BONAVENTURE, ROGER BACON AND RAYMOND LULL

BONAVENTURE

Texts

S. Bonaventurae Opera Omnia (Quaracchi, 1882–1902), 10 vols. This is a critical edition.

Questions disputées 'De Caritate', 'De Novimissimis', ed. P. Glorieux (Paris, 1950). Not contained in *Opera*.

Collationes in Hexaemeron, ed. F. Delorme (Quaracchi, 1934). A second redaction, not contained in *Opera*.

St Bonaventure's De reductione artium ad theologiam trans. E. T. Healy (St Bonaventure, N.Y., 1955). Latin and English texts.

St Bonaventure's Itinerarium mortis in Deum, trans. P. Boehner (St Bonaventure, N.Y., 1956). Latin and English texts.

Breviloquium by St Bonaventure, trans. E. E. Nemmers (St Louis and London, 1946).

Studies

J. M. BISSEN *L'exemplarisme divin selon saint Bonaventure* (Paris, 1929).

J. G. BUGEROL *Introduction à l'étude de S. Bonaventure* (Paris, 1961).

—— *S. Bonaventure et la sagesse chrétienne* (Paris, 1963).

M. M. DE BENEDICTIS *The Social Thought of Saint Bonaventure* (Washington, D.C., 1946).

E. GILSON *The Philosophy of St Bonaventure* (London, 1938). This is a translation of the first French edition of this classic work. The second French edition was published at Paris in 1943.

S. GRÜNEWALD *Franziskanische Mystik: Versuch zu einer Darstellung mit besonderer Berücktsichtigung des heiligen Bonaventura* (Munich, 1931).

E. LUTZ *Die Psychologie Bonaventuras* (Münster, 1909; *Beiträge*, VI, 4–5).

B. A. LUYCKX *Die Erkenntislehre Bonaventuras* (Münster, 1923; *Beiträge*, XXIII, 3–4).

C. M. O'DONNELL *The Psychology of St Bonaventure and St Thomas Aquinas* (Washington, D.C., 1937).

R. P. PRENTICE *The Psychology of Love according to St Bonaventure* (St Bonaventure, N.Y., 1957, 2nd ed.).

J. RATZINGER *Die Geschichtstheologie des hl. Bonaventura* (Munich, 1959).

P. ROBERT *Hylémorphisme et devenir chez S. Bonaventure* (Montreal, 1936).

B. ROSENMÖLLER *Religiöse Erkenntnis nach Bonaventura* (Münster, 1925; *Beiträge*, XXV, 3–4).

E. J. M. SPARGO *The Category of the Aesthetic in the Philosophy of St Bonaventure* (St Bonaventure, N.Y., 1953).

G. H. TAVARD *Transiency and Permanence: The Nature of Theology according to St. Bonaventure* (St Bonaventure, N.Y., 1954).

L. VEUTHEY *Sancti Bonaventurae philosphia christiana* (Rome, 1943).

ROGER BACON

Texts

Fratris Rogeri Baconi Opera quaedam hactenus inedita, ed. J. S. Brewer (London, 1859). Contains *Opus Tertium, Opus Minus* and some other writings. *Un fragment inédit de l'Opus Tertium de R. Bacon*, ed. P. Duhem (Quaracchi, 1909).

Part of the Opus Tertium of Roger Bacon, ed. A. G. Little (Aberdeen, 1912).

The Opus Maius of Roger Bacon, ed. J. H. Bridges (Oxford, 1897–1900), 3 vols.

The 'Opus Maius' of Roger Bacon, trans. R. B. Burke (Philadelphia, Pa, 1928, reprint New York, 1962).

Rogeri Baconis moralis philosophia, ed. F. Delorme and E. Massa (Zürich, 1953). Complete text of Part VII of Opus Maius.

The Greek Grammar of Roger Bacon and a Fragment of His Hebrew Grammar, ed. E. Nolan and S. A. Hirsch (Cambridge, 1902).

Fratris Rogeri Bacon Compendium Studii theologiae ed. H. Rashdall (Aberdeen, 1911).

Studies

C. BAEUMKER *Roger Bacons Naturphilosophie* (Münster, 1916).

R. CARTON *La synthèse doctrinale de Roger Bacon* (Paris, 1929).

—— *L'expérience mystique de l'illumination intérieure chez Roger Bacon* (Paris, 1929).

—— *L'expérience physique chez Roger Bacon, contribution à l'étude de la méthode et de la science expérimentale au XIIIe siècle* (Paris, 1924).

T. CROWLEY *Roger Bacon, the Problem of the Soul in His Philosophical Commentaries* (Louvain and Dublin, 1950).

S. C. EASTON *Roger Bacon and His Search for a Universal Science* (Oxford and New York, 1952).

E. HECK *Roger Bacon: Ein mittelalterlicher Versuch einer historischen und systematischen Religionswissenschaft* (Bonn, 1957).

A. G. LITTLE *Roger Bacon: Essays contributed by Various Authors on the Occasion of the Commemoration of the Seventh Centenary of His Birth* (Oxford, 1914).

For the position of Roger Bacon in the history of empirical science see A. C. Crombie *Robert Grosseteste and the Origins of Experimental Science 1100–1700* (Oxford, 1953), pp. 139–62.

RAYMOND LULL

Texts

Raymundi Lulli Opera Omnia, ed. I. Salzinger (Mainz, 1721–42), 8 vols.

Raimundi Lulli Opera Latina, critical edition by F. Stegmüller (Palma, 1959 f.).

Obras de Ramón Lull (Majorca, 1906–50). The writings in Catalan.

Blanquerna, trans. E. Allison Peers (London, 1926).

Studies

T. Y. J. CARRERAS Y ARTAU *Historia de la filosofía española*, Vol. I, pp. 231–640 (Madrid, 1939) and Vol. II (1943).
A. LLIMARÈS *Raymond Lull: philosophe de l'action* (Paris, 1963).
E. ALLISON PEERS *Ramon Lull: A Biography* (London, 1929).
E. W. PLATZECK *Raimund Lull* (Düsseldorf, 1962–4), 2 vols.
J. TUSQUETS *Ramón Lull, pedagogo de la cristianidad* (Madrid, 1954).
For bibliographies see Carreras y Artau (Vol. I) and Platzeck. There is a special review, *Estudios lulianos* (Palma, 1957 f.).

10 ALBERT THE GREAT AND THOMAS AQUINAS

ALBERT THE GREAT

Texts

Opera omnia, ed. A. Borgnet (Paris, 1890–99), 38 vols.
A critical edition of the *Opera Omnia*, under the editorship of B. Geyer, began publication at Cologne in 1951. Forty volumes are projected.
De animalibus, ed. H. Stradler (Münster, 1916; *Beiträge*, XV–XVI).
De vegetabilis, ed. C. Jessen (Berlin, 1867).

Studies

W. ARENDT *Die Staats – und Gesellschaftslehere Alberts des Grossen nach den Quellen dargestellt* (Jena, 1929).
H. BALSS *Albertus Magnus als Biologe* (Stuttgart, 1947).
F. J. CATANIA 'A Bibliography of St Albert the Great', in *The Modern Schoolman*, Vol. 37 (1959), pp. 11–28.
M. GRABMANN *Der hl. Albert der Grosse* (Munich, 1932).
—— 'Der Einfluss Alberts des Grossen auf das mittelalterliche Geistesleben', in *Mittelalterliche Geistesleben*, Vol. 2 (Munich, 1936).
R. LIERTZ *Der selige Albert der Grosse als Naturforscher und Lehrer* (Munich, 1931).
—— *Albert der Grosse* (Münster, 1948).
G. MEERSEMANN *Introductio in opera omnia beati Albert Magni, O.P.* (Bruges, 1931).
F. PELSTER *Kritische Studien zum Leben und zu den Schriften Alberts des Grossen* (Freiburg, 1920).
G. C. REILLY *Psychology of St Albert the Great compared with that of St Thomas* (Washington, D.C., 1934).

C. H. SCHEEBEN *Albertus Magnus* (Cologne, 1955).

A. SCHNEIDER *Die Psychologie Alberts des Grossen* (Münster, 1903–6; *Beiträge*, IV, 5–6).

T. M. SCHWERTNER *St Albert the·Great* (New York, 1932).

THOMAS AQUINAS
Texts

Opera omnia (Leonine edition, Rome, 1882 f.). This critical edition is still incomplete. The *Summa Theologiae* is contained in Vols. IV–XII (with Cajetan's commentary) and the *Summa contra Gentiles* in Vols. XIII–XV (with Sylvester of Ferrara's commentary).

Opera omnia (Parma, 1852–73), 25 vols. The Parma edition was reprinted at New York (1948–50).

Opera omnia (Paris, 1872–80), 34 vols. This is the Vivès edition.

The *Summa Theologiae* has been translated by the English Dominican Fathers (*The Summa Theologica*, London, 1912–36 22 vols.). A new translation with introduction and notes is in progress (Blackfriars Edition, London, 1964 f.).

The *Summa contra Gentiles* has been translated by A. C. Pegis, J. F. Anderson, V. J. Bourke and C. J. O'Neil (*On the Truth of the Catholic Faith*, New York, 1955–7, 5 vols.).

Among other works of Aquinas which have been translated into English we can mention: *De ente et essentia* (*On Being and Essence*, trans. A. Maurer, Toronto, 1949); *Quaestiones disputatae de veritate* (*Truth*, trans. R. W. Mulligan, Chicago, 1952–4, 3 vols.); *Quaestiones disputatae de potentia* (*On the Power of God*, trans. by L. Shapcote, Westminster, Md, 1952); *De Regno* (*On Kingship*, trans. G. B. Phelan and I. T. Eschmann, Toronto, 1949); *Compendium theologiae* (*Compendium of Theology*, trans. C. Vollert, St Louis, Mo., 1957); *Quaestio disputata de anima* (*The Soul*, trans. J. P. Rowan, St Louis, Mo., 1949); *Quaestiones dispututatae de malo* (*On Free Choice*, partially trans. A. C. Pegis, New York, 1945); *De unitate intellectus*, trans. P. E. Brennan, St Louis, Mo., 1946); and *De aeternitate mundi* (*On the Eternity of the World*, trans. C. Vollert, Milwaukee, 1965).

A number of Aquinas's commentaries on Aristotle have been translated into English. For example, *Aristotle's De Anima with the Commentary of St Thomas* (trans. K. Foster and S. Humphries, London and New Haven, 1951); *Commentary on the Nicomachean*

Ethics (trans. C. I. Litzinger, Chicago, 1964, 2 vols.); *Aristotle on Interpretation, Commentary by St Thomas and Cajetan* (trans. J. Oesterle, Milwaukee, 1962); *Commentary on the Metaphysics of Aristotle* (trans. J. P. Rowan, Chicago, 1961 2 vols.); and *Commentary on Aristotle's Physics* (trans. R. J. Blackwell and others, London and New Haven, Conn., 1963).

There are various books on selections, such as: *Basic Writings of Saint Thomas Aquinas* (ed. A. C. Pegis, New York, 1945, 2 vols.); *The Pocket Aquinas* (ed. V. J. Bourke, New York, 1960).

The *Thomas-Lexikon* by L. Schütz (Padeborn, 1895) was reprinted at New York in 1949.

Bibliographical

v. J. BOURKE *Thomistic Bibliography, 1920–1940* (St Louis, Mo., 1945).

P. MANDONNET and J. DESTREZ *Bibliographie Thomiste*, revised by M. D. Chenu (Paris, 1960).

M. GRABMANN *Die Werke des hl. Thomas von Aquin* (Münster, 1949, 3rd ed.).

And see the *Bulletin thomiste* (Paris, 1924 f.) and the *Répertoire bibliographique* (supplement to the *Revue philosophique de Louvain*).

Studies

F. BEEMELMANNS *Zeit und Ewigkeit nach Thomas von Aquin* (Münster, 1914; *Beiträge*, XVII, 1).

v. J. BOURKE *Aquinas' Search for Wisdom* (Milwaukee, 1965).

L. CALLAHAN *A Theory of Esthetic according to St Thomas* (Washington, D.C., 1927).

M. D. CHENU *Towards Understanding Saint Thomas* (Chicago, 1964). A fine introduction for serious study.

G. K. CHESTERTON *St Thomas Aquinas* (London, 1933).

F. C. COPLESTON *Aquinas* (Penguin Books, 1955 and reprints).

M. C. D'ARCY *Thomas Aquinas* (London, 1931).

E. DE BRUYNE *St Thomas d'Aquin: le milieu, l'homme, la vision du monde* (Brussels, 1928).

J. DE FINANCE *Être et agir dans la philosophie de St Thomas* (Paris, 1945).

M. DE WULF *Études historiques sur l'esthétique de S. Thomas d'Aquin* (Louvain, 1896).

C. FABRO *La nozione metafisica di partecipazione secondo S. Tommaso* (Turin, 1950, 2nd ed.).

A. FOREST *La structure métaphysique du concret selon S. Thomas d'Aquin* (Paris, 1931).

K. FOSTER *The Life of St Thomas Aquinas* (London and Baltimore, 1959).

R. GARRIGOU-LAGRANGE *Reality: A synthesis of Thomistic Thought* (St Louis, Mo., 1950).

L. B. GEIGER *La participation dans la philosophie de Saint Thomas* (Paris, 1942).

T. GILBY *The Political Thought of Thomas Aquinas* (Chicago, 1958).

E. GILSON *The Christian Philosophy of St Thomas Aquinas* (New York, 1956). Highly recommended.

M. GRABMANN *Der göttliche Grund menschlicher Wahrkeitserkenntnis nach Augustinus und Thomas von Aquin* (Cologne, 1924).

—— *Thomas Aquinas* (New York, 1928).

A. HAYEN *Saint Thomas d'Aquin et la vie de l'Église* (Louvain, 1952).

—— *La communication de l'être d'après saint Thomas d'Aquin* (Paris, 1957–9), 2 vols.

R. J. HENLE *Saint Thomas and Platonism* (The Hague, 1956).

A. KENNY (ed.) *Aquinas: A Collection of Critical Essays* (London, 1969).

—— *The Five Ways* (London, 1969).

G. P. KLUBERTANZ *St Thomas Aquinas on Analogy* (Chicago, 1960).

W. KLUXEN *Philosophische Ethik bei Thomas von Aquin* (Mainz, 1964).

O. LOTTIN *Le droit naturel chez S. Thomas et ses prédecesseurs* (Bruges, 1926).

A. MARC *L'idée de l'être chez S. Thomas et dans la scolastique postérieure* (Paris, 1931; *Archives de philosophie*, X, 1).

J. MARÉCHAL *Le point de départ de la métaphysique; Cahier V, Le thomisme devant la philosophie critique* (Louvain, 1926).

J. MARITAIN *The Angelic Doctor: the Life and Thought of St Thomas Aquinas* (New York, 1958, rev. ed.).

H. MEYER *The Philosophy of St Thomas Aquinas* (St Louis, Mo., 1944).

L. E. O'MAHONY *The Desire of God in the Philosophy of St Thomas Aquinas* (London, 1929).

J. OWENS *St Thomas and the Future of Metaphysics* (Milwaukee, 1957).

R. L. PATTERSON *The Concept of God in the Philosophy of Aquinas* (London, 1933).

A. C. PEGIS *St Thomas and the Problem of the Soul in the Thirteenth Century* (Toronto, 1934).

J. PIEPER *Guide to Thomas Aquinas*, trans. R. and C. Winston (New York, 1962).

K. RAHNER *Geist in Welt: Zur Metaphysik der endlichen Erkenntnis bei Thomas von Aquin* (Innsbruck, 1939).

H. REITH *The Metaphysics of St Thomas Aquinas* (Milwaukee, 1958).

P. ROUSSELOT *The Intellectualism of St. Thomas*, trans. F. James (London, 1935).

A. D. SERTILLANGES *S. Thomas d'Aquin* (Paris, 1925, 4th ed.), 2 vols.

—— *La philosophie morale de S. Thomas d'Aquin* (Paris, 1942, new ed.).

A. WALZ *Saint Thomas Aquinas*, trans. S. T. Bullough (Westminster, Md, 1951).

11 SIGER OF BRABANT AND THE CONDEMNATIONS

SIGER

J. J. DUIN *La doctrine de la providence dans les écrits de Siger de Brabant* (Louvain, 1954; *Philosophes médiévaux*, III).

C. A. GRAIFF *Siger de Brabant: Questions sur la métaphysique* (Louvain, 1948; *Philosophes médiévaux*, I).

P. MANDONNET *Siger de Brabant et l'averroisme latin au XIIIe siècle* (Fribourg, 1899; 2nd ed., Louvain, 1908–11, 2 vols; *Les philosophes belges*, VI–VII).

—— 'Nouvelles recherches sur Siger de Brabant et son école', in *Revue philosophique de Louvain* (1956), pp. 130–47.

F. VAN STEENBERGHEN *Siger de Brabant d'après ses œuvres inédites* (Louvain, 1931–42, 2 vols; *Les philosophes belges*, XII–XIII).

—— *Les œuvres et la doctrine de Siger de Brabant* (Brussels, 1938).

For further bibliographical material on Siger de Brabant see Duin and Van Steenberghen.

CONDEMNATIONS

C. BAEUMKER 'Zur Beurteilung Sigers von Brabant', *Philosophisches Jahrbuch* (1911), pp. 177–202.

D. A. CALLUS *The Condemnation of St Thomas at Oxford* (Oxford, 1946, *Aquinas Papers*).

G. C. CAPELLE *Autour du décret de 1210. Tome III: Amaury de Bène: Étude sur son panthéisme formel* (Paris, 1932; *Bibliothèque Thomiste*, 16).

T. CROWLEY 'John Peckham, O.F.M., Archbishop of Canterbury versus the New Aristotelianism', *Bulletin of the John Rylands Library*, Manchester (1951), pp. 242–55.

M. DAL PRA *Amalrico di Bène* (Milan, 1951).

P. DONCOEUR 'Notes sur les averroïstes latins: Boëce le Dace', *Revue des Sciences Philosophiques et Théologiques* (1910), pp. 500–11.

F. EHRLE 'John Peckham über den Kamf des Augustinismus und Aristotelismus in der zweiten Hälfte des dreizehnten Jahrhunderts', *Zeitschrift für katholische Theologie* (1889), pp. 172–93.

—— 'Der Kampf um die Lehre des hl. Thomas von Aquin in den ersten fünfzig Jahren nach seinen Tode', *Zeitschrift für katholische Theologie* (1913).

P. GLORIEUX 'Siger de Brabant' and 'Tempier (Étienne)' in the *Dictionnaire de Théologie Catholique*.

E. HOCEDEZ 'La condamnation de Gilles de Rome', *Recherches de Théologie Ancienne et Médiévale* (1932) (4), pp. 34–58.

JULES D'ALBI *Saint Bonaventure et les luttes doctrinales de 1267–1277* (Paris and Tamines, 1923).

J. KOCH *Giles of Rome: Errores Philosophorum*, critical text with introduction and notes, trans. J. O. Reidl (Milwaukee, 1944).

P. MICHAUD-QUANTIN 'La double-vérité des Averroistes: Un texte nouveau de Boèce de Dacie', *Theoria* (1956), pp. 167–84.

B. NARDI 'Note per una storia dell'averroisme latino', *Rivista di storia della filosofia* (1947–9).

C. OTTAVIANO *Tommaso d'Aquino. Saggio contro la dottrina averroistica dell'unità dell'intelletto* (Lanciano, 1930).

A. OTTO *Joannis Daci Opera* (Copenhagen, 1955).

G. J. SAJÓ 'Boetius de Dacia und seine philosophische Bedeutung', in *Die Metaphysik im Mittelalter* (Berlin, 1963), pp. 454–63.

E. SOMMER-SECKENDORFF *Studies in the Life of Robert Kilwardby, O.P.* (Rome, 1937).

C. TRESMONTANT *La métaphysique du Christianisme et la crise du treizième siècle* (Paris, 1964).

F. VAN STEENBERGHEN *The Philosophical Movement in the Thirteenth Century* (Edinburgh, 1955).

12 JOHN DUNS SCOTUS

TEXTS

Opera omnia, a critical edition prepared by the Scotist Commission at Rome and published by the Vatican City Press (1950 f.). Seven volumes have appeared up to date.

Opera omnia, ed. Luke Wadding (Lyons, 1639) and reprinted at Paris in the Vivès edition (1891–5). This edition contains a number of works which are not now attributed to Scotus, such as the *De rerum principio* and the *Grammatica speculativa*. But until the completion of the critical edition it is the only overall collection.

Tractatus de primo principio. There are three modern editions, edited respectively by M. Müller (Freiburg im B., 1941), E. Roche (St Bonaventure, N.Y., 1949) and B. Wolter (*A Treatise on God as First Principle*, Chicago, Ill., Forum Books, 1966). The two last include English translations, and Father Wolter's edition also contains two related questions from an early commentary by Scotus on the *Sentences*.

Duns Scotus: Philosophical Writings, a selection edited and translated by A. B. Wolter (Edinburgh, Toronto, New York and Paris, Nelson's Philosophical Texts, 1962). This volume contains both Latin and English texts. There is a paperback reprint of the English text (Indianapolis, Ind., 1964).

STUDIES

S. BELMOND *Essai de synthèse philosophique du Scotisme* (Paris, 1933).

E. BETTONI *L'ascesa a Dio in Duns Scotus* (Milan, 1943).

—— *Duns Scotus: The Basic Principles of His Philosophy*, trans. B. Bonansea (Washington, D.C., 1961).

J. E. BOLER *Charles Peirce and Scholastic Realism: A Study of Peirce's Relation to John Duns Scotus* (Seattle, Wash., 1943).

S. DAY *Intuitive Cognition: A Key to the Significance of the Later Scholastics* (St Bonaventure, N.Y., 1947).

D. DE BASLY *Scotus Docens ou Duns Scot enseignant la philosophie, la théologie, la mystique* (Paris, 1934).

R. EFFLER *John Duns Scotus and the Principle 'Omne quod movetur ab alio movetur'* (St Bonaventure, N.Y., 1962).

E. GILSON 'Avicenne et le point de départ de Duns Scot', *Archives d'histoire doctrinale et littéraire du moyen âge* (1927).

—— 'Les seize premiers Theoremata et la pensée de Duns Scot' (as above, 1937–8).

—— *Jean Duns Scot* (Paris, 1952).

M. GRAJEWSKI *The Formal Distinction of Duns Scotus* (Washington D.C., 1944).

—— 'Scotistic Bibliography of the Last Decade, 1929–39', *Franciscan Studies*, Vols. 1 and 2 (1941–2).

C. HARRIS *Duns Scotus* (Oxford, 1927), 2 vols. This work makes copious use of the unauthentic *De rerum principio*.

M. HEIDEGGER *Die Kategorien – und Bedentungslehre des Duns Scotus* (Tübingen, 1916).

W. HOERES *Der Wille als reine Vollkommenheit nach Duns Scotus* (Munich, 1962).

B. LANDRY *Duns Scot* (Paris, 1922).

E. LONGPRÉ *La philosophie du B. Duns Scot* (Paris, 1924). This work contains a reply to Landry's book.

R. MESSNER *Schauendes und begriffliches Erkennen nach Duns Scotus* (Freiburg im B., 1942).

N. MICKLEM *Reason and Revelation: A Question from Duns Scotus* (Edinburgh, 1953).

J. K. RYAN and B. BONANSEA (eds.) *Studies in Philosophy and the History of Philosophy. Vol. III: John Duns Scotus, 1265–1965* (Washington, D.C., 1965).

B. DE SAINT-MAURICE *John Duns Scotus: A Teacher for our Times*, trans. C. Duffy (St Bonaventure, N.Y., 1955).

O. SCHÄFER *Bibliographia de vita, operibus et doctrina Ioannis Duns Scoti Doctoris Subtilis et Mariani saeculorum XIX–XX* (Rome, 1955).

C. L. SHIRCEL *The Univocity of the Concept of Being in the Philosophy of John Duns Scotus* (Washington, D.C., 1942).

P. C. VIER *Evidence and its Function according to John Duns Scotus* (St Bonaventure, N.Y., 1951).

A. B. WOLTER *The Transcendentals and their Function in the Metaphysics of Duns Scotus* (St Bonaventure, N.Y., 1946).

—— 'Duns Scotus (John)', article in *The Encyclopedia of Philosophy*, ed. P. Edwards (New York and London, 1967), Vol. III, pp. 427–36.

The Acts of the Scotist Congress held at Oxford and Edinburgh to commemorate the seventh centenary of Scotus's birth have been published as *De Doctrina Ioannis Duns Scoti* (Rome, 1968).

13 OCKHAM

TEXTS

Theological and philosophical

Guillelmi de Ockham opera philosophica et theologica ad fidem codicum manuscriptorum edita, ed. S. Brown, O.F.M., and collaborators (St Bonaventure, N.Y., 1967 f.). This is the long awaited critical edition of Ockham's philosophical and theological writings. The first two volumes (1967 and 1970) of the *Opera Theologica* contain the Prologue to and the first three distinctions of the *Ordinatio*. Meanwhile the only complete edition of Ockham's commentary on the *Sentences* of Peter Lombard is *Super quattuor libros sententiarum subtilissimae quaestiones* (Lyons, 1495). Some of the material found in the *Reportatio* may not belong there, however.

Quaestio prima principalis Prologi in primum librum sententiarum cum interpretatione Gabrielis Biel, ed. P. Boehner (Paderborn, 1939).

Quodliberta septem (Paris, 1487 and Strasbourg, 1491).

The De sacramento altaris of William of Ockham, edited with an English translation by T. B. Birch (Burlington, Iowa, 1930).

The Tractatus de successivis, attributed to William Ockham, ed. P. Boehner (St Bonaventure, N.Y., 1944).

The Tractatus de praedestinatione et de praescientia Dei et de furturis contingentibus of William of Ockham, ed. P. Boehner (St Bonaventure, N.Y., 1945). This edition includes a study of 'the medieval problem of a three-valued logic' by the editor.

Summulae in libros physicorum (Bologna, 1494; Venice, 1506; Rome, 1637).

Ockham, Philosophical Writings, a selection edited and translated by P. Boehner (Edinburgh, Toronto, New York and Paris, Nelson Philosophical Texts, 1957). Contains Latin and English texts, and includes selections from logical writings.

Logical

Expositio aurea et admodum utilis super artem veterem (Bologna, 1496).

Expositio in librum Porphyrii de praedicabilibus ed. E. A. Moody (St Bonaventure, N.Y., 1965).

Summa totius logicae (Paris, 1488, and other old editions). There is a modern edition of the first and second parts and of the first part of the third part by P. Boehner (St Bonaventure, N.Y., 1951–4).

Political

Gulielmi de Ockham opera politica (Manchester, 1940 f.). The first volume of this critical edition appeared in 1940, edited by J. G. Sikes. The death of the editor caused an interruption. Vol. III, edited by H. S. Offler, appeared in 1956.

Gulielmi de Occam Breviloquium de potestate papae, a critical edition by L. Baudry (Paris, 1937).

Dialogus inter magistrum et discipulum (Lyons, 1493).

The De imperatorum et pontificum potestate of William of Ockham, ed. C. K. Brampton (Oxford, 1927).

Studies

N. ABBAGNANO *Guglielmo di Ockham* (Lanciano, 1931).

L. BAUDRY *Guillaume d'Occam: Sa vie, ses œuvres, ses idées sociales et politiques. Vol. I: L'homme et les œuvres* (Paris, 1949).

—— *Lexique philosophique de Guillaume d'Ockham* (Paris, 1958).

P. BOEHNER *Collected Articles on Ockham* (St Bonaventure, N.Y., 1956).

C. GIACÓN *Guglielmo di Occam* (Milan, 1941), 2 vols.

—— 'Occam (Guglielmo di)' in the *Enciclopedia Filosofica* (Florence, 1969), Vol. IV, cols. 1096–1105).

M. GOTTFRIED *Wilhelm von Ockham* (Berlin, 1949).

R. GUELLUY *Philosophie et théologie chez Guillaume d'Ockham* (Louvain and Paris, 1947).

E. HOCHSTETTER *Studien zur Metaphysick und Enkenntnislehre Wilhelms von Ockham* (Berlin, 1927).

G. DE LAGARDE *La naissance de l'esprit Laïque au déclin du moyen âge* (Paris): Vol. IV, *Ockham et son temps* (1942); Vol. V, *Ockham: Bases de départ* (1946); Vol. VI, *Ockham: La morale et le droit* (1946).

G. MARTIN *Wilhelm von Ockham: Untersuchungen zur Ontologie der Ordnungen* (Berlin, 1949).

E. A. MOODY *The Logic of William of Ockham* (London and New York, 1935).

—— *Truth and Consequence in Medieval Logic* (Amsterdam, 1953).

—— 'William of Ockham' in *The Encyclopedia of Philosophy* ed. P. Edwards (New York and London, 1967), Vol. VIII, pp. 306–17.

S. MOSER *Grundbegriffe der Naturphilosophie bei Wilhelm von Ockham* (Innsbruck, 1932).

R. SCHOLZ *Wilhelm von Ockham als politische Denker und sein Breviloquium de principatu tyrannico* (Leipzig, 1944).

H. SHAPIRO *Motion, Time and Place according to William Ockham* (St Bonaventure, N.Y., 1957).

C. VASOLI *Guglielmo d'Occam* (Florence, 1953).

P. VIGNAUX 'Nominalisme' and 'Occam' in the *Dictionnaire de Théologie Catholique*.

—— *Le nominalisme au XIVe siècle* (Montreal, 1948).

D. WEBERING *The Theory of Demonstration according to William Ockham* (St Bonaventure, N.Y., 1953).

14 SOME OTHER FOURTEENTH-CENTURY THINKERS

JOHN OF MIRECOURT AND NICHOLAS OF AUTRECOURT

Texts

A. BIRKENMAIER *Ein Rechtfertigungschreiben Johanns von Mirecourt* (Münster, 1922; *Beiträge*, XX, 5).

F. STEGMÜLLER 'Die zwei Apologien des Jean de Mirecourt', *Recherches de Théologie ancienne et médiévale* (1933), pp. 40–79, 192–204.

J. LAPPE *Nikolaus von Autrecourt* (Münster, 1908; *Beiträge*, VI, 1). Contains correspondence between Nicholas and Bernard of Arezzo and between Nicholas and Giles.

J. R. O'DONNELL 'Nicholas of Autrecourt', *Medieval Studies*, I (1939), pp. 179–280. Contains an edition of the *Exigit*.

Studies

M. DEL PRA *Nicola di Autrecourt* (Milan, 1951).

J. LAPPE: See above.

C. MICHALSKI *Les courants critiques et sceptiques dans la philosophie du XIVe siècle* (Cracow, 1927).

J. R. O'DONNELL 'The Philosophy of Nicholas of Autrecourt and His Appraisal of Aristotle', *Medieval Studies*, 4 (1942), pp. 97–125.

G. RITTER *Studien zur Spätscholastik* (Heidelberg, 1921–2), 2 vols.

P. VIGNAUX 'Nicholas d'Autrecourt' in the *Dictionnaire de Théologie Catholique*.

J. R. WEINBERG *Nicholas of Autrecourt: A Study in 14th Century Thought* (Princeton, N.J., 1948).

NICHOLAS ORESME AND THE SCIENTIFIC MOVEMENT
Texts

Johannis Buridani Quaestiones super libros quattuor de coelo et mundo,
ed. E. A. Moody (Cambridge, Mass., 1942).

'Maistre Nicole Oresme: Le livre du ciel et du monde', ed. A. D. Menut
and A. J. Denomy, *Medieval Studies,* 1941, pp. 185–280; 1942, pp.
159–297; 1943, pp. 167–333). The text and commentary are available
separately.

*Nicole Oresme: De proportionibus proportionum and Ad pauca res-
picientes,* ed. and trans. E. Grant (Madison, Wis., 1965).

Quaestiones super geometriam Euclidis, ed. H. L. L. Busard (Leiden,
1961).

Nicole Oresme and the Astrologers, ed. G. W. Coopland (Cambridge,
Mass., 1952). Contains two treatises against astrology.

De communicatione idiomatum, ed. E. Borchert (Münster, 1940;
Beiträge, XXXV, 4–5). A theological work.

The De moneta of Nicholas Oresme and English Mint Documents, ed.
C. Johnson (London, 1956).

For earlier editions of writings by Buridan, Albert of Saxony, Marsilius
of Inghen and Nicholas Oresme see, for example, the bibliographies in Ueberweg-Geyer, *Die patristische und scholastische
Philosophie.*

Studies

E. BOCKERT *Die Lehre von der Bewegung bei Nicolaus Oresme* (Münster,
1934; *Beiträge,* XXXI, 3).

M. CLAGETT *The Science of Mechanics in the Middle Ages* (Madison,
Wis., and London, 1959).

A. C. CROMBIE *Augustine to Galileo: The History of Science, A.D. 400–
1650* (London, 1952). Highly recommended.

—— *Robert Grosseteste and the Origins of Experimental Science*
(Oxford, 1953).

P. DUHEM *Le système du monde: histoire des doctrines cosmologiques de
Platon à Copernic* (Paris, 1913–59), 10 vols. A classical work.

C. A. HASKINS *Studies in the History of Medieval Science* (Cambridge,
Mass., 1924).

G. HEIDINGSFELDER *Albert von Sachsen* (Münster, 1926; *Beiträge,*
XXII, 3–4).

A. MAIER *Das Problem der intensiven Grösse in der Scholastik* (Leipzig, 1939).

—— *Die Impetustheorie der Scholastik* (Vienna, 1940).

—— *Studien zur Naturphilosophie der Spätscholastik* (Rome, 1949–58).

C. MICHALSKI *La physique nouvelle et les différents courants philosophiques au XIVe siècle* (Cracow, 1928).

E. A. MOODY 'John Buridan and the Habitability of the Earth', *Speculum* (1941), pp. 415–25.

G. RITTER *Studien zur Spätscholastik*. Vol. I: *Marsilius von Inghen und die okhamistische Schule in Deutschland* (Heidelberg, 1921).

L. THORNDIKE *A History of Magic and Experimental Science*. Vols. 3–4: *The Fourteenth and Fifteenth Centuries* (New York, 1934).

15 SPECULATIVE MYSTICISM

TEXTS

Eckhart

Meister Eckhart: Die deutschen und lateinischen Werke herausgegeben im Auftrage der deutsche Forschungsgemeinschaft (Stuttgart, 1936 f.). A critical edition.

Magistri Eckhardi Opera latina auspiciis Instituti Sanctae Sabinae ad codicum fidem edita (Leipzig): I, *Super oratione dominica*, ed. R. Klibansky (1934); II, *Opus tripartitum: Peologi*, ed. H. Bascour (1935); III, *Quaestiones Parisienses*, ed. M. A. Dondaine (1936).

Eine lateinische Rechtfertigungsschrift des Meister Eckhart, ed. A. Daniels (Münster, 1923; *Beiträge*, XXIII, 5).

Meister Eckhart: Das System seinier religiösen Lehre und Lebensweisheit: Textbuch aus den gedrückten und ungedrückten Quellen mit Einführung, ed. O. Karrer (Munich, 1926).

Meister Eckhart: A Modern Translation, ed. and trans. R. B. Blakney (New York, 1957). Selection.

Eckhart: Selected Treatises and Sermons, ed. J. M. Clark and J. V. Skinner (London, 1958).

Tauler

Die Predigten Taulers, ed. F. Vetter (Berlin, 1910).

Johannes Tauler. Predigten, ed. G. Hoffmann (Freiburg Im B., 1961).

Sermons de Tauler, ed. E. Hugueny, P. Théry and A. L. Corin (Paris, 1927–35), 3 vols.

Twenty-Five Sermons, trans. S. Winkworth (London, 1906, 2nd ed.).
The Sermons and Conferences of John Tauler, trans. W. Elliott (Washington, D.C., 1910).

Suso

Heinrich Seuse: Deutsche Schriften, ed. K. Bihlmeyer (Stuttgart, 1907), 2 vols.
L'œuvre mystique de Henri Suso: Introduction et traduction, ed. B. Lavaud (Fribourg, 1946–7), 4 vols.
Blessed Henry Suso's Little Book of Eternal Wisdom, trans. R. Raby (London, 1866, 2nd ed.).
The Life of Blessed Henry Suso by Himself, trans. T. F. Knox (London, 1865).

Ruysbroeck

Jan van Ruusbroec: Werke, nach der Standardschrift von Groenendal herausgegeben von der Ruusbroec-Gesellschaft in Antwerpen (Cologne, 1950, 2nd ed.), 4 vols.
The Adornment of the Spiritual Marriage, The Sparkling Stone, The Book of Supreme Truth, trans. C. A. Wynschenk Dom, and edited with introduction and notes by E. Underhill (London, 1951).
The Spiritual Espousals, trans. E. Colledge (London, 1952).

Gerson

Œuvres Complètes, ed. P. Glorieux (Paris, 1960 f.).
Johannis Gersonii Opera Omnia, ed. M. E. L. Du Pin (Antwerp, 1706).
Jean Gerson, commentateur dionysien: Les Notulae super quaedam verba Dionysii de Caelesti Hierarchia, ed. A. Combes (Paris, 1940).
Six sermons français inédits de Jean Gerson, ed. L. Mourin (Paris, 1946).
Ioannis Carlerii de Gerson: De mystica theologia, ed. A. Combes (Lugano, 1958).

STUDIES

General

J. BERNHART *Die philosophische Mystik des Mittelalters von ihren antiken Ursprüngen bis zur Renaissance* (Munich, 1922).
J. M. CLARK *The Great German Mystics* (Oxford, 1949).

H. DENIFLE *Das geistliche Leben: Deutsche Mystiker des 14 Jahrhunderts* (Salzburg, 1936, 9th ed. by A. Auer).

X. DE HORNSTEIN *Les grands mystiques allemands du XIVe siècle: Eckhart, Tauler, Suso* (Lucerne, 1920).

S. E. OZMENT *Homo Spiritualis: A Comparative Study of the Anthropology of Johannes Tauler, Jean Gerson and Martin Luther (1509–16) in the Context of Their Theological Thought* (Leiden, 1969).

R. C. PETRY *Late Medieval Mysticism* (Philadelphia, 1957).

P. POURRAT *Christian Spirituality in the Middle Ages, II* (Westminster, Md, 1953).

Eckhart

J. ANCELET-HUSTACHE *Master Eckhart and Rhineland Mysticism* (London, 1959).

J. M. CLARK *Meister Eckhart* (London, 1957).

G. DELLA VOLPE *Il misticismo speculativo di maestro Eckhart nei suoi rapporti storici* (Bologna, 1930).

A. DEMPF *Meister Eckhart: Eine Einführung in sein Werk* (Leipzig, 1934).

F. JOSTES *Meister Eckhart und seine Jünger* (Leipzig, 1915).

A. JUNDT *Essai sur le mysticisme spéculatif de Meister Eckhart* (Strasbourg, 1871).

O. KARRER *Mysticism East and West* (London, 1932).

V. LOSSKY *Théologie négative et connaissance de Dieu chez maître Eckhart* (Paris, 1960).

O. SPANN *Meister Eckhart's mystische Philosophie* (Vienna, 1949).

G. STEPHENSON *Gottheit und Gott in der spekulativen Mystik Meister Eckharts: Eine Untersuchung zur Phänomenologie und Typologie der Mystik* (Bonn, 1954).

Tauler

E. FILTHAUT (ed.) *Johannes Tauler: Ein deutscher Mystiker Gedenkschrift zum 600 Todestag* (Essen, 1961).

I. WEILNER *Johannes Taulers Bekekrungsweg: Die Erfahrungsgrundlagen seiner Mystik* (Regensburg, 1961).

Suso

J. A. BIZET *Henri Suso et le déclin de la scolastique* (Paris, 1946).
J. BÜKHMANN *Christuslehre und Christusmystik des Heinrich Seuse* (Lucerne, 1942).

Ruysbroeck

L. BRIGUÉ *'Ruysbroeck'* in the *Dictionnaire de théologie catholique*.
A. COMBES: See under *Gerson*.
B. FRALING *Der Mensch von dem Geheimnis Gottes. Unter suchungen zur geistlichen Lehre des Jan van Ruysbroeck* (Würzburg, 1967).
F. HERMANS *Ruysbroeck l'admirable et son école* (Paris, 1958).
E. UNDERHILL *Ruysbroeck* (London, 1915).
A. WAUTIER D'AYGALLIERS *Ruysbroeck l'admirable* (Paris, 1923).

Gerson

A. COMBES *Jean de Montreuil et le chancelier Gerson* (Paris, 1942).
Essai sur la critique de Ruysbroeck par Gerson (Paris, 1945–59), 3 vols.
J. L. CONNOLLY *John Gerson, Reformer and Mystic* (Louvain, 1928).
W. DRESS *Die Theologie Gersons. Eine Untersuchung zur Verbindung von Nominalismus und Mystik im Spätmittelalter* (Gütersloh, 1931).
J. B. MORRALL *Gerson and the Great Schism* (Manchester, 1961).
J. STELZENBERGER *Die Mystik des Johannes Gerson* (Breslau, 1928).

16 MARSILIUS OF PADUA

TEXTS

The Defensor Pacis of Marsilius of Padua, critical edition by C. W. Previté-Orton (Cambridge, 1928).
Marsilius von Padua, Defensor Pacis, critical edition by R. Scholz (Hanover, 1932–3), 2 vols.
Defensor Pacis, trans. A. Gewirth (New York, 1956).

Studies

A. CHECCHINI and N. BOBBIO (eds.) *Marsilio da Padova: Studi raccolti nel VI centenario della morte* (Padua, 1942).
A. GEWIRTH *Marsilius of Padua and Medieval Political Philosophy* (New York, 1951). Contains an extensive bibliography.

G. DE LAGARDE *Marsile de Padoue* (Paris, 1948). This is the second Cahier in *Naissance de l'esprit laïque au déclin du moyen âge.*
A. SABETTI *Marsilio da Padova e la filosofia politica del secolo XIV* (Naples, 1964).

17 NICHOLAS OF CUSA

TEXTS

Nicolai de Cusa Opera omnia iussu et auctoritate Academiae Heidelbergensis ad codicum fidem edita (Leipzig and Hamburg, 1932 f.). Critical edition.

Opera (Basel, 1565).

Opera (Paris, 1514, reprinted at Frankfurt am M., 1962), 3 vols.

Nicolaus von Cues: Texte seiner philosophischen Schriften, ed. A. Petzelt (Vol. I, Stuttgart, 1949).

De docta ignorantia libri tres: Testo latino con note di Paolo Rotta (Bari, 1913).

De pace fidei, ed. R. Klibansky and H. Bascour (London, 1956).

The Vision of God, trans. E. G. Salter (New York, 1928).

The Idiot, trans. W. R. Dennes (San Francisco, 1940).

Of Learned Ignorance, trans. G. Heron (London, 1954).

Unity and Reform: Selected Writings of Nicholas de Cusa, ed. J. P. Dolan (Notre Dame, Ind., 1962).

STUDIES

F. BATTAGLIA *Il pensiero giuridico e politico di Niccolò di Cusa* (Bologna, 1935).

H. BETT *Nicholas of Cusa* (London, 1932).

F. J. CLEMENS *Giordano Bruno und Nicolaus von Cues* (Bonn, 1847).

M. DE GANDILLAC *La philosophie de Nicolas de Cues* (Paris, 1941).

R. GRADI *Il pensiero del Cusano* (Padua, 1941).

G. HEINZ-MOHR *Unitas Christiana* (Trier, 1958).

K. JASPERS *Nikolaus Cusanus* (Munich, 1964).

J. KOCH *Nocolaus von Cues und seine Umvelt* (Heidelberg, 1948).

P. MENNICKEN *Nikolaus von Kues* (Trier, 1950).

P. ROTTA *Il cardinale Niccolò di Cusa, la vita ed il pensiero* (Milan, 1928).

—— *Niccolò Cusano* (Milan, 1942).

R. SCHULTZ *Die Staatsphilosophie des Nikolaus von Kues* (Hain, 1948).

P. E. SIGMUND *Nicholas of Cusa and Medieval Political Thought* (Cambridge, Mass., 1963).

E. VANSTEENBERGHE *Autour de la docte ignorance* (Münster, 1915; *Beiträge*, XIV, 2–4).

K. H. VOLKMANN-SCHLUCK *Nicolaus Cusanus* (Frankfurt am M., 1957).

M. WATANABE *The Political Ideas of Nicholas of Cusa, with Special Reference to his De Concordantia Catholica* (Geneva and Paris, 1963).

E. ZELLINGER *Cusanus-Konkordanz* (Munich, 1960).

Index